The Cash Dividend

The Cash Dividend
The Rise of Cash Transfer Programs in Sub-Saharan Africa

Marito Garcia and
Charity M. T. Moore

THE WORLD BANK
Washington, D.C.

© 2012 International Bank for Reconstruction and Development / International Development Association or
The World Bank
1818 H Street NW
Washington DC 20433
Telephone: 202-473-1000
Internet: www.worldbank.org

1 2 3 4   15 14 13 12

This volume is a product of the staff of The World Bank with external contributions. The findings, interpretations, and conclusions expressed in this volume do not necessarily reflect the views of The World Bank, its Board of Executive Directors, or the governments they represent.

The World Bank does not guarantee the accuracy of the data included in this work. The boundaries, colors, denominations, and other information shown on any map in this work do not imply any judgment on the part of The World Bank concerning the legal status of any territory or the endorsement or acceptance of such boundaries.

Rights and Permissions
The material in this work is subject to copyright. Because The World Bank encourages dissemination of its knowledge, this work may be reproduced, in whole or in part, for noncommercial purposes as long as full attribution to the work is given.

For permission to reproduce any part of this work for commercial purposes, please send a request with complete information to the Copyright Clearance Center Inc., 222 Rosewood Drive, Danvers, MA 01923, USA; telephone: 978-750-8400; fax: 978-750-4470; Internet: www.copyright.com.

All other queries on rights and licenses, including subsidiary rights, should be addressed to the Office of the Publisher, The World Bank, 1818 H Street NW, Washington, DC 20433, USA; fax: 202-522-2422; e-mail: pubrights@worldbank.org.

ISBN (paper): 978-0-8213-8897-6
ISBN (electronic): 978-0-8213-8898-3
DOI: 10.1596/978-0-8213-8897-6

Library of Congress Cataloging-in-Publication Data
Garcia, Marito
  The cash dividend : the rise of cash transfer programs in Sub-Saharan Africa / Marito Garcia and Charity Moore.
    p. cm.
  ISBN 978-0-8213-8897-6 — ISBN 978-0-8213-8898-3
  1. Transfer payments—Africa, Sub-Saharan—Case studies. 2. Economic assistance—Africa, Sub-Saharan. I. Moore, Charity II. World Bank. III. Title.
  HG3881.5.W57G367 2011
  399.5'22--dc23
                                                                                    2011028213

Cover photo: Dowa Emergency Cash Transfer program, Malawi. Sarah Molley / Concern Worldwide.

Contents

Foreword	*xiii*
Acknowledgments	*xv*
Abbreviations	*xix*

	Overview	1
	The Growing Use of Cash Transfer Programs in Sub-Saharan Africa	2
	The Review of Cash Transfers, an Emerging Safety Net in Africa	2
	Results of the Review	3
	Lessons Learned and the Road Ahead	8
	Note	9
	References	9
Chapter 1	**Cash Transfers**	11
	The Recent Increase in Cash Transfers around the World	11
	Increased Interest in Cash Transfers in Sub-Saharan Africa	12

v

	The Review of Cash Transfers, an Emerging Safety Net in Africa	13
	What Are Cash Transfer Programs?	18
	Cash Transfers within the Social Protection System	22
	Remainder of the Book	25
	Notes	26
	References	27
Chapter 2	The Rise of Cash Transfer Programs in Sub-Saharan Africa	31
	Social Protection in Sub-Saharan Africa	31
	Catalysts for the Growth of CT Programs in Sub-Saharan Africa	32
	Increased Focus on Social Protection and Cash Transfers within Sub-Saharan Africa	40
	Trends in Cash Transfer Implementation in Sub-Saharan Africa: Strategic Issues	46
	Conclusions	69
	Notes	69
	References	69
Chapter 3	Design and Implementation of Cash Transfers in Sub-Saharan Africa	75
	The Varying Objectives of Sub-Saharan Africa's CT Programs	75
	Targeting Features of Cash Transfers in Sub-Saharan Africa	80
	Client Registration: A Key Issue for Cash Transfers	92
	Program Benefits: How Much Was Transferred to Households?	94
	Cash Payment Systems	105
	Conditional versus Unconditional Cash Transfers	115
	Graduation from Cash Transfer Programs	128
	Monitoring and Accountability	130
	Communication to Ensure Program Impact: Building Understanding, Ownership, and a Constituency of Support	136

	Institutional Location, Coordination, and Capacity	138
	Evidence from Program Evaluations: Filling the Gaps in Knowledge	149
	Piloting of Cash Transfers before Expansion	170
	Program Cost	174
	Building the Constituency for Domestic Support: Easing the Path to Scaling Up Cash Transfers	188
	The Role of Development Partners in Program Initiation and Scale-Up	194
	Conclusions	199
	Notes	200
	References	201
Chapter 4	**Synthesis, Conclusions, and the Way Forward**	**215**
	Unique Program Characteristics of Cash Transfers in Sub-Saharan Africa	215
	Knowledge Gaps and Areas for Future Research	221
	Conclusions and the Road Ahead	224
	Notes	225
	References	225
Appendix A	**Detailed Reviews of Sub-Saharan Africa's Cash Transfer Programs**	**227**
	Botswana	227
	Burkina Faso	229
	Burundi	231
	Cape Verde	232
	Democratic Republic of Congo	232
	Eritrea	233
	Ethiopia	237
	Ghana	247
	Kenya	251
	Lesotho	264
	Malawi	268
	Mali	276
	Mauritius	277
	Mozambique	278

	Namibia	285
	Niger	291
	Nigeria	292
	Rwanda	297
	São Tomé and Príncipe	301
	Senegal	301
	The Seychelles	307
	Somalia	307
	Sierra Leone	307
	South Africa	309
	Swaziland	315
	Tanzania	317
	Zambia	322
	Zimbabwe	330
	Notes	332
	References	335
Appendix B	**Overview Tables**	**349**
	References	409

Boxes

1.1	Countries Included in the Desk Review	15
1.2	The Economic Rationale for Cash Transfer Programs	19
1.3	Additional References on Cash Transfer Programs	20
1.4	The Roles of Social Protection: Protection, Prevention, and Promotion	23
1.5	Additional References on Social Protection in Africa	25
2.1	The African Union's Social Policy Framework	41
2.2	The South African Grant System	52
3.1	Objectives of Sub-Saharan Africa's Cash Transfer Programs	76
3.2	The Targeting Dilemma and Additional References on Targeting	81
3.3	Cash versus Food Transfers	95
3.4	Experimentation in New Technologies for CTs in Africa	109
3.5	To Condition or Not to Condition? Discussion and Additional References	127
3.6	Impact Evaluations	128

| 3.7 | Results from Evaluations of Conditional Cash Transfer Programs | 155 |
| 3.8 | Results from a Cash Transfer Program Evaluation | 157 |

Figures

2.1	People Living on Less Than US$1.25 per Day, by Region, 2009	33
2.2	Malnutrition and Food Aid in Africa, 1990–2004	35
2.3	Orphanhood in Sub-Saharan Africa, 2005	38
2.4	African Attitudes Regarding Connection between Hard Work and a Better Life	43
2.5	Africans Who Believe That Helping the Poor Should Be a Top National Priority, 2008 and 2009	44
2.6	Consideration of Cash Transfers by Governments or Donors in Sub-Saharan Africa as of 2010	45
2.7	Sub-Saharan African Countries' Experiences with Cash Transfers, 2010	46
2.8	Start Dates and Durations of Sub-Saharan African Cash Transfer Programs, 1990–2010	47
2.9	Types of Programs Implemented by Countries of Different Wealth Levels, 2000–09	54
2.10	Approaches to Risk Used by Countries of Different Income Levels, 2000–09	57
2.11	Coverage of Cash Transfer Programs	59
2.12	Scale of Africa's Cash Transfer Programs by Countries' Income Classification	61
2.13	Focus of Programs by Countries' Income Classification	63
2.14	Life Stages Are Associated with Susceptibility to Specific Vulnerabilities	66
2.15	Program Beneficiaries by Countries' Income Classification	67
3.1	Groups Targeted in Conditional and Unconditional Cash Transfer Programs in Sub-Saharan Africa	84
3.2	Multiple Targeting Methods Used by Programs in Sub-Saharan Africa	85
3.3	Programs That Provide Only Cash Versus Programs That Provide Additional Benefits	98
3.4	Monthly Average Size of Cash Transfers Given at the Household Level	101

x Contents

3.5	Monthly Average Size of Cash Transfers Given at the Beneficiary Level	101
3.6	Monthly Average Size of Cash Transfers, Variable Transfers	102
3.7	Cash Distribution Systems in African CTs	107
3.8	Transfer Frequency	112
3.9	Cash Transfer Distribution by Gender	113
3.10	Results of CTs versus UCTs in Malawi	116
3.11	Changes in Relative Numbers of CT Programs: UCTs versus CCTs	117
3.12	Use of UCTs versus CCTs by Country Income Status	118
3.13	Conditions Used in Sub-Saharan Africa's CCT Programs	119
3.14	Institutional Location of CT Programs	139
3.8.A	Schooling Results from Zomba CT	158
3.8.B	Educational Achievement Results from Zomba CT	159
3.8.C	Marriage and Pregnancy Outcomes from Zomba CT	160
3.15	Evaluations Used in CT Programs in Africa	161
3.16	Impact of Tanzania's RESPECT CCT on Prevalence of Curable STIs	168
3.17	Annual Costs of CT Programs	176
3.18	Comparison of CT Cost and GNI per Capita for Programs around the World	177
3.19	Funding of Cash Transfers in Sub-Saharan Africa, by Country Income Status	180
3.20	Specific Funders of Cash Transfers	182
3.21	Comparison of Programs' Administrative Costs and Program Coverage	185

Tables

2.1	HIV Prevalence, Adults Age 15–49, circa 2007	37
2.2	Sub-Saharan African Countries by Income and Subregion	49
2.3	General Characteristics of Middle-Income and Low-Income/Fragile Cash Transfers: A Basic Typology	50
2.4	Classification by Program Duration and Focus	53
2.5	Selected Cash Transfers by Program Focus	56
3.1	Experimental Impact Evaluations Planned in Selected Cash Transfer Programs	169
B.1	Number of Cash Transfers Identified by Country, 2000–09	350

B.2	Focus of Selected Cash Transfer Programs	351
B.3	Presence of Conditional and Unconditional Transfers by Country	353
B.4	Conditional and Unconditional Transfers by Program	354
B.5	Program Approach, Selected Cash Transfers	355
B.6	Programs by Scale, Selected Cash Transfers	357
B.7	Programs by Life Stage Focus, Selected Cash Transfers	359
B.8	Approximate Number of Beneficiaries Covered by Programs	360
B.9	Groups Targeted, Selected Cash Transfers	362
B.10	Targeting Methods, Selected Cash Transfers	364
B.11	Frequency of Cash Transfer Distribution	368
B.12	Transfer Size, Selected Cash Transfers	370
B.13	Other Benefits Given, Selected Cash Transfers	374
B.14	Gender of Cash Recipient	375
B.15	Payment Mechanism by Program	377
B.16	Program Conditions	380
B.17	Monitoring of Conditions, Selected Cash Transfers	381
B.18	Other Internal Monitoring, Selected Cash Transfers	382
B.19	Communications Campaign and Strategy, Selected Cash Transfers	384
B.20	Institutional Home	386
B.21	Funders by Program, Selected Cash Transfers	390
B.22	Annual Estimated Program Costs	393
B.23	Total Estimated Program Costs, Various Years	397
B.24	Process Evaluation Information, Selected Cash Transfers	398
B.25	Completed Impact Evaluations by Program	399
B.26	Ongoing Experimental Evaluations by Program	401
B.27	Results from Evaluations of Cash Transfers in Sub-Saharan Africa	402
B.28	Key Contacts for Desk Review	406

Foreword

It is an exciting time in Africa! Although the continent faces unparalleled challenges, its potential to meet these obstacles has never been greater. Development policy has become increasingly concerned with the effect of vulnerability to adverse shocks on individuals' ability to escape poverty permanently. At a time when many policy makers want to understand how to create effective, cost-efficient safety net programs that address Africa's unique challenges, enthusiasm for conditional cash transfer programs in other regions has spilled over into the continent. Many policy makers are excited about how cash transfers can be used to meet Africa's poverty and development goals. Nevertheless, the potential for cash transfers, both conditional and unconditional, to work in Africa must be better understood. It is this issue—whether cash transfer programs can translate to Africa and be used to reduce vulnerability, build asset bases, increase food security, and encourage human capital accumulation—that this book addresses.

This book provides the results of a thorough investigation of the recent use of cash transfer programs in Sub-Saharan Africa. The review was aimed toward understanding the evolution and current state of the programs, their intended uses, and the unique challenges associated with using cash transfer programs in the Sub-Saharan environment.

The results of the review do not disappoint. The authors identified more than 120 cash transfer programs that were implemented between 2000 and mid-2009 in Sub-Saharan Africa. These programs have varying objectives, targeting, scale, conditions, technologies, and more. A sizable number of these programs conducted robust impact evaluations that provide important information, presented here, on the merits of cash transfer programs and their specific design features in the African context. The authors present summary information on programs, often in useful graphs, and provide detailed reference material in the appendixes. They highlight how many of the cash transfer programs in Africa that had not yet begun implementation at the time of writing will continue to provide important evaluation results that will guide the design of cash transfer programs in the region. In addition to presenting data and analysis on the mechanics of the programs, the authors discuss issues related to political economy. They highlight the importance of addressing key trade-offs in cash transfers, political will, and buy-in, and they emphasize the need to build evidence-based debates on cash transfer programs. Useful anecdotes and discussion illustrate how some programs have dealt with these issues with varying degrees of success.

This text will serve as a useful reference for years to come for those interested in large- and small-scale issues of cash transfer implementation, both in Africa and beyond. However, the book is not an end in itself. It also raises important questions that must be addressed and knowledge gaps that must be filled. Therefore, it is useful both in the information it provides and in the issues and questions it raises.

Lynne Sherburne-Benz
Sector Manager, Social Protection
Human Development Department, Africa Region
The World Bank

Acknowledgments

This review was prepared by a team led by Marito Garcia, lead economist in the Africa Human Development Department of the World Bank (AFTSP), and Charity M. T. Moore, consultant, with contributions from Vicente Paqueo and Alan Brody, consultants. The work was guided by Lynne Sherburne-Benz, sector manager, AFTSP, and the AFTSP sector leadership team: Anush Bezhanyan, Carlo Del Ninno, Yasser El-Gammal, Setareh Razmara, and Giuseppe Zampaglione. Overall guidance on structure and content of the review was provided by Margaret Grosh, lead economist in the Human Development Department of the Latin American and Caribbean Region and team leader of the World Bank Social Protection Global Expert Team. The authors are indebted to the support from the management team of the Africa Human Development Department, led by Ritva Reinikka, sector director, and Maureen Lewis, adviser.

Special thanks is extended to Cécile Cherrier, Mohammed Farooq (United Nations Children's Fund—UNICEF), Charlotte Harland (UNICEF), Sebastian Levine (United Nations Development Programme—UNDP), and Julianna Lindsey (UNICEF) for helping provide structure and improving the content of the report.

This review would not have been possible without assistance from many individuals, both within and outside the World Bank, who are working in social protection and cash transfer programs throughout Sub-Saharan Africa. Many people were gracious enough to provide us with contact information or to send us in the right direction as we investigated cash transfers in the region.

Besides relying on valuable information cited in the references, we are indebted to the following individuals who provided comments and additional information used in the review: Jane Maponga (Action Aid International, Zimbabwe); Nilsa Batalha (Angola's Ministry of Social Assistance and Reinsertion); Francisco Ayala, Paulina LaVerde, and Jason Thompson (Ayala Consulting); Jacy Braga Rodrigues (Bolsa Escola, São Tomé and Príncipe); Armando Barrientos (Brooks World Poverty Institute and Chronic Poverty Research Centre); Rene Ferreira (Centro Nacional de Pensões Sociais, Cape Verde); Darren Evans (Concern Worldwide); Gilberte Hounsounou (Conditional Cash Transfers for Orphans and Vulnerable Children, Senegal); Helen Appleton, Catherine Arnold, Ian Atfield, Joanne Bosworth, Isabelle Cardinal, Fagoon Dave, Gertrude Mapunda Kihunrwa, Dennis Paine, Sonya Sultan, Tim Waites, and Rachel Yates (Department for International Development); Philippe Bertrand, Jan Eijkenaar, Eliana Toro, Héloise Troc, and Marika Uotila (European Commission); Esther Schüring and Sanna Stockstrom de Pella (German Technical Cooperation); Kerina Zvobgo (GRM, Zimbabwe); Stephen Kidd (HelpAge International) Benjamin Roberts (Human Sciences Research Council); Paul Harvey (Humanitarian Outcomes); Melissa Andrade and Fábio Veras Soares (International Policy Centre for Inclusive Growth); Sammy Keter (Ministry of Arid and Semi-arid Lands, Kenya); Bestone Mboozi and Morris Moono (Ministry of Community Development and Social Services, Zambia); Harry Mwamlima (Ministry of Economic Planning and Development, Malawi); Nicola Jones (Overseas Development Institute); Camilla Knox-Peebles and Nupur Kukrety (Oxfam GB); Patrick Ward (Oxford Policy Management); Alex Rees (Save the Children UK); Foday Conteh (National Safety Net Program, Unconditional Cash Transfer for the Poor and Needy (Sierra Leone); Bernd Schubert (Team Consult); Carlos Alviar, Maggie Brown, Ben Davis, Tony Hodges, Mayke Huijbregts, Kumiko Imai, Theresa Kilbane, Dorothee Klaus, Roger Pearson, Rémy Pigois, and Tayllor Spadafora (UNICEF); Gelson Tembo (University of Zambia); Harold Alderman, Jeanine Braithwaite, Sarah Coll-Black, Damien de Walque, Shanta Devarajan, Pierre Fallavier, Ariel Fiszbein,

Emanuela Galasso, Florence Kondylis, Mungai Lenneiye, Maureen Lewis, Ida Manjolo, Michael Mills, Menno Mulder-Sibanda, Aidan Mulkeen, Suleiman Namara, Foluso Okunmadewa, Azedine Ougheri, Mirey Ovadiya, Berk Özler, Nadine Poupart, Ando Raobelison, Dena Ringold, Manuel Salazar, Riham Shendy, Wout Soer, Emma Sorensson-Mistiaen, Concha Steta-Gandara, Tshiya Subayi-Cuppen, Quy-Toan Do, Maurizia Tovo, Vincent Turbat, Will Wiseman, and Ruth Wutete (World Bank); and Mads Lofvall and Waheed Lor-Mehdiabadi (World Food Programme). The time these individuals have taken to share documentation, comments, and other information is greatly appreciated.

Finally, although an attempt has been made to ensure that the information presented in this report is accurate, any errors are those of the authors.

Abbreviations

AIDS	acquired immunodeficiency syndrome
ATM	automated teller machine
CARE	Cooperative for Assistance and Relief Everywhere
CB-CCT	Community-Based Conditional Cash Transfer (Tanzania)
CCT	conditional cash transfer
CF-SCT	Child-Focused Social Cash Transfer (Senegal)
CGP	Child Grants Programme (Lesotho)
CIDA	Canadian International Development Agency
COPE	In Care of the Poor (Nigeria)
CT	cash transfer
DANIDA	Danish International Development Agency
DECT	Dowa Emergency Cash Transfers (Malawi)
DFID	U.K. Department for International Development
DCO	District Children Office (Kenya)
DPT	diphtheria, pertussis, tetanus (vaccine)
FAO	Food and Agricultural Organization of the United Nations
FACT	Food and Cash Transfers (Malawi)

GAPVU	Gabinete de Apoio à População Vulnerável, or Office for Assistance to the Vulnerable Population (Mozambique)
GDP	gross domestic product
GFATM	Global Fund to Fight AIDS, Tuberculosis, and Malaria
GNI	gross national income
GPS	global positioning system
GSM	Global System for Mobile Communications
HAMSET II	Second HIV/AIDS/STI, Tuberculosis, Malaria and Reproductive Health Project (Eritrea)
HIPC	Heavily Indebted Poor Countries (Initiative)
HIV	human immunodeficiency virus
HSNP	Hunger Safety Net Programme (Kenya)
HSV-2	herpes simplex virus type 2
IDA	International Development Association
ILO	International Labour Organization
IPC-IG	International Policy Centre for Inclusive Growth
LEAP	Livelihood Empowerment Against Poverty (Ghana)
MDG	Millennium Development Goal
MIS	management information system
NGO	nongovernmental organization
OVC	orphans and vulnerable children
PRP	Protracted Relief Programme
PSA	Programa de Subsidio de Alimentos, or Food Subsidy Program (Mozambique)
PSM	propensity score matching
PSNP	Productive Safety Net Programme (Ethiopia)
PSNP-DS	Productive Safety Net Programme–Direct Support component (Ethiopia)
RBF	Results-Based Financing (Eritrea)
RESPECT	Rewarding STI Prevention and Control in Tanzania
SASSA	South African Social Security Agency
SCT	social cash transfer
Sida	Swedish International Development Cooperation Agency
SIM	Subscriber Identity Module
STI	sexually transmitted infection
TASAF	Tanzania Social Action Fund
TIMSS	Trends in International Mathematics and Science Study
UCT	unconditional cash transfer

UNDP	United Nations Development Programme
UNESCO	United Nations Educational, Scientific, and Cultural Organization
UNHCR	Office of the United Nations High Commissioner for Refugees
UNICEF	United Nations Children's Fund
USAID	U.S. Agency for International Development
VUP	Vision 2020 Umurenge Programme (Rwanda)
WFP	World Food Programme

Overview

The challenges facing Sub-Saharan Africa are daunting. Although the continent experienced strong economic growth in the beginning of the 21st century, poverty and poor human capital indicators still characterize many countries in the region. Challenges related to environmental degradation, agricultural production and food security, climate change, natural and humanmade disasters, volatile prices and terms of trade, high unemployment and population growth, HIV/AIDS and other diseases, and other problems all demand strong responses.

The vulnerability of Africans to this myriad of challenges has increased as traditional support systems have struggled to protect individuals faced with idiosyncratic and covariate shocks. Increasing migration, urbanization, the HIV/AIDS epidemic, and the evolution of traditional family structures have weakened informal safety nets. Certain groups, such as orphans and vulnerable children (OVC), have been especially vulnerable to these changes.

These issues, along with recent economic crises and downturns, have increasingly led governments and donors in Africa to examine whether social protection in general—and cash transfer (CT) programs in particular—can address some of the region's challenges.

The Growing Use of Cash Transfer Programs in Sub-Saharan Africa

Traditional responses to disasters in Sub-Saharan Africa, such as emergency food aid in times of food shortages, have increasingly been seen as inadequate. Emergency food aid responds to famines but has failed to clearly contribute to food security. Many households receiving food aid are in a state of chronic, rather than temporary, food insecurity. Governments and groups that recognized these issues were some of the first to begin experimenting with transferring cash instead of food. Major CT programs in Ethiopia (the Productive Safety Net Programme's Direct Support component, or PSNP-DS) and Kenya (the Hunger Safety Net Programme, or HSNP) were developed to address this ongoing food insecurity. It is hoped that regular emergency aid eventually will not be needed if mechanisms are in place to help households manage risk in good times and cope with it in downturns.

Using regular cash transfers to decrease the need for emergency food aid is only one way that CT programs are being used to protect the region's poor and vulnerable population. The success of CT programs around the world has led Africans and the donor community to examine whether cash transfers can be used to address additional challenges in the region.

Support for CT programs—and for social protection in general—is growing within the region. Since late 2004, the African Union has provided encouragement to countries to develop their own social policy frameworks, and a Plan of Action supported by governments commits member states to expanding and empowering social protection programs. Individual governments are also taking the initiative in their own countries.

The Review of Cash Transfers, an Emerging Safety Net in Africa

In 2009, growing interest in the use of CT programs in Sub-Saharan Africa led the World Bank to initiate a comprehensive desk review of the CT programs that had been used recently in the region. This book presents the results of the review.

The review was conducted with assistance from, and in order to benefit, those working in social protection—especially CT programs—within Sub-Saharan Africa. Its intended audience is those in the development community with an interest in the region's experience with cash transfers.

Programs included in the review provided noncontributory transfers of cash from formal institutions to targeted individuals or households, usually to satisfy minimum consumption needs. The transfers could be conditional or unconditional and could be provided for emergency or development purposes. The review excluded public works programs, in-kind transfer programs, and voucher-based programs unless they also had a CT component.

The review consisted of several activities. Public documentation related to CT programs that existed in Sub-Saharan Africa since 2000, as well as related information on social protection, was reviewed. It is believed that almost all of the major relevant public documentation available at that time was considered. More than 200 individuals working in the identified cash transfer programs or related organizations were asked to provide additional information, with approximately half of these individuals providing more details on the programs and political economy issues.

This book summarizes the results of the review by examining how cash transfers have been used in Sub-Saharan Africa, analyzing and discussing program components, and highlighting lessons learned. Although useful in itself, the book cannot take the place of more in-depth assessments generated by those intimately familiar with the dynamics of each program's unique environment.

Results of the Review

A total of 123[1] cash transfer programs were identified in the review, although only a subset of these programs is described in detail in this book. The programs are diverse, ranging from emergency one-time transfers, to unconditional noncontributory social pensions, to conditional cash transfer programs (CCTs) with human capital development objectives similar to the vanguard Latin American CCTs.

Middle-Income and Low-Income Cash Transfers

Two distinct types of CT programs clearly emerge in the region. In general, upper-middle-income countries in Sub-Saharan Africa have implemented similar CT programs (known here as *middle-income CT programs*), while low-income countries and fragile states have operated programs that share many common characteristics (known here as *low-income* or *fragile CT programs*). Cash transfers in lower-middle-income countries fall into both categories: CT programs of lower-middle-income countries in Southern Africa are more similar to those of their upper-middle-income neighbors, whereas CT programs of lower-middle-income countries in the region are more similar to those of other low-income countries.

The middle-income CTs, often referred to as *cash grants*, are established programs expected to continue indefinitely. They are typically part of rights-based social assistance systems, sometimes stemming from systems established in the colonial era. They are usually based in government institutions and are domestically funded. These CT programs often focus on assisting individuals in poverty, and their stable nature allows them to proactively focus on the ex ante preventive and promotive roles of social protection. They typically cover a wide range of vulnerable groups and a significant portion of the population through coordinated registration and information systems. Their widespread coverage is often achieved through near-universal targeting of vulnerable groups (that is, categorical targeting), such as the elderly.

Conversely, low-income and fragile CTs are often short-term projects, or they aim to graduate beneficiaries from the program within a relatively short time frame. They are typically seated outside of the government and are partially or fully funded by donors. They often focus on combating food insecurity or building human capital. Another large group of these CT programs simply addresses emergencies—whether natural disasters or events caused by humans—once they have occurred. These projects often target a very limited portion of the population or a certain vulnerable group, which is often influenced by donor preferences. Since these CT programs are not seated in a central organization, their management information systems are usually ad hoc, are not linked to other programs, and are often of poor quality. The fragmented nature and patchy coverage of these CT programs reflect their lack of domestic ownership and coordination.

Despite the major differences across the two groups, some low-income countries are headed down a path similar to that followed by the wealthier countries in the region. There is a growing trend in low-income countries toward institutionalization of some major CT programs. Many pilot programs hope to become large-scale, permanent programs, and they are working toward this end. Government ownership of these programs is relatively strong, and key investments are being made to establish the core systems (targeting, payments, monitoring, and so on) necessary for their success.

Distinguishing Characteristics of Sub-Saharan Africa's Cash Transfer Programs

Sub-Saharan Africa's CT programs share many characteristics with CT programs around the world. However, they clearly stand out as unique in certain areas. Some of these features effectively address the unique context of Sub-Saharan Africa, others are not inherently positive or negative, and still others have arisen as CTs are used to confront challenges of greater frequency or depth than those seen in other regions. They are an attempt at a best response, given the current challenges of the specific context.

Programs are responding to Sub-Saharan Africa's unique challenges. Although many CT programs—especially conditional cash transfer programs—often address households' lack of human capital, programs in Sub-Saharan Africa recognize that even more basic issues, such as food security and survival, must first be addressed in their beneficiary populations. Therefore, their objectives often focus more directly on households' immediate needs.

Some programs in Sub-Saharan Africa also focus on sexual activities and outcomes, such as early marriage and sexually transmitted infection (STI) status. These types of objectives, though similar in part to those of some other CT programs, are relatively unique, and they reflect a programmatic variation that can address Sub-Saharan Africa's challenges in these areas. Programs that focus on supporting OVC also help to systematically deal with the OVC crisis affecting many countries in the region.

Most cash transfer programs have a high level of community involvement. Although many CT programs around the world require communities to support program activities, the programs in Sub-Saharan Africa often rely on communities in ways beyond those found in other regions. Communities are involved in identifying and selecting potential beneficiaries, collecting data, verifying information about beneficiaries, distributing cash, monitoring beneficiaries' use of cash (even in unconditional transfers), and addressing grievances. This extensive community involvement often is driven by capacity limitations in the programs' implementing bodies.

Although community involvement can raise new concerns about the management of cash transfers, it has been indispensable to the programs in Sub-Saharan Africa. When correctly managed, community involvement can lower costs, improve implementation, and help sustain traditional support systems that have been weakened by constant pressure and a changing environment. Because communities can sometimes be a source of exclusion and discrimination to individuals not favored by traditional authorities or powers, community involvement needs to be appropriately monitored to ensure that abuses do not occur.

Programs often do not require cash payment recipients to be females. In contrast to many other CT programs around the world, many programs in Sub-Saharan Africa do not specify that a woman should be the recipient of the cash. This trend is partially driven by the number of programs that transfer cash to individuals rather than households (for example, social pensions). Even so, this explanation does not fully explain this tendency, and it is not clear that this programmatic variation is a first-best approach.

Empirical work and anecdotal evidence have pointed to the benefits that can accrue to children as women's control of household resources increases. For instance, Duflo (2003) has found such beneficial impacts in South Africa, and Quisumbing and Maluccio (2000) have found qualified evidence of such benefits in Ethiopia and South Africa. However, assuming that women should automatically receive all CTs in the region also could be naive. Fortunately, programs are testing how results differ when transfers are distributed to males rather than females in Burkina Faso and, outside of the region, in Morocco and the Republic of Yemen, which share some gender dynamics similar to parts of Sub-Saharan Africa.

Use of and application of conditions for cash transfers are relatively flexible. Conditional cash transfer programs in Sub-Saharan Africa apply conditions and monitoring with a level of flexibility not seen as frequently outside of the region. Many CCT programs in Sub-Saharan Africa use "soft" conditions, which impose no penalties for noncompliance. Even in programs that enforce hard conditions, most apply those conditions flexibly. For example, conditions may be applied only in locations with adequate supply-side infrastructure or in areas that receive additional supply-side investments. In some cases, only households that are judged capable of fulfilling conditions are required to abide by them. Conditions are often monitored less frequently than they are in other regions, and warnings and partial payment penalties are often applied when beneficiaries do not comply with conditions to ensure that benefits are not inappropriately kept from needy households.

This hesitancy to apply conditions in the traditional sense reflects valid concerns about the beneficiaries' ability to fulfill conditions, the capacity of supply-side institutions to handle increased demand, and the programs' capacity to monitor conditions. Once again, these issues are being tested by evaluations in the region, and they deserve further analysis.

New leapfrog technologies are used in cash transfer operations in Africa. Cash transfer programs in Sub-Saharan Africa are investigating how to use advanced technologies to overcome traditional capacity constraints. Some of these technologies address challenges that are relatively unique to the region. Biometric identification can overcome traditional difficulties in identifying beneficiaries without appropriate documentation; point-of-sale devices or mobile phones can be used to transfer cash to nomadic or hard-to-reach beneficiaries; mobile phones may be used for data collection, social marketing, communication, or monitoring purposes; web-based management information systems may be able to integrate program databases across remote locations; and more. The possibility for technology to address capacity constraints in the region is still being investigated. Although there is excitement about the possibility of using advanced technologies, this excitement should be tempered with a realistic understanding of whether and how these technologies will deliver what they promise.

Institutional location and funding of CTs are both governmental and nongovernmental. Unlike the leading CT programs in other regions, almost half of the identified Sub-Saharan African programs were located outside government institutions, and one in two were funded entirely by nongovernmental funds. Although these programs have been valuable and generated important information, continuing this trend in the long run would be inefficient.

Programs that remain outside of domestic governments fail to capitalize on potential economies of scale needed for cost-effective implementation of targeting, registration, monitoring, and evaluation systems. Meanwhile, duplication of effort occurs as each program establishes its own systems and procedures. Impacts are limited and resources wasted, while portions of the potential beneficiary population may remain unsupported. The programs fail to develop capacity within government institutions, while they remain subject to the whims of donors and short funding cycles. They also face challenges of balancing domestic and external priorities.

Although weak macroeconomic conditions have often discouraged African leaders from funding major CTs or similar programs, certain signs suggest that increased fiscal space may be available for domestic funding of CTs in the medium to long term. Regional economic growth before the recent downturn, combined with stable macroeconomic policies, increased revenue collection, foreign investment, and potential natural resource revenues (if managed correctly), suggest that many countries may be increasingly able to fund CT programs, provided that they have the will to do so. Improvements in governance help make these goals more feasible.

That being said, many CT programs will continue to require external financing and support, and development partners can make important contributions by adopting long-term, coordinated approaches to funding cash transfers and supporting long-term capacity building and technical support for CTs.

Lessons Learned and the Road Ahead

Much can already be learned from Sub-Saharan Africa's experience with cash transfer programs. Evaluations of unconditional programs have found significant impacts on household food consumption (for instance, Miller, Tsoka, and Mchinji Evaluation Team 2007 for Malawi's Social Cash Transfer Program; Soares and Teixeira 2010 for Mozambique's Food Subsidy Program); nonfood consumption (for instance, RHVP 2009 for Zambia's Social Cash Transfer); and children's nutrition and education (including Agüero, Carter, and Woolard 2007 and Williams 2007 for South Africa's Child Support Grant). A recent experimental evaluation found that a program for adolescent girls conditioned on their school attendance improved enrollment, attendance, and test scores in Malawi. Unconditional transfers in the same program decreased early marriage and pregnancy among girls who had already dropped out of school (Baird, McIntosh, and Özler 2011). Another experimental evaluation of a conditional program in Tanzania found that a relatively large transfer conditioned on STI status helped keep adults from contracting STIs, thereby pointing to the potential of CT programs to help fight HIV (de Walque and others 2011).

This information is useful, but more needs to be learned. Results from evaluations already under way will continue to provide information on the usefulness of conditions in CT programs in Sub-Saharan Africa, the impact of paying transfers to female or male household representatives, and the impact of transfers when programs benefit from previous community investments or other coexisting successful programs.

Impact evaluations will provide important information for program design, but more can also be learned from case studies and experience sharing across programs. Knowledge gaps remain in key areas, including, among others, collecting data in settings with limited financial and human resource capacity, targeting individuals who may not be easily identified because of stigma or inaccessibility, dealing with soft issues related to conditions, using communities effectively, monitoring and coordinating among involved groups in limited-capacity settings, and coordinating donor funding while supporting government priorities and systems.

Cash transfer programs are not a panacea. They are not always an appropriate tool, they cannot address all vulnerabilities or problems, and they face steep challenges to their effective implementation. Nevertheless, excitement over the potential use of CTs in Sub-Saharan Africa is not unmerited. Experiences—many relatively successful—reveal that the question is not *whether* cash transfers can be used in the region, but *how* they should be used, and how they can be adapted and developed to meet social protection and development goals. Cash transfers may well prove to be an important tool for addressing the region's development, poverty alleviation, and human rights aspirations.

Note

1. The total is 134 if programs with unofficial sources or unclear 2009 start dates are included.

References

Agüero, Jorge, Michael Carter, and Ingrid Woolard. 2007. "The Impact of Unconditional Cash Transfers on Nutrition: The South African Child Support Grant." Working Paper 39, International Poverty Centre, Brasília.

Baird, Sarah, Craig McIntosh, and Berk Özler. 2011. "Cash or Condition? Evidence from a Cash Transfer Experiment." World Bank, Washington, DC. http://ipl.econ.duke.edu/bread/papers/0511conf/Baird.pdf.

de Walque, Damien, William H. Dow, Rose Nathan, Carol Medlin, and RESPECT Study Team. 2011. "Evaluating Conditional Cash Transfers to Prevent HIV and Other STIs in Tanzania." PowerPoint presentation, World Bank, Washington, DC, May 4.

Duflo, Esther. 2003. "Grandmothers and Granddaughters: Old-Age Pensions and Intrahousehold Allocation in South Africa." *World Bank Economic Review* 17 (1): 1–25.

Miller, Candace, Maxton Tsoka, and Mchinji Evaluation Team. 2007. "Evaluation of the Mchinji Cash Transfer: Report II—Targeting and Impact." Center for International Health and Development, Boston University, Boston, and Centre for Social Research, University of Malawi, Zomba.

Quisumbing, Agnes R., and John A. Maluccio. 2000. "Intrahousehold Allocation and Gender Relations: New Empirical Evidence from Four Developing Countries." FCND Discussion Paper 84, Food, Consumption, and Nutrition Division, International Food Policy Research Institute, Washington, DC.

RHVP (Regional Hunger and Vulnerability Programme). 2009. "Impact of Social Cash Transfers on Household Welfare, Investment, and Education in Zambia." Wahenga Brief 17, RHVP, Johannnesburg. http://www.wahenga.net/node/223.

Soares, Fábio Veras, and Clarissa Teixeira. 2010. "Impact Evaluation of the Expansion of the Food Subsidy Programme in Mozambique." Research Brief 17, International Policy Centre for Inclusive Growth, Brasília.

Williams, Martin J. 2007. "The Social and Economic Impacts of South Africa's Child Support Grant." Working Paper 39, Economic Policy Research Institute, Cape Town, South Africa.

CHAPTER 1

Cash Transfers
An Effective Means to Promote Equitable Growth and Protect the Poor in Sub-Saharan Africa?

Over the past decade, interest has increased around the world in the use of cash transfers (CTs) as a means to promote inclusive growth. Although many of the most well-known CT programs are based in Latin America or parts of Asia, experience with the programs has not been limited to these regions. Increasingly, cash transfers have been used in Sub-Saharan Africa. A growing interest in the use of CTs and the lessons that can be learned from them has led to this comprehensive review of the experiences of Sub-Saharan African countries with these programs. This book synthesizes the results of that review for the benefit of development practitioners working in Sub-Saharan Africa and around the world.

The Recent Increase in Cash Transfers around the World

The use of CT programs has steadily increased around the globe, and these programs now exist in countries in Africa, Asia, Central Europe, and Latin America. The rise of CTs coincides with the *quiet revolution,* a term used to describe the rapid increase in social protection programs on development agendas around the world (Barrientos and Hulme

2008b). As of 2008, Barrientos and Hulme estimated that cash transfers benefited 150 million households throughout the developing world. The proliferation of CTs is a phenomenon that has arisen within the global south, where countries have created programs that suit their own unique needs (Hanlon, Barrientos, and Hulme 2010).

Increased Interest in Cash Transfers in Sub-Saharan Africa

In part, cash transfers arose in Sub-Saharan Africa as recognition grew that some other types of aid were not effectively achieving their goals. For example, emergency food aid was responding to famines, but it was failing to contribute to food stability. Over time, the chronically poor became increasingly dependent on food aid. Such trends became a major concern in countries such as Ethiopia, whose emergency food aid cost an average of US$265 million from 1997 through 2002, reaching more than 5 million people each year (Hoddinott n.d.). Other Sub-Saharan African countries with early experiences with CTs, such as Malawi, had also faced this problem and turned to cash transfers.

Increasing migration, urbanization, and the evolution of traditional family structures have also weakened traditional safety nets in Sub-Saharan Africa. Individuals who formerly would have been cared for by family members have increasingly been left to fend for themselves. The ability of informal safety nets to protect individuals has weakened considerably in the face of increased demands brought on by the HIV/AIDS crisis. Certain groups—especially orphans and vulnerable children (OVC)—have been especially vulnerable to these changes.

These problems are compounded when considered jointly with other sources of vulnerability and poverty in the region, such as exclusion, patronage politics, insecure property rights and landlessness, environmental degradation, and conflict stemming from ethnic differences.

Finally, recent financial crises and price volatility have sharpened the interest of certain policy makers, notably Africans themselves (see box 2.1 in chapter 2), in using different methods to address persistent and often deepening vulnerabilities. Noting the success of cash transfers in other parts of the world, stakeholders have increasingly asked whether CT programs could address the complex challenges present in Sub-Saharan Africa. Key questions include whether CTs are appropriate in Sub-Saharan Africa and, if so, what factors increase a program's probability of success and maximize its potential outcomes.

The Review of Cash Transfers, an Emerging Safety Net in Africa

Growing excitement over the potential impacts of cash transfers in Sub-Saharan Africa needs to be balanced by a thorough understanding of the way CT programs work in different contexts throughout the continent. The success of CTs in Asia or Latin America does not necessarily imply that CT programs would be just as successful in Sub-Saharan Africa. Additionally, the design of programs in other regions may not be entirely appropriate when transferred to Sub-Saharan Africa. An assessment of the programs' feasibility requires an understanding of the broader status of social protection in the region and a closer look at how well existing CTs have worked in specific contexts of different Sub-Saharan African countries.

Scope and Role of the Review

In 2009, this growing interest in the use of cash transfers in Sub-Saharan Africa led the World Bank to initiate a desk review of all CT programs in the region. Important overviews of social protection in Africa have already been completed (for example, Ellis, Devereux, and White 2009; Taylor 2010). Other reviews have provided excellent information about CTs (such as Andrade 2008; Barrientos and Holmes 2007; Barrientos, Niño-Zarazúa, and Maitrot 2010). However, the scope of prior reviews has not been as comprehensive as that attempted here, both in its identification of CTs and its analysis of program components. This review attempts to supply up-to-date information on countries' experiences with CTs throughout the region, as well as to provide a comprehensive overall analysis of the region's programs. Sub-Saharan Africa has significant experience with various types of CTs, and such experiences will be useful as other countries, both within and outside the region, continue to develop their own programs.

The initial review of the CT programs was conducted from April 2009 to June of 2009. The analysis in this book includes only those programs with official information sources that were known to have started by the end of June of 2009, unless otherwise specified. Supplementary information for the review was collected through the end of 2010, but new programs were not added to the analysis.[1]

The review was conducted with assistance from those working in social protection within Sub-Saharan Africa, and it is meant to benefit that group. Its intended audience is those in the development community with an interest in the past experiences and current state of cash transfers within Sub-Saharan Africa. Therefore, the book assumes that the reader is familiar with the basic components of social protection and CTs. Although a cursory review of major relevant concepts is provided, throughout the text the reader is referred to other sources for further information.

Programs Covered in the Review

The decision regarding which types of programs to include in the review was driven by the need to understand how cash-based programs provided by formal institutions (the state, donors, nongovernmental organizations, and so forth) have been used in Sub-Saharan Africa. Therefore, other social assistance programs that solely provide food or in-kind transfers, as well as voucher-based programs, are not covered. Because interest was based on programs that provided benefits to individuals or households only, grants given to communities or other groups were not included in the analysis. All types of CT programs were included, regardless of their focus on emergency assistance or economic development.

The parameters of the study were also driven by a wider World Bank review of social assistance programs, which divided the review of CTs from that of public works and other programs that some might include under the definition of cash transfers. For this reason, cash-based public works programs were excluded from the review. Nevertheless, some CTs are part of larger programs that provide in-kind transfers or vouchers or that have a public works component. Because these programs also provide the type of cash transfers covered by this review, they are included in the current analysis, with attention directed to their CT components.

A total of 123 CT programs were identified,[2] though only a subset of these programs is described in detail in this book. The CTs uncovered in the region are diverse. They range from emergency one-time transfers to unconditional, noncontributory social pensions to conditional cash transfer programs with human capital development objectives similar to the flagship Latin American programs.

Activities in the Review

The review comprised several activities. Initially, public documentation related to Sub-Saharan African CT programs that existed since 2000 was reviewed. (The list of countries included in the desk review is provided in box 1.1.) This portion of the study included examining documents that discussed program components, execution, and evaluation; loan agreements; and the political economy. It is believed that almost all of the

> **Box 1.1**
>
> ### Countries Included in the Desk Review
>
> | | |
> |---|---|
> | Angola | Madagascar |
> | Benin | Malawi |
> | Botswana | Mali |
> | Burkina Faso | Mauritania |
> | Burundi | Mauritius |
> | Cameroon | Mozambique |
> | Cape Verde | Namibia |
> | Central African Republic | Niger |
> | Chad | Nigeria |
> | Comoros | Rwanda |
> | Congo, Dem. Rep. | São Tomé and Príncipe |
> | Congo, Rep. | Senegal |
> | Côte d'Ivoire | Seychelles |
> | Equatorial Guinea | Sierra Leone |
> | Eritrea | Somalia |
> | Ethiopia | South Africa |
> | Gabon | Sudan |
> | Gambia, The | Swaziland |
> | Ghana | Tanzania |
> | Guinea | Togo |
> | Guinea-Bissau | Uganda |
> | Kenya | Zambia |
> | Lesotho | Zimbabwe |
> | Liberia | |

major relevant public documentation available at that time was accessed and reviewed. Additional supporting documentation was also examined in an effort to understand the state of social protection in Sub-Saharan Africa and to ascertain the interest of countries and development partners in certain types of CTs.

In an effort to supplement the review of program-related documentation, key individuals working in the identified CT programs were contacted via e-mail to solicit additional information on the programs. These individuals were informed of the nature of the project and asked if they had additional information or documentation regarding the program of interest or pertaining more generally to CTs throughout the region. The individuals contacted were those listed on public documentation, as well as others known to play a role in CTs in Sub-Saharan Africa. They included high- and mid-level officials in relevant programs and their lead ministries, members of the donor community, and other researchers.[3]

More than 200 individuals were contacted during this process, with a response rate of approximately 50 percent. Many individuals provided supplemental program documentation that had not been accessed already, complemented by their written insights into the relevant programs. More than 25 individuals agreed to and completed telephone interviews, which typically lasted between 30 minutes and one hour. Several others were interviewed in person. Interviews covered additional details about the programs and how they functioned, as well as issues related to political will and program perception, which were more difficult to obtain from the program literature.

Limitations of the Review

Support and insight from African policy makers were invaluable to the review. However, in general, responses were more readily elicited from the donor community than from individuals within specific programs on the ground. Difficulties associated with contacting and communicating with some policy makers and program implementers within countries have led some discussion in this book to be driven relatively more by the perspectives of the supporting community of donors and academics than by the perspectives of Africans themselves (particularly those in lower-level positions). This potential bias has been kept in mind, and every attempt has been made to fairly represent programs in light of this limitation.

Obviously, more information was available on programs that have existed for several years or that are larger in scale. Also, documentation was more easily obtained for programs that have received strong external support. Any tendency to focus on programs that have greater ties to the donor community is driven by the comparatively greater availability of information on those programs rather than any sort of preference for them.

Likewise, documentation and information on emergency one-off or short-lived transfers were more difficult to obtain, and it is not clear that every single program of this type from 2000 or later has been identified. These short-term programs often lack the documentation that larger, long-term programs have. In some cases, very little information was obtained about these programs, which limited the extent to which they could be included in the analysis in chapter 3. Despite this limitation, a major effort was made to ensure that all of these programs were identified. Whenever relevant information was uncovered, it was used in the analysis. However, these programs are often not discussed at length, and detailed information provided in the appendixes does not cover most of these CT programs because of their small size, their short duration, and the dearth of official information about them.

Charts and descriptions in chapters 2 and 3 may also be biased by the availability of information on specific program characteristics. To the extent that programs without available information differed systematically from those with data, the analysis will be biased. In light of these limitations, the analysis presented is intended to provide a general look at the state of CTs in the region rather than to provide a definitive breakdown on all programs in Sub-Saharan Africa.

The insights this book provides are primarily in the general analysis of program characteristics in chapters 2 and 3. Because information on some program aspects, particularly those related to softer issues, was sometimes limited, the discussion in these chapters varies between numerical analysis of program components and more general descriptions and anecdotal evidence. This variation in approach was driven by the availability of information on each topic.

An additional weakness of the review was its inability to incorporate many details of how the political economy affected the programs. Although this limitation caused the analysis to focus on many of the more easily quantified program features, readers should be aware that soft issues also played a role in the programs' success in the region. Context is of utmost importance, and CTs should be designed with that in mind. Politics—at both the local and national levels—remain key to the success of all programs. The analysis presented here should be interpreted with the understanding that these softer political issues are paramount and that simply getting program basics right (that is, targeting, monitoring, payment systems, and so forth) may not be sufficient if these other issues are not fully addressed.

Finally, this review of country experiences with CTs in Sub-Saharan Africa provides a useful starting point for readers who want to understand the scope and design of CT programming in the region. It claims only to broadly summarize experiences and provide data and insights that may shed light on cross-cutting and cross-country issues of program design and implementation. Although useful in itself, it cannot take the

What Are Cash Transfer Programs?

Before moving on, readers will find it important to clarify what the term *cash transfer program* refers to throughout the remainder of the book. For the purposes of the review, such programs provide noncontributory cash grants to selected beneficiaries to satisfy minimum consumption needs. Sometimes these programs are also known as *social cash transfer* or *social transfer programs*. The transfers are noncontributory in the sense that beneficiaries do not pay into a system that later awards them the transfers. By definition, they exclude partially or wholly self-funded pension systems or other forms of deferred compensation. This definition includes noncontributory pensions, poverty-based transfers, and family grants. Beneficiaries do not need to work to receive transfers; therefore, public works and guaranteed employment programs are excluded.[4] However, other requirements or conditions may be placed on beneficiaries before they are allowed to receive their CTs. The source of the transfers is the state or other public entities; remittances and other private transfers are not included.

CTs are typically provided with relief or development goals in mind. Emergency CTs are provided to help households smooth consumption in the face of a major crisis, whereas CTs for development are usually given at regular intervals for an extended period of time with longer-term goals in mind. Many CTs in Sub-Saharan Africa contain elements intended for both of these purposes. For additional information on the economic rationale for the use of cash transfer programs, see box 1.2. Box 1.3 also provides some additional references on the topic.

Some program design or implementation features are common across CTs. For instance, similar to other safety net programs, CT programs typically target beneficiaries in chronic or transient poverty or people belonging to vulnerable groups, such as those who lose out in reforms (Grosh and others 2008). Well-designed CTs are also characterized by objective targeting, payment, and monitoring and evaluation systems.

Conditional and Unconditional Transfers and In-Kind Transfers

Cash transfer programs may be conditional or unconditional. Unconditional cash transfers (UCTs) provide cash to all eligible and registered beneficiaries. Conditional cash transfers (CCTs) provide benefits only to beneficiaries

Box 1.2

The Economic Rationale for Cash Transfer Programs

Several arguments have been made in support of CT programs. First, it is argued that distributing cash to the poor can be a more effective poverty-fighting instrument than other public sector investments. Other investments in areas such as infrastructure or public services can tend to be regressive, benefiting wealthy individuals more than the poor. Whether public investments are better spent on infrastructure, public services, governance reform, other social protection programs, or otherwise is not easily answered, and countries will have to weigh these trade-offs carefully.

A second argument is that CTs can be used to lessen the impact of failures in credit and insurance markets. CTs can allow beneficiaries to make investments or purchases they could not otherwise make, given credit market imperfections, and they can help beneficiaries smooth income and consumption, given limitations in insurance markets. Such a role for CTs is particularly important once an adverse shock has occurred. Similarly, providing (nonemergency) transfers at predictable intervals can help beneficiaries manage risks of idiosyncratic or systemic shocks ex ante. It is argued that cash transfers may significantly reduce the impact of market imperfections—and at a lower cost than intervening to fix the market.

From the perspective of utility maximization, CTs provide beneficiaries with as much or greater utility than any type of in-kind transfer, because the beneficiary can choose to spend the cash in the way that is most useful for him or her. Likewise, a CT allows households to achieve (weakly) higher utility than they could from a subsidy.

The rights-based perspective argues that CTs allow the state to redress inequalities in groups disadvantaged by exogenously determined characteristics, such as ethnicity, gender, or parents' poverty levels. Individuals born into poverty have fewer opportunities than others, and the state may address this problem by providing CTs. The rights-based rationale also argues that a CT is less paternalistic than other government-provided benefits, particularly in-kind transfers, because it does not decide which bundle of goods or services will be most useful to the beneficiary.

Taken together, these arguments suggest that CTs can increase efficiency (that is, by replacing more regressive programs, reducing the costs of market failures, and allowing beneficiaries to achieve higher utility levels) and equity (that is, by acting as a redistribution mechanism).

(continued next page)

Box 1.2 *(continued)*

Cash transfers may also be linked to programs that encourage productivity-enhancing or income-generating activities that will decrease poverty and vulnerability, and they are thought to play a productivity-increasing role themselves. They are seen as important for addressing short-term problems (such as a shortage of income in households with young children) that could have long-term deleterious consequences (such as malnutrition, which could lead to lower long-term productivity).

For additional references on cash transfer programs, see box 1.3. For more information about the economic rationale for CCTs, and additional references on the topic, refer to box 3.3 in chapter 3.

Source: Fiszbein and Schady 2009.

Box 1.3

Additional References on Cash Transfer Programs

Multiple valuable resources are available on various aspects of cash transfers. Fiszbein and Schady (2009) discuss the rationale for cash transfers and CCTs and examine results from CCTs around the world. Arnold, Conway, and Greenslade (2011) provide evidence on the impact of CTs around the world. Hanlon, Barrientos, and Hulme (2010) also present arguments for the use of CTs around the world. They emphasize the importance of program context, as well as methods to improve CTs, particularly those that receive significant donor funding. Samson, van Niekerk, and Mac Quene (2006) highlight issues to consider when designing and implementing social cash transfers. They also provide a good overview of how CTs fit into various conceptual frameworks for social protection. Samson (2009) discusses the potential of CTs to stimulate pro-poor growth.

Harvey (2007) examines the role of CTs for humanitarian relief, as well as the ties between emergency transfers, development, and social protection. References for how to set up emergency CTs include Harvey and others (2010) and International Red Cross and Red Crescent Movement (2007).

Devereux and Pelham (2005) review unconditional cash transfers used in Southern and Eastern Africa and discuss lessons learned. Holmes and Barrientos (2009) examine how CTs can be used to address child poverty in West Africa.

who have fulfilled prescribed conditions, known also as *co-responsibilities*. Common conditions include the requirement that children regularly attend school; that they obtain prescribed medical checkups; or that a household adult attend educational seminars covering basic nutrition, health, and other topics. Throughout the remainder of this book, the term *CTs* will refer to both unconditional and conditional cash transfers.

Typically, most CCTs—and some UCTs—provide benefits to female, rather than male, adult household members. This design feature is expected to increase females' household bargaining power and to improve children's well-being. It is based on empirical evidence suggesting that greater control of household resources by females is associated with larger expenditures on items for children (see Quisumbing and Maluccio 2000 for just one example).

Whether CTs should be conditioned has been hotly debated. It is generally recommended that conditions be used when households are investing in suboptimal levels of human capital or when conditions help garner political support for the program. However, even when these conditions exist, the cost of imposing conditions should be weighed against the benefits they are expected to generate.[5] For additional information regarding the rationale for using conditions in CTs, see box 3.5 in chapter 3.

Although this review does not discuss extensively whether cash or in-kind transfers are more appropriate in a given setting, this aspect is important to consider. In general, cash transfers are recognized as more efficient than food or other in-kind transfers, both from a logistic and from a utility-maximizing point of view. However, additional important issues should be considered before CTs are used, particularly during times of food shortages, droughts, or other natural disasters. When food supplies are extremely limited, food transfers are preferable to cash, because CTs may drive up local food prices and not protect consumption levels. The value of CTs can also erode significantly in a high-inflation environment. Unless the CTs are indexed to food prices, food transfers may be more appropriate. Thus, CTs are not a universal solution, and local factors affecting their effectiveness need to be carefully considered. For more information about the use of food and cash transfers, see box 3.3 in chapter 3.

Other Commonly Recognized Benefits of CTs

Relatively strong evaluation designs and program monitoring systems have contributed to the measurement of the clearly beneficial effects of

CTs on poverty, school enrollment and attendance, per capita consumption, children's growth indicators, and more. CTs have also been found to increase investment in productive activities (see box 3.7 in chapter 3 for results from selected CCTs).

A generally recognized benefit of CCTs is their potential to combat short-term poverty by ensuring that minimum consumption levels are met, while encouraging households to invest in human capital, which will provide many long-term benefits. UCTs can do the same to a potentially different degree.

Other commonly mentioned benefits of CTs include their ability to maintain relatively low administrative costs and encourage interinstitutional coordination and institutional strengthening. CTs have also played a key role in developing more coherent, coordinated national social protection policies and strategies. In addition, some CTs may encourage inclusion of the poor in the financial system. Depending on local markets and infrastructure, transfers have varying multiplier effects on local economies (Sabates-Wheeler, Devereux, and Guenther 2009). Finally, some countries, such as Ethiopia, have been able to scale up their programs in response to crises, thereby establishing that appropriately designed CTs may be able to provide a temporary, wide-scale response to crises.[6]

Cash Transfers within the Social Protection System

Although they are important programs on their own, CTs are a vital component of a country's social protection system (when it exists). Many authors have thoughtfully addressed the concepts of social protection and safety net programs. Such detailed discussions are beyond the scope of this book. However, for the purposes of the review, this book relies on a recent World Bank definition of *social protection* as "private (both formal and informal) and public initiatives that connect men and women to labor markets, reduce people's exposure to risks, and enhance their capacity to protect themselves against hazards and loss of income that threaten their present and future well-being" (World Bank 2011, 9).

Programs classified as social protection include social assistance, social insurance, social funds, social services, and public policies related to issues such as labor or gender (Ellis, Devereux, and White 2009; Grosh and others 2008; Slater and others 2008). These categories include noncontributory and contributory transfer schemes ranging from subsidies and transfers to unemployment insurance and pensions.

Box 1.4

The Roles of Social Protection: Protection, Prevention, and Promotion

Social protection is often envisaged as providing ex post *protection* to those who have suffered shocks to ensure that they maintain a basic level of well-being and do not suffer irreversible losses; ex ante *prevention*, which decreases the probability that shocks, given that they occur, will have an adverse impact on those experiencing them; and ex ante *promotion* of individuals and households into increased and higher-return investments in assets, human capital, and livelihoods (see the accompanying figure). It is also mentioned as capable of transforming social risks and inequalities to empower marginalized and vulnerable groups for a more just society (Devereux and Sabates-Wheeler 2004).

Examples of social protection for individuals include food aid, subsidies, and transfers. Preventive programs include crop, weather, health, unemployment, or disability insurance; pensions; and public works programs. Promotive programs include nutrition programs, extension programs, vocational training,

The Roles of Social Protection

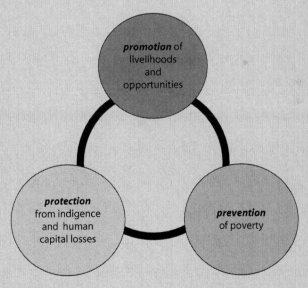

Source: World Bank 2011.

(continued next page)

> **Box 1.4** *(continued)*
>
> microcredit programs, and CCTs. Transformative social protection includes policy making and information campaigns to influence individuals' attitudes or behaviors.
>
> Other often-discussed features of social protection include its potential to reduce aggregate poverty and promote macroeconomic growth. The role of social protection as a component of the social contract is also important, as the state then ensures its citizens will maintain a basic level of welfare. In countries recovering from civil conflict, social protection is considered important for consolidating peace and strengthening the state (Blank and Handa 2008). Social protection interventions are seen as complementary to market-based mechanisms: they are able to provide protection from market failures and adverse market-based corrections (European University Institute 2010).

Social assistance programs, also known as *safety nets*, are defined as "noncontributory transfer programs targeted in some manner to the poor and those vulnerable to poverty and shocks" (Grosh and others 2008, 514). Programs in a country's safety net system could include cash transfers, in-kind transfers, subsidies or fee waivers, and public works programs of various types. Others consider safety nets more narrowly, limiting them to programs that provide minimal benefits at minimum cost and that support beneficiaries only when markets fail to provide for their basic needs (Ellis, Devereux, and White 2009). The definition of safety nets used in this book represents the broader perspective.

CTs are part of safety net programs or systems and, therefore, are part of social protection in general. Depending on their specific features, CTs can play a protective role for individuals who have experienced an adverse shock (emergency or relief CTs); they can reduce the potential negative effect of shocks before they occur (that is, CTs that have been used to replace emergency food aid); they can play a promotive role by increasing investments in assets or human capital (CCTs and UCTs); and they may transform individuals' attitudes to increase social justice and inclusion of excluded groups and minorities (women, OVCs, and so forth) (Blank and Handa 2008; Slater and others 2008). Although CTs can potentially address all the major roles of social protection, they should not necessarily be used to do so; instruments besides CTs should perhaps be used instead.

A well-executed CT typically does not stand alone but serves a country's goals of protecting vulnerable groups and promoting growth. CTs

> **Box 1.5**
>
> ### Additional References on Social Protection in Africa
>
> Key references discussing the roles of social protection include Barrientos and Hulme (2008a), Devereux and Sabates-Wheeler (2004), and Guhan (1994). Another influential approach to understanding social protection has been the social risk management framework developed by Holzmann and Jørgensen (2001), which illustrates how social protection deals with risks.
>
> Information about the presence and design of social assistance programs around the world can be found in Barrientos, Niño-Zarazúa, and Maitrot (2010). For additional information about the rationale for, and appropriate implementation of, safety net programs and their accompanying systems, the reader is referred to Grosh and others (2008).
>
> Specific literature on social protection programs in Africa includes a study by Ellis, Devereux, and White (2009), who motivate the use of social protection programs in Africa and describe how social protection programs have functioned. Niño-Zarazúa and others (2010) discuss whether social protection, and especially cash transfers, will take root across Africa. Their focus is on the importance of political economy issues.
>
> Holmes and Jones (2009) discuss the role of social protection in protecting children in West and Central Africa, whereas Blank and Handa (2008) examine the role of social protection in Eastern and Southern Africa. Sabates-Wheeler, Devereux, and Guenther (2009) discuss the relationship between social protection policies and agricultural policies for small producers, with a focus on Africa. Finally, European University Institute (2010) and Taylor (2010) provide additional useful information and discussions on social protection in Sub-Saharan Africa.

should be designed to complement other safety net and social protection programs to achieve synergies, reduce costs, and more effectively achieve national goals. For instance, CTs are often linked to income-generating programs or projects that help engage the poor in the financial system or the formal economy. For more information about social protection and safety net programs, see boxes 1.4 and 1.5.

Remainder of the Book

The rest of this book will provide the reader with in-depth information about Sub-Saharan Africa's experience with CTs. Chapter 2 provides additional information on the increase in CTs throughout the region, along with a more in-depth explanation of the reasons for this growth. It also provides a general typology of cash transfers in Sub-Saharan Africa and highlights important strategic issues.

Chapter 3 provides a more detailed analysis of the CTs identified in terms of implementation and design features. It incorporates a summary analysis of programs' components, as well as information on individual programs. The analysis is intended to paint a broad picture of the state of CTs throughout the region, to uncover some of the lessons already learned from existing programs, and to highlight areas where additional information would be useful. Chapter 4 synthesizes the information gained and concludes.

The review uncovered a large amount of information about many CTs, some of which is available in this book's appendixes. Appendix A provides in-depth information about the major programs covered in the review and is useful for those seeking additional information about a specific program. Appendix B provides tables with summary information on program specifics as an additional reference to chapter 3.

Notes

1. Obviously, as discussions and programs are progressing throughout Sub-Saharan Africa, the data contained here have changed since the time they were gathered.
2. The total is 134 if programs with unofficial sources or unclear 2009 start dates are included.
3. See table B.28 in appendix B for the list of individuals who provided information for the review.
4. However, some cash transfers are part of larger public works programs.
5. The discussions here and elsewhere in the text regarding the appropriateness of CCTs or UCTs, as well as food or cash transfers (see the next paragraph in the main text), are obviously generalized and somewhat naive. Some of these issues are highlighted later in the text, but the bulk of this discussion is left to others as it is not the focus of the current book.
6. Some characteristics of CCTs, more so than of UCTs, render them less appropriate for rapid scale-up in times of crisis. However, having an established CT program, whether conditional or unconditional, in place before a crisis can help mitigate the effects of the crisis itself (Fiszbein, Ringold, and Srinivasan 2010).

References

Andrade, Melissa. 2008. "Social Protection in Africa: A Mapping of the Growing Cash Transfer Experiences in the Region." Presented at the International Poverty Centre, Brasília, May 20.

Arnold, Catherine, Tim Conway, and Matthew Greenslade. 2011. *DFID Cash Transfers Evidence Paper*. London: U.K. Department for International Development.

Barrientos, Armando, and Rebecca Holmes. 2007. Social Assistance in Developing Countries Database. Version 3.0. Brooks World Poverty Institute, University of Manchester, Manchester, U.K., and Overseas Development Institute, London.

Barrientos, Armando, and David Hulme, eds. 2008a. *Social Protection for the Poor and Poorest: Concepts, Policies and Politics*. London: Palgrave Macmillan.

———. 2008b. "Social Protection for the Poor and Poorest in Developing Countries: Reflections on a Quiet Revolution." Brooks World Poverty Institute Working Paper 30. School of Environment and Development, University of Manchester, Manchester, U.K.

Barrientos, Armando, Miguel Niño-Zarazúa, and Mathilde Maitrot. 2010. Social Assistance in Developing Countries Database. Version 5.0. Brooks World Poverty Institute, University of Manchester, Manchester, U.K.

Blank, Lorraine, and Sudhanshu Handa. 2008. "Social Protection in Eastern and Southern Africa: A Framework and Strategy for UNICEF." United Nations Children's Fund, New York.

Devereux, Stephen, and Larissa Pelham. 2005. "Making Cash Count: Lessons from Cash Transfer Schemes in East and Southern Africa for Supporting the Most Vulnerable Children and Households." Save the Children UK, HelpAge International, and Institute of Development Studies, London. http://www.ids.ac.uk/go/idsproject/making-cash-count.

Devereux, Stephen, and Rachel Sabates-Wheeler. 2004. "Transformative Social Protection." IDS Working Paper 232, Institute of Development Studies, Brighton, U.K.

Ellis, Frank, Stephen Devereux, and Philip White. 2009. *Social Protection in Africa*. Northampton, MA: Edward Elgar.

European University Institute. 2010. *Social Protection for Inclusive Development: A New Perspective in EU Cooperation with Africa*. San Domenico di Fiesole, Italy: Robert Schuman Centre for Advanced Studies, European University Institute.

Fiszbein, Ariel, Dena Ringold, and Santhosh Srinivasan. 2010. *Cash Transfers and the Crisis: Opportunities and Limits*. Washington, DC: World Bank.

Fiszbein, Ariel, and Norbert Schady, with Francisco H. G. Ferreira, Margaret Grosh, Nial Kelleher, Pedro Olinto, and Emmanuel Skoufias. 2009. *Conditional Cash Transfers: Reducing Present and Future Poverty*. Washington, DC: World Bank.

Grosh, Margaret, Carlo del Ninno, Emil Tesliuc, and Azedine Ouerghi. 2008. *For Protection and Promotion: The Design and Implementation of Effective Safety Nets*. Washington, DC: World Bank.

Guhan, Sanjivi. 1994. "Social Security Options for Developing Countries." *International Labour Review* 133 (1): 35–53.

Hanlon, Joseph, Armando Barrientos, and David Hulme. 2010. *Just Give Money to the Poor: The Development Revolution from the Global South*. Sterling, VA: Kumarian.

Harvey, Paul. 2007. *Cash-Based Responses in Emergencies*. Humanitarian Policy Group Report 24. London: Overseas Development Institute.

Harvey, Paul, Katherine Haver, Jenny Hoffmann, and Brenda Murphy. 2010. "Delivering Money: Cash Transfer Mechanisms in Emergencies." Save the Children UK, London.

Hoddinott, John. n.d. "Ethiopia's Productive Safety Net Programme." PowerPoint presentation, International Food Policy Research Institute, Washington, DC.

Holmes, Rebecca, and Armando Barrientos. 2009. "The Potential Role of Cash Transfers in Addressing Childhood Poverty and Vulnerability in West and Central Africa." Regional Thematic Report 3 for the Study on Social Protection in West and Central Africa, Overseas Development Institute, London.

Holmes, Rebecca, and Nicola Jones. 2009. "Child-Sensitive Social Protection in West and Central Africa: Opportunities and Challenges." Synthesis Report for the Study on Social Protection in West and Central Africa, Overseas Development Institute, London.

Holzmann, Robert, and Steen Jørgensen. 2001. "Social Risk Management: A New Conceptual Framework for Social Protection, and Beyond." *International Tax and Public Finance* 8 (4): 529–56.

International Red Cross and Red Crescent Movement. 2007. *Guidelines for Cash Transfer Programming*. Geneva: International Committee of the Red Cross and International Federation of Red Cross and Red Crescent Societies.

Niño-Zarazúa, Miguel, Armando Barrientos, David Hulme, and Sam Hickey. 2010. "Social Protection in Sub-Saharan Africa: Will the Green Shoots Blossom?" Brooks World Poverty Institute Working Paper 116, University of Manchester, Manchester, U.K.

Quisumbing, Agnes R., and John A. Maluccio. 2000. "Intrahousehold Allocation and Gender Relations: New Empirical Evidence from Four Developing Countries." FCND Discussion Paper 84, Food, Consumption, and Nutrition Division, International Food Policy Research Institute, Washington, DC.

Sabates-Wheeler, Rachel, Stephen Devereux, and Bruce Guenther. 2009. "Building Synergies between Social Protection and Smallholder Agricultural Policies." FAC Working Paper SP01. Future Agricultures Consortium Secretariat, Institute of Development Studies, University of Sussex, Brighton, U.K.

Samson, Michael. 2009. "Social Cash Transfers and Pro-Poor Growth." In *Promoting Pro-Poor Growth: Social Protection*, 43–55. Paris: Organisation for Economic Co-operation and Development.

Samson, Michael, Ingrid van Niekerk, and Kenneth Mac Quene. 2006. *Designing and Implementing Social Transfer Programmes*. Cape Town: Economic Policy Research Institute.

Slater, Rachel, John Farrington, Rebecca Holmes, and Paul Harvey. 2008. "A Conceptual Framework for Understanding the Role of Cash Transfers in Social Protection." Project Briefing 5, Overseas Development Institute, London.

Taylor, Viviene. 2010. *Social Protection in Africa: An Overview of the Challenges*. Addis Ababa: African Union.

World Bank. 2011. "Managing Risk, Promoting Growth: Developing Systems for Social Protection in Africa—Africa Social Protection Strategy 2011–2021." Concept Note, World Bank, Washington, DC.

CHAPTER 2

The Rise of Cash Transfer Programs in Sub-Saharan Africa

This chapter describes some of the factors motivating the growth of cash transfers (CTs) throughout Sub-Saharan Africa, as well as a general framework that can be used to classify and understand CTs in the region. Before examining the growth and use of CTs in Sub-Saharan Africa, the chapter describes the extent of formal social protection in the region. Although illustrative, the following brief discussion on social protection in Sub-Saharan Africa simplifies very complex situations, and it is intended purely to sketch general tendencies in the region, rather than to characterize the state of social protection in every country.

Social Protection in Sub-Saharan Africa

Historically, social protection in Africa has been implemented in a piecemeal manner. Many countries traditionally had no social protection strategy, or the strategy was not strongly supported by the government. Ministries in charge of social protection in Sub-Saharan Africa have usually been weak, both politically and technically. Such weakness is evident in governments' budget allocations: spending on social protection has typically been about 0.1 percent of gross domestic product (GDP) in

Sub-Saharan African countries, whereas this number is approximately 5.7 percent of GDP for North Africa and the Middle East (Coudouel and others 2002).

The traditional focus of social protection in Sub-Saharan Africa has been on infrastructure, such as social funds, or on social protection as a means of coping with emergencies. Consistent with this historical tendency, both CTs and other social protection programs have been implemented in an ad hoc manner in many countries reviewed in the current study. However, both governments and development partners have expressed increasing interest in improving social protection and safety nets.

Growing recognition that social protection is important, both for the well-being of vulnerable groups and for a country's overall economic health, has led to increased attention to how programs can protect the vulnerable and encourage their inclusion in the economy. The trend toward establishing national social protection strategies and policies may provide a needed framework to facilitate institutionalization and scaling up of work on CTs in the region.

Catalysts for the Growth of CT Programs in Sub-Saharan Africa

Interest in Social Protection Spurred by Global Economic Crises

The increase in social protection and CT programs in Sub-Saharan Africa has occurred partly in response to intense pressures faced by the continent's poor and vulnerable populations. For instance, from 2007 through early 2009, threats of financial collapse and global recession, food shortages, and rising food and fuel prices drew donors' attention to the need to mitigate the effects of these crises on vulnerable groups. Global leaders and individuals on the ground called for increased social protection for groups affected by the crises to help them cope with current and potential future adverse shocks. Better social protection measures were seen as a means to achieve pro-poor growth and the Millennium Development Goals (European University Institute 2010).

Concerns over Persistent Poverty, Low Human Capital, and Food Insecurity

Although many individuals and households around the world were hit hard by recent downturns, the African continent fared relatively well considering the potential effect of the crises. However, the negative effects of the economic downturn and crises in Sub-Saharan Africa have been compounded by poor human development outcomes and persistent poverty in many countries in the region.

It is widely recognized that, overall, the gains from economic development have been slower to arrive in Africa than in other regions. The share of people living on less than US$1.25 purchasing power parity per day in Sub-Saharan Africa is consistently higher than in all other regions of the world (see figure 2.1). In 22 of the 42 Sub-Saharan African countries examined, more than half the population lives on less than US$1.25 per day (World Bank 2009c).

These poverty indicators are accompanied by poor human development outcomes in many countries. Despite making significant achievements in primary education, child mortality, and access to clean water, among other indicators, most countries in Sub-Saharan Africa are not expected to achieve many of the Millennium Development Goals (World Bank 2010).

Recurrent famines exacerbate vulnerability in Sub-Saharan Africa. Drought and famine increase susceptibility to malnutrition, which remains a major concern for children under five in many countries in the region. Nutrition deficits are a major concern for young children, for whom food crises can have irreversible consequences in cognitive ability and future productivity and wages. Despite receiving significant amounts of

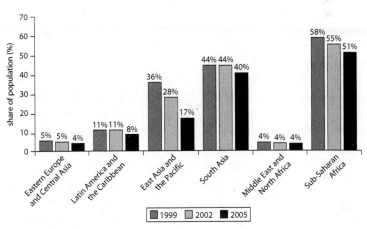

Figure 2.1 People Living on Less Than US$1.25 per Day, by Region, 2009

Source: World Bank 2009c.
Note: US$1.25 is 2005 purchasing power parity value.

food aid to combat the effects of food crises, many countries have seen persistently high malnutrition levels (see figure 2.2).

Even in countries not specifically affected by recurrent famines, food security is a concern. Some factors contributing to food insecurity include ethnic and political conflicts, low agricultural productivity and environmental degradation, a changing climate, and poor or changing terms of trade (Niño-Zarazúa and others 2010). Limited diversity in livelihoods increases households' reliance on subsistence agriculture for their survival and leaves them exposed to serious food security risks.

Another major factor in food insecurity is food price increases and volatility. This problem has taken a toll on vulnerable groups and has led to the creation of several CT programs. For instance, Senegal's Child-Focused Social Cash Transfer was created as a temporary response to sharp increases in food staple prices that resulted, in part, from rising world prices. Food prices remain structurally higher than in the past, and a cash transfer is now seen as an appropriate instrument to address these changes. Other Sub-Saharan African countries are also using CTs in an attempt to cushion vulnerable populations from continuing food price volatility.

From Food Aid to Cash Transfers

Changes in the provision of transfers in Sub-Saharan Africa have occurred in two distinct areas: from emergency food aid to emergency CTs, and from emergency food or cash transfers to regular, predictable transfers (Niño-Zarazúa and others 2010).

The transition from food aid to emergency CTs has occurred as the limitations of emergency food aid have been recognized. Food aid was expensive, and logistic challenges meant that it often arrived after households had sold or depleted productive assets to obtain food. Governments and groups that recognized these issues were some of the first to begin experimenting with transferring cash instead of in-kind goods. Early CT pilots by nongovernmental organizations (NGOs) in Malawi and Ethiopia established that CTs were a viable alternative to in-kind support.[1] These transfers, though made in cash, were often given in emergency situations.

The transition from emergency short-term transfers to predictable long-term transfers has also occurred in part because of dissatisfaction with emergency food aid. Countries, development partners, and civil society organizations have increasingly recognized that many households receiving food aid are in a state of chronic, rather than temporary, food insecurity. Major CT programs in Ethiopia (the Productive Safety Net

Figure 2.2 Malnutrition and Food Aid in Africa, 1990–2004

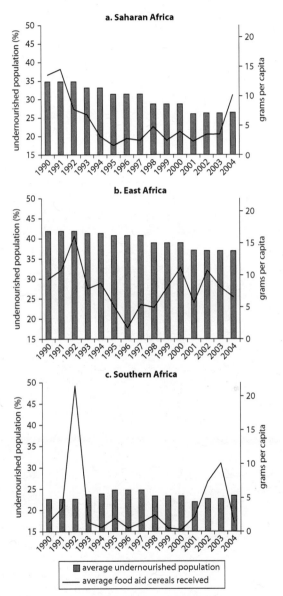

Sources: FAO 2007, 2008.
Note: Undernourishment data are reported for a three-year period. Saharan Africa comprises Chad, Mali, Mauritania, Niger, and Sudan. East Africa comprises the Comoros, Eritrea, Ethiopia, Kenya, Madagascar, Malawi, Mauritius, Mozambique, the Seychelles, Somalia, Tanzania, and Uganda. Southern Africa comprises Botswana, Lesotho, Namibia, South Africa, Swaziland, and Zimbabwe.

Programme's Direct Support component, or PSNP-DS[2]) and Kenya (the Hunger Safety Net Programme, or HSNP) have been developed to address this ongoing food insecurity. Notably, the transition from food to cash is not total; the PSNP-DS, for example, still provides some transfers in food rather than cash.

Kenya's HSNP helps illustrate the issue. In areas later targeted by Kenya's HSNP, 60 percent of the population had relied on emergency food aid for their survival for more than 10 years, and acute malnutrition was consistently as high as 30 percent. Although aid was emergency based, the hunger was predictable, and many believed that it could be addressed using regular CTs (HSNP n.d.).

This paradigm shift in the provision of aid to Sub-Saharan Africa was epitomized by the mantra of "predictable funding for predictable needs" (Ellis, Devereux, and White 2009, 16). Underlying this philosophy is the belief that regular emergency aid to Sub-Saharan Africa will not be needed if mechanisms are in place to help households manage risk in good times and cope with it in downturns. The programs most favored to replace emergency transfers have included predictable cash transfers.

Other Catalysts for the Growing Use of Cash Transfers in Sub-Saharan Africa

Several other factors have also influenced the use of CTs in Sub-Saharan Africa.

The HIV/AIDS crisis and orphans and vulnerable children. An additional challenge for many countries in Sub-Saharan Africa is the HIV/AIDS crisis, with estimated prevalence rates reaching over 20 percent in the hardest-hit countries (UNAIDS and WHO 2008; see also table 2.1). The AIDS crisis is one factor driving an increase in the number of orphans and vulnerable children (OVC) in countries with major generalized epidemics (figure 2.3). School attendance by orphans is often lower than that of nonorphans, a source of concern for the economic development of future generations.

One response by African countries to the HIV/AIDS crisis has been to begin CT programs. For instance, Kenya's Cash Transfer for Orphans and Vulnerable Children Project was created to systematically support Kenya's OVC and to prevent their institutionalization (World Bank 2009b). Zambia's social cash transfers were started to help poor households,

Table 2.1 HIV Prevalence, Adults Age 15–49, circa 2007

Country	Prevalence (%)
Angola	2.1
Benin	1.2
Botswana	23.9
Burkina Faso	1.6
Burundi	2.0
Cameroon	5.1
Central African Republic	6.3
Chad	3.5
Congo, Rep.	3.5
Congo, Dem. Rep.	1.3
Côte d'Ivoire	3.9
Equatorial Guinea	3.4
Eritrea	1.3
Gabon	5.9
Gambia, The	0.9
Ghana	1.9
Guinea	1.6
Guinea-Bissau	1.8
Kenya	4.9
Lesotho	23.2
Madagascar	0.1
Malawi	11.9
Mali	1.5
Mauritania	0.8
Mozambique	12.5
Namibia	15.3
Niger	0.8
Nigeria	3.1
Rwanda	2.8
Senegal	1.0
Sierra Leone	1.7
Somalia	0.5
South Africa	18.1
Swaziland	26.1
Togo	3.3
Uganda	5.4
Tanzania	6.2
Zambia	15.2
Zimbabwe	15.3

Sources: UNAIDS and WHO 2008; WHO Global Health Atlas database, http://apps.who.int/globalatlas/dataQuery/default.asp.

Figure 2.3 Orphanhood in Sub-Saharan Africa, 2005

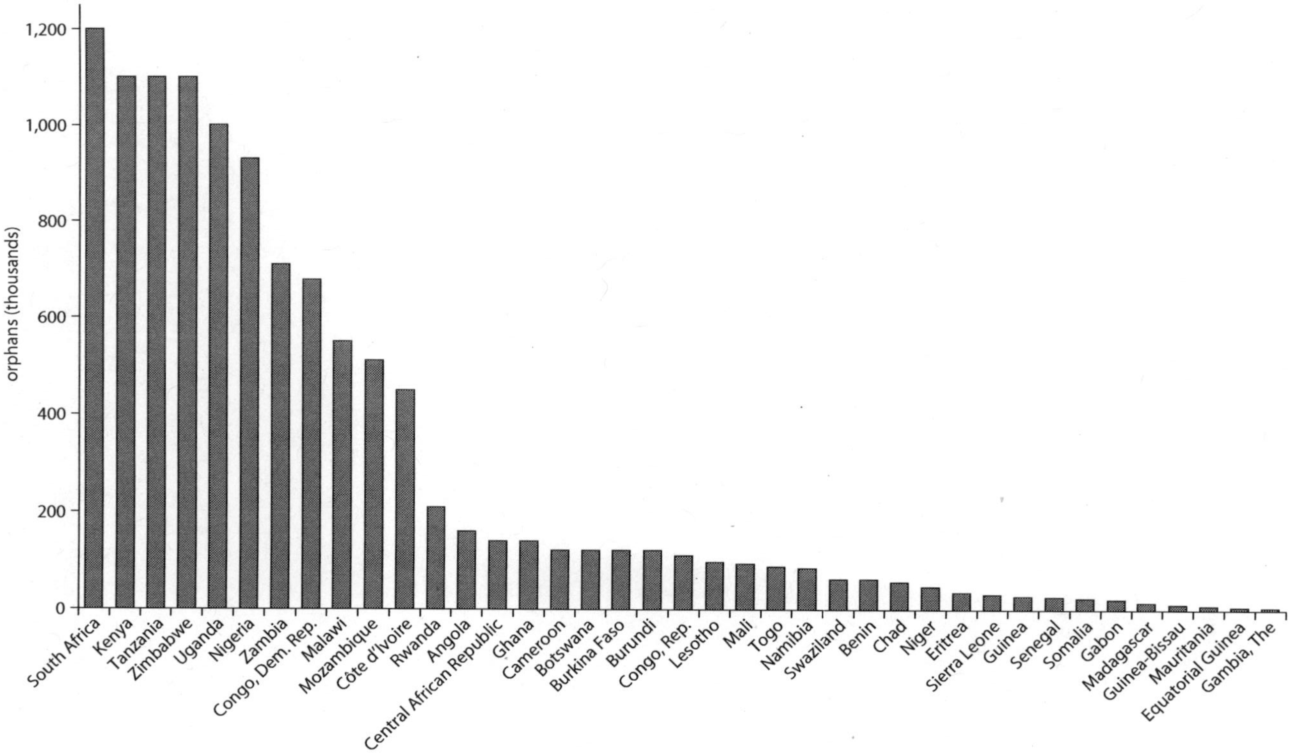

Source: UNAIDS and WHO 2008.

including those affected by AIDS (for example, households without adult members capable of participating in the labor force as a result of disease or death), that were not receiving help from other labor-based or microcredit programs (Schüring 2010).

Concerns that informal safety nets do not adequately protect individuals. Although family, clan, and other mutual support systems have traditionally played an important role in protecting individuals faced with adverse shocks, these support systems cannot necessarily deal with large, multiple covariate shocks. Furthermore, traditional systems can exclude marginalized groups or individuals, who are left with incomplete risk-coping mechanisms (European University Institute 2010).

The deterioration of informal safety nets is felt acutely within families, where skipped-generation households have become more common. The effects of HIV/AIDS, various ethnic and political conflicts, and high migration levels have induced a demographic shift in Sub-Saharan Africa not experienced in other parts of the world. Although infant and elderly mortality rates have slowly declined, deaths of prime-age adults have rapidly increased. The number of elderly household members caring for children has grown quickly, either because children have been orphaned or because their parents have migrated in search of job opportunities (Kakwani and Subbarao 2005). This shift of responsibilities to the elderly is one source of the weakening of traditional mutual support arrangements in the region.

In Namibia, a combination of multiple shocks has weakened traditional emergency responses and generated greater reliance on existing CTs. In 2002 and 2003, an increasing number of OVC were affected by the drought and food security crisis that hit Southern Africa, overwhelming the capacity of already-taxed informal safety net systems. In response to that crisis, 110,000 OVC residing in areas with high HIV seroprevalence levels received emergency food aid through a joint program of the World Food Programme (WFP) and the Food and Agriculture Organization of the United Nations, which was later extended to deal with chronic hunger. The government soon determined that consistent, longer-term assistance through cash grants was warranted, and Namibia's Ministry of Gender, Equality, and Child Welfare set out to transition children from WFP food aid to government-funded cash grants (Levine, van der Berg, and Yu 2009).

The deterioration of informal safety nets has also led some countries to begin CTs. For example, Swaziland began its Old Age Grant to address the growing vulnerability of poor elderly Swazis, particularly in light of the damaging effect of HIV/AIDS on informal support systems (Dlamini 2007). Mozambique initially targeted its Food Subsidy Program (Programa de Subsidio de Alimentos) to urban dwellers, whom they believed lacked the informal community and family-level safety nets available to rural Mozambicans (Devereux and Pelham 2005). The program has since expanded to rural areas, reflecting the recognition that traditional safety nets are also lacking in those areas for certain individuals.

Potential growth in financing for social protection. Although weak macroeconomic conditions in Sub-Saharan Africa have often discouraged leaders from trying to address the plight of the vulnerable, there are signs that increased funds will be available for countries to implement CT programs. Sub-Saharan Africa's economic growth before the recent downturn—combined with stable macroeconomic policies, increased revenue collection, foreign investment, and potential natural resource revenues (if managed correctly)—suggest that many countries may be able to fund CTs in the medium to long term. Improvements in governance help make these goals increasingly feasible. Funding from donors in the form of debt relief, increased sector support, and longer-term financing mechanisms may allow countries to more easily provide predictable, long-term CTs that fit within domestic strategies.

Increased Focus on Social Protection and Cash Transfers within Sub-Saharan Africa

The change of approach to social protection and CTs is accepted within the continent. Since late 2004, the African Union has encouraged countries to develop their own social policy frameworks. In 2006, meetings in Livingstone, Zambia, led to the Livingstone Call for Action. In 2007 came the Yaoundé Declaration, in which governments were encouraged to fit plans for social protection into their national budgets and development plans (Taylor 2010). In Windhoek, Namibia, in 2008, meetings for African ministers in charge of social development led to the creation of the Social Policy Framework for Africa. The recommendations generated in these meetings, including the Social Policy Framework, were endorsed in early 2009 by the 14th African Union Executive Council (African Union 2009). A plan of action supported by governments commits member states to increasing and empowering social protection programs and increasing coverage to excluded households. See box 2.1 for additional details on the African Union's support for social protection and CTs.

Box 2.1

The African Union's Social Policy Framework

The Social Policy Framework, created by the First Session of the African Union Conference of Ministers in Charge of Social Development at Windhoek, Namibia, in 2008, recognizes the important role that social development plays as a complement to economic growth in Africa. Its recommendations are to be used to guide member states as they prioritize and strengthen national social policies related to issues including, but not limited to, social protection, labor, population, infectious diseases, education, health and nutrition, agriculture, migration, gender equality, environmental issues, conflicts and civil unrest, foreign debt, crime, and life-cycle and disability-related vulnerabilities.

The framework asserts that social policy should be implemented by the state, and it recognizes the importance of social policy for improving living standards as a key goal of development. It encourages member states to recognize the importance of social protection in contributing to economic growth and human capital accumulation, breaking intergenerational cycles of poverty, and reducing inequality. Important principles of the Social Policy Framework include its rights-based motivation; its focus on long-term development goals; its emphasis on the coordination of social, economic, and political policy; and its endorsement of grassroots-led approaches to ensure ownership of policies at the local level (African Union 2008).

Plans for social protection throughout the continent are to allow for incremental increases in programs and can include "introducing and extending public-financed, non-contributory cash transfers" (African Union 2008, 17). Although countries have been encouraged to develop strategies that best fit their unique context, a minimum package of assistance has also been outlined, which the countries have agreed is affordable when financed with assistance from development partners (Taylor 2010). Countries endorsing the Social Policy Framework for Africa have agreed to create, implement, and determine costs for national plans in accordance with this minimal package, which includes health care and targeted assistance for children, workers in the informal sector, the elderly, people living with disabilities, and the unemployed. Countries have been encouraged to include social protection in their Poverty Reduction Strategy Papers and National Development Plans, to reform and support existing programs, to determine costs for a minimum social package, and to use social protection to protect impoverished peoples from adverse systemic shocks (African Union 2008; Schubert and Beales 2006).

(continued next page)

> **Box 2.1** *(continued)*
>
> An Implementation Strategy Proposal, created by the second session of the African Union Conference of Ministers in Charge of Social Development, goes beyond the recommendations of the Social Policy Framework to provide assistance in prioritizing, sequencing, and implementing social policies. Regarding social protection, the proposal encourages member states to create their own "social protection floors," which define basic service and income thresholds, and to place these floors within the context of national social protection strategies and relevant programs (African Union 2010).

Individual governments are also taking the initiative in their own countries. For example, Rwanda's government examined its existing social protection programs and concluded they were fragmented, often worked outside of the national budget, and did not reach their full potential (World Bank 2009a). The Rwandan cabinet officially approved and began to implement the Vision 2020 Umurenge Programme (VUP), in 2007, in an effort to speed up poverty reduction, spark growth in rural areas, and strengthen social protection (Republic of Rwanda 2009). In Ghana, the government realized that its economic growth alone was not enough to bring the extremely poor out of poverty or to protect other vulnerable groups from falling into it. More needed to be done to address the challenges these groups faced (Sultan and Schrofer 2008), and the government determined that a CT program was a potential solution to these issues.

Opinions among Africans have reflected increased recognition of vulnerabilities to shocks. Data from the World Values Survey Association (2009) show Africans' responses to a question regarding whether they believe hard work can help them achieve a better life. In 2007, respondents were less convinced that hard work could bring them a better life, compared with responses prior to 2007, perhaps reflecting individuals' growing recognition of their vulnerability to forces beyond their control (see figure 2.4). What is more, a majority of Africans believe their government's most important national priority is improving the economic lives of the poor (see figure 2.5).

Some of the reasons for the increase in CTs throughout Sub-Saharan Africa, as laid out in the preceding sections, illustrate that the changing

Figure 2.4 African Attitudes Regarding Connection between Hard Work and a Better Life

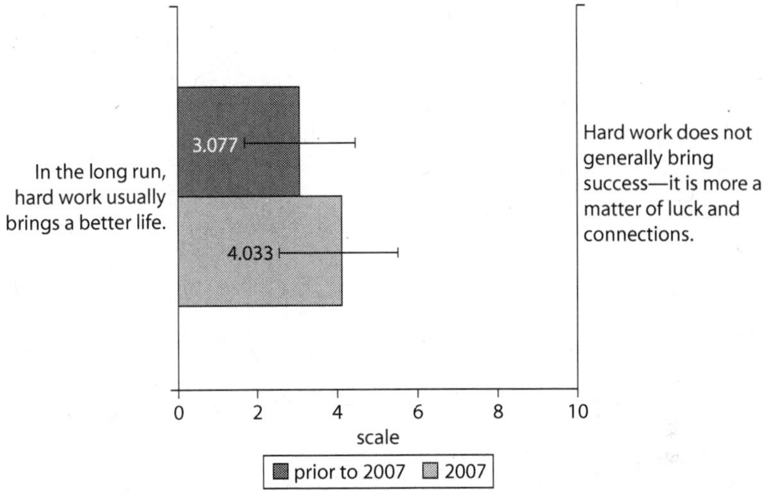

In the long run, hard work usually brings a better life. — 3.077

Hard work does not generally bring success—it is more a matter of luck and connections. — 4.033

scale 0–10

■ prior to 2007   ■ 2007

Source: World Values Survey Association 2009.
Note: Figure shows the extent to which survey respondents agree with the two statements. Standard deviations are represented by error bars. The sample prior to 2007 comprised 8,561 respondents; the sample for 2007 comprised 11,808 respondents. Respondents were from Burkina Faso, Ethiopia, Ghana, Mali, Nigeria, Rwanda, South Africa, and Zambia.

focus and modality are embraced within the continent. The next sections turn to the specifics of the programs identified in the review.

Interest of Sub-Saharan Countries in Cash Transfer Programs and Limited Implementation of Programs

The map in figure 2.6 illustrates the extent to which CTs have received recent attention in Sub-Saharan Africa, as uncovered in the desk review. Of 47 countries reviewed, 39 had engaged in some sort of formal dialogue surrounding CTs, whether it was initiated by the government or by development partners. Although the extent of programming throughout the region is less extensive, the map reveals the definite interest of many countries to learn what role CTs may play in their country's social protection programs.

Interest in CTs is not limited to high-level discussions: potential beneficiaries express appreciation for the programs as well. Some early programs, often administered by international NGOs, asked beneficiaries whether they preferred to receive cash or food transfers. Overall, results

Figure 2.5 Africans Who Believe That Helping the Poor Should Be a Top National Priority, 2008 and 2009

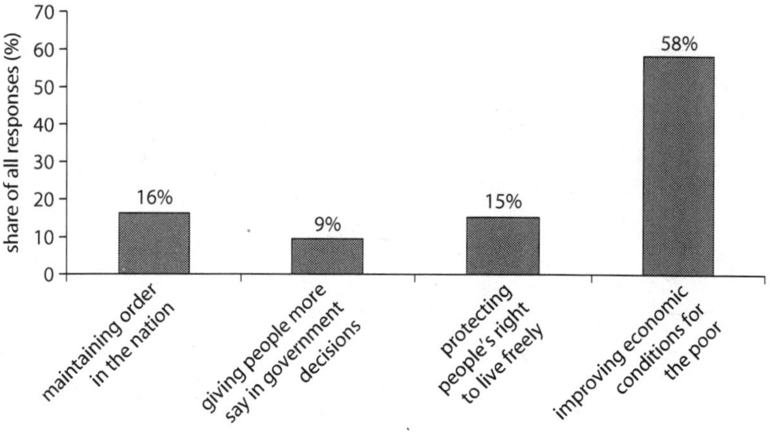

Category	Share (%)
maintaining order in the nation	16%
giving people more say in government decisions	9%
protecting people's right to live freely	15%
improving economic conditions for the poor	58%

Question: If you had to choose, which of the following is most important as a national priority?

Source: Afrobarometer database, http://next.pls.msu.edu/index.php?option=com_content&view=article&id=132&ltemid=80.
Note: Total is less than 100 percent because other responses were allowed. A total of 27,713 people responded. Respondents were from Benin, Botswana, Burkina Faso, Cape Verde, Ghana, Kenya, Lesotho, Liberia, Madagascar, Malawi, Mali, Mozambique, Namibia, Nigeria, Senegal, South Africa, Tanzania, Uganda, Zambia, and Zimbabwe. All surveys were conducted in 2008, except for the surveys in Zambia and Zimbabwe, which were conducted in 2009.

pointed to the potential role for CTs. For instance, an evaluation of Save the Children Canada's cash and in-kind transfer program in Isiolo district, Kenya, found that recipients preferred cash to in-kind transfers because of cash's greater fungibility (O'Donnell 2007).

That said, beneficiary endorsement of CTs is not unqualified. After the purchasing power of CTs in Ethiopia's PSNP deteriorated significantly, most beneficiaries preferred receiving food over CTs. Food transfers ensured that they could meet minimum consumption needs in a situation of critical food insecurity (Sabates-Wheeler and Devereux 2010). On the whole, it appears that beneficiaries often appreciate receiving cash, provided that benefits are adjusted to keep pace with inflation.

The Dramatic Increase in African Cash Transfer Programs after 2000

Interest in CTs has already translated into program implementation, with a multitude of CTs under way throughout most areas of the region (see figure 2.7).

Figure 2.6 Consideration of Cash Transfers by Governments or Donors in Sub-Saharan Africa as of 2010

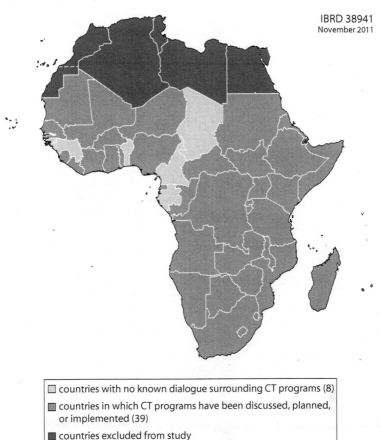

- countries with no known dialogue surrounding CT programs (8)
- countries in which CT programs have been discussed, planned, or implemented (39)
- countries excluded from study

Source: Authors' representation.
Note: Countries with no known dialogue surrounding CTs at the time of the study were the following: Benin, Cameroon, Chad, the Comoros, Gabon, The Gambia, Guinea, and Guinea-Bissau. Countries in which CTs have been discussed, planned, or implemented were as follows: Angola, Botswana, Burkina Faso, Burundi, Cape Verde, Central African Republic, Democratic Republic of Congo, Republic of Congo, Côte d'Ivoire, Equatorial Guinea, Eritrea, Ethiopia, Ghana, Kenya, Lesotho, Liberia, Madagascar, Malawi, Mali, Mauritania, Mauritius, Mozambique, Namibia, Niger, Nigeria, Rwanda, São Tomé and Príncipe, Senegal, the Seychelles, Sierra Leone, Somalia, South Africa, Sudan, Swaziland, Tanzania, Togo, Uganda, Zambia, and Zimbabwe.

Of the ongoing programs highlighted in this review, most began after 2000. A graphical depiction of the initiation and duration of some of Sub-Saharan Africa's CTs illustrates how the number of CT programs has increased rapidly within the past few years (figure 2.8). This growth reflects the global increase in CTs around the world since 2000.

Figure 2.7 Sub-Saharan African Countries' Experiences with Cash Transfers, 2010

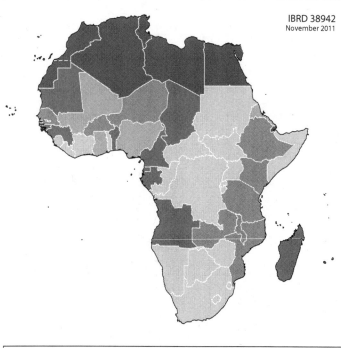

- countries that have had unconditional CT programs only (21)
- countries that have had conditional CT programs only (5)
- countries that have had both conditional and unconditional CT programs (9)
- countries with no known CT programs (12)
- countries excluded from study

Source: Authors' representation.
Note: Countries in which only conditional CT programs were identified were the following: Eritrea, Ghana, Mali, Nigeria, and São Tomé and Príncipe. Countries in which only unconditional CT programs were identified were as follows: Botswana, Burundi, Cape Verde, Central African Republic, Democratic Republic of Congo, Republic of Congo, Côte d'Ivoire, Lesotho, Liberia, Mauritius, Namibia, Rwanda, the Seychelles, Sierra Leone, Somalia, South Africa, Sudan, Swaziland, Togo, Uganda, and Zimbabwe. Countries that were identified as having had both conditional and unconditional CT programs were as follows: Burkina Faso, Ethiopia, Kenya, Malawi, Mozambique, Niger, Senegal, Tanzania, and Zambia. Countries with no known CT programs were as follows: Angola, Benin, Cameroon, Chad, the Comoros, Equatorial Guinea, Gabon, The Gambia, Guinea, Guinea-Bissau, Madagascar, and Mauritania.

Trends in Cash Transfer Implementation in Sub-Saharan Africa: Strategic Issues

This section of the chapter sketches several general typologies that can be used to understand CT programs in Sub-Saharan Africa.

Figure 2.8 Start Dates and Durations of Sub-Saharan African Cash Transfer Programs, 1990–2010

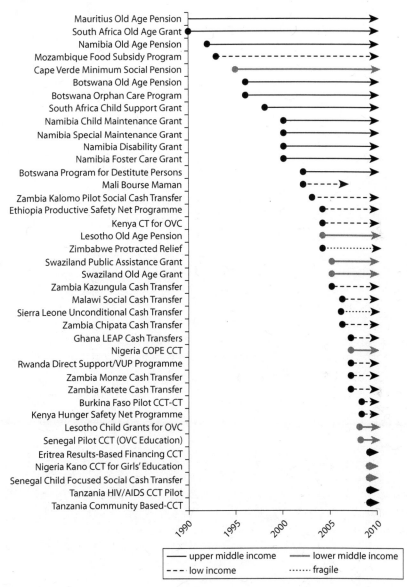

Source: Authors' representation.

Middle-Income and Low-Income Cash Transfers

Two distinct pictures of CTs emerge when CT programming in Sub-Saharan Africa is examined. In general, upper-middle-income countries have implemented similar CT programs, and low-income countries and countries designated as fragile states have operated programs that share many common characteristics. CTs in lower-middle-income countries fall into both categories. In lower-middle-income countries in Southern Africa, CT programs are similar to those in their upper-middle-income neighbors, whereas in lower-middle-income countries in the rest of the region, the programs are similar to those of low-income countries. See table 2.2 for a list of countries by their official classification and region.

Admittedly, there are exceptions to this rule. For instance, Gabon and Equatorial Guinea's lack of CTs tracks more closely with some other low-income countries, and Zimbabwe has remnants of a welfare system similar to that of the wealthier Southern African countries. However, this framework generally describes the situation in the region well.

Although for the following discussion the programs are most easily divided into these two general divisions, tables throughout this book are shown using official World Bank income classifications, which allow a separate examination of characteristics of lower-middle-income countries and fragile states. The book was designed in this manner to allow the analysis to be based on an official classification system and to illustrate that some of these characteristics of CTs are better represented by a continuum than by a black-and-white division.

A summary of the characteristics of the two groups of CTs, which are known as the *middle-income CTs* and the *low-income or fragile CTs*, is provided in table 2.3.

Similar distinctions between programs have been noted by Niño-Zarazúa and others (2010), who distinguish between what they call the "Southern Africa model" and the "Middle Africa model." The Southern Africa model corresponds to rights-based CTs awarded on the basis of categorical criteria. Initially, such CTs were given to the elderly, and they are now expanding to include children. These programs are based in government institutions, are domestically funded, and have strong legislative backing. The similar cash grants and social protection programs in the region reflect the countries' economic links and shared labor markets.

CT programs in the Middle Africa model provide transfers, but in some cases they use conditional cash transfers (CCTs) to promote the use of services, such as health or education. Other unconditional programs in the second group focus on human capital in their objectives.

Table 2.2 Sub-Saharan African Countries by Income and Subregion

Income classification	Central Africa	East Africa	Saharan Africa	Southern Africa	West Africa
Upper-middle-income countries	Equatorial Guinea[a] Gabon[a]	Mauritius Seychelles		Botswana Namibia South Africa	
Lower-middle-income countries (excluding fragile states)	Angola[a]			Lesotho Swaziland	Cameroon[a] Cape Verde Nigeria[a] Senegal
Low-income countries (excluding fragile states)	Rwanda Zambia	Comoros Ethiopia Kenya Madagascar Malawi Mozambique Tanzania Uganda	Chad[a] Mali Mauritania Niger		Benin Burkina Faso Gambia, The Ghana[a] Guinea Guinea-Bissau
Fragile states	Burundi Central African Republic Congo, Rep.[a] Congo, Dem. Rep. São Tomé and Principe	Eritrea Somalia	Sudan[a]	Zimbabwe	Côte d'Ivoire Liberia Sierra Leone Togo

Source: Authors' compilation.
Note: This table uses World Bank income classifications as of January 2011.
a. The country is an oil-producing country.

Table 2.3 General Characteristics of Middle-Income and Low-Income/Fragile Cash Transfers: A Basic Typology

Program characteristics	Middle-income CTs	Low-income and fragile CTs
Program start date	Before 2000 (colonial era in many cases)	2000 and later
Duration of program	Long term	Short term
Objectives	Poverty focused	Focused on food security, human capital, or emergency response
Approach to social protection	Ex ante prevention and promotion	Ex post protection
Coverage	Wide-scale coverage of vulnerable and poor population	Limited coverage of select vulnerable groups
Targeting	Universal or near-universal coverage of eligible group	Limited target group
Use of communities	Limited	Often involved in targeting, monitoring, payment distribution
Conditions	None	Sometimes
Institutional base	Government	Outside of government
Legal support and enabling legislation	Yes; rights-based programs	Still incipient
Monitoring systems	Established; appeals mechanisms in place	Variable quality and sometimes very weak
Funders	Government	Donor or government plus donor
Complementary programs	Usually part of a social assistance system	Usually stand-alone

Source: Authors' compilation.

These Middle Africa programs are typically shorter-term projects that are donor financed and delivered through multiple groups within and outside of the government. The proliferation of implementing agencies reflects the vacuum in state-led CT programs, in part because of the weak institutions in charge of social protection in Sub-Saharan Africa. Domestic commitment to social protection in many of these countries is weaker than that found in the first group, although it appears to be on the rise in many of these countries (Niño-Zarazúa and others 2010).

Middle-income CTs began earlier and have a longer-term focus than most low-income CTs. As can be seen by the arrows in figure 2.8, most of the middle-income CTs were established earlier than the low-income and fragile CTs. The middle-income CT programs are established programs with long-term duration; the low-income and fragile CT programs are often projects of limited duration, or they provide benefits for a limited time before beneficiaries are expected to move out of the program. Many of them simply address emergencies. Others hope to become large-scale, permanent programs, and they are working to this end.

The objectives of the middle-income CTs often focus on assisting individuals in poverty, whereas the objectives of the low-income and fragile CTs focus on combating food insecurity, responding to emergencies, or building human capital. Even semantics for the programs vary: middle-income CTs are often referred to as cash grants, and low-income and fragile CTs are referred to as cash transfers or social cash transfers.

The middle-income CT programs are often part of rights-based social assistance systems that have their base in systems established in the colonial era. In Namibia and South Africa, the countries' cash grant systems are a carryover from earlier welfare systems that provided fairly generous benefits to the minority ruling group while giving smaller grants to members of the majority population.[3] Despite the obvious flaws of these systems, the programs generated an expectation that the government had a responsibility to provide support to vulnerable members of society. When rights and privileges were extended to all citizens or residents in an equitable manner, the early cash grants generated a greater demand for social protection systems and paved the way for large-scale CTs. This experience created an expectation that governments should provide minimum protection for citizens. In South Africa, the government holds that its constitution has mandated the right to social security. Provided it is able to do so, the government must provide social assistance to vulnerable groups without other means of support (Republic of South Africa 2004). For more information about the South African system, the largest in the region, see box 2.2.

Sub-Saharan Africa's CTs can be divided on the basis of their expected duration. For the purposes of the review, CTs were considered short term if they lasted a year or less; all other programs were classified as long term. Admittedly, the long-term designation also includes midlength programs. Although not ideal, the terms are used for illustrative purposes.

Programs were also classified according to their focus, which was determined primarily by the CTs' stated objectives and, to a lesser extent,

> **Box 2.2**
>
> ## The South African Grant System
>
> The extensive coverage of South Africa's grant system provides an illustration of the cash grant systems often present in upper-middle-income countries in Sub-Saharan Africa. The South African system cost 3.2 percent of GDP in 2007/08 and reaches a significant proportion of the population—13 million of South Africa's most vulnerable people—either directly or indirectly. It includes an Old Age Pension, a Disability Grant, a Care Dependency Grant, a Foster Care Grant, and a Child Support Grant. Other less prominent grants in the system include the Grant for Carers of the Aged, the War Veterans Grant, and Social Relief of Distress. Specific information about the major grants is provided in the accompanying table.
>
> **Overview of the South African Grant System**
>
> | Benefit | Year started | Eligible population | Coverage | Transfer size |
> |---|---|---|---|---|
> | Old-Age Pension | 1928 | Elderly (women over 60 and men over 65 who pass a means and asset test) | 2,400,000 (5% of South Africans; 80% of the elderly) | US$112 monthly |
> | Disability Grant | 1946 | People living with disabilities who pass a means and asset test | 1,300,000 (3% of South Africans) | US$112 monthly |
> | Care Dependency Grant | Unknown | Children up to age 18 with disabilities who do not live in an institution and whose household passes a means test | 107,000 | US$117 monthly |
> | Foster Care Grant | Unknown | State-approved foster parents of OVC up to age 18, for children who pass a means test | 484,000 | US$76 monthly |
>
> *(continued next page)*

Box 2.2 *(continued)*

| Child Support Grant | 1998 (replaced the State Maintenance Grant) | Children through age 14 who live in households that pass a means test | 8,800,000 (70% of children) | US$27 monthly |

Sources: European University Institute 2010; Plaatjies 2006; SASSA 2009; South African Government Services 2009; Streak 2007; U.S. Social Security Administration 2009.
Note: Transfer size and coverage are current as of April 2009. Only major grants are shown.

by the program components. Within longer-term programs, most CTs were focused either on poverty and food security objectives or on human capital investments. Those programs that focused on human capital investments tended to be CCT programs, whereas the programs focused on poverty and food security usually involved unconditional transfers. Most short-term programs focused on addressing crises brought on by natural disasters, such as famines or floods, or human-caused disasters, usually as a result of conflicts. Short-term CTs that focused on natural disasters often had a food security focus, because such disasters typically have a major impact on food security (see table 2.4).

Figure 2.9 shows that, as expected, wealthier countries (with their concomitant rights-based social assistance systems) implement long-term programs. These programs had a poverty or food security emphasis. Lower-middle-income countries (excluding fragile states) also tend to implement long-term CT programs. Approximately three out of four lower-middle-income CT programs were long term, and most had a food security or poverty focus. Still, almost one in four CTs in this group was short term and addressed natural disasters. In low-income countries (excluding low-income fragile states), half of programs were long term and half were short term. Most short-term programs focused on natural

Table 2.4 Classification by Program Duration and Focus

	Program duration			
	Long term		Short term	
Program focus	Poverty or food security	Human capital	Natural disaster or food security	Humanmade disasters

Source: Authors' compilation.

Figure 2.9 Types of Programs Implemented by Countries of Different Wealth Levels, 2000–09

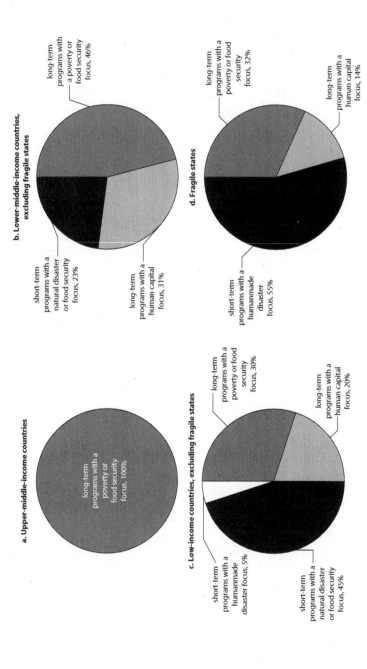

Source: Authors' representation.

Note: The sample size is 17 for upper-middle-income countries, 13 for lower-middle-income countries, 40 for low-income countries, and 22 for fragile countries. Sample size is limited to programs that could be classified into one of the categories.

disasters. Over half of programs in fragile states were short term, and all these short-term programs addressed human-caused disasters. Table 2.5 provides a list of selected CTs classified according to this framework.

Program ownership and reactive or proactive focus have gone hand in hand. Another fundamental difference between the two groups is that of ownership: middle-income CT programs are almost exclusively based in government institutions and are domestically funded, whereas low-income and fragile CT programs are often seated outside of the government and are supported by donors. Low-income and fragile CTs can often be characterized as donor driven. Their fragmented nature and patchy coverage reflect the lack of domestic ownership and coordination of many of these programs.

Unsurprisingly, middle-income CTs and low-income and fragile CTs tend to focus on different roles of social protection. Figure 2.10 shows how middle-income CTs focus on the ex ante preventive and promotive roles of social protection. Low-income and fragile CTs in the region have a larger protective focus, meaning a greater percentage of the programs are responding to shocks once they have already occurred. These findings illustrate that wealthier countries are more successful in proactively confronting risks; lower-income countries are reacting to crises ex post. This trend coincides with the patchy, short-term implementation of CT programs in lower-income countries, and it reflects those programs' reliance on donors who select priority crises for intervention based on the donors' own institutional mandates and priorities.

Scale of coverage remains very different between middle-income and low-income CT programs. Within a given country, the middle-income CTs typically cover a wide range of vulnerable groups and a significant portion of the population. In contrast, the low-income and fragile CTs often cover a very limited part of the population and only certain vulnerable groups, such as OVC. The widespread coverage of middle-income CTs is often achieved through near-universal targeting (that is, categorical targeting) of vulnerable groups, such as the elderly, whereas low-income and fragile CTs often use more detailed proxy- or community-based targeting methods to identify beneficiaries.

To coordinate benefits across the country's various CT programs, middle-income programs often use centrally coordinated registration and information systems. Management information systems for low-income and fragile CT programs are usually more ad hoc, unconnected

Table 2.5 Selected Cash Transfers by Program Focus

Long-term focus		Short-term focus	
Poverty or food security	Human capital	Natural disaster or food security	Humanmade disasters
• Botswana Old Age Pension • Botswana Program for Destitute Persons • Cape Verde Minimum Social Pension • Ethiopia PSNP-DS • Ghana Livelihood Empowerment against Poverty • Kenya HSNP • Lesotho Child Grants Programme • Lesotho Old Age Pension • Malawi Social Cash Transfer • Mauritius Food Aid • Mozambique Food Subsidy Program • Namibia Grants System • Nigeria COPE (In Care of the Poor) Conditional Cash Transfer • Rwanda VUP • South African Grants System • Zambia Social Cash Transfers • Zimbabwe Care for the Elderly • Zimbabwe Drought Relief • Zimbabwe Protracted Relief Program • Zimbabwe Support to Families in Distress	• Burkina Faso Conditional Cash Transfer or Cash Transfer • Eritrea Results-Based Financing • Kenya Cash Transfer for Orphans and Vulnerable Children • Malawi Zomba Cash Transfer • Mali Bourse Maman • Nigeria COPE Conditional Cash Transfer • Nigeria Kano Conditional Cash Transfer for Girls' Education • São Tomé and Príncipe Bolsa Escola • Senegal Conditional Cash Transfer for Orphans and Vulnerable Children • Tanzania Community-Based Conditional Cash Transfer	• Kenya Isiolo Emergency Drought Transfers • Lesotho Cash and Food Transfers Pilot Project • Malawi Dowa Emergency Cash Transfer Project • Malawi Food and Cash Transfer Programme • Malawi Oxfam Emergency Transfers • Mozambique Cash Grants for Disaster Response • Mozambique Emergency Flood Transfers • Niger CARE Disaster Risk Reduction Transfers • Niger Tanout Cash Transfer Project • Swaziland Emergency Drought Response • Tanzania Save the Children UK Transfers • Zambia Cash Grants I (Mongu and Kaoma Transfers) • Zambia Flood Cash Grants I	• Burundi UNHCR (Office of the United Nations High Commissioner for Refugees) Cash Grants • Central African Republic UNHCR Repatriation Grants • Republic of Congo Repatriation Grants • Côte d'Ivoire Repatriation Grants • Democratic Republic of Congo Emergency Cash Grants • Liberia Cash Grants for Ex-combatants • Liberia Repatriation Cash Grants • Rwanda Child Soldiers Reintegration Grant • Sierra Leone Reinsertion Benefits • Somalia UNHCR Transfers • Sudan Cash Transfer for Ex-combatants • Togo UNHCR Grants

Source: Authors' compilation.

Figure 2.10 Approaches to Risk Used by Countries of Different Income Levels, 2000–09

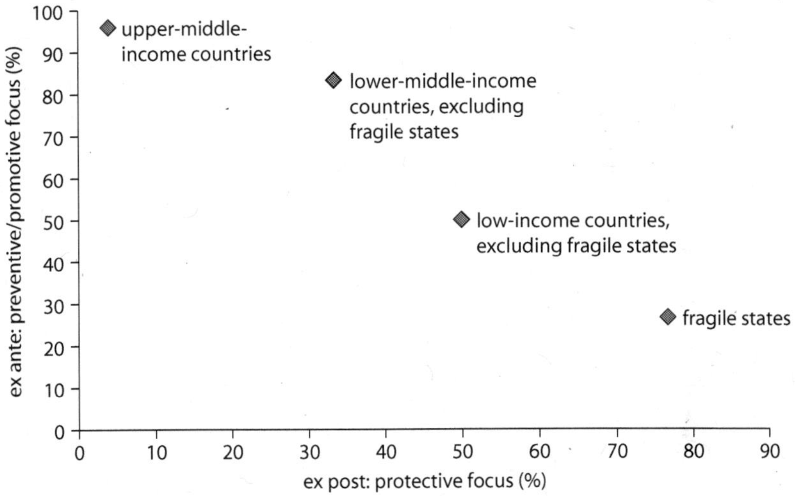

```
100
 90  ◆ upper-middle-
       income countries
 80           ◆ lower-middle-income
                countries, excluding
 70             fragile states
 60
 50              ◆ low-income countries,
                   excluding fragile states
 40
 30                                ◆ fragile states
 20
 10
  0
    0   10   20   30   40   50   60   70   80   90
              ex post: protective focus (%)
```
(y-axis: ex ante: preventive/promotive focus (%))

Source: Authors' representation.
Note: Total of program percentages can exceed 100 percent because some programs have both an ex ante and an ex post role. Sample size of 111 includes only those CTs for which the program could be clearly classified into a protective, preventive, or promotive rationale. Programs directed to individuals in distress are considered protective because the program is responding to a specific adverse shock to the beneficiary. Programs targeting vulnerable groups such as orphans, widows, or the poor are considered preventive because they are not responding to a specific shock to the household. Programs with the words *human capital or livelihood development* in the name or program objectives are considered promotive. Programs can be classified in multiple categories if objectives suggest classification is appropriate.

to other programs, and often of worse quality than those of the middle-income programs. (Some of the newest CT programs in low-income countries promise to be exceptions to this rule.) The middle-income CTs that are part of a larger system aim to provide complementary benefits to various groups. For instance, Botswana's Program for Destitute Persons covers children with terminally ill parents who cannot care for them, and its Orphan Care Program covers these children once they become orphans. Theoretically, communication between the two programs should ensure that newly orphaned children do not fall through the cracks (BFTU 2007).[4]

Reflecting their typically pilot or stand-alone nature, most of the reviewed programs in the low-income CT group had fewer than 50,000 estimated beneficiaries, and they typically covered individuals or households within a limited geographic area. The middle-income CTs covered larger numbers of beneficiaries. The largest of the middle-income CT programs was South Africa's Child Support Grant, which covered approximately 8.8 million children; South Africa's entire grant system reached more than 13 million beneficiaries in 2008/09 (SASSA 2009).

In contrast, the largest cash transfer in the low-income CTs was Ethiopia's PSNP-DS, which covered approximately 1.2 million beneficiaries and was many times larger than most other CTs in low-income countries. Other exceptions to the typically small low-income CTs included Mozambique's Food Subsidy Program and the Democratic Republic of Congo's Emergency Cash Grants for Ex-combatants. Panel a in figure 2.11 illustrates the wide range of beneficiaries and households covered in selected CTs in Sub-Saharan Africa. Panel b illustrates that the average number of beneficiaries per program was smallest in lower-middle-income countries and fragile states. CT programs in low-income countries had an average of more than 100,000 beneficiaries per program, although this number is skewed by the PSNP-DS. This average, though still much larger than the lower-middle-income and fragile averages, is still almost seven times smaller than the average number of beneficiaries in the upper-middle-income country CT programs.

Although most low-income CT programs cover just a small percentage of the population, middle-income programs provide benefits to sizable groups. South Africa's grant system reaches approximately 27 percent of the population,[5] and Namibia's CT program covers 12 percent (Levine, van der Berg, and Yu 2009). Swaziland's Old Age Grant reached 6 percent of the population in 2006/07 (RHVP 2007).

Exceptions to this rule do occur, however. In addition to Ethiopia's PSNP-DS, a few other low-income CT programs cover or hope to cover significant portions of the population. In terms of their target populations, Kenya's HSNP plans to reach 40 percent of the poorest households in selected districts (HSNP n.d.), and its Cash Transfer for Orphans and Vulnerable Children Project expects to cover 50 percent of extremely poor OVC by 2012 (World Bank 2009b). Mozambique's Food Subsidy Program reached 15 percent of poor elderly Mozambicans in 2006 (Ellis 2007). Although coverage of those programs' target populations is not as high as Mexico's Oportunidades or Brazil's Bolsa Família, which covered 72 percent and 84 percent of the countries' poor populations (Johannsen, Tejerina, and Glassman 2009), respectively, the expected coverage is still substantial, particularly in light of unique challenges the programs face in identifying, enrolling, and maintaining beneficiaries.

Figure 2.11 Coverage of Cash Transfer Programs

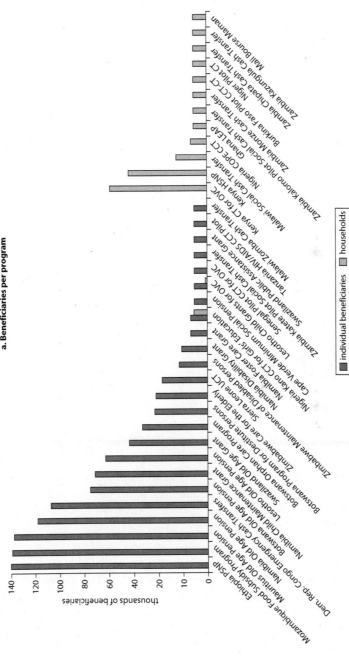

a. Beneficiaries per program

(continued next page)

Figure 2.11 (continued)

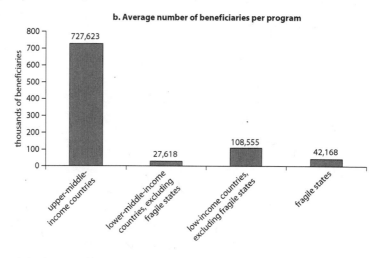

Source: Authors' representation.
Note: Ethiopia's PSNP-DS reached approximately 1.2 million individuals in 242,383 households in 2010. Mozambique's Food Subsidy Program reached 287,454 individuals at the end of 2008. Numbers are based on most recent data available. Sample for average number of beneficiaries per program is 19 for upper-middle-income countries, 9 for lower-middle-income countries, 15 for low-income countries, and 8 for fragile states. Data are limited to those programs for which information was available.

Low-income CT programs may become more similar to middle-income CT programs. Despite the major differences seen across the two groups, some low-income countries appear to be headed down a similar path as that followed by the wealthier countries in the region. Leaders in these countries increasingly recognize the need for social assistance to ensure the survival of vulnerable groups and to support economic development and growth. Major CT programs have been launched in low-income countries, some with significant domestic support and ownership, such as Ethiopia's PSNP, Ghana's Livelihood Empowerment against Poverty, Kenya's Cash Transfer for Orphans and Vulnerable Children and HSNP, and Rwanda's VUP. Some of these programs are planning, or have achieved, significant coverage, and they have invested in strong monitoring systems. They are based in government institutions that are working to build capacity for implementation, and they are intended to last beyond a single project cycle or funding tranche.

This trend is visible in figure 2.12, which shows the current and anticipated scale of CT programs. The identified middle-income CTs are exclusively large scale. Many low-income CTs have been started as small

Figure 2.12 Scale of Africa's Cash Transfer Programs by Countries' Income Classification

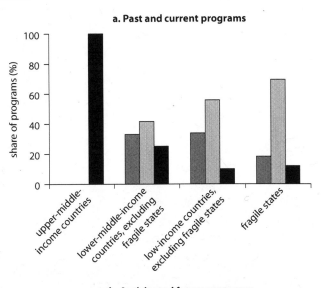

a. Past and current programs

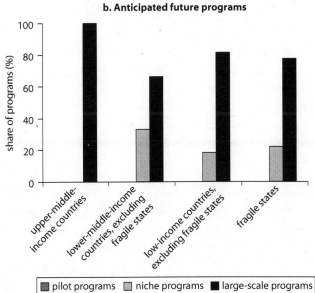

b. Anticipated future programs

■ pilot programs ■ niche programs ■ large-scale programs

Source: Authors' representation.
Note: Panel a includes only programs whose scale could be determined; future CTs are included only if their future form could be clearly determined. Sample size is 119 for past or current programs (24 for upper-middle-income countries, 12 for lower-middle-income countries, 50 for low-income countries, and 33 for fragile states). Sample size is 54 for anticipated future programs (25 for upper-middle-income countries, 9 for lower-middle-income countries, 11 for low-income countries, and 9 for fragile states).

pilots that provide benefits to a limited number of beneficiaries. Those pilots are typically undertaken for one of two reasons: (a) to test and evaluate whether a CT will work in the given setting (that is, for research purposes) or (b) simply to test systems and components before a large-scale rollout. Of programs that currently exist in lower-middle-income and low-income countries, all pilots are expected to transition either to niche or to large-scale programs. Most programs aspire to future coverage that is national or large scale, reflecting a growing focus in the region on establishing national social protection systems in which CTs are expected to play a major role.

Only slightly more than 1 in 10 programs (out of all programs) have niche-like goals. These niche programs, even after reaching full scale-up, extend benefits to only a limited number of individuals or households. Such households have unique characteristics not common to much of the population, allowing a side-scale targeting of a limited number of people. An example of such a niche program is Nigeria's Kano Conditional Cash Transfer for Girls' Education, which provides benefits to girl students in one state. The smaller percentage of niche programs projected for the future also reflects the short-term nature of many niche programs, such as emergency transfers to victims of a crisis. However, new niche programs probably will be developed in the future to address new crises as they arise.

Focus of Most Programs on Vulnerability Rather Than Poverty

Notwithstanding their major differences, the middle-income and low-income CT programs exhibited certain commonalities, as well as other areas in which no clear distinctions could be seen. First, most CTs in Sub-Saharan Africa can be classified as transfers given to specific vulnerable groups, rather than poverty-targeted social assistance (see figure 2.13). A higher percentage of low-income CTs (in low-income and fragile states) focus on vulnerability criteria than do middle-income CTs, but the majority of all CTs focus on vulnerabilities rather than simply on poverty. Vulnerability-focused CTs protect at-risk groups, such as orphans, the elderly, or the HIV-affected, from specific shocks. They usually do not explicitly focus on the individuals' actual poverty levels. Such programs target individuals who may or may not be poor at the time, with transfers aiming to decrease beneficiaries' vulnerability to adverse shocks.

Other CT programs in Sub-Saharan Africa provide poverty-targeted social assistance, which seeks to help the extremely poor without regard to the specific problems to which beneficiaries may be vulnerable. Such

Figure 2.13 Focus of Programs by Countries' Income Classification

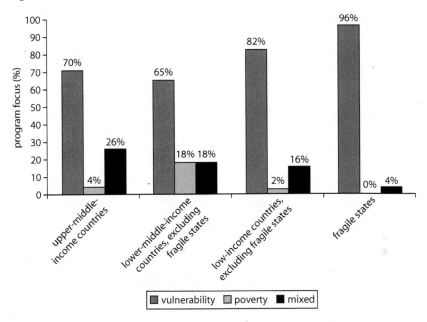

Source: Authors' representation.
Note: Sample size is 114. This number is less than the total number of identified programs because of limited information about some programs.

programs have targeting mechanisms that focus on poverty indicators, and program goals also focus on poverty. Lower-middle-income CT programs took this focus most frequently; very few programs in low-income countries—and none in fragile states—gave exclusively poverty-focused transfers. Approximately one in four upper-middle-income countries implemented programs with a mixed (poverty and vulnerability) focus; the percentage of programs with a mixed focus was lower for all other groups.

The tendency to focus on vulnerabilities rather than poverty may reflect, in part, the high poverty rates and deep poverty gaps throughout the region. There are concerns that CTs targeting a certain percentage of the poor will face opposition from those not targeted by the program but who perceive themselves (or others) as poor people in similar need of transfers. When the majority of the population is poor or nearly poor, poverty-based targeting may exclude individuals from a program on the basis of a few cents difference in income or expenditure. Given high poverty headcounts and small differences between the lowest income or consumption deciles, for instance, the concern is that poverty-focused transfers will be met with opposition because many people believe that coverage should reach a greater percentage of the poor population.

Because fiscal limitations in most countries restricted the percentage of the poor population that could be covered by CTs, programs often used vulnerability-focused targeting criteria for inclusion in programs that are relatively easy to identify and are perceived as fair by the general population. Targeting of vulnerable groups may also put less strain on administrative capacity. In some cases, the program's underlying goal may still be to combat poverty rather than specific vulnerabilities. The more that poverty correlates with certain easily identifiable vulnerability characteristics, the more easily categorical or vulnerability-based targeting can directly attack poverty.[6] In practice, the line between poverty-targeted and vulnerability-focused approaches is often blurred.

A vulnerable group commonly targeted in the region includes individuals living in HIV-affected households. Programs focused on these individuals include Burkina Faso's Pilot CCT-CT program, Kenya's Cash Transfer for Orphans and Vulnerable Children, Lesotho's Child Grants Programme, and Senegal's Conditional Cash Transfer for Orphans and Vulnerable Children. Transfers for people living with disabilities are also commonly given. Middle-income CT programs, such as those found in Namibia and South Africa, often separate disability grants from other transfers. In countries such as Malawi and Zambia, transfers for extremely poor people living with disabilities have been awarded within a broader transfer program focused on households that do not have a member capable of participating in the labor force.

Other vulnerable groups commonly targeted in Sub-Saharan Africa's CTs (and especially in low-income CTs) are those affected by natural disasters, such as floods. Emergency CTs are commonly given to address victims of these disasters. For example, CARE (Cooperative for Assistance and Relief Everywhere) and two Mozambican microfinance institutions gave CTs ranging from US$47 through US$100 in 2000 in response to floods in Mozambique through a program known as Cash Grants for Disaster Response (Meyer 2007). Also in Mozambique, the U.S. Agency for International Development funded a one-time transfer to victims of floods in 2001 (Waterhouse 2007). In 2007, Concern Worldwide and Oxfam GB (2007) administered a program in Zambia for flood victims. These are just several examples of emergency programs addressing victims of natural disasters; others have addressed droughts and flooding in West Africa.

Conflicts or potential conflicts have exacerbated vulnerabilities in some Sub-Saharan African countries, and these conflicts are burdens in themselves. To address vulnerabilities induced by conflicts, some (low-income) programs give CTs to encourage repatriation of refugees and reintegration of former combatants. These programs typically provide a one-off transfer to help individuals who are making a major investment by relocating or beginning a new occupation. In Burundi, a major CT repatriation program was expected to reach more than 50,000 beneficiaries to encourage their repatriation (IRIN 2009). Most of these programs are rather small and are not discussed in detail in this book, but they are known to have been used in Burundi, the Central African Republic, the Democratic Republic of Congo, the Republic of Congo, Côte d'Ivoire, Eritrea, Liberia, Mozambique, Rwanda, Sierra Leone, Somalia, Sudan, and Togo. The extent of these programs shows the popularity of using CTs in postconflict situations.

Cash Transfers That Target Individuals in Various Life Stages

Middle-income and low-income CTs also focused on individuals in various life stages. Similarities were seen in their life-stage focus, but nuances across the middle-income and low-income CTs did emerge. Because each life stage has accompanying risks, often unique to the stage, these programs not only target different age groups, but also may provide different benefits, maintain varying conditions, or even have distinct distribution mechanisms. Major life stages include birth and early childhood, primary school age, secondary school age and young adulthood, adulthood, and old age. The life stages are associated with various vulnerabilities, which may correlate with poverty, though some individuals in each group obviously will not be poor. Figure 2.14 lists some of the vulnerabilities associated with life stages.

The decision to address a specific life stage and its corresponding vulnerabilities is typically based on an analysis of the scope and long-term consequences of the vulnerabilities within the CT's potential program area. For instance, the long-term impact of a poor diet is greater for a young child than for a young adult or adult male. Moreover, CT programs are not always appropriate for addressing certain vulnerabilities related to life stage. Although adults are vulnerable to lack of employment opportunities, a public works program, rather than a CT, may more adequately address underemployment in labor-capable adults.

Figure 2.14 Life Stages Are Associated with Susceptibility to Specific Vulnerabilities

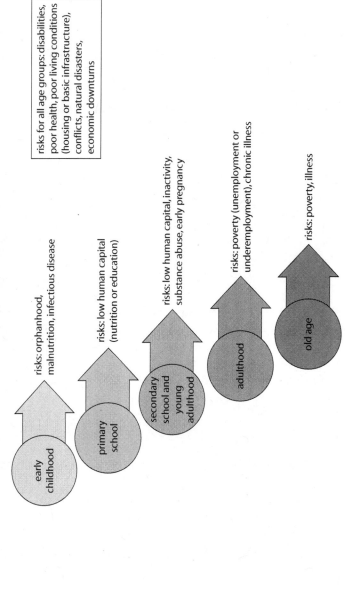

Source: Authors' representation.

A summary of CT programs in Sub-Saharan Africa, classified by the stage of the life cycle they address and the country's income status, is provided in figure 2.15. Overall, more than one in three programs in Sub-Saharan Africa specifically target children, young adults, or both; however, this number is approximately one in four for the middle-income CTs, and one in two for the low-income CTs. Most child-focused programs target school-age children, rather than very young children, a surprising result given the major vulnerabilities known to exist in early childhood. The second most common life stage targeted is old age, and targeting is accomplished mainly through social pensions. Middle-income CTs are more likely to target the elderly than are low-income CTs, probably because of the popularity of social pensions in those countries. Mothers are targeted relatively rarely, and few programs specifically target other life-stage combinations.

The major CT programs in Sub-Saharan Africa that focus on children take varying approaches. For instance, Eritrea has recently started a

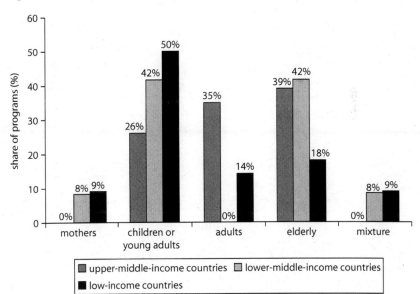

Figure 2.15 Program Beneficiaries by Countries' Income Classification

Source: Authors' representation.
Note: Sample size is 57. Programs were not included in this chart if they did not focus on one or more life stages. For instance, programs targeted to refugees are not included, as they may include individuals in all life stages. Because many CTs in fragile states do not target individuals in a specific life stage, fragile states are not broken out in this analysis.

program intended to combat the relatively poor health of mothers and young children in rural areas. Senegal's Conditional Cash Transfer for Orphans and Vulnerable Children targets one vulnerable group—OVC—by addressing education-related vulnerabilities affecting primary and secondary schoolchildren. Kenya's Cash Transfer for Orphans and Vulnerable Children also targets OVC while attempting to condition transfers on human capital investment in children's health and education. The middle-income CTs tend to award some of the few poverty-focused transfers as grants for children living in poverty.

Most CTs that focus on adult household members determine program eligibility on the basis of household adults' ability to participate in the labor force. If a household adult has a disability or a chronic debilitating illness, these programs award transfers to the household. If a household adult could participate in the labor force or in a public works program, the household is usually excluded from the CT. This approach has been taken in Malawi and Zambia. Other programs that provide benefits to adults in households in which adults are capable of participating in the labor force tend to focus on the need to use cash for food consumption or to benefit children in the household.

Transfers targeted to the elderly are also common in many parts of Sub-Saharan Africa. Social pension programs typically focus on meeting consumption needs of the elderly or reducing poverty in elderly households. As Kakwani and Subbarao (2005) point out, poverty in many Sub-Saharan African countries tends to be deeper in households with elderly members. In addition, the number of skipped-generation households, in which elderly individuals must care for children without the support of other adults, has increased in the region. Countries sometimes use social pensions to target both the elderly and vulnerable children, because many children in skipped-generation households are OVC.

It is important to note that using social pensions in the hopes of benefiting children is not the most efficient means of targeting children. Some researchers have used Duflo's (2003) study, among others, to point out that pensions benefit grandchildren in households. This interpretation is not the main point of Duflo's study, which instead shows that granddaughters benefit from pensions that their grandmothers, but not grandfathers, receive. (Girls, but not boys, had a significant improvement in anthropometric outcomes.) A program, such as a pension, with a high leakage rate to individuals other than children would be considered poor in terms of its ability to target children.

Conclusions

The identified CT programs can be clearly divided into a general typology that is based somewhat loosely on a country's income levels. Although this framework is useful for painting a high-level picture of how CTs have been used throughout the region, it masks significant differences in program components and implementation issues. These dynamics are the focus of the next chapter, which examines lessons that can already be learned from Sub-Saharan Africa's experience with CT programs.

Notes

1. This is not to say that food transfers are not without merit or that CTs are always superior to in-kind transfers. For instance, an evaluation of one of these programs, the Dedza Safety Nets Pilot Programme, recommended that cash be used in combination with in-kind transfers (Levy, Nyasulu, and Kuyeli 2002). Later evaluations of Ethiopia's Productive Safety Net Programme have found that beneficiaries preferred food transfers to cash when the value of the cash deteriorated (Sabates-Wheeler and Devereux 2010).
2. Because the Productive Safety Net Programme (PSNP) contains both a public works component and the Direct Support cash transfer, the term PSNP is used here to refer to the entire program, including the public works component. PSNP-DS is used to refer to only the Direct Support component of the PSNP. This distinction is important because much of the literature on the PSNP highlighted in this book refers to the entire program and not simply the CT component.
3. Niño-Zarazúa and others (2010) discuss some of the political dynamics of the earliest transfers in the middle-income Southern African countries.
4. The program is still known to underserve orphans.
5. Authors' calculation taking April 2009 grant coverage divided by the estimated population for 2009.
6. Despite this tendency, for classification purposes in this book, all programs that focus on vulnerable groups are classified as such, regardless of their motivation.

References

African Union. 2008. "Social Policy Framework for Africa." First Session of the African Union Conference of Ministers in Charge of Social Development, Windhoek, October 27–31.

———. 2009. "Decisions and Declarations." Executive Council, 14th Ordinary Session, Addis Ababa, January 26–30.

———. 2010. "Social Policy Framework for Africa: Implementation Strategy Proposal." Second Session of the African Union Conference of Ministers in Charge of Social Development, Khartoum, November 21–25.

BFTU (Botswana Federation of Trade Unions). 2007. "Policy Position Paper on Social Security and Social Protection in Botswana." BFTU, Gaborone.

Concern Worldwide and Oxfam GB. 2007. "Cash Transfers as a Response to Disaster: Lessons from Oxfam GB and Concern Worldwide Responses in Western Zambia." Oxfam GB, Oxford, U.K. http://www.oxfam.org.uk/resources/countries/downloads/zambia_cash_transfers_200805.pdf.

Coudouel, Aline, Kene Ezemenari, Margaret Grosh, and Lynne Sherburne-Benz. 2002. "Social Protection." In *PRSP Sourcebook of Poverty Reduction: Volume 2—Macroeconomic and Sectoral Approaches*. Washington, DC: World Bank.

Devereux, Stephen, and Larissa Pelham. 2005. "Making Cash Count: Lessons from Cash Transfer Schemes in East and Southern Africa for Supporting the Most Vulnerable Children and Households." Save the Children UK, HelpAge International, and Institute of Development Studies, London. http://www.ids.ac.uk/go/idsproject/making-cash-count.

Dlamini, Armstrong. 2007. "A Review of Social Assistance Grants in Swaziland: A CANGO/RHVP Case Study on Public Assistance in Swaziland." Regional Hunger Vulnerability Programme, Johannesburg.

Duflo, Esther. 2003. "Grandmothers and Granddaughters: Old-Age Pensions and Intrahousehold Allocation in South Africa." *World Bank Economic Review* 17 (1): 1–25.

Ellis, Frank. 2007. "Food Subsidy Programme, Mozambique." REBA Case Study Brief 7, Regional Evidence Building Agenda, Regional Hunger Vulnerability Programme, Johannesburg.

Ellis, Frank, Stephen Devereux, and Philip White. 2009. *Social Protection in Africa*. Northampton, MA: Edward Elgar.

European University Institute. 2010. *Social Protection for Inclusive Development: A New Perspective in EU Cooperation with Africa*. San Domenico di Fiesole, Italy: Robert Schuman Centre for Advanced Studies, European University Institute.

FAO (Food and Agriculture Organization of the United Nations). 2007. "Food Aid Shipments: World Food Programme Certified Data as of 30 June 2007." FAO Statistics Division, Rome.

———. 2008. "Prevalence of Undernourishment in Total Population." FAO Statistics Division, Rome.

HSNP (Hunger Safety Net Programme). n.d. "Welcome to Hunger Safety Net Programme." HSNP, Nairobi. http://www.hsnp.or.ke/.

IRIN (Integrated Regional Information Networks). 2009. "Burundi: Repatriation of Refugees from Tanzania Resumes." IRIN, Nairobi. http://www.irinnews.org/Report.aspx?ReportID=84089.

Johannsen, Julia, Luis Tejerina, and Amanda Glassman. 2009. "Conditional Cash Transfers in Latin America: Problems and Opportunities." In *Social Assistance and Conditional Cash Transfers: Proceedings of the Regional Workshop*, ed. Sri Wening Handayani and Clifford Burkley. Manila: Asian Development Bank.

Kakwani, Nanak, and Kalanidhi Subbarao. 2005. "Ageing and Poverty in Africa and the Role of Social Pensions." Working Paper 8, International Poverty Centre, Brasília.

Levine, Sebastian, Servaas van der Berg, and Derek Yu. 2009. "Measuring the Impact of Social Cash Transfers on Poverty and Inequality in Namibia." Stellenbosch Economic Working Paper 25/09, Department of Economics and Bureau for Economic Research, University of Stellenbosch, Stellenbosch, South Africa.

Levy, Sarah, Gerald Nyasulu, and Jaynet Kuyeli, with Carlos Barahona and Cathy Garlick. 2002. "Dedza Safety Nets Pilot Project: Learning Lessons about Direct Welfare Transfers for Malawi's National Safety Nets Strategy." Calibre Consultants, Concern Universal, and Statistical Services Centre, University of Reading, Berkshire, U.K.

Meyer, John. 2007. "The Use of Cash/Vouchers in Response to Vulnerability and Food Insecurity: Case Study Review and Analysis." World Food Programme, Rome.

Niño-Zarazúa, Miguel, Armando Barrientos, David Hulme, and Sam Hickey. 2010. "Social Protection in Sub-Saharan Africa: Will the Green Shoots Blossom?" Brooks World Poverty Institute Working Paper 116, University of Manchester, Manchester, U.K.

O'Donnell, Michelle. 2007. "Project Evaluation: Cash-Based Emergency Livelihood Recovery Programme." Save the Children Canada, Toronto.

Plaatjies, Daniel. 2006. "Conditional Cash Transfer Programs in South Africa." Presented at the Third International Conference on Conditional Cash Transfers, Istanbul, June 26–30.

Republic of Rwanda. 2009. "Vision 2020 Umurenge Programme (VUP): Direct Support Operational Framework and Procedure Manual." Ministry of Local Government, Good Governance, Community Development, and Social Affairs, Kigali.

Republic of South Africa. 2004. "Social Assistance Act, 2004." *Government Gazette* 468 (26446): 2–30.

RHVP (Regional Hunger and Vulnerability Programme). 2007. "Old Age and Public Assistance Grants, Swaziland." REBA Case Study Brief 6, Regional Evidence Building Agenda, RHVP, Johannesburg.

Sabates-Wheeler, Rachel, and Stephen Devereux. 2010. "Cash Transfers and High Food Prices: Explaining Outcomes on Ethiopia's Productive Safety Net Programme." *Food Policy* 35 (4): 274–85.

SASSA (South African Social Security Agency). 2009. "Statistical Report on Social Grants." Report 17, Strategy and Business Development Branch, Monitoring and Evaluation Department, SASSA, Pretoria.

Schubert, Bernd, and Sylvia Beales. 2006. "Social Cash Transfers for Africa: A Transformative Agenda for the 21st Century—Intergovernmental Regional Conference Report, Livingstone, Zambia, 20–23 March 2006." HelpAge International, London.

Schüring, Esther. 2010. "Strings Attached or Loose Ends? The Role of Conditionality in Zambia's Social Cash Transfer Scheme." Maastricht Graduate School of Governance, Maastricht, Netherlands.

South African Government Services. 2009. "Social Services." South African Government Services, Pretoria. http://www.services.gov.za/.

Streak, Judith. 2007. "Brief Overview of Cash Transfer System in South Africa and Introduction to HSRC Going to Scale Research Project." PowerPoint presentation at the Africa Regional Workshop on Cash Transfer Programmes for Vulnerable Groups, Mombasa, Kenya, February 26–28.

Sultan, Sonya M., and Tamar T. Schrofer. 2008. "Building Support to Have Targeted Social Protection Interventions for the Poorest: The Case of Ghana." Presented at the Conference on Social Protection for the Poorest in Africa: Learning from Experience, Kampala, September 8–10.

Taylor, Viviene. 2010. *Social Protection in Africa: An Overview of the Challenges*. Addis Ababa: African Union.

UNAIDS (Joint United Nations Programme on HIV/AIDS) and WHO (World Health Organization). 2008. *2008 Report on the Global AIDS Epidemic*. Geneva: UNAIDS.

U.S. Social Security Administration. 2009. *Social Security Programs throughout the World: Africa 2009*. Washington, DC: Office of Retirement and Disability Policy, Office of Research, Evaluation, and Statistics.

Waterhouse, Rachel. 2007. "The Political and Institutional Context for Social Protection in Mozambique: A Brief Overview." International Policy Centre for Inclusive Growth, Brasília.

World Bank. 2009a. "Program Document on a Proposed Grant in the Amount of SDR 4 Million (US$6 Million Equivalent) Funding to the Republic of Rwanda for a First Community Living Standards Grant (CLSG-1)." Human Development III, Eastern Africa Country Cluster II, Africa Region, World Bank, Washington, DC.

———. 2009b. "Project Appraisal Document for a Cash Transfer for Orphans and Vulnerable Children Project." World Bank, Washington, DC.

———. 2009c. *2009 World Development Indicators*. Washington, DC: World Bank.

———. 2010. "Africa's Future and the World Bank's Support to It." Draft, World Bank, Washington, DC.

World Values Survey Association. 2009. "1981–2008 Official Aggregate." Version 20090901. World Values Survey Association, Uppsala. Aggregate File Producer: ASEP/JDS, Madrid. http://www.worldvaluessurvey.org.

CHAPTER 3

Design and Implementation of Cash Transfers in Sub-Saharan Africa
Trends, Lessons, and Knowledge Gaps

Although chapter 2 provided a high-level view of strategic issues related to cash transfers (CTs) in Sub-Saharan Africa, this chapter examines the nuances of CT design and implementation, and it sketches a more complete picture of how CTs have worked in Sub-Saharan Africa. It is intended to highlight trends in program implementation, lessons that have already been learned, and areas where existing knowledge needs to be improved to enhance program outcomes. The chapter begins with one of the most basic questions: What are the objectives of the reviewed CTs in Sub-Saharan Africa?

The Varying Objectives of Sub-Saharan Africa's CT Programs

CT programs in the region address a remarkably wide range of objectives. As already mentioned, some have specific human capital goals or aim to encourage peace consolidation in a postconflict situation. Others state that they are working to combat both acute and chronic food insecurity or to ensure that targeted beneficiaries are able to meet subsistence consumption needs. An objective of a number of CTs is simply to determine how well the programs function in the given environment. A sample of CT program objectives in the region is given in box 3.1.

Successful programs rely on analytical background work that helps to determine the needs in a given area and the type of program or CT that can best respond to those needs. Program objectives should reflect those analyses, which consider both quantitative factors, such as the number or

---

Box 3.1

Objectives of Sub-Saharan Africa's Cash Transfer Programs

Sub-Saharan Africa's CT programs have a wide variety of objectives:

- *Botswana Program for Destitute Persons.* To ensure that the government provides minimum assistance to genuinely destitute persons to ensure their good health and welfare.
- *Botswana Old Age Pension.* To financially assist elderly people who do not have other support as a result of the deterioration of support from the extended family.
- *Burundi UNHCR (Office of the United Nations High Commissioner for Refugees) Cash Grants.* To encourage and support repatriation of Burundian refugees residing in Tanzania.
- *Eritrea Results-Based Financing.* To improve the health outcomes of mothers and children in rural areas of Eritrea by increasing the use of health facilities and services, improving children's health outcomes, and increasing the coverage and quality of health services.
- *Ethiopia Productive Safety Net Programme.* To provide households with cash or food transfers to help meet their food needs and protect them from depleting their assets, and to build productive assets in communities to decrease the causes of chronic food insecurity.
- *Ghana LEAP.* To supplement the subsistence needs of the extremely poor, connect beneficiaries to related services to improve their welfare, and encourage comprehensive social development through the use of public-private partnerships.
- *Kenya CT for OVC.* To provide regular cash transfers to households with orphans and vulnerable children to encourage fostering and retention of such children in households within communities and to promote their human capital development.

(continued next page)

Box 3.1 *(continued)*

- *Malawi Social Cash Transfer.* To decrease poverty, hunger, and starvation in all households that are ultrapoor and, at the same time, labor constrained.
- *Mozambique Food Subsidy Program.* To ensure that consumption levels do not fall to levels insufficient for survival.
- *Nigeria Kano Conditional Cash Transfer for Girls' Education.* To increase education levels of girls in Kano state to improve progression toward the Millennium Development Goals of universal primary education and gender equality.
- *Senegal Conditional Cash Transfer for Orphans and Vulnerable Children.* To support education and vocational training of 5,000 orphans and vulnerable children by ensuring that they have access to education or vocational training; supporting their financial needs; and financially supporting their psychosocial, family, educational, and professional sustenance.
- *South Africa Grant System.* To provide appropriate social assistance to those without access to social security and to reduce poverty and promote social development.
- *Tanzania Community-Based Conditional Cash Transfer.* To increase access of the poor and vulnerable to basic services, to increase school attendance and health care visits of beneficiaries, to determine how a conditional cash transfer relying on community-driven development and functioning within a social fund can be effectively implemented, and to see how such a transfer can be used to lessen the impact of AIDS in communities.
- *Zambia Kalomo Social Cash Transfer.* To decrease poverty, starvation, and hunger of targeted households, and to generate information about the viability of a social cash transfer program in Zambia.

Source: Authors' compilation based on various sources.

proportion of individuals with given vulnerabilities, and "soft" issues, such as capacity constraints. One country in which analytical work has been crucial in formulating a CT's specific objectives is Senegal, whose conditional cash transfer (CCT) for orphans and vulnerable children (OVC) arose in response to report recommendations that community groups needed support to improve education and vocational training for OVC (Document de Cadrage Technique 2009). Kenya also relied on analytical work to focus the objectives of its first major CT, the CT for OVC. In 2005, analysis determined that approximately 12 percent of Kenyan households were headed or maintained by orphans, whose school attendance (among 10- to 14-year-olds) was markedly lower than that of nonorphans (Government of Kenya 2005). Because these OVC represent 30 percent of all poor children in Kenya, addressing their needs was vital for the country (World Bank 2009d).

Similar to some of the vanguard CCT programs in Latin America, some CCTs in Sub-Saharan Africa have objectives related to specific human capital objectives: Mali's Bourse Maman and Nigeria's Kano CCT for Girls' Education focus on improving educational attainment of vulnerable groups, Eritrea's Results-Based Financing (RBF) program focuses on improving health outcomes for mothers and children, and Nigeria's COPE (In Care of the Poor) CCT and Tanzania's Community-Based Conditional Cash Transfer (CB-CCT) have human capital objectives in both education and health care.

Other CTs in Sub-Saharan Africa are being used to address challenges more specific to the region. For instance, many Sub-Saharan African programs have objectives related to food security. Those objectives reflect the region's relatively recently begun transition from emergency food aid to regular cash transfers and the recurrent extreme food insecurity confronted by many on the continent. Many programs, including several short-term cash-for-relief programs in Ethiopia, Kenya, Malawi, Swaziland, and Tanzania, have objectives related to ensuring the survival of beneficiaries or decreasing hunger for those in danger of malnutrition or starvation. Longer-term programs with such objectives include Kenya's Hunger Safety Net Programme (HSNP), Mozambique's Food Subsidy Program (Programa Subsidio de Alimentos, or PSA), Senegal's Child-Focused Social Cash Transfer (CF-SCT) program, and Zambia's Social Cash Transfer (SCT) program. Still other programs want to help households meet their food consumption needs while protecting their productive assets, such as the Direct Support component of Ethiopia's Productive Safety Net Programme (PSNP-DS) and the Direct Support component in Rwanda's Vision 2020 Umurenge Programme (VUP), or to encourage household productivity, such as Ethiopia's PSNP-DS and Zimbabwe's Protracted Relief Program.

Other CTs relatively unique to Sub-Saharan Africa are those that have been developed to combat HIV or the effects of the AIDS crisis. Kenya aims to avoid the institutionalization of orphans and vulnerable children through its CT for OVC, and Senegal recognizes the vulnerability of OVC, particularly in regard to school desertion, in its CCT for OVC. Tanzania has a CCT that tries to slow the spread of sexually transmitted infections (STIs), HIV, and unintended pregnancies among young adults, with conditions specifically tied to recipients' remaining free from curable STIs.

African CT objectives can reflect diversity within countries and over time. Given Sub-Saharan Africa's extreme ethnic, economic, and cultural diversity, there is usually no one-size-fits-all program for all vulnerable groups in a country. Although ensuring that programs not become fragmented and incoherent is important, room must also be made for addressing the needs of different vulnerable groups within a country. Kenya's CT programs—the CT for OVC and HSNP—address two major vulnerable groups (OVC and people living in arid and semiarid lands) in ways that suit the groups' differing needs. Likewise, Nigeria's COPE CCT differs in objectives, targeted beneficiaries, and benefits across the 12 diverse states where it is being implemented. An altogether separate Nigerian CCT, the Kano CCT for Girls' Education, directly addresses the lower education levels of girls in a limited area.

Several countries have found that combining a CT with a public works program suits their program goals. Ethiopia's PSNP takes this form. A public works program alone would exclude households without any members able to participate in the labor force. By including a direct CT component in the PSNP-DS, the program is able to reach extremely vulnerable households that would be overlooked by the public works program. Rwanda's VUP operates similarly.

Linking program components and objectives is imperative. A necessary, but not sufficient, condition of a successful CT is that the program's components align with the program's objectives. When components align with program goals, they work in a complementary fashion, expanding the program's potential effects. Obviously, programs that aim to provide cash to combat food insecurity should have different components than those that aim to encourage human capital investment in education or health or those that have specific goals of improving households' productive capacity. When confusion arises regarding whether CT components are appropriate, the objectives provide direction for the program. For instance, Ethiopia's PSNP has had to work to maintain an appropriate balance between its development and welfare components; its stated objectives help provide direction and lessen confusion about the program's role. Objectives also provide a clear measure by which the program can be assessed.

Specific program components are outlined in the following sections, with attention paid to those most crucial to the success of any CT. Although program features will differ depending on the CT's objectives, each program must address the following major components, which serve as key foundations on which to build. Any well-designed CT will have well-thought-out targeting, payment, monitoring, and evaluation systems. Other design components are included in the following summaries as well, where experiences have shown that their alignment with program objectives is important to the CT's success.

Targeting Features of Cash Transfers in Sub-Saharan Africa

A CT program's objectives should guide who should be selected as program beneficiaries. If objectives focus on poverty, impoverished households or individuals are the program's ideal beneficiaries. If food security is a primary objective, households vulnerable to food insecurity should be targeted. If human capital investment is the program's main focus, the individuals who would benefit the most from improved investment in human capital (or who could provide the greatest benefit to society)—typically certain children—are targeted. However, deciding who the ideal beneficiaries is often easier than ensuring that benefits are distributed to those individuals.

A program's targeting system is the method it uses to select beneficiaries or households to be included in the program. Targeting can be completed using geographic locations; basic demographic or categorical indicators, such as gender or age; community members (such as committees or entire villages); means-tested information about household income; proxy means methods that use indicators related to poverty or well-being;[1] or self-targeting, when potential beneficiaries must apply for a program on their own (Coady, Grosh, and Hoddinott 2004b). Targeting is used to focus funds to maximize their effect, given resource limitations. When targeting is analyzed, inclusion and exclusion errors are typically reported in light of the ideally targeted beneficiary or household. An inclusion error occurs when a program provides benefits to an ineligible person. Exclusion errors occur when eligible beneficiaries are not allowed in the program; such errors often reflect constraints on the program's budget. Exclusion errors may also arise from failures of program implementers to adequately communicate benefits and procedures when self-targeting is involved. Programs try to minimize both types of errors, though a trade-off is often inherent between the two. For more information on the issues involved in targeting and additional references, see box 3.2.

Box 3.2

The Targeting Dilemma and Additional References on Targeting

Whether CT programs should be targeted has been an ongoing debate. At one extreme lie those who believe that targeting is inappropriate: transfers should be universally provided to all of a country's citizens. To universalists, targeting has not been successful as a redistributive mechanism, and it can generate only limited budget support. Those in favor of targeting believe it can achieve its goals. They also believe that universal benefits are not a feasible objective (Grosh and others 2008). Although universality is a philosophical ideal, most policy makers accept that universality cannot currently be achieved in most Sub-Saharan African countries and that some degree of targeting must be used. Therefore, the debate regarding targeting of CTs in Sub-Saharan Africa lies between those in favor of near-universal transfers and targeted transfers.

Near-Universal Transfers

Some policy makers favor universal or near-universal transfers to certain portions of the population. Such transfers are also known as *categorical transfers*, because they are based on simple categorical criteria, such as age or disability. Many of the transfers focus on protecting people from risks related to their life stage, including risks in childhood, adulthood (disability), or old age (European University Institute 2010). Those in favor of categorical targeting point out that it is administratively simple. When compared with more restrictive targeting methods, categorical targeting more easily generates broad-based political support. Communities may also be more likely to support categorical targeting as a motivation for providing benefits to certain groups, such as the elderly or OVC, over others (Slater and Farrington 2009).

Categorical targeting is also appropriate to those who consider social protection a basic human right that should be guaranteed by the state to its citizens.[a] Many of the middle-income African countries, such as Botswana, Mauritius, Namibia, and South Africa, approach their CTs from this framework, and they have legislation supporting their social grants system. According to this view, denying certain individuals transfers may be a violation of their human rights.

Despite their advantages, categorical transfers are subject to greater errors of inclusion (White and others 2009), and they tend to place greater demands on

(continued next page)

Box 3.2 *(continued)*

the domestic budget because individuals receive benefits regardless of their economic need. A final problem with categorical transfers is that needy individuals who do not meet basic eligibility criteria may not receive necessary support if the social protection system fails to cover all potentially needy groups (European University Institute 2010).

More Restrictive Targeting Methods
Those in favor of more strictly targeted transfers (or poverty targeting) point out that stricter targeting can decrease inclusion errors. Poverty targeting can support multiple needy or vulnerable groups, and targeted transfers can be more progressive than near-universal transfers. Programs with poverty-related targeting can save money by providing transfers to a smaller portion of the population, thereby making better use of limited resources (White and others 2009).

Despite these benefits, costs are involved in implementing poverty-related targeting (White and others 2009). Although measuring those costs is not always easy, Grosh and others (2008) found that means and proxy means targeting costs in a sample of programs studied in Central Asia, Eastern Europe, and Latin America averaged approximately 4 percent of program costs and between 25 percent and 75 percent of administrative costs. Targeting costs as a percentage of benefits transferred for a group of programs in Latin America averaged below 1.5 percent. Within Sub-Saharan Africa, targeting costs as a percentage of total costs will depend on transfer size, program coverage, and the extent to which the program is well established.

In addition, targeting of transfers may be difficult to administer correctly: eligible households may be difficult to identify and data collection may be expensive (Jones 2009), particularly in some low-capacity Sub-Saharan African settings. Households may have difficulty understanding targeting criteria and may not believe those criteria are fair. When targeting criteria are well understood, households may adjust their composition or behaviors to meet those criteria. Programs with targeted transfers also have to be careful to avoid leapfrogging of beneficiary income over nonbeneficiary income, and retargeting will need to occur at certain intervals (White and others 2009). An additional concern about targeting is its potential to create social tensions or stigmatization (Jones 2009). This issue is important in countries with widespread poverty.

Whether a program identifies beneficiaries using categorical or near-universal methods or chooses beneficiaries through more selective methods should be

(continued next page)

Box 3.2 *(continued)*

based on a calculated decision regarding the expected costs and benefits of the methods chosen. The expected future size of targeted groups will also have implications for the CT's long-term fiscal sustainability and must be considered. Analysis of household survey data can help outline the empirical trade-offs associated with the targeting method chosen.

Of course, sometimes targeting is not open to discussion; beneficiary groups may have already been decided before the analytical work began (Slater and Farrington 2010). Targeting choices must ultimately be pragmatic decisions that weigh the various administrative, private, social, and political costs involved with the potential targeting methods (Grosh and others 2008).

Recommended References on Targeting
For further information on issues associated with appropriate targeting, see Grosh and others (2008) and Coady, Grosh, and Hoddinott (2004b) for a thorough treatment of the topic. See also Slater and Farrington (2009), who highlight important issues to consider when targeting in low-income, low-capacity countries, and Slater and Farrington (2010), who provide a quick reference guide on key targeting principles, particularly in very low-income settings.

a. Notably, Niño-Zarazúa and others (2010) point out that countries in Southern Africa with universal social pensions have Gini coefficients greater than 0.5. They argue that this inequality has generated a desire for social protection while helping to keep transfer leakage low and providing fiscal space for redistribution using transfers.

Groups Targeted

Groups commonly targeted in Sub-Saharan Africa include OVC or other HIV-affected individuals, the elderly, and people with disabilities or those who are unable to participate in the labor market. Other vulnerable groups often targeted include the extremely poor, potentially malnourished preschool children, and pregnant or lactating mothers. Targeted groups are not mutually exclusive, and significant overlap across the groups may occur. Some programs target a combination of these groups, such as OVC and extremely poor elderly people.

Figure 3.1 depicts targeted groups, broken down between conditional and unconditional CTs. Many CCTs target children or OVC. Several target the unemployed, mothers and young children, and young adults, and one in four CCTs targets a combination of these groups.

Figure 3.1 Groups Targeted in Conditional and Unconditional Cash Transfer Programs in Sub-Saharan Africa

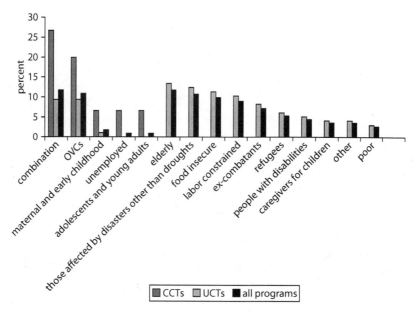

Source: Authors' representation.
Note: Sample size is 15 for CCTs, 96 for UCTs, and 111 for all programs. Samples are based on programs with known information about the targeted group.

Unconditional cash transfers (UCTs) target a wider variety of groups. The elderly are the most frequently targeted group, followed by victims of disasters and people with insecure food sources. Households without members capable of participating in the labor force are targeted slightly less frequently, at approximately 10 percent of the time. OVC, refugees, ex-combatants, and people living with disabilities are targeted in 5 percent to 10 percent of the UCTs.

Targeting Methodology

Most CTs in Sub-Saharan Africa combine several targeting methods to select beneficiaries. For instance, many select households using community or proxy means targeting within selected geographic regions. In some cases, targeting criteria could logically be classified into multiple categories.

A summary of the most commonly used targeting methods in the reviewed programs is found in figure 3.2. Multiple targeting methods are counted for programs that used more than one method. Panel a shows that categorical targeting is the most widely used method in both CCTs

Figure 3.2 Multiple Targeting Methods Used by Programs in Sub-Saharan Africa

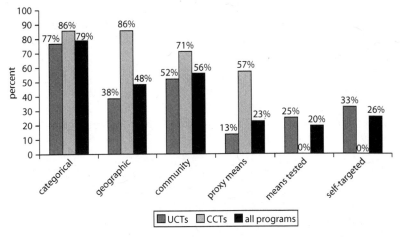

a. Conditional and unconditional programs

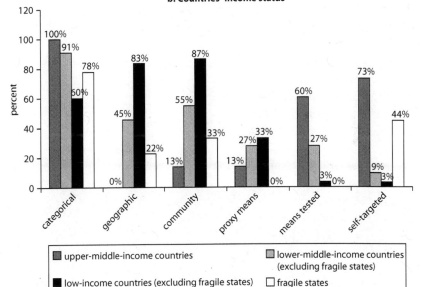

b. Countries' income status

Source: Authors' representation.
Note: In panel a, totals for CCTs and UCTs are greater than 100 percent because multiple targeting methods were used in many programs. Sample size is 14 for CCTs and 52 for UCTs. Samples are based on programs for which specific targeting information was available.
In panel b, totals add up to greater than 100 percent by income category because multiple targeting methods were allowed per program. Sample size of CTs is 15 for upper-middle-income countries, 11 for lower-middle-income countries (excluding fragile states), 30 for low-income countries (excluding fragile states), and 9 for fragile states. Samples are restricted to programs for which specific targeting information was available.

and UCTs. Geographic targeting and community targeting are also used frequently in most programs, especially CCTs. A little over one in five programs applies means tests, proxy means tests, or self-targeting. Proxy means tests are much more common in CCTs, a practice similar to CCTs outside of Sub-Saharan Africa, and means testing and self-targeting are more popular in UCTs.

Some social pensions in the region are universal or categorically targeted (as in Botswana, Cape Verde, Lesotho, and Mauritius), whereas others are means or proxy means tested, meaning that they have criteria in addition to the age requirement (as in Namibia, South Africa, and Swaziland). This mixture is similar to that found in pension programs around the world.

Examining targeting methodologies by countries' income status reveals significant differences across the groups (figure 3.2, panel b). Upper-middle-income countries practice categorical, means testing, and self-targeting methods most frequently. Lower-middle-income and low-income countries frequently use categorical and geographic criteria. More than half of CTs in lower-middle-income countries use community-based targeting, and almost 9 out of 10 do the same in low-income countries. One in two programs in lower-middle-income countries uses means or proxy means testing, and one in three programs in low-income countries uses proxy means testing. Very little means testing is used in low-income countries. CTs in fragile states use categorical and self-targeting methods in many programs; community targeting is a fairly common targeting method for these countries as well.

Widespread use of community-based targeting. One of the most salient features of targeting methods used in the reviewed CTs is the widespread use of community-based targeting systems, which are used to a more limited extent in comparable CTs around the world. Community targeting has obvious benefits. Those in the immediate community are easily able to identify vulnerable households that should receive benefits. They are familiar with households' needs and recent shocks they have faced, and they are likely to know whether households will use cash in a manner they deem responsible. Community-based targeting is relatively inexpensive, and it has the additional benefit of informing community members about the CT and involving them in it. Conversely, community-based targeting may impose additional costs on communities in terms of opportunity costs or social and political costs of carrying out the targeting at the local level.

A commonly cited concern associated with community-based targeting is the danger of nepotism or other types of favoritism leading to inclusion of persons who should not be eligible (and therefore the potential exclusion of eligible individuals or households). Favoritism in community-based targeting has been identified as an issue affecting CT programs in Malawi and Zambia. Miller, Tsoka, and Reichert (2010) report that village heads were sometimes able to inappropriately influence community members involved in selecting beneficiaries for Malawi's SCT program, perhaps because community members were not able or confident enough to navigate local political dynamics. Across Sub-Saharan Africa, the strength of traditions of extended family responsibilities and obligations creates an environment favorable to the emergence of such problems.

Even when communities attempt to implement fair and accurate targeting, inconsistent application of targeting rules may arise when eligibility criteria have room for interpretation. Clear targeting criteria and training of community committees or members involved in targeting should help ease this problem, at least to an extent. Finally, even when community members objectively target households, community-based targeting may still be perceived as unfair or inconsistent. This issue may be especially contentious in the poorest areas, where very small material differences separate beneficiaries and nonbeneficiaries.

Some Sub-Saharan African countries have taken steps to combat targeting errors when using community-based targeting. Malawi's SCT does not allow village heads to be on community social protection committees, which are in charge of targeting (Miller, Tsoka, and Reichart 2010). The SCT has also recently added a verification round to its targeting process. Extension workers are now involved in verifying targeting decisions, as they know community members well and may be more impartial than others, given that they are usually from outside the community and extended family system. Zambia allows local leaders to be involved in targeting but has taken steps to create a confidential appeals process to ensure that targeting is as fair as possible (Hamonga 2006).

In some cases, communities have already received training and have the capacity to implement targeting relatively easily. In Rwanda, for example, information gathered by existing *Ubudehe*[2] committees about local households' relative welfare is used for targeting purposes in the Direct Support program. In Ethiopia's PSNP, communities already had relevant experience targeting households for food aid, which has facilitated the program's community-based targeting (World Bank

2010a). Other programs first sensitize communities and then provide training to enable them to participate more effectively in the targeting process.

Additional checks on community-based targeting should be clearly understood by community members. Kenya's CT for OVC uses community-based targeting combined with geographic, categorical, and even proxy means testing. Although the process has reduced targeting errors, the complicated method has also generated confusion surrounding beneficiary selection, leaving some households feeling unfairly excluded or unsure of why they are beneficiaries. This confusion may easily become a source of tension among community members.

Other community targeting in Sub-Saharan Africa is conducted in a more indirect manner. Some programs encourage key community members, such as health workers, to identify potential beneficiaries on a case-by-case basis (Mozambique's PSA). Others target OVC—children who may not identify themselves because of the stigma associated with HIV/AIDS—by relying on local organizations that already are in contact with them (Senegal's CCT for OVC).

Other issues to consider in targeting. In some of Sub-Saharan Africa's CT programs, a major concern is that beneficiaries' incomes will "leapfrog" over those of nonbeneficiaries. This issue is especially important when CTs are implemented in areas with a relatively flat income distribution. The size of a poverty-targeted transfer must be chosen carefully to ensure that it meets program goals but does not suddenly make beneficiaries substantially better off than nonbeneficiaries who had a similar standard of living before the CT began. If the program fails to address this possibility, leapfrogging may generate significant social tension (Ellis 2008, as cited in Slater and Farrington 2010).

This issue will not affect every country equally. In an analysis of Ghana and Malawi, leapfrogging was found to be a major concern in Malawi, where the distribution of income was very flat (especially in rural areas), whereas it was not as problematic in Ghana, where the income distribution was more unequal (White and others 2009). In Malawi, only US$9 or US$10 per capita monthly divided the lowest income decile from the sixth income decile, highlighting the potential of transfers to cause significant leapfrogging (Ellis 2008, as cited in Slater and Farrington 2010).

Care must also be taken when poverty targeting is accompanied by categorical targeting. For instance, although Malawi and Zambia target ultrapoor, labor-constrained households in their major CTs, ultrapoor households with available labor may be even worse off than labor-constrained households if employment is unavailable, given that ultrapoor households may need more calories per person than do labor-constrained households (Ellis 2008, as cited in Slater and Farrington 2010). Those issues suggest the importance of using analytical work to drive CT designs.

Some programs in Sub-Saharan Africa use quotas to restrict the number of beneficiaries targeted by geographic location. In Malawi and Zambia, surveys determined that 10 percent of households were ultrapoor and labor constrained. On the basis of this determination, the 10 percent worst-off households that fit the labor-constrained definition were selected as beneficiaries in each given locality. However, even in areas with a relatively equal spatial income distribution, such quotas can be problematic, excluding eligible households in areas with greater than 10 percent eligible households, and including ineligible households in areas with eligible populations of less than 10 percent (White and others 2009).

Also important is understanding who may benefit indirectly from a CT based on the targeting scheme. For instance, old-age pensions in Lesotho and South Africa are known to provide significant support to OVC who live with their grandparents. This support is especially helpful in Lesotho, which is still in the process of trying to put more significant support in place for OVC. Samson (2007) calculated that 65 percent of the pension money in Lesotho is actually used by the elderly to care for children. The significant size of the transfer provides a major boost to household income, and it may benefit children. However, this scheme does not negate the need for programs directed to children, because any pension obviously targets the elderly first and will miss many OVC.

Finally, targeting in Sub-Saharan Africa may also need to deal with local cultural and social traditions, such as targeting of polygamous households. This issue arose in Ethiopia's PSNP. In that case, the government decided that the best approach was to use a standard procedure in which wives and their children should each be registered as separate households (Devereux, Sabates-Wheeler, and others 2008), although implementation across locations has varied in practice (World Bank 2010a).

Data Collection for Targeting
Often household surveys, censuses, administrative data, and birth and death records are out of date or nonexistent in Sub-Saharan African

countries. Institutional capacity and financial backing for data collection may be weak, and access to some communities may be difficult at best. This lack of data can be a significant obstacle in the targeting process. Beyond leaving knowledge gaps about households' program eligibility, the lack of data can put CTs in danger of overlooking some vulnerable households entirely. Various programs have confronted such data limitations differently as they attempt to collect data for program purposes. The collection methods often are limited by time and financial constraints that affect data accuracy and, consequently, targeting precision. The constraints also make it difficult to maintain up-to-date information about households that are excluded from programs, another key piece of information for targeting and program implementation.

Even information allowing for broad-scale geographic targeting is limited in some Sub-Saharan African countries. Despite the relative dearth of detailed information by region, general geographic targeting is possible in most cases. What is more, the usefulness of data collection exercises, such as detailed poverty mapping in parts of the country where a potential CT program may function, can provide an impetus for a country to develop and maintain more current data.

Community help in collecting data. Programs in Sub-Saharan Africa have typically relied on ad hoc community-level data collection methods to acquire necessary information for targeting households and individuals. For instance, community members identify potential beneficiaries of Botswana's Orphan Care Program, and social workers must then assess each case (BFTU 2007). In lieu of relying on an up-to-date census, Malawi's SCT has collected necessary data for targeting by using community members' knowledge of where households reside (Miller, Tsoka, and Reichart 2010). Similarly, Eritrea relies on village health committees to identify potential RBF beneficiaries and invite them to enrollment meetings (Ayala Consulting 2009). In program areas of Kenya's CT for OVC, local committees identify potential beneficiary households, which are then visited by enumerators, who collect additional information about the households to help determine whether they are eligible for the CT (Government of Kenya 2006).

Malawi's experience illustrates some of the potential difficulties encountered when using community members to collect data for the program's targeting system. Community-level knowledge of the presence of households within a given area was often inaccurate, with leaders estimating as much as 43 percent more or 44 percent fewer households than those encountered in a systematic canvassing activity. Estimating household numbers incorrectly affected how many beneficiaries would be included in the program in a given location. Listings were sometimes affected by nonrandom exclusion of households because of their remote or relatively inaccessible location or their lack of community ties and by purposeful inclusion of ghost households (Miller, Tsoka, and Reichert 2010).

Data collection through other agencies or means. Some programs identify potential beneficiaries—and, therefore, collect data about them—as the individuals initiate contact with other official support systems. Potential beneficiaries are identified through their contact with a local official in health, education, or social services who then helps to enroll the individual in the program. This method of identification occurs in Mozambique's PSA, where health centers may identify potential beneficiaries and local program officials verify their information. The officials receive small payments as an incentive for recommending or enrolling beneficiaries (Datt and others 1997). Similarly, nongovernmental organizations (NGOs) and other groups that provide support to OVC identify potential beneficiaries for Senegal's CT for OVC. In some countries, such targeting mechanisms have the tendency to overlook individuals who hide because of the stigma associated with a condition such as HIV. In Senegal's case, this concern is lessened; OVC should be more easily identified by NGOs, because they are used to identifying and assisting them.

Still other programs (including multiple programs in the upper-middle-income countries of Mauritius, Namibia, and South Africa) leave the onus of providing data on potential beneficiaries, who are required to submit information to program offices to receive benefits. With this type of design, beneficiaries who are not connected to relevant support systems will be excluded from the CT program. Given that some of those individuals will typically be the ones who most need the program's assistance, this method of identifying eligible beneficiaries can lead to undercoverage of the eligible population. Awareness campaigns have been important in increasing coverage for many of these programs.

Although data collection using community members and incidental data collection are not a first-best practice in many cases, they may be the most appropriate methods, given program constraints. Over time, CT programs may be able to generate increased support and a rationale for regularly collecting microlevel data as programs expand and are concerned with households' ongoing eligibility and recertification.

Knowledge Gaps in Targeting Systems

Information about the execution and effectiveness of targeting systems in CT programs throughout Sub-Saharan Africa is still fairly limited. The difficulties associated with effective targeting suggest that case studies analyzing targeting and its effectiveness—in terms of success in reaching intended beneficiaries, implementation successes and failures, inclusion and exclusion outcomes, and costs—will be helpful to other programs throughout the region. Specific areas where knowledge will be helpful include the following: collecting data in limited financial and human resource capacity settings; targeting individuals who may not be easily identified because of stigma or inaccessibility; improving the implementation of community-based targeting, particularly with respect to effectively training communities in targeting practices and successfully navigating local political and cultural dynamics; and effectively communicating targeting criteria to program beneficiaries and nonbeneficiaries.

Targeting in Sub-Saharan Africa faces a set of particular challenges in data collection in terms of weaknesses in available population data and statistics, weak institutional capacities for collecting and analyzing data, and problems with access and cooperation from populations to be surveyed. Balancing the financial and social costs of targeting with the desire to achieve targeting accuracy can be a delicate issue, which further analysis and experience will be able to inform.

Client Registration: A Key Issue for Cash Transfers

A validated registration system needs to be in place to enroll transfer recipients once eligible beneficiaries have been identified for inclusion in a CT. A key issue in low-income countries is how to reliably identify eligible beneficiaries for enrollment purposes. Problems arise where procedures are not in place to correctly identify beneficiaries. Individuals may register for multiple grants (when they are not supposed to do so), or someone may wrongly receive grants in another person's name. For example, Swaziland has found that its Old Age Grant has more recipients than the number of eligible Swazis, a sign that large-scale fraud is occurring. The government blames this corruption on early implementation errors that allowed multiple proofs to be used to identify an individual in the initial enrollment period (RHVP 2007).

Challenges That Arise When Requiring Official Documentation

Requiring beneficiaries to register for CTs using a national identification card or a birth certificate is one way to reduce the incidence of fraud. Unfortunately, vital registration data, such as date of birth, are often limited in low-income countries, and the poor tend to have lower coverage levels of birth registration. In some countries, the integrity of vital registration systems themselves may be compromised. Strict requirements regarding identification documents may end up excluding the neediest beneficiaries, who ought to be eligible, without providing adequate protection against fraud. Consequently, the stricter such requirements become, the greater they contribute to errors of exclusion that can undermine programs' objectives.

The strict documentation requirements of Namibia's cash grant system, for example, have made it difficult for some extremely poor individuals to benefit from certain programs. The system requires potential beneficiaries to present birth documents, identification documents, and proof of marriage, among other items (Republic of Namibia 2007). This system is a significant obstacle to the registration of many individuals who would otherwise be eligible for the programs. This issue also caused problems when Namibia tried to move children out of long-term food aid to cash transfers. Difficulties arose because many of the most vulnerable children targeted for transition lacked formal registration records or proof of parentage. The personnel required for this transition taxed the capacities of Namibia's existing grant system.

Orphans and vulnerable children may face particular difficulties satisfying formal documentation requirements, especially in countries where large-scale illnesses and deaths from AIDS have left many households headed by children or the elderly, and documents have been lost with the death of parents or the movement of children between homes. Others often vulnerable to inadvertent exclusion from programs include refugees, foreign nationals, and children of those individuals.

Steps Taken to Facilitate Registration

Some countries have taken steps to alleviate identification and validation problems. Kenya's HSNP will use smart cards along with fingerprints to identify beneficiaries. This information can be recorded at a registration meeting, and it does not require beneficiaries to obtain identity cards (HSNP n.d.). Lesotho's Old Age Pension enrolled beneficiaries using voter registration cards (issued during the 2002 elections), and local chiefs verified identities and ages of individuals (Croome, Nyanguru, and

Molisana 2007). Malawi's SCT provides beneficiaries with photo identification cards (Schubert 2007a). Mozambique's PSA has worked to help potential beneficiaries obtain national identity cards. In lieu of the official cards, the program now increasingly accepts proof of application for identity cards or voter registration cards (Ellis 2007).

Although rolling registration is not practiced in many programs that are not self-targeted, some CTs make clear efforts to continue to identify and register vulnerable households. Frequent retargeting in Ethiopia's PSNP and Rwanda's VUP allows communities to identify potential new beneficiaries for the programs (Devereux and others 2006; Republic of Rwanda 2009). Community committees in Zambia's Kalomo SCT were allowed to identify households to fill newly opened positions twice annually to bring other vulnerable households into the program (Ministry of Community Development and Social Services 2008).

Another important issue in client registration is the time that elapses from when beneficiaries have their first contact with the program until they begin receiving transfers. Client demand combined with capacity constraints can cause this time to be longer than hoped. In Mozambique's PSA, a decision on program eligibility was supposed to occur within 15 days of the individual's application. However, in 2007, this process was reported to take months to complete (Ellis 2007). Similarly, it can take up to three months to be registered for a child-related grant in Namibia (Republic of Namibia 2007).

Program Benefits: How Much Was Transferred to Households?

Benefits provided by the reviewed CT programs vary widely. Approximately three in four programs provide only cash transfers. The most common benefits given in addition to cash were in-kind transfers. Some programs, such as Botswana's Orphan Care Program, primarily provide in-kind transfers and supplement this transfer with a small cash transfer. Other programs provide a mixture of food and cash transfers. Ethiopia's PSNP recognizes that recipients will sometimes benefit more from food than from cash. Therefore, the program has distributed both kinds of benefits, although it is attempting to transition mainly to cash. For more on the use of food versus cash transfers in an emergency setting, see box 3.3.

Other benefits that have accompanied CTs in the region include health care (Cape Verde's Minimum Social Pension), fee waivers (Malawi's Zomba CT and Botswana's Program for Destitute Persons), and psychosocial support (Botswana's Orphan Care Program and

Box 3.3

Cash versus Food Transfers

Potential Advantages of Cash Transfers

Whether a program should provide cash or food transfers must be carefully considered, as many factors play into the effectiveness of each type of transfer. From the perspective of delivery agencies, simplified logistics and storage are key advantages of cash transfers over food. Delivery of food aid is an extremely complex enterprise that involves donation or procurement of appropriate stocks (both nutritionally and culturally); contracting of transportation (in some cases, both internationally and locally); maintenance of temporary storage at each end; assurance of timely delivery; and finally, physical distribution of the stocks, in appropriate quantities, to the right beneficiaries. All these steps require ongoing monitoring to ensure quality, safety, and security throughout the entire chain of delivery. At the recipient's end, the beneficiary receives a good that may be lifesaving during extremely dire circumstances but, at some point in the crisis, may need to be traded at a discount to allow the beneficiary to buy something even more desperately needed.

Food transfers can also create distortions in local markets that undermine production incentives for local farmers, thereby initiating a cycle of increasing dependency on imports that have a dampening effect on economic growth. Cash, on the other hand, has the ability to stimulate local markets—a benefit that has both short- and long-term positive effects. The infusion of cash into local economies may have multiplier effects: it can help farmers reestablish local food production more quickly and efficiently by using some cash for productive inputs, and it can improve their prospects of finding buyers of their produce in local markets.

Where markets are operating efficiently, cash transfers are argued to be the superior choice. They leave almost all the logistic and security functions to competing private sector and state entities that specialize in those functions and give the beneficiary power to choose what and how much to buy and eat.

Despite the many positive aspects of cash transfers, major potential pitfalls can be associated with using cash. The most obvious problem with cash is that its value will erode in a high-inflation environment. Care should also be taken when distributing cash in environments with limited markets, because cash infusions may temporarily increase local prices until supply can adjust to keep up with new demand.

(continued next page)

Box 3.3 *(continued)*

Programs That Provide Both Cash and Food Transfers

Some programs are not dogmatic about their use of cash or food; they value what works best, including a mix of food and cash within the same program. Ethiopia's PSNP has taken such a flexible approach. The decision of when and where to provide food aid is based on the program's mix of available food and cash, the community's preferences, the local availability of food and markets, and the capacity of districts to distribute cash. In practice, limited district-level capacity to administer cash has often driven decisions of which locations should receive cash or food (World Bank 2010a).

The PSNP's flexibility has allowed it to address local needs as they evolve and to use a mixture of food and cash to help households manage spatially or seasonally based risk. Balancing food and cash transfers, as the PSNP has done, also requires officials to differentiate seasonal price changes from the price volatility that results from idiosyncratic shocks and market failures and to consider the effect of their decisions on local production systems (Sabates-Wheeler, Devereux, and Guenther 2009).

The cash transfers distributed in Ethiopia's PSNP lost significant purchasing power between 2006 and 2008, leading to an increasing proportion of beneficiaries who stated that they preferred food transfers to cash (Sabates-Wheeler and Devereux 2010) and increasing requests by districts for food transfers. To deal with this issue, the PSNP negotiated its resource mix and provided cash transfers for three months, followed by food transfers for three months, thereby allowing households to better deal with price fluctuations and food insecurity.

If it had the available resources to do so, the PSNP could have dealt with the price volatility and eroding purchasing power by increasing the size of CTs along with price increases and adjusting transfers for local prices (World Bank 2010a). This practice would not have been new to the continent: Malawi's Food and Cash Transfers and the Dowa Emergency Cash Transfers successfully experimented with indexing CTs to food prices to avoid this problem (Davey 2007; Mvula 2007). Other solutions could have included temporarily providing vouchers that were guaranteed to cover the cost of certain commodity bundles and increasing the duration of the cash transfers (Sabates-Wheeler and Devereux 2010).

Although some programs can transition between food and cash, that approach may present significant challenges if the existing system is not prepared to do so.

(continued next page)

> **Box 3.3** *(continued)*
>
> The transition from emergency food aid to regular CTs, in particular, can be a long-term endeavor that requires significant coordination to ensure that no gaps in coverage occur.
>
> Outside of the PSNP, other programs have found that many households in food crisis situations prefer a combination of cash and food transfers. Such a combination ensures that they can meet their nutritional requirements but gives them the flexibility of spending cash in the ways most profitable to them. In 2007 and 2008, the United Nations World Food Programme worked with World Vision to test the value of food and cash transfers during a drought in Lesotho. Analysis of the program showed that more beneficiaries preferred the combination of cash and food aid, followed by those who preferred strictly cash. The program evaluation found the effect of the CTs would have been greater still had the transfers been properly indexed to the price of food (Devereux and Mhlanga 2008).
>
> In Swaziland's Emergency Drought Response Program, 9 out of 10 respondents to a postprogram survey said that they preferred transfers of both food and cash to one modality only. Preference for food aid, the common transfer modality, decreased as a result of the program (Devereux and Jere 2008). Beneficiaries' favorable opinions of cash transfers suggest that CTs may become an important, but not always appropriate, solution for future emergency aid, provided that market conditions are appropriate.
>
> **Further Reading**
>
> This brief discussion is not intended to be exhaustive. For an overview of the issues involved in deciding whether to use food or cash transfers, see Barrett and Maxwell (2005) and Gentilini (2007).

Senegal's CCT for OVC). Before enrolling in Namibia's Old Age Pension and Disability Pension, beneficiaries must purchase a life insurance policy to cover funeral expenses. Most additional benefits provided by the programs are used to enhance the effect of the cash and to help beneficiaries graduate from the program and move into productive activities. The appropriateness of these benefits depends on the program's objectives, the beneficiaries served, and the opportunities for beneficiaries once outside the program. See figure 3.3 for a breakdown of types of program benefits distributed in the identified programs.

Figure 3.3 Programs That Provide Only Cash Versus Programs That Provide Additional Benefits

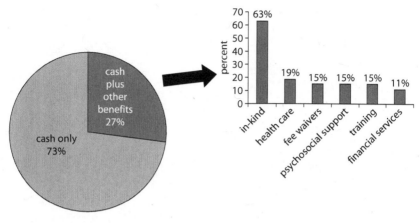

Source: Authors' representation.
Note: Graph on right adds to greater than 100 percent because some programs provide more than one type of benefit in addition to cash. Sample size is 101 for pie chart; number reflects programs with available data about specific benefits. Sample size is 26 for graph.

Transfer Size: A Delicate Issue

All else held constant, larger transfers reach fewer beneficiaries than smaller transfers. However, if transfer sizes are too small, programs will not have their intended effect and the ratio of administrative to benefit costs will be rather high. Factors to consider when determining transfer sizes include the minimal transfer size that will achieve the program's stated goals, the anticipated pool of eligible beneficiaries, and the program's budget (Grosh and others 2008). Other important considerations are whether the transfers will be adjusted to keep pace with inflation and how the population of eligible beneficiaries is expected to evolve.

Deciding on transfer levels is often an iterative process in which data projecting how to fulfill the program's goals meet head to head with the program's budget constraints (Grosh and others 2008). Difficult decisions must be made: Should benefit sizes be decreased? How would such a decrease affect expected outcomes? Should transfers be given to a smaller group of eligible recipients? If so, who is in this group, and how should such people be targeted? Final factors to consider are whether transfer size should vary by household size, composition, location, gender of the head, or other characteristics, and whether the scheme can be implemented given existing program capacity.

Therefore, decisions about transfer size should be based on empirical work that reflects an understanding of the potential beneficiary population and determines how to maximize transfer effectiveness and achieve program objectives while balancing financial and capacity constraints. Provided that transfer income is treated the same as other household income (that is, it is entirely fungible), ex ante simulations can help determine what transfer sizes are needed to meet program goals. Strong impact evaluations can inform how effective various transfer sizes are in meeting the program's specific goals.

Linking of Benefit Composition to Program Objectives: Transfers and Trade-offs

It is important that program benefits align with the program's specific objectives. For programs with objectives related to food security, including other benefits in addition to cash may be important to ensure that households can achieve this objective. Programs whose objectives include productivity-enhancing activities may include training components or means to increase access to financial services. Programs that seek to increase human capital investments may also relax constraints on households by providing health care free of charge or by giving certain fee waivers to households.

CT programs that aim to eliminate food insecurity in Sub-Saharan Africa have typically tried to set transfers at a level that allows eligible households to meet their nutritional needs. For instance, Kenya's HSNP selected its transfer level on the basis of the five-year average price of cereals (HSNP 2008), and the Zambian SCTs set transfers to allow households to purchase a 50-pound bag of maize monthly, presumably enough to allow a household of six to eat a second meal each day (Schüring 2010b). Although Ethiopia's PSNP originally considered varying transfer levels depending on the size of the household's food gap, capacity constraints led it to provide a uniform transfer (World Bank 2010a).

If the program's goal is to reduce poverty, an appropriate measure to determine transfer levels is the size of the poverty gap for eligible households. Malawi's SCT provides an average transfer value of MK 1,700 (US$13) per household monthly, which was deemed large enough to fill the extreme poverty gap in target households (Schubert and Huijbregts 2006).

In line with its objectives specific to the OVC crisis, Kenya's CT for OVC chose transfer levels that were believed to cover enough of the needs of OVC to help keep them in their households (World Bank 2009d).

A final way that programs have used transfer size to achieve their objectives is to break the transfers into different components. Nigeria's COPE CCT envisions providing monthly CTs, known as the *Basic Income Grant*, in addition to a lump-sum payment that is supposed to be used for major household investments. This component, known as the *Poverty Reduction Accelerator Investment*, sets aside approximately US$60 monthly for households into a savings account. It is to be given to the household annually only after households have received training to help them create a microenterprise (World Bank n.d.a).

Although larger transfers may result in stronger outcomes, there are also concerns that transfers not be so large as to cause unintended effects. Lesotho's Child Grants Programme (CGP) decided to provide a relatively small transfer in response to concerns that a larger transfer would encourage dependency in beneficiary households. The CGP also limited transfer size in light of concerns over the government's future capacity to finance the grants (PlusNews 2009). This decision reflects the importance of undertaking empirical work to understand how large the eligible population could become and how the expected program budget could cover this population. It also suggests that political economy issues may play a role in transfer size; in this case, smaller transfers were also more politically palatable.

The lack of data about beneficiary households in many programs makes it difficult to make standardized comparisons of transfer size across the identified programs. Ideally, data on the distribution of expenditure or consumption of beneficiary households or another relevant group could be compared to transfer sizes. Because this information is not available, relative transfer sizes are shown in figures 3.4, 3.5, and 3.6.

Figure 3.4 compares the average monthly transfer levels of programs that provide cash at the household level. The monthly value of the transfers shown ranges from US$8 through US$15. (This range assumes that the transfers are spread evenly over 12 months, which is not true in all cases.)

Many other identified CT programs awarded a flat transfer to households, but these CTs were typically one-time or short-term transfers. The one-time transfers tended to be larger than the transfers shown in figure 3.4, with values ranging from approximately US$40, in the case of the Burundi UNHCR (Office of the United Nations High Commissioner for Refugees) Cash Grants, to several hundred dollars, in the case of cash grants to ex-combatants in Liberia and Côte d'Ivoire.

Other transfers are given at the individual level (see figure 3.5). These transfers are often social pensions, although some CCTs directed to adolescents or young adults are also included in this category, as in the

Figure 3.4 Monthly Average Size of Cash Transfers Given at the Household Level

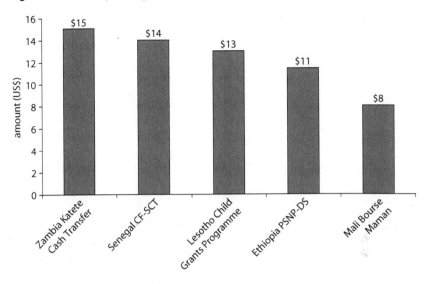

Source: Authors' representation.
Note: Transfer size was calculated using the average exchange rate during the time of program implementation.

Figure 3.5 Monthly Average Size of Cash Transfers Given at the Beneficiary Level

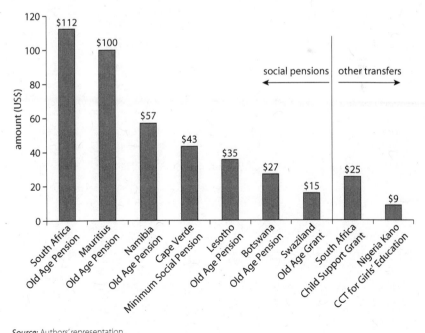

Source: Authors' representation.
Note: Transfer size was calculated using the average exchange rate during the time of program implementation.

Figure 3.6 Monthly Average Size of Cash Transfers, Variable Transfers

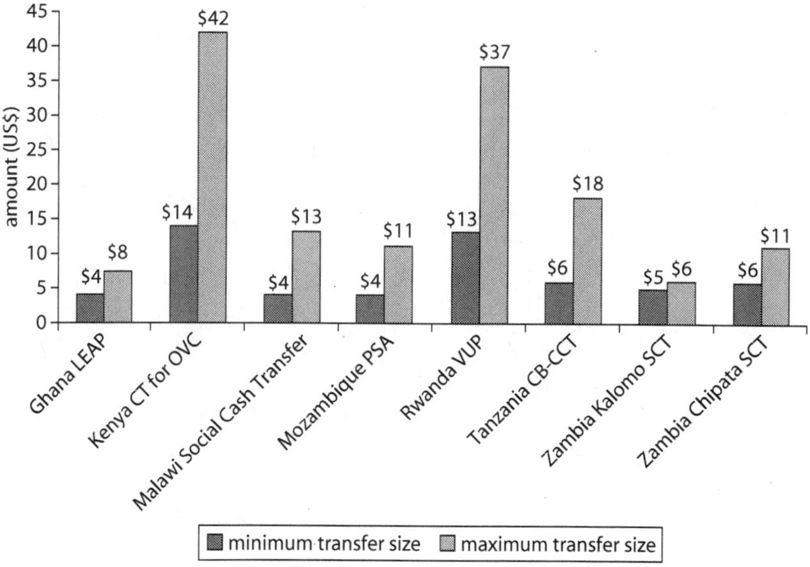

Program	minimum transfer size	maximum transfer size
Ghana LEAP	$4	$8
Kenya CT for OVC	$14	$42
Malawi Social Cash Transfer	$4	$13
Mozambique PSA	$4	$11
Rwanda VUP	$13	$37
Tanzania CB-CCT	$6	$18
Zambia Kalomo SCT	$5	$6
Zambia Chipata SCT	$6	$11

Source: Authors' representation.
Note: Transfer size was calculated using the average exchange rate during the time of program implementation.

case of Nigeria's Kano CCT for Girls' Education. These transfer values vary substantially. The wealthiest countries provide the largest transfers through their social pensions, which are US$100 monthly or more in some cases. The size differences in part reflect cost-of-living differences between the less wealthy and wealthier countries.

Still other programs award cash transfers on a graduated system. This design provides households with a base transfer that is supplemented according to the number of household members. The marginal increase in transfers often decreases from the first to the second and subsequent household members, usually with a cap on the total possible transfer size. Many of the CT programs reviewed, outside of social pensions, used this strategy to link household size to transfer values. The range of minimum and maximum monthly transfers for several programs that use this graduated system is found in figure 3.6. As the figure shows, the range of transfers varies greatly among different programs; for some transfers, the maximum amount is less than double the minimum transfer, whereas for many others, it is approximately three times the minimum transfer value.

Ad hoc descriptions of transfer size. Additional information on the value of CTs is also available. For instance, the following comparisons have been made in terms of households' consumption or expenditures:

- Kenya's CT for OVC equals approximately 20 percent of poor Kenyan households' expenditures (World Bank 2009d).
- Kenya's HSNP is between 30 percent and 40 percent of beneficiary households' food expenditures (HSNP n.d.).
- Ghana's LEAP (Livelihood Empowerment Against Poverty) transfers are equal to 20 percent of the bottom quintile's average household consumption (World Bank 2010c).
- Malawi's Zomba cash transfer was set to equal approximately 15 percent of eligible households' total monthly consumption (Baird and others 2010).

In size, those transfers are comparable to transfers in other CT programs around the world.

In terms of wages or income, information on transfer size includes the following:

- Mauritius's Old Age Pension was worth approximately 20 percent of the average wage in the country in 2008 (Central Statistics Office 2007).
- Mozambique's PSA equaled between 4 percent and 6 percent of the country's minimum wage in 2007 (Ellis 2007).
- South Africa's Old Age Pension and Disability Grant each equal 1.75 times median income. South Africa's Foster Care Grant is 1.15 times median per capita income, and the Child Support Grant is 0.4 times the value of the median per capita income (Woolard and Leibbrandt 2010).

These statistics can obscure the transfers' relative value to beneficiaries. Despite the apparent low value of Mozambique's PSA, a 2008 evaluation determined that the average benefit received by beneficiary households equaled 21.8 percent of the households' current consumption levels, a number comparable to those found in similar programs. However, the transfers were still low in comparison with the minimum value of the monthly food basket outlined by the government of Mozambique (Soares, Hirata, and Rivas n.d.).

In terms of gross domestic product (GDP) per capita, the following was found:

- Transfers in Burkina Faso's Pilot CCT-CT do not surpass 7.5 percent of GDP per capita in one household with one child in the oldest group (de Walque 2009).
- Nigeria's Kano CCT for Girls' Education was set to equal approximately 20 percent of GDP per capita in 2007 (Ayala 2009).

Several programs outline transfer size in relation to poverty or food poverty, which is appropriate if the program has food security or related goals, as follows:

- Ethiopia's PSNP-DS household transfer equals approximately 10 percent of the basket represented by the 2007/08 national poverty line (World Bank 2010a).
- Senegal's CF-SCT transfer equals about 14 percent of the average food basket value in households with four adults (World Bank 2009a).
- Tanzania's CB-CCT provides benefits that equal half of the food poverty line for each child and benefits that equal the food poverty line for the elderly (Evans 2008).
- Lesotho's Old Age Pension was originally set to cover the cost of meeting 75 percent of the minimal caloric needs of a household of five (Croome, Nyanguru, and Molisana 2007).
- Zambia's Kalomo SCT base transfer of approximately US$10 per household was considered insufficient to cover the poverty gap but enough to pull people from extreme poverty (Ministry of Community Development and Social Services and German Agency for Technical Cooperation 2007).

Once again, these descriptions may obscure the real potential effects of the transfer. For instance, Ethiopia's PSNP-DS transfers covered more than 10 percent of needs for many households. Recent evidence in PSNP communities suggests transfers cover about 40 percent of annual food needs (World Bank 2010a).

Some programs indexed transfer size to inflation, such as Malawi's Food and Cash Transfers (FACT) and Dowa Emergency Cash Transfers (DECT) programs, and others, such as Kenya's HSNP, have planned to do so. Budget constraints are a major factor keeping other programs from doing so. In the presence of price volatility or high inflation, not indexing transfers to a basket of prices—particularly local food staple prices—can undermine the program's effects (see box 3.3).

Knowledge gaps related to transfer sizes. These ad hoc comparisons provide limited information about relative transfer sizes across Sub-Saharan Africa's CT programs. Clearly, having additional information about transfer sizes that is comparable across programs would be useful, perhaps through multicountry studies using household data. Information about transfer size in relation to eligible households' pretransfer consumption or expenditure would be helpful when examining the relationship between transfer sizes and key outcomes.

In CCTs and UCTs alike, the influence of a transfer of a particular size on beneficiary behavior will depend on the elasticity of a given outcome, such as investments in education or health, with respect to the transfer size. Although some limited analysis on such issues has been completed in programs in other regions, only a few studies have examined these elasticities of demand within Sub-Saharan Africa. Results from CTs in Sub-Saharan Africa will provide useful information regarding these questions in the near future.

Finally, the size and structure of transfers may have the potential to alter household composition, particularly given the fluid nature of household membership in many Sub-Saharan African countries. Evaluations should be designed in such a way as to determine the potential effect of the transfers on practices related to household composition, such as child fostering. The effect of transfers on household composition needs to be understood because it may, in turn, affect intrahousehold bargaining, household investments, the welfare of specific household members, and outcomes for those members.

Cash Payment Systems

Cash payment systems must take into account methods of distributing cash, transfer mechanisms, frequency of cash transfers, and recipients of transfers.

Distribution of Cash
In terms of the technology used to deliver cash, payment mechanisms in Sub-Saharan Africa range from the basic to the relatively sophisticated. Some beneficiary groups receive payments at a designated time, whereas others may receive payments whenever they choose to retrieve them.

Paypoint distribution, used in Ethiopia, Malawi, Mozambique, and Zambia, among others, requires beneficiaries to arrive at a designated place to retrieve their transfers within a short time frame (for example, on a certain day). Those paypoints often vary their location to increase security. The location and day of the distribution are usually announced only shortly before the transfer day.

Other simple payment methods include the following: retrieval of transfers at local offices by beneficiaries who have had program booklets filled out by CT personnel (Eritrea's RBF); delivery through the post office or post bank systems (Ghana's LEAP, Kenya's CT for OVC, and Lesotho's Old Age Pension); distribution by community committees (Burkina Faso's Pilot CCT-CT and Tanzania's CB-CCT); and payment by a community leader such as a teacher or health worker, who must travel to a nearby urban area to retrieve the money before distributing it to beneficiary households (Zambia's multiple SCTs).

Other programs, such as those in South Africa, use more sophisticated methods, such as direct deposit into beneficiaries' bank accounts. Point-of-service machines have also been used to distribute cash to beneficiaries in Sub-Saharan Africa. The point-of-service devices rely on both smart cards and fingerprint verification to identify beneficiaries. They are portable and work offline but must be taken to connect into a mobile network to update financial records. This method is being used in Kenya's HSNP, which provides transfers to nomadic households in areas where bank branches are unavailable. Similar operations are used in parts of South Africa and Namibia.

Many payment arrangements require coordination and support from personnel involved with distribution. For example, the point-of-service agents for Kenya's HSNP are selected by Equity Bank; they must be local shopkeepers with a trusted record and enough liquidity to finance transfers for approximately 100 individuals each month. When intermediary agents pay cash to beneficiaries, a bank account for the point-of-service agent is automatically paid the amount of the transfer plus a fee. The agent must then retrieve any cash from an Equity Bank branch. The point-of-service machines are also able to function as miniature automated teller machines (ATMs) for beneficiaries and others. No fee is charged to beneficiaries for their first four cash withdrawals per month (HSNP n.d.).

Other innovative transfer mechanisms have been used successfully in Sub-Saharan Africa, particularly in remote areas that are difficult to reach with large sums of cash. The Democratic Republic of Congo's Emergency

Cash Grant program distributed cash monthly for one year to ex-combatants through mobile phones. In 2007, an emergency CT program used to respond to postelection violence in Kenya transferred cash through mobile phones using unique SIM (Subscriber Identity Module) cards (that is, portable memory chips). Groups of 10 beneficiaries shared a mobile phone and received support from a literate cluster leader (del Ninno 2009).

As shown in figure 3.7, the majority of CT programs in Sub-Saharan Africa allow beneficiaries to retrieve benefits through a local office, such as a post bank or commercial bank. Slightly over one-third of programs require beneficiaries to travel to designated paypoints to obtain their cash. Just over 1 in 10 programs use direct deposit to bank accounts or mobile ATMs, and slightly fewer than 10 percent of programs provide cash through community-level distribution to beneficiaries or mobile phone payments. Many programs use a combination of payment mechanisms, relying on the methods that function best in a given location.

Appropriate Transfer Mechanisms

In choosing transfer mechanisms, programs should keep burdens on beneficiaries and others in mind: the transfer mechanism chosen should be

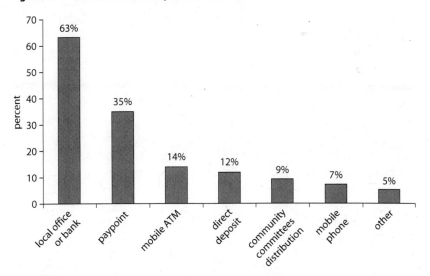

Figure 3.7 Cash Distribution Systems in African CTs

Source: Authors' representation.
Note: Sample size is 57. Data are limited to those programs whose specific distribution mechanism could be determined. Total is greater than 100 percent because some programs have multiple distribution systems.

appropriate to beneficiaries' circumstances. If retrieving transfers is too costly or difficult for beneficiaries, they may opt not to take them. For instance, the Swazi government distributes CTs through bank checks, which is the most convenient approach for the responsible department. Unfortunately, this mechanism places a heavy burden on elderly and destitute beneficiaries, who must collect and cash their checks. In some instances, beneficiaries are unfamiliar with checks, and they often have to travel to offices located far from their homes to collect and cash the transfers (RHVP 2007).

Distribution decisions may affect beneficiaries differently. An evaluation of Ethiopia's PSNP found substantial variability in beneficiaries' ease of access to payments. In some localities, beneficiaries were paid close to their homes, whereas up to one in three beneficiary households were forced to sleep away from home when retrieving transfers (Gilligan and others 2009b).

Namibia and South Africa use several transfer mechanisms to ensure that accessible methods are available to all households. Namibia's Old Age Pension makes payments through bank deposits, post offices, or mobile banking units that use smart cards. Two-thirds of beneficiaries receive their payments through mobile banks and smart cards (ELCRN 2007; Levine, van der Berg, and Yu 2009). This type of setup may be the most effective solution for maintaining high coverage in remote areas.

Programs that rely on community members to retrieve and distribute CTs may ultimately place significant costs on those community members, especially in terms of time expenditure. In Zambia, for example, teachers often close school for a day or more each month to retrieve transfers.[3] Kenya's CT for OVC has relied on district children officers to deliver transfers to households in some districts; the feasibility of this arrangement has decreased as coverage per district has increased.

Because many potential beneficiaries of CTs in Sub-Saharan Africa do not have banks, distributing cash into bank accounts may not always be feasible. However, Swaziland's Emergency Drought Response program tested the use of direct deposit transfers for previously unbanked individuals and found it to be fairly successful. Households in the program received training on financial basics to help them understand the purpose of banking and how to use their bank accounts. Save the Children contracted with the Standard Bank of Swaziland to distribute transfers into bank accounts for beneficiaries, and Standard Bank worked with Swazi Post to deliver transfers. Recipients were able to withdraw funds from the post office using point-of-sale machines or an ATM card.

They were free to withdraw funds whenever they chose (Devereux and Jere 2008).

Almost 6,100 beneficiaries,[4] most of them female, opened bank accounts as a result of the program. The program evaluation found that beneficiaries adopted the bank account and concomitant technology with few problems (Beswick 2008; Devereux and Jere 2008). That experience suggests that using the formal banking system to deliver transfers should not be ruled out simply because the beneficiary population is unbanked. However, programs that want to distribute cash through the financial system to the unbanked should plan to spend resources to educate beneficiaries and bring them into the formal system.

These examples illustrate that transfer mechanisms should be considered in light of the burdens that they place on both program administrators and beneficiaries. The examples also highlight that technology, if harnessed correctly and marketed appropriately, can be used to improve program execution and perhaps even draw the unbanked into formal financial systems. For more on the potential (and hazards) of using technology to improve CTs in Sub-Saharan Africa, see box 3.4.

Frequency of Cash Transfers

The majority of the identified cash transfers are given on a monthly or bimonthly basis. Transfers are awarded quarterly and annually in less than

---

Box 3.4

Experimentation in New Technologies for CTs in Africa

Cutting-edge information and communication technologies were for many years viewed as too advanced to be used in developing countries. In some of those countries, however, new systems that are being developed are skipping generations of obsolescent technologies, and more advanced technologies are being introduced than those used in some wealthier countries, which often use outdated legacy systems in which they have large investments.

Advanced technologies have the potential to improve efficiencies in CT programs, especially in the areas of registration, transfer payment, and program monitoring. However, program policy makers and planners must be careful not to be dazzled by high-tech approaches. Drawbacks of each type of technology

(continued next page)

Box 3.4 *(continued)*

must be carefully assessed. Building on existing infrastructures of established systems with national coverage, such as postal banks, should still be considered.

Biometric Systems and Smart Cards

Biometric systems and smart cards hold promise for Sub-Saharan African CT programs. Biometric systems using fingerprinting can improve registration and identification of beneficiaries in some Sub-Saharan African CT programs. They also add security and checks against fraud in registration and payment processes.

Technology is also being tested to improve distribution of payments in remote, hard-to-access environments or in situations where the beneficiaries' location may change over time. This flexibility is important for a program such as Kenya's Hunger Safety Net Programme, where nomadic beneficiaries use smart cards and biometric identification to retrieve benefits from locations of their choice (HSNP n.d.).

Mobile Phones

Mobile phone technology has multiple uses in CT programs. The fast-expanding coverage of cell phone systems throughout much of the African continent may allow mobile phone technology to be used in CT programs. Nigeria's Kano CCT for Girls' Education will test how mobile phones can be used in a limited-capacity environment to distribute transfers and send messages to beneficiaries (Gerelle 2009). Field workers also use mobile phones to request a class register and record girls' school attendance for monitoring purposes. When mobile networks are unavailable, data are stored on the phone until reception is available and the information can be transmitted (Mobenzi Researcher 2011a).

Mobile phones may also be used to conduct research. For instance, mobile researcher technology allows smart phones to be used to conduct household surveys. The technology is able to walk enumerators through complex skip and repeat patterns one question at a time, immediately noting data inconsistencies and reducing data entry errors. Collected data can be sent in real time to a central information system, and communication between central offices and enumerators allows problems to be addressed as they occur. No data entry personnel are needed, and survey data can be exported and analyzed immediately. The controls in the system improve data integrity, because there is a clear record of who has dealt with and altered data. Phones can be used to take pictures of survey respondents and record GPS (global positioning system) locations

(continued next page)

Box 3.4 *(continued)*

of households to discourage ghost respondents. This technology allows for a 40 percent reduction in required supervision staff members. Costs of the technology include the phones (less than US$200), data transfer costs, and training and payment of enumerators and supervisors (Mobenzi Researcher 2011b). Mobile researcher technology has already been used in multiple countries in Sub-Saharan Africa.

Web-Based Management Information Systems
Web-based management information systems also may prove useful. This technology lets officials access a single system from decentralized locations, thus allowing for more up-to-date recordkeeping and facilitating communication and the transmission of data among program offices. In this way, central offices can stay better apprised of field-level implementation.

The Need for Appropriate Infrastructure, Training, and Communication
Key issues affecting the willingness to adopt new technologies are ease of use and comfort with the modality. Adoption of new technologies depends on well-designed training that addresses all obstacles to proper use by the specific beneficiary group. When users refuse to adopt, a wise approach is to look into what those who introduced the technology did (or failed to do) in communicating it.

Program officials using sophisticated technology need to have reliable access to technical assistance and support for problem solving when inevitable glitches and problems arise. Access to support is especially important when officials have little experience with the technology and are working in a low-capacity environment. The need for support was noted for Ethiopia's PSNP (World Bank 2010a). Without the necessary technical assistance, technology can become more of a hindrance than an enabling force.

In considering innovative approaches, program managers must also keep in mind that a technology that is appropriate in some settings may prove inappropriate in others. A small CT in Malawi known as Dowa Emergency Cash Transfers encountered many difficulties while trying to use a distribution mechanism very similar to the one being used in Kenya's HSNP. The difficulties stemmed from poor coverage of the appropriate cell phone network (Global System for Mobile Communications, or GSM) and from the lack of compatible sites to retrieve cash. Rather than improving accessibility, the technology actually made it harder for beneficiaries to retrieve transfers (Langhan, Mackay, and Kilfoil 2008).

10 percent of reviewed programs. Other programs, such as Mali's Bourse Maman, provide regular transfers through only a portion of the year (in Bourse Maman's case, the school year). Still others, such as Eritrea's RBF, award transfers only after households have fulfilled certain requirements. (RBF transfers are given to women after they complete a certain number of medical checkups.) Figure 3.8 shows how often the reviewed CTs are distributed.

Several factors must be weighed when deciding the frequency of transfer distribution, including the cost and timing of distribution and the ability of households to incorporate transfers of a given frequency into their income stream. In particular, when a program intends to help rural agricultural households, CTs should be distributed at appropriate times in the production cycle (Sabates-Wheeler, Devereux, and Guenther 2009). For instance, cash should not arrive at a time when labor demands on household members discourage them from retrieving transfers, and it should arrive in time, or frequently enough, to allow households to use transfers to purchase time-sensitive agricultural inputs.

Just as appropriately timing the transfer schedule is important, transfers must be distributed as planned. Some Sub-Saharan African programs

Figure 3.8 Transfer Frequency

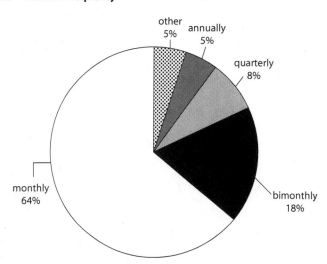

Source: Authors' representation.
Note: Sample size is 61. Data are limited to programs that provide more than one transfer and for which specific information on frequency of transfers was available. Some programs give benefits monthly, but the benefits are not given for the entire year (for example, they are given during the school year only). In that case, they are classified as monthly, because they are given every month during the time when transfers are distributed.

mentioned that transfer delivery was unreliable. This unreliability can undercut the stability that households need to incorporate the additional cash as a regular part of their income. An evaluation of Ethiopia's PSNP found that program impacts were significantly dampened in households that received either low or irregular transfers (Gilligan and others 2009a). Although timeliness of distributions has gradually improved, only a little over one-quarter of PSNP households said that they were able to plan for their transfers. Improving this indicator has been a key goal of the program. It has required significant capacity building, monitoring, and continuous adjustments and improvements to help improve on-time transfer delivery (World Bank 2010a).

Transfer Recipients

Many CT programs (and especially CCT programs) throughout the world have provided benefits primarily to female beneficiaries; however, the reviewed CT programs in Sub-Saharan Africa showed less preference for distributing cash exclusively to women. Almost half of CCT programs and 9 in 10 UCTs distributed cash to either male or female beneficiaries (see figure 3.9). Some of this distinction is due to the individual nature of many transfer programs, such as social pensions, in the region. Other transfers do not specifically direct cash to women, although in practice,

Figure 3.9 Cash Transfer Distribution by Gender

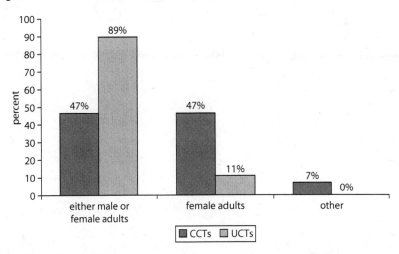

Source: Authors' representation.
Note: Figure shows the intended beneficiary (payee) of cash transfers. Sample size is 15 for CCTs and 38 for UCTs. Results are limited to those programs that clearly explain which household member should receive cash.

women are the primary recipient in most households. Despite this inclination, slightly over 20 percent of all programs indicated that transfers should be given to women whenever possible. This tendency is markedly greater in CCTs than in UCTs.

Burkina Faso's Pilot CCT-CT is studying which household member should be the transfer recipient. Some transfers in the experimental evaluation are being given to male adults, and others are being given to female adults in the household. The results of the evaluation will inform this feature in other CTs in Sub-Saharan Africa. Programs in Morocco and the Republic of Yemen, not covered in this review, are also testing how program outcomes change depending on whether mothers or fathers receive transfers. Results from these programs may be especially helpful in African countries that share relatively similar cultures.

More recently, CT programs have begun distributing some benefits to adolescent beneficiaries, a practice that has been used in education-focused CCT programs in Bangladesh and Colombia (Fiszbein and Schady 2009), among others. This program feature is being tested experimentally in Malawi's Zomba CT to assess any variations in impact based on the proportion of transfers given to parent versus adolescent beneficiaries. After two years of program implementation, evaluation results showed that increasing the share of the transfer given to adolescent girls did not affect the schooling, marriage, or fertility outcomes examined (Baird, McIntosh, and Özler 2010).

Areas for Further Analysis in Cash Payment Systems

Sub-Saharan African countries are currently investigating several issues important to the design of CTs, including differences in outcome based on which household member receives the cash. An important factor to keep in mind is that the intrahousehold dynamics in Sub-Saharan Africa are different from those in other regions. The dynamics may vary greatly even within countries, so decisions about the transfer recipient need careful attention and evaluation. Both quantitative and qualitative methods should be used to gather information about what arrangements are most conducive to the desired program outcomes. Care should be taken to understand how receipt of the CT, especially by women, affects intrahousehold relationships. Transferring cash to women rather than to men may improve household welfare and give women greater household bargaining power. Conversely, it could also be counteracted in the household. These questions are currently being tested within Sub-Saharan Africa, and additional analysis in this area will be helpful.

Many programs in Sub-Saharan Africa are also experimenting with novel means of delivering cash to beneficiaries, and these experiences will be helpful to others seeking to implement programs, particularly in remote rural settings. Although the optimal frequency of cash distribution merits further analysis, much of this decision rests on pragmatic questions of human resource availability and program capacity to process payments and deliver cash. Therefore, case studies and other information related to improving on-time delivery of transfers may be more useful.

Conditional versus Unconditional Cash Transfers

Conditions have the potential to enhance transfer-related outcomes, but context matters. The decision to condition transfers depends on multiple factors, and conditions may or may not be cost-effective in various countries in Sub-Saharan Africa. Even if conditions are important for program impacts in countries outside the region, this result may not translate similarly to Sub-Saharan Africa. For example, returns to certain education levels may be lower in certain Sub-Saharan African countries than they are in other parts of the world, which could affect how beneficiaries use CTs with and without education-related conditions attached. The true value of applying conditions in CTs within the region needs to be, and currently is being, tested. If the benefit of enforcing conditions outweighs the costs, a more appropriate approach for most programs is to focus on conditional CTs, unless they have another reason for not imposing conditions.

Most studies have been inconclusive on the exact effect of conditions. Fiszbein and Schady (2009) have summarized existing evidence, which includes economic theory, simulations, and empirical analysis from natural experiments, on the effect of conditions in CCTs. They suggest that conditions may increase positive impacts on children's education and health. Until the recent evaluation of Malawi's Zomba CT was completed, evidence on conditions was not based on any experimental evaluations.

Malawi's Zomba CT provided transfers conditional on school enrollment to some female adolescent beneficiaries and unconditional transfers to others. The CCT has proved to be more effective than the UCT in improving schooling outcomes, including enrollment, attendance, and test scores (see figure 3.10). At first glance, the UCT, but not the CCT, appears to decrease the probability of teenage pregnancy and early marriage. However, those results are more nuanced than they first appear, and

Figure 3.10 Results of CTs versus UCTs in Malawi

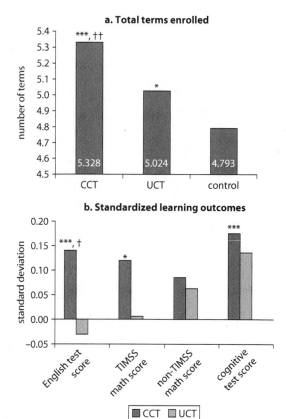

Source: Baird, McIntosh, and Özler 2010, table III (panel a) and table XI (panel b).
Notes: Sample size is 852 for panel a and 2,057 for panel b. Dependent variable equals total number of school terms enrolled in during the program out of six possible terms for panel a. In panel b, test scores are standardized with a mean equal to zero and standard deviation of one in the control group. Math and English tests were created on the basis of Malawi school curriculum. The TIMSS score is based on five questions from the 2007 TIMSS. Both panels show results from ordinary least squares regressions using baseline values of age dummies, strata dummies, a household asset index, highest grade attended, a dummy for ever had sex, and a dummy for whether respondent participated in development of tests in pilot (learning outcomes regressions only). Results for both panels are based on regressions run with robust standard errors clustered at the local (enumeration area) level and are weighted so that results are representative of the target population in the enumeration areas. * indicates the result is statistically different from that of the control group at the 90 percent level; ** indicates the result is statistically different from that of the control group at the 95 percent level; *** indicates the result is statistically different from that of the control group at the 99 percent level; † indicates that the CCT result is significantly different from the UCT result at the 90 percent level; †† indicates that the CCT result is significantly different from the UCT result at the 95 percent level.

they highlight some of the trade-offs between providing CCTs and UCTs. An additional question raised by the experiment is whether such results could be replicated outside of the experimental setting. See box 3.8, later in this chapter, for an explanation of program results.

Prevalence of Conditional Programs

Conditions are applied in a number of Sub-Saharan African countries, including, but not limited to, Burkina Faso, Ghana, Kenya, Malawi, Nigeria, and Tanzania. In many cases, programs take a significant amount of time to build sufficient capacity to regularly enforce program conditions. Enforcing conditions has often depended on the capacity and buy-in of relevant line ministries to work with program units to monitor fulfillment of conditions.

The majority of CTs started in Sub-Saharan Africa since 2000 have been unconditional (see figure 3.11). However, the percentage of CCTs is not insignificant: one in four CTs were conditional. Newer programs are more likely to be conditional than programs that were established earlier. Of the identified programs established in 2007 or later, 40 percent were designed as CCTs. If the experience of the past several years reflects an ongoing trend, the relative representation of CCTs in the region is expected to continue to grow.

In terms of the general typology described in chapter 2, the region's wealthier countries rely on UCTs (see figure 3.12). This tendency partially

Figure 3.11 Changes in Relative Numbers of CT Programs: UCTs versus CCTs

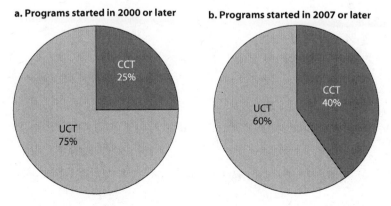

Source: Authors' representation.
Note: Data are current as of June 2009. Panel a has a sample size of 72; panel b has a sample size of 30. Samples are limited to programs that began in 2000 or later and that provided enough information to be confidently classified.

Figure 3.12 Use of UCTs versus CCTs by Country Income Status

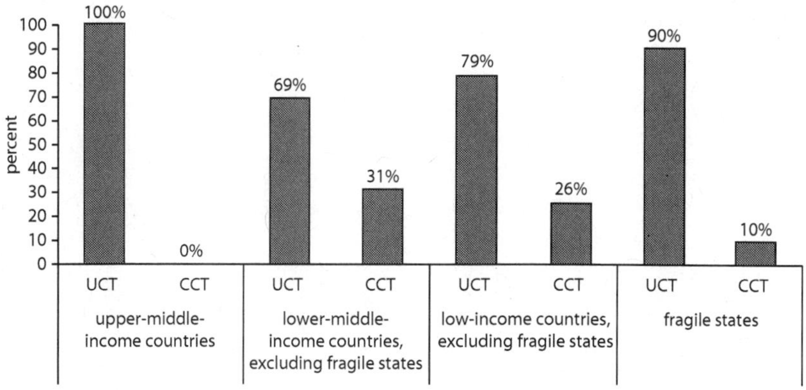

	UCT	CCT
upper-middle-income countries	100%	0%
lower-middle-income countries, excluding fragile states	69%	31%
low-income countries, excluding fragile states	79%	26%
fragile states	90%	10%

Source: Authors' representation.
Note: Sample size is 25 for upper-middle-income countries, 13 for lower-middle-income countries, 43 for low-income countries, and 20 for fragile states. Total for low-income countries adds to greater than 100 because two programs are both UCTs and CCTs.

reflects the belief held in some wealthier countries that rights-based social assistance is not compatible with CCTs. The lower-middle-income countries have the highest relative representation of CCTs (approximately one in three programs), while just over one in four programs in low-income countries are CCTs. The greater representation of CCTs in lower-middle-income countries than in low-income countries probably reflects some of the greater capacity constraints involved with enforcing conditions in the poorest countries. Fragile states have primarily implemented UCTs, as would be expected given their weak institutions and frequent emergency-focused CTs.

Although an increasing proportion of programs in the region are designed as CCTs, this shift does not necessarily indicate that all programs will head in this direction. Some relatively new programs have purposefully decided that conditioning transfers is not currently the best option. For example, Senegal's CF-SCT was designed without any conditions attached for several reasons. An unconditional transfer was justified, given that the program was dealing with an acute crisis caused by rising food prices. The program's designers assumed that if targeting correctly identified vulnerable households, the transfer would be used appropriately and conditions would be unnecessary. A strong communications strategy supporting maternal and children's nutrition was also expected to help beneficiaries make appropriate investments in nutrition and health without the need for conditions. That being said, the program's designers remained open to the idea of imposing soft conditions, and they planned to examine this possibility (World Bank 2009a). (Soft conditions require that beneficiary households agree verbally or in writing that they will abide by listed conditions; however, no penalty is charged if they do not comply.) Ethiopia's PSNP-DS, though unconditional, has also left itself open to conditioning future transfers on attendance at literacy classes or participation in relatively undemanding labor activities (World Bank 2010a).

Variation in Approach to Conditionality throughout Sub-Saharan Africa

Conditions that have commonly been used in Sub-Saharan Africa are similar to those in CCTs around the world. The most common conditions are education- and health-related requirements for children (see figure 3.13). Additional common conditions require household adults to attend educational or training sessions and pregnant women to fulfill health-related requirements.

Figure 3.13 Conditions Used in Sub-Saharan Africa's CCT Programs

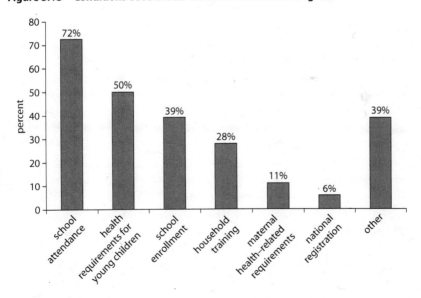

Source: Authors' representation.
Note: Sample size is 18. Total adds to greater than 100 percent because most programs have multiple conditions. "Other" includes elderly members' medical checkups, successful school progression, avoidance of child labor, and formation of community committees to improve local sanitation. CCTs were excluded if specific data on conditions did not provide enough information for classification.

Several CCT programs in Sub-Saharan Africa have adapted programmatic variations that reflect the constraints present in many low-capacity settings, as well as concerns that conditions are too heavy a burden to place on many beneficiaries. These programs try to strike a compromise between conditional and unconditional transfers by imposing soft conditions, with no penalty charged if beneficiaries do not comply with the requirements. In the reviewed CTs, it was not always clear whether beneficiaries believed they would be penalized for noncompliance with soft conditions.

Some programs use both soft and hard conditions. Such a mixture of conditions is used in Nigeria's Kano CCT for Girls' Education. If the hard condition of 80 percent school attendance is not met, benefits are forfeited. Soft conditions are as follows: girls are expected to pass their classes and obtain birth certificates, siblings under age five must receive immunizations and attend medical checkups, mothers must attend pre- and postnatal classes, and mothers and partners must attend awareness-raising seminars (Gerelle 2009). The program's experimental evaluation will shed light on the extent to which both types of conditions help to achieve the program's goals.

Other Sub-Saharan African programs approach conditions from a similarly less punitive perspective. Rather than setting transfer levels and conditions and then deducting from transfer levels for noncompliance, they set a base transfer level that is given regardless of the household's behavior. If the household chooses to engage in conditioned activities, it then receives a bonus payment. This design is used in Zambia's Chipata district, where a bonus is supposed to be awarded to those who fulfill nonrequired criteria (Ministry of Community Development and Social Services and German Agency for Technical Cooperation 2007). Using bonuses rather than conditions is thought to help create a positive attitude toward the conditioned behavior and increase the likelihood that the behavior will continue over the long term. The difference between this design and that of a traditional CCT appears to be mainly semantic and ideological.

Conditions have been flexibly applied in practice. In reality, the line between unconditional transfers, transfers with soft conditions, and transfers with hard conditions is often blurred. For example, Kenya's CT for OVC has conditions outlined but recognizes that requiring households to fulfill conditions is not always feasible. In those cases, the CT is supposed to operate as a UCT. A similar plan is in place for Tanzania's CB-CCT;

conditions will not be enforced when education and health centers are far from program communities. Nigeria's Kano CCT for Girls' Education focuses on girls' completion of primary school or transition to junior secondary school, and conditions depend on the local availability of the schools (Bouchet 2009). Eligible schools also must be receiving support under the national and state education plans (Ayala 2009). The programs just mentioned conduct supply-side capacity inventories to understand where to apply conditions.

Even in areas with an adequate supply of schools and health clinics, conditions are sometimes only gradually enforced. Monitoring of conditions in Kenya's CT for OVC has been incrementally phased in over time. Only education conditions were being enforced by mid-2009. Even though some conditions are still not enforced, households are encouraged, through community awareness campaigns, to invest in their children's education and health care whenever possible.

Penalties for noncompliance and frequency of monitoring reflect concerns for beneficiaries' well-being. Although programs in Sub-Saharan Africa share human capital objectives with other programs around the world, it is crucial that the cost to households of complying with conditions is carefully considered before a decision regarding conditioning is made. In a study of a Zambian SCT, Schüring (2010b) found that the poorest households reported that they would be most likely to forgo receiving a conditional transfer, presumably because of the burdens the conditions would place on the household. This result is a common concern about conditional programs, and it must be examined.

Concerns about the demands that conditions place on beneficiaries are addressed in Tanzania's CB-CCT, which exempts children who are household heads and the chronically ill from fulfilling conditions. In addition, households receive transfers for one year before they can be financially penalized for not complying with conditions. In all households, failure to comply with conditions initially results in a warning and a visit to the household to determine if there is a valid reason for noncompliance. Further noncompliance results in another warning and a payment reduction for each noncomplying household member (equivalent to 25 percent of elderly persons' payments and 50 percent of children's payments). Continuing noncompliance eventually results in suspension from the program, although beneficiaries may return later. This flexibility, combined with the fact that some payments are automatically paid without penalty because of the timing of monitoring, helps to ensure that households are not inappropriately excluded from the program (Ayala Consulting 2008).

Other CCTs in the region still provide transfers, albeit reduced, to households that do not comply with conditions. In Kenya's CT for OVC, a household will forfeit K Sh 400 (US$5.60) of their total transfer for every child or adult not complying with conditions. When households fulfill conditions, they receive transfers of K Sh 1,000 (US$14) for households with one or two OVC, K Sh 2,000 (US$28) for households with three to four OVC, and K Sh 3,000 (US$42) for households with five or more OVC (World Bank 2009d). This reduction for noncompliance with conditions theoretically allows households to receive at least K Sh 200 (US$2.80) in households with seven or fewer noncomplying members.

Frequency of monitoring is another issue that should be considered in Sub-Saharan Africa's conditional programs, keeping in mind both the demands every round of verification will place on the program and the constraints beneficiary households face in fulfilling conditions. For instance, Zambia's Monze SCT was expected to verify compliance with education conditions only once per school term, rather than monthly. This plan was put in place to allow rural agricultural households to use household labor during key parts of the agricultural season without failing to meet the 80 percent school attendance requirement (Schüring 2010b).[5]

In some countries, communities support conditions. In some cases, Africans support conditioning transfers. Communities benefiting from the pilot of Kenya's CT for OVC requested that transfers be conditioned. In general, the argument that conditions are politically appealing is based on the idea that conditions satisfy the tax base that their money is being spent well, although the Kenyan communities' request was unrelated to this argument.

Similar support for conditional transfers was found in households of varied income levels and urban-rural locations in Zambia. The support was attributed to the conditions' ability to help beneficiaries know how to spend transfers and avoid misusing them. Favorable opinions of conditions were not unqualified, however. Individuals' support for CCTs depended on the group targeted for the transfers and the availability of necessary supply-side infrastructure (Schüring 2010b).

Interestingly enough, the same study found that most beneficiaries thought conditions were empowering. This finding was particularly true in the case of illiterate households. The conditions guided beneficiaries toward behaviors that they may have had little information about previously. The conditions also helped beneficiaries bargain over household expenditures with their spouses because of the clear expectations about households' responsibilities with respect to transfer receipt. The study noted, however, that the sense of empowerment may have been generated through another, possibly more cost-effective method, such as an awareness campaign (Schüring 2010b).

Issues to consider when using soft conditions include credibility, communications, and cost-benefit assessments. Programs interested in using soft conditions must consider several factors. A program that does not expect to enforce conditions but says it will do so is willingly being disingenuous and is potentially undermining trust between the state and citizens. Programs that plan to enforce conditions but do not make progress toward that goal should keep in mind that the relevant ministry's credibility may decrease if it does not align its communication and practices (Regalia 2006).

Programs that plan to enforce conditions but are unable to immediately do so have to make a strategic decision regarding how to present the conditions. They can initially present the conditions as highly encouraged behaviors without threatening beneficiaries with penalties for noncompliance. A communication campaign alerting beneficiaries to the conditional nature of the program could be launched once the program is able to monitor conditions. However, the program may have to deal with opposition from beneficiaries whose transfers shift from UCTs to CCTs.

If a CT program makes the strategic decision to use soft conditions because of concerns that the cost of compliance with hard conditions would be too high for beneficiaries, it should be careful not to present soft conditions in a way that is counterintuitive to the program rationale. To the extent that beneficiaries feel obliged to keep their commitment, even when no penalty for noncompliance is threatened, the program may be inadvertently placing conditions on beneficiaries.

Either way, programs interested in using soft conditions should consider the costs and benefits involved with this approach versus those of a simple social marketing campaign.

Concurrent Supply-Side Initiatives in Conditional Cash Transfer Programs: The African Approach

Cash transfers often uncover weaknesses in service delivery systems. When a CT's major objective is to increase human capital investments, supply-side issues often need to be addressed. CTs, and especially CCTs, may expose limitations of the current services as increased demand is placed on those services. Such weaknesses may affect programs' long-term results. Fiszbein and Schady (2009) assessed evidence on the effects of CCTs throughout the world and found that though intermediate effects of such programs are often positive, final outcomes, such as children's height-for-age or test scores, are often more mixed. They suggest that one factor contributing to this result is that CCTs may place more children in inferior health and education services, thereby resulting in poorer outcomes.[6] This issue is particularly important to address in Sub-Saharan Africa, where supply-side infrastructure is often not capable of meeting increased demand.

Rather than not enforcing conditions in areas with limited supply-side capacity, CCT programs may simply limit their coverage to areas with sufficient supply-side infrastructure. For example, Eritrea's RBF recognizes that quality of health services is crucial to program outcomes, and eligible sublocations must have at least one health center with proper sanitation practices, a clean water source, and proper lighting (Ayala Consulting 2009). Alternatively, NGOs or other agencies are sometimes engaged to improve supply-side infrastructure and services.[7] However, this practice can generate conflict with line ministries or other involved parties when other organizations appear to encroach on territory within their jurisdiction. Engaging NGOs is a stopgap measure rather than a long-term solution.

Other CT programs have capitalized on potential synergies with successful supply-side programs already being implemented. Although it is a UCT, Senegal's CF-SCT provides a helpful example. It uses some of the systems already developed in the successful Nutrition Enhancement Program to lessen the programming burden on the CT, and it confines its work to areas that have already received extensive support for maternal and children's health (World Bank 2009a). The health care system, which was recently expanded at the community level, is able to support the increased demand that the SCT is expected to generate. Similarly, Eritrea's RBF is expected to complement a World Bank–funded project known as HAMSET-II (the Second HIV/AIDS/STI, Tuberculosis, Malaria and Reproductive Health Project), which is working to improve the health sector through training employees, providing supplies, and promoting appropriate behavioral changes (Ayala Consulting 2009).

Another strategy that deals with supply-side constraints is to work to improve service delivery infrastructure through the program itself.

Although this approach may be successful, it places significant pressure on programs, especially those at the pilot stage, and the programs require agreement and significant coordination between the CT and line ministries. Each such layer of organizational complexity introduces new variables and risks that will have to be managed if the program is to succeed.

Once again, Eritrea's RBF provides a good example of a program that is addressing supply-side weaknesses. The RBF includes a component of CCTs that are paid to local health officials provided that they fulfill agreed-on health targets. Individual outcome-based payments to frontline workers are combined with larger supplemental transfers to health systems. Considerable flexibility is given to local managers to allow them to decide how to use these additional funds. Those efforts can motivate local providers to find ways to decrease access costs to health care. RBF's supply-side investment is supposed to help health providers meet the increased demand generated by the program's transfers, which are conditioned on use of the health system (Ayala Consulting 2009).

Services may sometimes be available but underused owing to other constraints that CTs may be able to address. Eritrea's RBF CCT also recognized that a major limitation keeping women from giving birth in an appropriate facility was a lack of timely transportation to medical institutions. In addition to providing traditional CCTs to women, the program raises awareness among transport providers and awards vouchers to individuals who transport women to health facilities when they are about to give birth or are facing complications (Ayala Consulting 2009).

Although CCTs will ideally be able to work with line ministries to coordinate increasing demand and supply for health care, education, and more, these efforts often take significant time, resources, and patience to achieve. Ministries may need to expand their collaboration with other agencies both at the top and at the ground levels and both vertically and horizontally. Buy-in of significant political players at multiple levels of government must be won, and this support has to be backed with appropriate resources that allow civil servants to execute mandates of increased interagency coordination. Additional personnel may need to be hired and trained, and spheres of responsibility must be negotiated. Coordination efforts must be ongoing. Although the most obvious capacity issue with CCTs is often seen at local supply-side bottlenecks, capacity at the central level in human resources, planning, logistics, and execution is just as important for improving delivery of key services crucial to program outcomes.

Areas for Future Study Related to Conditions and Supply-Side Capacity

Given the challenges inherent in applying conditions in many Sub-Saharan African countries, the use of conditions in Sub-Saharan Africa must be analyzed more thoroughly and within a wider variety of contexts. Early quantitative analysis of CCTs versus UCTs in Sub-Saharan Africa suggests that conditions may be important to achieve certain outcomes, although a CCT is not necessarily the right instrument to achieve all goals (see box 3.5). Results may be closely tied to which activities are conditioned.

Although traditional impact evaluations (box 3.6) are important to understand the effectiveness of CCTs and UCTs on specific outcomes, other studies are also important. An example of such a study has been completed for Zambia's Monze District SCT (Schüring 2010b). This study combines multiple methods, including secondary data, beneficiary and nonbeneficiary surveys, in-depth interviews, community games, and administrative data, to address important issues regarding the use of conditions in Zambia. It covers many soft issues related to conditioning, including beneficiary and public perceptions of conditions, the challenges in applying conditions, the potential exclusionary role of conditions, and the political economy dynamics that ultimately affect the usefulness of conditions. It also addresses beneficiaries' preferences with respect to altruism and risk aversion, time discounting, and potential information asymmetries, to determine whether those factors played a role in suboptimal human capital investments.

Although this study found that many Zambians supported conditioning transfers, it ultimately concluded that applying conditions was not optimal at that time. The conclusion was driven by the conditions' potential tendency to exclude the worst-off beneficiaries, the setting's low implementation capacity, and the conclusion that conditions had a relatively small potential to significantly change beneficiaries' health and education behaviors. This type of analysis, combined with rigorous quantitative evaluations, will prove useful for other countries that are trying to determine whether and how conditions should be applied in their own programs.

Another area of study that may prove fruitful is the question of which conditions should be applied—and how often conditions should be monitored—in CCT programs. Many of the vanguard CCT programs condition benefits on school attendance, which must be monitored relatively frequently, and Sub-Saharan African CCT programs are following in their footsteps. However, if a program can encourage children to continue

Box 3.5

To Condition or Not to Condition? Discussion and Additional References

Fiszbein and Schady (2009) provide a thorough discussion on when placing conditions on human capital investments may be appropriate for cash transfer programs. They suggest that conditions may be useful when households underinvest in human capital or when adding conditions increases the program's political acceptability and sustainability.

Households may underinvest in human capital for several major reasons. Investments may be privately suboptimal as a result of imperfect information, myopic decision making, or incomplete altruism of parents toward their children. Incomplete altruism may result from inefficient intrahousehold bargaining outcomes or excessively high parental discount rates in the presence of credit market failures. Even if households invest in privately optimal levels of human capital, this level may still be socially suboptimal because of the presence of positive externalities in human capital investment (Fiszbein and Schady 2009).

Despite their benefits, conditional transfers present potential problems. These problems include the possibility that conditions will be too costly for the most destitute households to comply with, in essence excluding them from program benefits, or that the quality of education or health services will be too low to provide significant benefits to households. Other concerns are that schools and health centers will be unable to support increased demand created by the CCTs, and that the CCT program will not have adequate capacity to monitor and enforce conditions. Additional opposition to conditions stems from the belief that the government should not withhold benefits from citizens who are entitled to a state transfer (Fiszbein and Schady 2009).

Those interested in learning more about the rationale for, implementation of, and known impacts of CCTs throughout the world are referred to Fiszbein and Schady (2009). Fiszbein and Schady also highlight how CCTs should work in tandem with other social protection programs. Readers interested in the issues involved in deciding whether to condition CTs are also referred to Schüring (2010a). Other key references on CCTs include Das, Do, and Özler (2005), who discuss the tension between equity and efficiency objectives in CCTs as they balance redistributing resources with increasing investments in human capital, and Rawlings and Rubio (2005), who discuss programs and evaluation results for some of the earliest Latin American CCTs.

> **Box 3.6**
>
> **Impact Evaluations**
>
> Although many programs in Sub-Saharan Africa have tried to determine the impact of CTs on key outcomes, some of the evaluations have lacked the credible counterfactual necessary to determine the program's causal effect on beneficiaries. To have an impact evaluation in the truest sense, a program must be able to identify treatment and control groups. *Experimental evaluations* randomly assign beneficiaries or households into these groups, often exploiting the program's need to conduct a phased rollout (because of fiscal, capacity, or political constraints) to ensure that potential beneficiaries are not unfairly excluded from the program. A *quasi-experimental* or *nonexperimental* method does not work from intentionally randomized assignment of treatment and control groups. Instead, these evaluations use econometric methods, including matching, difference-in-difference regressions, and instrumental variables, to try to isolate program impacts. For more information on program evaluations, see Ravallion (1999, 2005).

in school by monitoring grade progression or final exam grades, rather than by monitoring daily attendance, this knowledge would be useful.

Similarly, conditions may be most important at key junctures, such as the transition to the second cycle of primary school or to junior secondary school. If a program has difficulty applying conditions that require frequent monitoring, it could instead learn what value can be added by monitoring only the groups with the highest risk for suboptimal behaviors (for example, school desertion during major transitions). This analysis should consider which conditions have the greatest effect on beneficiary behavior and what unintended consequences monitoring these conditions might have, such as the potential for increased automatic promotion in the case of a grade progression condition.

Finally, additional case studies and knowledge sharing will offer useful information on how Sub-Saharan African CCTs have helped encourage the improvement of condition-related service delivery. Such findings will be particularly relevant for low-income countries trying to implement CCTs in areas that face severe capacity constraints.

Graduation from Cash Transfer Programs

The concept of beneficiaries' graduation from CT programs has received considerable attention in Sub-Saharan Africa. In some cases, beneficiaries graduate only after they have also received support in income-generating opportunities. Beneficiaries may be connected to a public works or microfinance program, or they may have completed a vocational training course and received a lump sum for capital investment. Other beneficiaries may graduate after receiving important psychosocial support that should help them in the future. Households that graduate from a CT program may continue to benefit from other social support at a level commensurate with their need and ability. Rwanda's VUP and Ethiopia's PSNP, for example, have strategies that encourage capable households to graduate from their CT components into public works or other income-generating activities.

Graduation is not a requirement of social assistance. In Sub-Saharan Africa, where skipped-generation households are increasingly common, program graduation is not always feasible as a short- or even medium-term goal. Governments that have clear vision about vulnerability among different groups in the country and that fully understand the purpose of their CTs will maintain realistic expectations regarding graduation. In Rwanda, which has looked into social protection issues in great depth, the government recognizes that some households, such as those composed only of the elderly or of the elderly and young children, should not be expected to quickly graduate from its state-sponsored CT program. In some cases, graduation is not expected to occur. Either the transfers or some other form of social protection will be needed indefinitely to sustain individuals who cannot maintain their own livelihood. The status of households is closely monitored in Rwanda's VUP, with targeting reviewed every six months at the local level, thereby ensuring that households are correctly categorized with respect to social protection issues (Republic of Rwanda 2009).

Ethiopia's PSNP has struggled to encourage graduation when possible, while still covering beneficiaries who should remain in the program. Initially, some households were graduated after acquiring significant assets, even if the assets were purchased on credit (Devereux and others 2006). The practice pushed beneficiaries from the program before they were able to survive without the transfers. This dilemma highlighted the program's need to clarify its role in development (for those able to work) and in welfare (for PSNP-DS beneficiaries, who were unable to participate in public works). Over time, expectations have become more realistic about the time required for households to be able to graduate. Increasingly, the government understands that graduation depends not just on the success of the CT program, but also on the program's ability to link households to other support that will help increase their asset base, mitigate the effect of shocks, and link them into well-functioning markets (World Bank 2010a).

Monitoring and Accountability

Monitoring plays an important role in all CTs, providing officials with information on how funds are spent, how well the program is carrying out its duties, and whether and how many beneficiaries are being reached.

The Management Information System: A Building Block to Improve Program Credibility and Enhance Impact

Establishing a strong management information system (MIS) early in a CT's life is critical to the program's success and its potential to scale up. Programs that use manual information systems or other relatively inefficient systems are unable to grow in the way that a program with an appropriate electronic system can. For instance, Kenya's CT for OVC was slowed down by its MIS for a time because the system was not designed to handle data for a program as large as Kenya's became. Its MIS eventually began to create implementation bottlenecks that had to be addressed.

Many of the small CTs in Sub-Saharan Africa have monitoring systems with at least some manual components. For instance, at payment distributions of the Lesotho CGP, a payment coupon and receipt are stamped in a Child Grant coupon book, which identifies the household through a unique number (Blank 2008). Similarly, most documentation of Zambia's pilot SCTs has been filed manually. However, a beneficiary database and payment registrar are maintained on computers. This information is transported to and from districts and headquarters on compact discs (Ministry of Community Development and Social Services 2008). Other programs rely on computer databases that may or may not be able to communicate with other monitoring systems.

In an ideal world, programs will establish and properly implement a comprehensive monitoring system that is wholly assimilated into program processes. However, given limited capacity and resources, Africa's CT programs will often begin and work with limited monitoring capacity. In such situations, the program should focus on primary monitoring priorities instead of requiring exhaustive tests at all levels of the system, while working to improve capacity at identified bottlenecks. Stopgap monitoring should be put in place when necessary as program capacity is developed. This approach has been used successfully by Ethiopia's PSNP, which established initial monitoring processes (such as quarterly external roving financial audits and an information center) that have provided important information to program officials while other existing monitoring processes are being improved (World Bank 2010a). Capacity building in monitoring has been an ongoing process for the program.

Technology, management information systems, and coordinating social protection programs and policies. As technological capacity increases in Sub-Saharan Africa, MISs are increasingly being designed with web-based capabilities. Programs that enable officials to enter data at decentralized levels, without having to transmit information physically to program headquarters, reap benefits of up-to-date reports and the ability to respond quickly to emerging problems. Kenya's HSNP has established such a web-based system that should be capable of coordinating with other databases in the future (HSNP n.d.). This important feature can benefit the government as it creates a coherent social protection strategy. Senegal's CF-SCT is on the receiving side of similar benefits; it is making use of a monitoring system already developed by the Nutrition Enhancement Program (World Bank 2009a).

Some MISs are already able to communicate with other systems, which encourages intersectoral coordination and program efficiencies. In Eritrea's RBF, information on health centers will be entered into the project's MIS and into a broader-level MIS that follows the health facilities (Ayala Consulting 2009). This type of communication across systems is crucial.

Ghana plans to create a single registry modeled on Brazil's to harmonize various social protection programs at work in the country (World Bank 2010c). This type of setup is still fairly rare in Sub-Saharan Africa's CTs, especially outside of the upper-middle-income countries. As countries increasingly embrace coherent national social protection strategies, single registries will probably become more common.

An MIS should be able to accommodate future program expansion and integration with other systems. If and when programs do scale up or increase coordination with relevant line ministries or other social protection programs, the necessary increase in MIS capacity is then incremental, and systems do not have to be completely re-created to allow for the new features. Compatible designs save both financial and human resources. Compatibility is an important issue for Kenya's CT for OVC, which wants to link the postal system to a new financial MIS module (World Bank 2009d).

Other vital monitoring activities. Other important monitoring activities in Sub-Saharan Africa's CTs include production of regular reports on costs, activities, outputs, beneficiaries, and so forth. These reports are created through the programs' MIS.

Random spot-checks to verify that monitoring is proceeding correctly are essential. In Sub-Saharan Africa, lists of eligible households are sometimes published to maintain program accountability with communities (for example, in Lesotho's CGP; Blank 2008). Checks completed by external groups, as well as financial audits, are also important to gain and maintain program credibility. All of these additional controls are important, especially when implementers or government agencies handle larger budgets than those to which they are accustomed, and concerns of corruption must be addressed (World Bank 2010a).

CTs can undertake various activities to limit fraud. Budget controls and procedures should be in place. As much as possible, given resource constraints, transfer payments should be reconciled at all levels. Risks can also be reduced by including controls in the program's design and by keeping implementation as uncomplicated as possible, given program goals. Automated programs should search for and report basic inconsistencies such as duplicate beneficiaries. When possible, report results should be cross-referenced with data available from other sources. When grant beneficiary lists were compared with records of public service employees in South Africa, fraud was uncovered and addressed (DFID 2006).

Monitoring in emergencies. For programs that cover beneficiaries in emergencies or potential crises, monitoring systems must be designed to collect real-time information that will inform major programmatic decisions. For instance, since Ethiopia's PSNP works in areas of extreme food insecurity that previously relied on emergency aid, program officials have had to keep apprised of local food security, inflation, and the timeliness of transfer delivery. While government systems to handle these demands are being developed, the program has had to use innovative monitoring systems to ensure it has the information it needs. To do so, it has created an information center, which uses random auditing of various districts, and it relies on rapid response teams to help respond to realities on the ground as they develop (World Bank 2010a).

Additional monitoring requirements of CCTs. CCTs have additional monitoring requirements that verify whether beneficiaries have abided by conditions. These activities are important, as payment levels will depend on the outcome of the monitoring. Fulfillment of conditions should be monitored at regular intervals that coincide with the frequency with which conditions are supposed to be fulfilled.

Several methods of monitoring conditions are used, or will be used, in Sub-Saharan Africa. In Eritrea, health and growth monitoring cards are marked by local health officials for women who fulfill conditions. The women then take the cards to local administrative offices for verification and transfer payments (Ayala Consulting 2009). In Nigeria's COPE, households typically turn in forms signed by relevant institutions to local program offices (World Bank n.d.a). In Burkina Faso and Kenya, individuals in health centers and schools fill in booklets that track the fulfillment of conditions (CNLS 2008; Government of Kenya 2007). In some cases, the centers turn the information in to relevant officials; in other cases, another group such as an NGO collects data for the program.

Monitoring as a feed-in to program decision-making. Data from monitoring should help officials understand if the CT's objectives are being met. Properly aligning monitoring with programmatic goals will provide key information needed to analyze the CT and adjust it as necessary. Programs that are donor funded need to ensure that the CT's monitoring systems collect data that are useful to domestic decision makers as well as to donors. When all program partners agree on the program's objectives and logical framework, they are able to more clearly decide what criteria should be monitored, and they can coalesce around those common criteria (World Bank 2010a).

This approach, taken in Ethiopia's PSNP, avoids creating inefficiencies in the monitoring process and placing unnecessary burdens on program officials (World Bank 2010a). The PSNP has been able to use monitoring and reviews to direct improvements in the program. Information collected has led the PSNP to expand its coverage and increase budget support for capacity building at the regional level ("Productive Safety Nets Programme in Ethiopia" n.d.). When information from monitoring and reviews is continuously incorporated to improve the CT, it can lead to better program design and more effective implementation.

Design Features That Encourage Accountability and Transparency

Just as properly functioning data systems are important for monitoring purposes, key individuals or groups may also be vital for monitoring. In Sub-Saharan Africa, communities may be involved in monitoring beneficiaries during payment distributions and in monitoring beneficiaries' use of cash or fulfillment of conditions. For instance, Lesotho's CGP plans to use community groups to monitor how beneficiaries use the unconditional transfers (PlusNews 2009). Community groups also may know about changes in beneficiaries and households that affect their eligibility for benefits. If used correctly, this information may help maintain targeting integrity.

Community leaders may play an important role as arbiters when program abuses arise; therefore, they must be adequately informed about the CT program. Miller, Tsoka, and Reichert (2010) found that traditional authorities sometimes lacked important information about Malawi's SCT that could have allowed them to stop community committee members from gleaning parts of transfers from beneficiaries and later disqualifying beneficiaries from the program when they refused to provide money to committee members.

However, using communities for monitoring purposes presents its own challenges. If communities are used to enhance program monitoring, these groups should be properly trained, and steps should be taken to avoid any sort of favoritism. Some programs that involve communities in monitoring find that they appreciate a small cash or in-kind remuneration for the work they complete. Kenya's CT for OVC has found this strategy to boost morale among community volunteers (Government of Kenya 2006).

Community groups and individuals that are used for monitoring should themselves be monitored by higher-level groups to ensure that they are correctly carrying out their duties. One issue that arose in Zambia's SCTs was that some local schools told beneficiaries they were supposed to use transfers to pay parent-teacher associations. Community welfare assistance committees also pressured beneficiaries to use CTs to invest in livestock or in other areas they deemed important (Schüring 2010b). Monitoring of such groups should help limit those activities.

Ongoing monitoring of local groups by higher-level program officials, though sometimes difficult to practice because of personnel, fiscal, and temporal constraints, may improve CT implementation. Monitoring may also allow for communication with, and continual training of, local program implementers. It can help community members with program-related responsibilities feel supported by those at central levels. For instance, Malawi's SCT receives local support through its community social protection committees. The committees have voiced the desire for higher-level officials to have a stronger presence in their activities (Miller, Tsoka, and Reichart 2010).

Other program components may play a role in monitoring. Beneficiaries of Namibia's Old Age and Disability Pensions are required to purchase life insurance benefits of up to N$2,000. In addition to helping family members cover the beneficiary's funeral costs, this component helps discourage individuals from trying to collect benefits after the beneficiary dies (Levine, van der Berg, and Yu 2009).

Other Features Used to Monitor Community and Beneficiary Satisfaction

Many programs use appeal or complaint processes to monitor community and beneficiary satisfaction. The independence of these processes from other program decision-making bodies is important. Such arrangements may need special attention in Sub-Saharan African CT programs that rely heavily on community-based targeting, because ensuring impartial, nonretributive judgments by community-based appeal committees may be difficult. Ethiopia's PSNP navigates the issue by allowing appeals of targeting decisions by community food security task forces to be taken to higher levels for consideration.

Some programs are using innovative methods to ensure that beneficiaries are able to air their grievances. World Vision's Cash and Food Transfer Pilot Project in Lesotho addressed complaints by using traveling community help desks, which beneficiaries could visit at local paypoints to deal with their complaints (Devereux and Mhlanga 2008). The process appeared to function well. South Africa's grant system has a hotline that individuals can call to file complaints and provide information about fraud or abuse.

Kenya's CT for OVC will use external organizations to conduct community censuses to evaluate the quality of local OVC committees. The organizations will also assess beneficiary and nonbeneficiary opinions and satisfaction with the program using "citizen report cards" (World Bank 2009d). Tanzania's CB-CCT will also use a community scorecard, which will assess local opinions of the program through focus groups. In addition, community management committees are expected to complete self-assessments to improve their own performance (TASAF 2008). These methods and others will be useful in maintaining awareness of community and beneficiary perceptions of CTs.

Knowledge Gaps in Monitoring, Accountability, and MISs

Information regarding how to effectively implement monitoring systems in a limited-capacity setting will be helpful to policy makers in

Sub-Saharan Africa. Some information is available on this topic, but additional information from established programs may be helpful as new programs begin and attempt to scale up. Case studies on how to overcome technological constraints in monitoring and how to increase capacity of program personnel to improve monitoring will be important, as will additional support on how to establish social registries in such settings.

Information for programs that use community members for monitoring of targeting, distribution, and other program components will also be helpful. More cost-effective means of monitoring communities involved in CT programs need to be identified. Additional information on the effectiveness of various monitoring levels would be useful. For instance, is continuous, planned monitoring of community groups or data systems more cost-effective than less frequent monitoring combined with random spot-checks on systems and processes? Also, who are the best individuals to perform this type of monitoring?

A final issue that needs further study is how to monitor who actually resides in beneficiary households. This issue is particularly important if benefits are tied to household size. After returning to beneficiary households between three and five times during the course of a year, researchers determined that 9 percent of beneficiaries listed in households receiving Malawi's SCT were actually ghost members used to inflate household transfers (Miller, Tsoka, and Reichert 2010). Given the fluctuations in household size and composition over time in many parts of Sub-Saharan Africa, cost-effective monitoring of who belongs to households may be difficult to achieve.

Communication to Ensure Program Impact: Building Understanding, Ownership, and a Constituency of Support

Cash transfers are a relatively new development programming concept in Sub-Saharan Africa. As with any innovation, communication about CTs will influence how well they are accepted and whether they will succeed. Communication is vital to explain the purpose, components, and outcomes of programs; to improve understanding and buy-in; and to complement programmatic goals through social marketing campaigns.

Communication tools are being used, but planning needs to improve. Senegal's CCT for OVC has recognized that sensitization and communication must be undertaken to increase support for the program (CNLS and World Bank n.d.). Support may be crucial even before a program begins: Eritrea's RBF was supposed to begin only after national and local promotional activities increased awareness and understanding of the program (Ayala Consulting 2009). Such communication with beneficiaries and nonbeneficiaries alike can help generate and maintain support for a CT program.

Once a CT program is established, the program must provide the general population with information about how it is functioning. At the very least, it should make this information available on request. Such information could include statistics on program coverage and expenditures, results of independent program audits, and findings from impact and process evaluations (DFID 2006).

Communication campaigns can also be used to increase program coverage. Namibia has combated significant undercoverage of its grants by launching an awareness campaign that informed the public about grant eligibility (Republic of Namibia 2007).

Similarly, programs must communicate information about payments. Some CTs publicize lists of beneficiaries, such as the publicly posted lists in Lesotho's CGP (Blank 2008), and many announce payment days, for example, through radio announcements in Namibia (ELCRN 2007; Levine, van der Berg, and Yu 2009).

Communicating with beneficiaries is important to help them understand what benefits they are entitled to and to minimize fraud. An evaluation of Mozambique's PSA revealed that households often did not know how much cash they should receive. On average, households' transfers were approximately two-thirds of the value for which they were qualified. This low payout was due, in part, to poor household awareness of benefit eligibility (Datt and others 1997).

Communication can also help maintain beneficiary satisfaction. Although overall satisfaction of beneficiaries of Ethiopia's PSNP was 75 percent, the sample of households that reported they had sufficient information to understand how the program functioned had a 90 percent satisfaction rate (Urban Institute and Birhan Research and Development Consultancy 2008, as cited in World Bank 2010a).

CT programs can learn from and adopt communication strategies used by other successful programs. Kenya's CT for OVC has attempted to improve its transparency and increase understanding of the CT through a strong communication plan. The campaign provides information about the CT to participating communities and holds meetings for relevant stakeholders in program areas. The communication campaign will support a program website, pamphlets, posters, and more. Some of the plans used in the communication strategy have been taken from lessons learned in other programs, especially Kenya's Free Primary Education Programme (World Bank 2009d).

Some Sub-Saharan African programs are exploring innovative communication strategies to influence actions related to the CT's objectives. Eritrea, for example, plans to implement a Healthy Mothers campaign to increase awareness related to maternal and child health. The campaign will include a contest in which women who have fulfilled certain conditions are entered in drawings that award prizes on National Women's Day (Ayala Consulting 2009). In the hopes of increasing the CT's impacts, Nigeria's Kano CCT for Girls' Education plans to use a communication campaign in program localities to combat cultural opposition to girls' education (World Bank 2008).

Communication is an area of CT design that often receives due attention only later in the implementation process, after problems emerge. Evaluations of current communication strategies and experience sharing across countries may highlight the need to put an appropriate strategy in place from the outset.

Institutional Location, Coordination, and Capacity

The institutional location of CT programs will affect many facets of its design and performance. The institutional home of a program must have both the capacity to implement a CT program and the ability to coordinate among stakeholder groups.

Institutional Location of Cash Transfers

The programs reviewed had a wide range of institutional homes (see figure 3.14). Almost half of the reviewed CT programs operated outside the jurisdiction of government ministries. Those programs tended to be short-term emergency transfers, often with NGO or donor involvement. Outside of this group, most programs examined were based in a department related to social welfare or labor. (Social pensions tend to be based in labor departments.)

CT programs' institutional homes track closely with a country's income status. The reviewed upper-middle-income countries' CTs all have homes in government departments. As income levels decrease, programs are increasingly seated outside of the government. Approximately three in four CTs in lower-middle-income countries have government homes; this number is reduced to one in three for low-income countries. The breakdown for fragile states is similar to that for low-income

Figure 3.14 Institutional Location of CT Programs

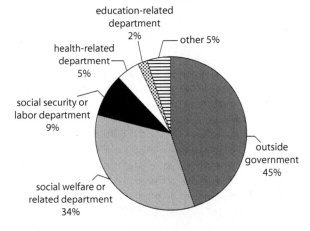

a. All countries

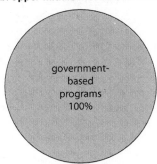

b. Upper-middle-income countries

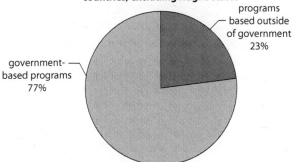

c. Lower-middle-income countries, excluding fragile states

(continued next page)

Figure 3.14 *(continued)*

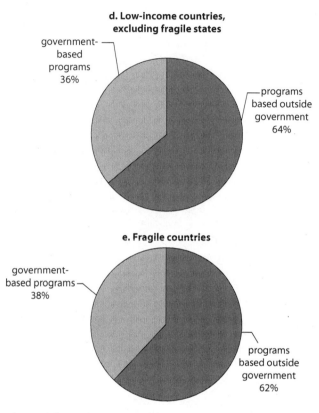

Source: Authors' representation.
Note: Sample size is 107 for panel a, 23 for panel b, 13 for panel c, 45 for panel d, and 26 for panel e. Analysis is limited to those programs whose institutional home was clear from available information.

countries; however, this result is driven by Zimbabwe's government-based programs, whose influence appears to have diminished significantly in recent years. Excluding all Zimbabwean CTs, 85 percent of programs in fragile states are based outside of the government. This situation clearly illustrates why there are concerns that CTs in low-income countries are donor driven.

Programs with a very specific focus have sometimes been placed within a line ministry directly related to its focus. For instance, Eritrea's RBF is based within the Ministry of Health (Ayala Consulting 2009), and Ethiopia's PSNP is based in the country's Office of Food Security under the Ministry of Agriculture and Rural Development (Andrade 2008).

Programs that support OVC or fight HIV are sometimes based in a country's National Council against AIDS—for example, Burkina Faso's Pilot CCT-CT (CNLS 2008) and Senegal's CCT for OVC (Document de Cadrage Technique 2009). A more recent program, Tanzania's CB-CCT, has its institutional home in the Tanzania Social Action Fund (TASAF). This arrangement has the potential to capitalize on knowledge and community capacity where the social fund has been at work.

Strategic Location Matters
Very few CT programs in Sub-Saharan Africa are located in institutional settings that carry out higher-level coordinating functions, such as are found in some of the large-scale cross-sectoral Latin American CCTs that operate under the office of the president. In Sub-Saharan Africa, such arrangements are unlikely in the short term in the absence of widespread national social protection policies and programs.

That being said, CT programs' institutional locations are still very important in terms of their ability to obtain resources and coordinate with other groups. In Eritrea, RBF's institutional arrangement allows it to complement the work of the Ministry of Health, where it is seated under the direction of the Family and Community Health Division's Family and Reproductive Health Unit (Ayala Consulting 2009). Other programs should similarly leverage the influence that they do have.

Institutions' Capacity for CT Programs
Building up the capacity of CT institutional homes is needed to ensure long-term effectiveness. A frequent complaint about CT programs—and social protection programs more broadly—is that they are located in weak institutional homes. The structures of government administrations created during the colonial period generally reflected little or no concern for social protection of the colonized population. Responsibility for social protection was left to informal institutions—particularly the extended family—that had traditionally fulfilled those functions. For a long time, postindependence national governments left social protection largely to those traditional institutions.

Increasingly, conflict; migration; AIDS; and economic, demographic, and social change have eroded the strengths of those traditional systems. At the same time, they have created vast new vulnerabilities and urgently increased the need for social protection. Current Sub-Saharan African government structures for social protection—often departments or directorates of social welfare nested inside other ministries that themselves lack political clout—are often not up to the challenges posed by the rapid-onset social crises with which they are often asked to deal.

The capacity of officials and other individuals within the CT program's implementing institution is crucial to the program's success. Commentary on the reviewed CTs highlighted the limitations placed on CTs when involved members lacked skills crucial to carrying out their responsibilities. Such issues arose, for instance, when program employees (or civil service employees who were implementing programs) lacked computer literacy. Other challenges faced by some government ministries involved in CTs stem from their previous focus on helping individuals in need of support (that is, through case-based legal support, adoption, and so forth), rather than addressing the collective needs of vulnerable groups. This concern was a challenge in Ghana, where training and a change of focus were needed to reorient officials to meet the demands of LEAP (Jones 2009).

Longer-term approaches to institutional development for CT programs have been shown to save time in the long run. A short-term solution that is sometimes used to address limited institutional capacity in social protection–related ministries is to locate CTs within a different, politically stronger institution. This approach is often taken to solve some immediate problems but may give rise to a new set of dilemmas. As awareness grows regarding social protection, availability of new resources from donors may lead to a proliferation of new small programs competing for those resources, each finding a home in a different institution. The institutions themselves may be competing for resources. Each CT program then seeks to expand and separately sets out to address capacity constraints, so that social protection strategies and programming become a confused arena of overlapping responsibilities, conflict, and coordination challenges. Unfortunately, bypassed from the start because of its weaknesses, the institutional home with the rightful government mandate for such coordination remains without capacity to fulfill its responsibilities.

The weaknesses of this strategy have been recognized. The African Union's Social Policy Framework advises member states to enhance the capacity of ministries in charge of social protection (African Union 2008). When possible, a longer-term approach is preferred to solve the problem of the weak institutional home. Even when urgent issues require shortcuts, significant efforts should be made to increase stability and capacity in the longer-term institutional home. Such an approach has been taken within Kenya's Ministry of Gender, Children, and Social Development and within the CT program unit, even as the CT for OVC continues to expand. In this ministry, consistent efforts have been made to develop capacity and the ability to function autonomously, all while the program has scaled up rapidly (World Bank 2009d).

The home ministry of Ghana's CT program, LEAP, also faces major capacity constraints. However, in contrast to the Kenyan case, the ministry has tried to scale up the CT program at a pace that can allow for, and encourage, commensurate capacity building and institutional strengthening within the ministry. Ghana has also dealt with this issue by requesting development partners to invest in institutional strengthening in the ministry, while allowing the government to provide actual CT funds (Sultan and Schrofer 2008).

Coordination among Stakeholder Groups: Not an Easy Matter

CT programs often must rely on other ministries or groups to implement program components. Much of the important day-to-day work is conducted by decentralized entities that work for the CT program—and often for other programs. These low-level groups must coordinate among themselves to ensure that the program is correctly implemented. Coordination is also important at higher levels, which can encourage cooperation in the lower echelons and mobilize support for large, long-term investments required to put effective systems in place.

Because line ministries are often involved in monitoring conditions, coordination among program units, decentralized line ministries, and other partners is crucial for CCT programs. For example, village committees against AIDS and decentralized line services monitor the fulfillment of conditions in Burkina Faso's Pilot CCT-CT. Coordination is required between provincial and regional committees against AIDS, local committees, and representatives of the line ministries (CNLS 2008). Senegal's CCT for OVC must work with local NGOs to identify OVC, implement the program, and coordinate with schools. It has found such coordination among the various groups to be essential, especially at decentralized levels (CNLS and World Bank n.d.; Document de Cadrage Technique 2009).

Coordination is also important in UCT programs, which often rely on lower-level officials and groups for help implementing the program. In Malawi's SCT, district social welfare committees are composed of members from various sectors. The committees play a role in approving lists of potential beneficiaries (Miller, Tsoka, and Reichert 2010). Rwanda's VUP also delegates responsibilities to groups at various levels, making coordination indispensable. Districts are responsible for financial administration of VUP, including contracting with partners and making payments (Republic of Rwanda 2009).

Programs that work with outside entities, such as NGOs, also must coordinate activities. Kenya's HSNP works with various outside organizations that are in charge of administration, payments, complaints, monitoring, and evaluation. Many of these groups are NGOs. This structure requires communication among all groups, as well as higher-level coordination by a secretariat within the Ministry for the Development of Northern Kenya (HSNP n.d.). In Senegal's CF-SCT, the local governments, which must support nutrition in their (typically) infrastructure-focused local development plans, are supposed to contract with organizations to work in communities. The Coordination Unit for the Fight against Malnutrition decides on local transfer providers by location (World Bank 2009a). Within communities, executing agencies can be NGOs, civil society organizations, or other groups that implement the community-level nutrition program and verify lists of local beneficiaries. Once again, coordination among involved groups is integral to the CT program's success.

Coordination is required to exploit program synergies. Coordination is also important for CTs that want to link beneficiaries to complementary programs. In Kenya's CT for OVC, an advisory area council has district-level officials involved in various activities, beyond simply the CT, that assist children and help coordinate support for OVC. Lesotho's CGP will use district child protection teams, which will work with community committees to implement the CGP and coordinate other child social services across the district (Blank 2008).

Coordination between CTs and other programs is particularly important when CTs have productive objectives and aim to graduate beneficiaries from the transfers. Those links have proved vital to the effectiveness of Ethiopia's PSNP, where program outcomes were muted when beneficiaries did not have access to related programs supporting their food security (Gilligan and others 2009a; World Bank 2010a). Over time, the PSNP has improved its ability to link beneficiaries to other programs that help increase their income and assets (Slater and others 2006).

Similarly, Ghana's LEAP purports to provide numerous services to beneficiaries to help improve their livelihoods; in reality, this coordination is not developed, and LEAP has very limited capacity to generate synergies with other programs. (Complementarities are expected in livelihoods and income generation, health care, education, emergency support, and other areas.) Program managers expect that high-level coordination and political support will be necessary to create these connections, and both planning and implementation will be crucial. The first steps in this direction include high-level meetings and identification and costing of local-level activities and services that can support beneficiaries (Jones 2009). The hope is that improved coordination can help exploit these synergies over time.

Some programs using decentralized groups allow local-level implementation variations. When programs rely on decentralized bodies to implement the program on a daily basis—whether within their program unit, in line ministry offices, in NGOs or community-based organizations, or with other community-based groups and leaders—execution of the program may vary based on local needs.

In Ethiopia's PSNP-DS, some districts *(woredas)* provide smaller Direct Support transfers to a greater number of beneficiaries, and others choose to provide larger transfers to fewer beneficiaries. Criteria for payment also vary across woredas. Lower-level administrative units *(kebeles)* also have significant authority. Kebeles establish safety net plans for their area and create and direct community food security task forces (Gilligan and others 2009b). This autonomy generates differences in the PSNP at the local level, which is theoretically tailored to local needs.

Mozambique's PSA uses paid individuals known as *permanentes* to provide crucial support at the community level. Communities select these individuals, who serve between 15 and 25 beneficiaries (Ellis 2007). Their duties include informing communities about the PSA, assisting at paydays, verifying cash recipients, and visiting beneficiaries. As might be expected, the value of permanentes' assistance varies substantially, generating local implementation differences (Waterhouse 2007).

Formal arrangements among groups are growing. When CT programs rely on other organizations to implement programs, formal agreements between the involved groups are helpful. Roles and responsibilities are agreed on and clearly outlined, and the agreement gives the CT program authority to expect decentralized line ministry officials to cooperate on specific tasks. Some Sub-Saharan African programs have made official agreements between the program unit and other ministries. For instance, the project coordinating unit in Ghana's LEAP CT has a memorandum of understanding with the line ministries with which it works (World Bank 2010c).

Memorandums can encourage officials in other departments or ministries to recognize the legitimacy of their CT-related responsibilities.

An important aspect of the memorandum is to ensure that those assigned the duty of implementing the program see their duties related to the CT as part of their core responsibilities (World Bank 2010a). If they view their CT duties as nonessential or as an additional burden on top of their normal obligations, implementation will probably suffer.

Although some programs have formal agreements with other groups, this type of coordination is still the exception and not the rule. Most reviewed programs did not discuss having any sort of official agreement with related agencies. However, some programs recognize this need. The lack of official agreements across involved agencies was cited in a review of the Zambian SCTs. The review stated that if the programs were to enforce conditions, official district-level agreements between the Department of Social Welfare and the Department of Education would be necessary to ensure that teachers carried out monitoring responsibilities (Schüring 2010b).

Coordination improves over time. In many cases, official coordination between programs is apparently being developed. Coordination between agencies often takes time to establish, because officials may be accustomed to thinking and working within their own areas, and they may find communicating and working across ministries or other organizations difficult. As CTs strive to work with other units, coordination may naturally improve. For instance, coordination has improved over time in Zambia's SCTs (Schüring 2010b).

Although interinstitutional coordination is vital to the success of a CT, an important point is not to let coordination become so complicated that it is an obstacle to the program's success. An exceptionally complicated institutional arrangement can cause confusion over roles within programs. Roles and responsibilities among centralized and decentralized entities may need to be clarified to make sure each body works to its respective strengths and uses resources effectively.

Finally, interinstitutional coordination will be affected by a country's political structure. Nigeria's federal design has generated some confusion over roles and responsibilities of stakeholders at the federal and state levels. This ambiguity has led the program to examine how Brazil's CCT functions within its federal structure (World Bank 2009b).

Institutional and Managerial Capacity of Involved Groups

Dealing with capacity constraints in supporting groups. Just as capacity issues are critical in the CT program's institution, capacity of other involved groups and community members is extremely important. Local implementation will be flawed at best if, for instance, the CT program relies on community members with program-related responsibilities requiring the use of basic skills—such as literacy or numeracy—that they lack. If they are involved in implementing the program, community members and cross-sectoral officials need appropriate program-related training and capacity building to help them carry out their specific duties. The need for training is ongoing, both to remind and update existing staff and to instruct new officials.

Likewise, involved institutions need to be capable of fulfilling their CT-related duties in addition to the obligations for which they are already responsible. They should be prepared to transfer knowledge to incoming officials and other supporting groups.

When programs encounter capacity-related bottlenecks, they must determine how to improve capacity or work around constraints. Ethiopia's PSNP was begun using a simple design to ensure that the basics could be achieved. Program officials approached capacity constraints head on by classifying districts on the basis of districts' implementation ability and working within those parameters. Regional budgets were increased to support district-level capacity building ("Productive Safety Nets Programme in Ethiopia" n.d.). The PSNP has added complexity to its systems as it is able to in order to meet increased demands (World Bank 2010a).

Zambia's Kalomo SCT has had to deal with limited capacity in the Public Welfare Assistance Scheme, an institution that existed before the CT and through which the CT is implemented. Capacity was limited because of low literacy levels and the need for increased training and equipment. Providing additional training and information about the program has lessened some of these problems (Hamonga 2006).

Speaking about Malawi, Miller, Tsoka, and Reichert (2010) report that almost half of the SCT's community social protection committee members did not fully understand which beneficiaries were to be included or excluded from the program. Since learning this, the program has taken steps to increase understanding of the SCT and capacity for targeting—a crucial step when local community members play a major role in the program.

Leveraging previous community-level investments. Other programs rely on community members and groups that have received training from other sources since such training allows them to more easily carry out

CT-related duties. Tanzania's CB-CCT requires that participating communities pass certain criteria: they must have successfully implemented a subproject for TASAF, and they must have a functioning community management committee (Evans 2008). Those requirements capitalize on investments already made in communities. By using local capacity as a screening mechanism, the program also expects to enhance its impacts. Nigeria's COPE CCT is also building on successful community-driven development projects that are supposed to improve program implementation (World Bank n.d.a).

Rwanda's VUP is able to rely on community groups because of previous local-level investments, combined with a strong community sensitization and training component (DFID 2009). Villages use the *Ubudehe* method, which is already being used in many locations of the country for various purposes, to qualitatively identify and classify households for targeting (Republic of Rwanda 2009). VUP hopes that by building on the achievements of Rwanda's Decentralization and Community Development Project, the CT is more likely to be successful (World Bank 2009c). By taking advantage of existing decentralized groups, VUP is also expected to keep administrative costs to about 8 percent (DFID 2009).

Degree of Institutionalization of Programs: Enabling Legislation Can Be a Catalyst

Many programs are only beginning in Sub-Saharan Africa, and the concept of social protection is still gaining traction; thus, legal support for social protection programs is still incipient in many countries. Other countries, however, have legal support that has helped to institutionalize their social protection programs. Unsurprisingly, much of this support is based in upper-middle-income countries. For instance, South Africa provides for social protection in its constitution. Legal protections for its cash grants are afforded through the Aged Persons Act of 1967, the Child Care Act of 1983, and the Social Assistance Act of 2004 (Plaatjies 2006). Similarly, Namibia's Old Age Pension was established by an act in 1928, and in 1992, following independence, it was legally established through the National Pension Act (Levine, van der Berg, and Yu 2009).

Swaziland's Old Age Grant and Public Assistance Grant are provided for in the Swazi bill of rights, which places responsibility on the government to protect the welfare of children, people with disabilities, and the elderly. However, the Public Assistance Grant, which enjoys less political capital than the Old Age Grant, is limited by the funds available to the government, and coverage varies according to annual funding (Dlamini

2007). Therefore, official support for social protection is not always a mandate for action.

Although few countries have legal support for their CTs, some countries support CT programs through national social protection strategies or other frameworks, such as Poverty Reduction Strategy Papers. This support, as well as related national legislation, is encouraged in the African Union's Social Policy Framework, which advises member states to recognize their responsibility in providing social protection by enacting relevant legislation (African Union 2008).

The Rwandan government recognizes the importance of social protection programs and the Direct Support CT, which is part of the Vision 2020 Umurenge Programme, in national poverty reduction. The Rwandan cabinet officially approved VUP, which is a leading program in the government's National Economic Development and Poverty Reduction Strategy for 2008 through 2012 (Republic of Rwanda 2009).

Van Domelen (2010, as cited in World Bank 2011) suggests that over one-third of countries in Sub-Saharan Africa have their own social protection strategies. For example, Senegal's two CTs are supported by the country's National Social Protection Strategy for 2005–15. The strategy emphasizes the need to increase social protection and protect groups and individuals vulnerable to adverse systemic shocks (Basic Training Course 2009).

National social protection strategies can make room for high-level cross-sectoral steering committees and technical committees that can help coordinate social protection programs within a country. Devereux, Ellis, and White (2008) highlight how Malawi and Zambia have each been able to use these strategies and committees to promote coordination of coverage and sharing of information on vulnerable groups within the country. Given the growing role of CTs in many Sub-Saharan African countries, this type of support for programs is expected to increase.

Evidence from Program Evaluations: Filling the Gaps in Knowledge

Several types of evaluations can be used to review program performance, including targeting, process, and impact evaluations. These evaluations are distinct from the monitoring practices already discussed in that they occur less frequently, they involve greater time to complete, and their results feed into major programmatic decisions (Burt and Hatry 2005, as cited in Grosh and others 2008).

Evaluations can go a long way in determining whether programs are worthwhile and how they can be improved. Their importance has been recognized by African leaders as well as by development partners. The African Union's Social Policy Framework recommends that monitoring, evaluation, and impact evaluations of social protection programs be effectively designed and implemented (African Union 2008).

The effectiveness of evaluations should be decided in light of how they measure and inform program objectives. Do the evaluations measure whether CTs are achieving their stated goals, and is this measurement defensible? They also should be judged according to whether they feed into domestic understanding of program dynamics and outcomes, in addition to contributing to the global knowledge base on CTs.

The Role of, and Results from, Targeting Evaluations

Targeting evaluations determine whether CTs are reaching their intended beneficiary population and examine how beneficiaries compare with nonbeneficiaries. Such evaluations assess the extent of errors of inclusion and exclusion, and they determine the share of benefits being transferred to the poor, along with measuring other indicators. Targeting evaluations can be conducted using representative household survey data, sometimes supplemented with additional survey information collected by the CT program itself. These evaluations, similar to process evaluations, require less time and funding than do impact evaluations. More information on how to properly implement targeting evaluations is available from Grosh and others (2008) and Ravallion (2007).

A few studies have analyzed targeting effectiveness in CT programs in Sub-Saharan Africa. Their results are primarily based on data collected from the programs, and many of them simply examine errors of inclusion and exclusion. Therefore, most are not comprehensive targeting evaluations. Nevertheless, they provide useful information on the effectiveness of targeting.

Depending on the program's definition of eligibility, exclusion errors in Malawi's SCT communities ranged from 37 percent to 68 percent. This outcome reflects the size of the budget as well as the quality of targeting. Estimates of the inclusion error ranged from 16 percent to 34 percent, depending on definitions of eligibility (Miller, Tsoka, and Reichert 2008). These numbers are comparable to targeting errors in other similar programs around the world, and they are commendable considering the financial and human constraints the program faces. Nevertheless, improving them is still in the program's interest, given the extent of abject poverty in some excluded households (Miller, Tsoka, and Reichert 2010).

An analysis of targeting in Kenya's CT for OVC revealed that most selected households contained an orphan or vulnerable child (98 percent), and most of these households were poor. However, the extremely poor were underrepresented in the program (Hurrell, Ward, and Merttens 2008).

Using data from 2008, Soares and Teixeira (2010) determined that targeting of Mozambique's PSA was successful at selecting the worst-off households within localities. Soares and Teixeira used a version of the targeting index developed by Coady, Grosh, and Hoddinott (2004a), in which the percentage of the beneficiary population that falls in the bottom quintile of a reference distribution is divided by 20.[8] The index equals 1 for a program that achieves no net redistribution; higher numbers indicate the program is more pro-poor. The index calculated for households treated by the PSA was 2.69. Even when compared only with rural households that were potentially eligible for the PSA, the index for beneficiary households was still 1.88. In comparison, Coady, Grosh, and Hoddinott (2004a) calculated an average index of 1.8 for the CT programs they reviewed.

Despite the PSA's effective targeting within localities, Soares and Teixeira (2010) found that localities treated by the PSA were better off than other areas. Their evaluation highlighted that geographic targeting of localities could be improved. However, this result may partially be driven by nonrandom selection of data on comparison households in localities not treated by the PSA (Soares and Teixeira 2010).

South Africa's grant system has been found to effectively reach a large proportion of households in the poorest quintiles, and the grant income is a primary income source for these households. In 2008, 70 percent of households in South Africa's bottom three quintiles said they received cash grants (Woolard, Harttgen, and Klasen 2010, as cited in European University Institute 2010).

Evaluations of Ethiopia's PSNP, conducted in 2006 and 2008, found that the program correctly placed beneficiaries in the public works and CT components (Devereux and others 2006; Gilligan and others 2009b). In 2006, almost 60 percent of surveyed households that received Direct Support cash transfers were unable to work, and one-quarter were elderly. In general, Direct Support beneficiaries had lower incomes, fewer assets, and less land than the households participating in the public works arm of the PSNP (Devereux and others 2006). In 2008, between 50 percent and 65 percent of households believed the community-level targeting was fair (Gilligan and others 2009b).

Given that these programs also conducted impact evaluations when they analyzed their targeting, a more extensive targeting evaluation was not necessary. Once a CT program has proven its effectiveness through an impact evaluation, there is a role for the type of targeting assessments previously mentioned, which can be used to generate data about the CT's potential impact when a large-scale impact assessment is not possible or necessary (Grosh and others 2008).

Further analysis of the effectiveness of targeting systems of other CT programs in Sub-Saharan Africa will be helpful for understanding the programs' success in reaching their intended beneficiaries and ultimately in improving outcomes.

The Role of Process Evaluations

Process evaluations examine whether the CT is effectively carrying out its duties, and they highlight areas for improvement. The evaluations consist of thorough reviews of program implementation, and they should occur in addition to the regular monitoring that is part of daily job responsibilities. Procedurally, they can involve internal random audits or spot-checks of documentation and activities at various levels; information gathering from beneficiaries and program officials (that is, through interviews or focus groups); and analysis of administrative data.

Process evaluations may also involve external assistance. Regular (financial and process) audits by independent agencies can provide information that helps improve programs, develop program credibility and accountability with the public, and discourage or address fraud or corruption.

Grosh and others (2008) highlight that process evaluations are used to examine implementation problems as they arise, to supplement information obtained from impact evaluations, to inform stakeholders about how the program is operating, and to fill in for inefficient monitoring systems. The last role of process evaluations is the least preferred function.

Areas addressed in CT process evaluations can include (a) timeliness of program inscription; (b) timeliness of financial distributions and associated bottlenecks, both directly for the CT and between agencies involved in the CT; (c) accessibility of transfers to beneficiaries; (d) beneficiaries' and other stakeholders' knowledge of program rules and procedures; (e) presence and performance of equipment and personnel at CT program offices; and (f) receipt of complaints or appeals to determine whether problems have been resolved, uncover recurring problems, and find out whether specific groups are differentially affected by those problems.

Many CT programs in Sub-Saharan Africa have undertaken process evaluations of some sort, whether minor or extensive. Results from these reviews are interspersed throughout this book.

Process evaluations have been essential in helping programs such as Ethiopia's PSNP recognize important bottlenecks and make adjustments to improve the program. Information gathered from the PSNP's process evaluations is determined by a set of objective performance goals. Those goals allow the program to determine how well it is functioning within each locality, generate objectives around which implementers can work, and provide a basis by which progress can be determined (World Bank 2010a).

Although large-scale process evaluations will be helpful for Sub-Saharan Africa's CT programs, ad hoc evaluations of identified bottlenecks can also be undertaken at a relatively low cost with a potentially high return. Of course, process evaluations are useful only to the extent that the data gleaned from them feed into decision making and drive programmatic improvements. Results from process evaluations—and the subsequent steps taken by officials to address identified problems—can also feed into the regional and global knowledge bases on effective implementation of CTs. Sharing of case studies and specific insights gained from process evaluations has been, and is expected to continue to be, useful for CT programs in Sub-Saharan Africa.

Use of Rigorous Impact Evaluations to Inform Program Designs and Accelerate Scaling Up

Impact evaluations attempt to isolate a program's causal effects on outcomes in beneficiary households, thereby quantifying the effects of the CT. Before the relatively recent wave of evaluations of CCT programs, strong program impact evaluations (that is, with a credible counterfactual) were not commonly conducted for safety net programs (Grosh and others 2008). Although the bulk of the evidence about CTs is found outside Sub-Saharan Africa, results from major programs in the region are beginning to fill this gap. This trend will encourage discussions, driven by empirical evidence, of the usefulness of CTs and their impacts on key outcomes.

CCT programming in Latin America has benefited from strong evaluation components included by program designers. The resulting evidence base for the effectiveness of the CTs, as well as insights into design issues, has benefited work on CTs around the world (see box 3.7). Perhaps just as important is how the credibility of findings based on high-quality evaluations has helped to quiet theoretical, ideological, or political critiques of the programs, thereby allowing the programs to stand—and expand—on their own merits. The Latin American experience illustrates that although a strong impact evaluation does not guarantee that a program will gain or maintain political support or funding, it is certainly helpful.

Many evaluations of CT programs in Sub-Saharan Africa have lacked key criteria needed for a causal interpretation. Such evaluations are unable to determine if changes in trends over time are due to the program, time (secular) trends, nonrandom differences between treatment and comparison groups (selection), or a combination of factors. Results must be interpreted in light of such limitations. Fortunately, several ongoing evaluations in Sub-Saharan Africa will be able to assign a causal effect to transfers, allowing for a better understanding of CTs' impacts. An example of a well-designed and well-executed experimental evaluation is provided in box 3.8.

Figure 3.15 provides a graphical representation of the type of evaluations used in reviewed CTs. It highlights how CCTs have been more likely to use experimental evaluations than have UCTs, with almost three in four CCTs using experimental methods and three in four UCTs using nonexperimental methods. More than one in three UCTs have incorporated qualitative components in their evaluations, a slightly higher rate than that found in CCTs. Although the trend of using experimental methods in CCTs and nonexperimental methods in UCTs is interesting, this tendency may simply reflect the simultaneous growth in the use of CCTs and experimental evaluation methods throughout the region. In fact, all known evaluations that were being conducted at the time of writing were experimental.

Another important point is that the total number of programs with information about evaluations was fewer than 40 out of more than 120 possible programs. This limited sample reflects the tendency of many smaller programs to forgo official evaluations—or at least not to provide publicly available information regarding their evaluations that could be used in the review.

Impact evaluations have more value if done right the first time. One rationale for establishing a strong impact evaluation design from the outset is to ensure that when implementation achieves results and

Box 3.7

Results from Evaluations of Conditional Cash Transfer Programs

Although evaluations of Sub-Saharan Africa's CT programs have provided initial information on the programs' effectiveness, the bulk of evidence on CT programs' impacts is found in studies outside of Africa. CCT programs, particularly those in Latin America, are especially well known for their rigorous impact evaluations. A summary of results from some CCT programs is presented here to provide a glimpse of the information gained from their evaluations, which have contributed important insights to the global knowledge base on CCTs.

CCTs, Consumption, and Poverty

Using data from various years from Brazil, Cambodia, Colombia, Ecuador, Honduras, Mexico, and Nicaragua, Fiszbein and Schady (2009) find that these countries' CCT programs increased per capita consumption for the median household by between 7 percent and 29 percent. The programs had varying effects on the poverty headcount, poverty gap, and squared poverty gap. The programs with the largest effects on consumption were associated with decreases in all of these measures.

Consumption has also shifted in favor of improved quality: Colombia's Familias en Acción, Mexico's Oportunidades, and Nicaragua's Red de Protección Social increased the diversity and quality of food eaten in beneficiary households (Attanasio and Mesnard 2006; Hoddinott, Skoufias, and Washburn 2000; Maluccio and Flores 2005).

CCTs, Household Investments, and Labor Supply

Gertler, Martínez, and Rubio-Codina (2006) found that Oportunidades had a significant positive effect on households' investments in agriculture and microenterprises. They suggest that the transfers helped overcome credit constraints and allowed beneficiaries to make higher-risk, higher-reward investments. In contrast, Nicaragua's Red de Protección Social did not have much effect on agricultural investments (Maluccio 2010). However, it helped beneficiaries—especially those hit hardest by the crisis—smooth expenditures during a negative covariate shock, the downturn in coffee prices (Maluccio 2005).

Many CCTs have decreased child labor, although some programs showed no effect (Fiszbein and Schady 2009). For example, beneficiary children in Cambodia's Education Sector Support Project were 10 percentage points less likely to participate in paid work than nonbeneficiaries (Ferreira, Filmer, and Schady 2009).

(continued next page)

Box 3.7 *(continued)*

Most reviewed CCTs have not negatively affected adult labor supply (Fiszbein and Schady 2009).

CCTs and Human Capital Investment

Many CCTs in Latin America and the Caribbean have had positive, significant impacts on school enrollment; most reviewed CCTs in other regions have had similar effects (Fiszbein and Schady 2009). Enrollment impacts of Latin American and Caribbean CCTs reviewed by Fiszbein and Schady ranged from an insignificant 0.6 percent enrollment increase for seventh through ninth graders for Mexico's Oportunidades (contrasted with an 8.7 percent increase for sixth graders) to an overall enrollment increase of 12.8 percent for Nicaragua's Red de Protección Social (Maluccio and Flores 2005; Schultz 2004). Outside of Latin America, Cambodia's Education Sector Support Project was found to increase school enrollment by 21.4 percent and attendance by 25 percent (Ferreira, Filmer, and Schady 2009).

The effect of Latin America's CCTs on the use of health services is more mixed, although some programs still had significant positive results. Oftentimes, impacts have varied by beneficiary characteristics and by outcome. For instance, Colombia's Familias en Acción caused a 33.2 percent increase in attendance to well visits of children ages two to four. However, the program's impact on children four and up was only 1.5 percent and significant at the 10 percent level. Improved compliance with the DPT (diphtheria, pertussis, tetanus) vaccination protocol was only marginally significant for children under two years old, and it was insignificant for older children (Attanasio and others 2005).

CCTs and Health and Cognitive Outcomes

Many CCT programs have improved intermediate outcomes in health and education; effects on final outcomes are not as clear cut. Despite some of these mixed results, major health improvements have been attributed to some CCTs. For instance, Nicaragua's Red de Protección Social decreased stunting in children under age five by five percentage points within the first two years of the program (IFPRI 2005). Improvements in cognitive skills among young children have also been attributed to CCTs. After nine months participating in another Nicaraguan CCT program known as Atención a Crisis, young children had significantly higher language proficiency and personal and behavioral skills (Macours, Schady, and Vakis 2008). Impacts in these areas suggest CCTs have the potential to protect children from irreversible underinvestments with major long-term implications.

Taken together, results suggest that CCTs can improve important indicators in development and human capital.

Box 3.8

Results from a Cash Transfer Program Evaluation

The impact evaluation of a small CT in Malawi's Zomba district illustrates the power of an experimental design to determine a CT's effects, as well as to parse out nuances of impacts relevant for program design. The Zomba CT, which was designed explicitly for research purposes, tested the impact of conditional and unconditional transfers on educational, marriage, and fertility outcomes for female adolescents.

Schooling Impacts of the CCT and UCT Arms

Results two years into the program showed that the conditionality in the transfers was driving key educational outcomes. Although enrollment improved in both the UCT and CCT beneficiary groups, the improvement for the UCT was less than half (43 percent) of the improvement of the CCT group. School attendance also improved in the CCT arm over that in the UCT and control arms (see box figure 3.8.A and Baird, McIntosh, and Özler 2010).

Notably, the enrollment effects examined in the two-year evaluation were based on schools' reports of girls' enrollments. When the girls themselves reported their enrollment, the UCT arm appeared to be more successful in increasing school enrollment than the CCT arm. This difference suggests that external verification of data that may be subject to bias may be a worthwhile use of funds in impact evaluations.

Furthermore, the study found that the CCT raised enrollment more cost-effectively than the UCT could. The CCT could use smaller transfer sizes to achieve the same impacts that could be achieved through a larger UCT. It also saved money by not paying transfers when girls did not comply with conditions. These factors provided cost savings in the CCT that more than covered the additional costs involved in implementing a conditional program (Baird, McIntosh, and Özler 2011).

The two-year results also revealed that the CCT improved learning outcomes (see box figure 3.8.B). The UCT was not found to improve these scores.

Impacts on Pregnancy and Marriage

Finally, after two years, the evaluation found that the CCT was not effective in preventing teen pregnancy and marriage. The UCT arm, however, was able to significantly decrease the probability that girls would become pregnant or get married (see box figure 3.8.C). This result was primarily due to the UCT's effect on

(continued next page)

Box 3.8 *(continued)*

Box Figure 3.8.A   Schooling Results from Zomba CT

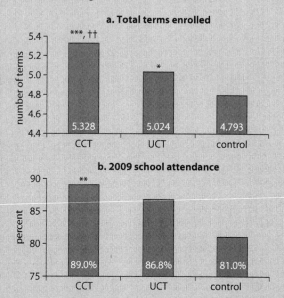

Sources: For panel a, Baird, McIntosh, and Özler 2010, table III; for panel b, Baird, Chirwa, and others 2010, table V.
Note: Sample size in panel a is 852. In panel a, the dependent variable equals the total number of school terms (out of six possible) in which the beneficiary was enrolled during the program. Sample size in panel b is 319. In panel b, the sample is composed of all respondents with attendance information for at least one of the three school terms. Overall attendance is determined by dividing number of days attended out of number of possible term days for terms with available data. For both graphs, results are from ordinary least squares regressions run with robust standard errors clustered at the local (enumeration area) level. Controls included are age dummies, strata dummies, a household asset index, highest grade attended, and a dummy for never had sex, all at the baseline. Regressions are weighted to be representative from the enumeration area target populations.
*** indicates that the result is statistically different from that of the control group at the 99 percent level; ** indicates that the result is statistically different from that of the control group at the 95 percent level; * indicates that the result is statistically different from the control group at the 90 percent level; †† indicates that the CCT result is statistically different from the UCT result at the 95 percent level.

adolescent girls who dropped out of school after the program began. No effects of the UCT or CCT were found on girls who remained students (Baird, McIntosh, and Özler 2011).

Given that school abandonment is associated with early marriage and pregnancy in this setting, those girls who remained in school were less likely to marry

(continued next page)

Box 3.8 *(continued)*

Box Figure 3.8.B   Educational Achievement Results from Zomba CT

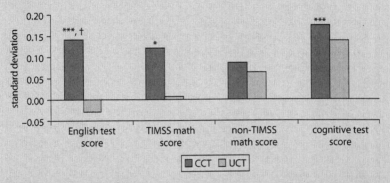

Source: Baird, McIntosh, and Özler 2010, table XI.
Note: Sample size is 2,057. Test scores are standardized with a mean equal to zero and standard deviation of one in the control group. Math and English tests were created on the basis of Malawi school curriculum. The TIMSS score is based on five questions from the 2007 Trends in International Mathematics and Science Study (TIMSS). Ordinary least squares regressions controlled for baseline values of age dummies, strata dummies, a household asset index, highest grade attended, a dummy for ever had sex, and a dummy for whether respondent participated in development of tests in pilot. Regressions used robust standard errors clustered at the local (enumeration area) level and were weighted to be representative of the target population in the enumeration areas.
*** indicates that the result is statistically different from that of the control group at the 99 percent level; * indicates that the result is statistically significant at the 90 percent level; † indicates that the CCT result is statistically different from the UCT result at the 90 percent level.

or become pregnant regardless of what type of transfer they received. Therefore, CCTs did not have an additional impact on marriage and pregnancy outcomes for girls who would have remained in school even if they received only UCTs. Obviously, CCTs also did not affect marriage and pregnancy rates for girls who dropped out of school and forfeited the transfers. Therefore, CCTs reduced marriage and pregnancy only by keeping girls from dropping out of school, something that they did accomplish. The large differential effect of UCTs was driven by the income effect of the transfers and the large number of girls who were not affected by CCTs (that is, those girls who would abandon school regardless of the type of transfer they received). These indicators would have been still lower had the girls remained in school, but the UCT impact was still large (Baird, McIntosh, and Özler 2011).

This outcome highlights a trade-off inherent in CCT and UCT programs. The CCT program was able to encourage human capital formation among girls who

(continued next page)

Box 3.8 *(continued)*

Box Figure 3.8.C   Marriage and Pregnancy Outcomes from Zomba CT

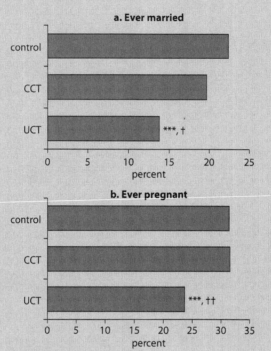

Source: Baird, McIntosh, and Özler 2010, table VII.
Notes: Sample size of unique observations was 2,089. Figure shows the results from individual fixed-effects regressions using robust standard errors clustered at the local (enumeration area) level and weighted to represent the target population in relevant enumeration areas.
*** indicates that the result is significantly different from that of the control group at the 99 percent level; † indicates that the UCT arm differs from the CCT arm at the 90 percent confidence level; †† indicates that the CCT and UCT arms are significantly different at the 95 percent level.

complied with its requirements, but it kept transfers from girls who were more vulnerable to adolescent pregnancy and early marriage (that is, CCT noncompliers). The CCT was also able to keep girls from dropping out of school and reduced marriage through this channel, but the overall income effect of the UCT on girls' marriage was larger, given the large group of noncompliers. As Baird, McIntosh, and Özler (2011, 35) conclude, their study "makes clear that while CCT programs may be more effective than UCTs in obtaining the desired behavior change, they can also undermine the social protection dimension of cash transfer programs."

Figure 3.15 Evaluations Used in CT Programs in Africa

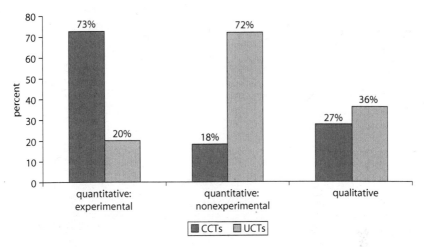

Source: Authors' representation.
Note: Sample size is 11 for CCTs and 25 for UCTs. Analysis is limited to programs for which information is clearly provided on the type of evaluation used by a program. Totals for each type of program exceed 100 percent because multiple evaluation types were used in some programs.

resolves contentious issues, the credibility of the evaluation will lay those issues fully to rest. Otherwise, arguments may continue, giving rise to pressures and compromises in the form of further piloting and a new evaluation. Zambia's original pilot evaluation for the Kalomo SCT faced such problems. The evaluation design was not defensible to critiques; therefore, its conclusions could not serve as a basis for national policy changes and program expansion. Instead, new pilots were undertaken, expansion has been slow, and a more rigorous impact evaluation is only now being completed.

A particular challenge to ensuring that a defensible evaluation is conducted arises for programs implemented in geographic areas served by multiple partners and development programs. When governments or other organizations introduce new programs or variations across evaluation control and treatment localities, direct program impacts become more difficult to ascertain, although econometric techniques can control for some of those issues. Such issues have already been encountered in some Sub-Saharan African programs, and policy makers should be aware of the potential complications that can arise when implementing impact evaluations.

The demands that evaluations may place on program officials also need to be kept in mind. Designing and successfully executing an impact evaluation requires significant financial and staff resources, including time. Such demands can be especially daunting at the outset of the CT program, when it is being designed and when baseline data must be collected. Important decisions have to be made that will have significant consequences for impact evaluations, including whether using a phased program rollout is more appropriate than another method, who will conduct the evaluation, and how the evaluation will affect the job responsibilities of program officials.

When evaluations will place significant additional burdens on certain officials or groups, extra support should be provided for these entities. In externally funded programs, partners that are financing evaluations should be sensitive to the additional burdens that evaluations will place on the program's staff, and they should ensure that adequate support is available for officials. For example, the evaluation of Zambia's Monze SCT was plagued by unrealistic expectations of program officials, which affected both the implementation and evaluation of the CT (Schüring 2010b). Evaluation designs also need to allow for the inevitable delays and personnel, budget, capacity, and time constraints present in any program, particularly as the program begins. Designs should be pragmatic rather than idealistic.

Given the strategic decisions that must be made related to impact evaluations and the multiple groups invested in an evaluation's success, reaching a consensus is important regarding what should be measured, how the evaluation should be conducted, and what the timing should be. Both domestic officials and donors must support these decisions. When donors are driven by short-term financing deadlines, project officials may be pressured to roll out the CT program at a pace that is difficult, given capacity constraints, but necessary because of the timing of follow-up surveys. This dynamic can generate tension, although it may also serve as an impetus to maintain program timelines, which have ideally been agreed to by all involved groups.

One concern sometimes expressed about impact evaluations is their cost. However, evaluation designs can be rigorous without being excessively complex and costly. Over the long run, the costs of implementing a good impact evaluation often prove to be lower than the costs of not doing so. Such costs do not always have to be borne by the project or government. Development partners will often fund evaluations, viewing the knowledge to be gained as useful not only in terms of the

Interpretation of Results from Africa's CT Evaluations: Important Caveats

One must keep several caveats in mind when reviewing the evidence of impacts of CT programs.[9] First, a common observation is that results are more likely to be published when significant program impacts are found, particularly if the results are positive. CTs that do not have significant impacts on key indicators, or that have outcomes that are negative or insignificant, may tend to be glossed over. Therefore, even an attempt to provide a neutral evaluation of programs may slant in favor of programs whose results are reported in published papers and gray literature.

Another consideration when determining the value of a CT program is the opportunity cost of implementing a CT rather than another intervention. Is a CT the most cost-effective means of achieving specific objectives (such as poverty reduction), or would another intervention, such as school feeding, public works, investment in education or health services, or infrastructure, achieve those goals more effectively? That question is even more pressing, given the extent and depth of poverty in many Sub-Saharan African countries, combined with the region's significant fiscal limitations. Evaluations of CT programs should also consider that such programs may create long-term commitments to deliver transfers that are politically difficult to discontinue. Therefore, opportunity costs of CTs should be considered in light of both the present and expected future demand on resources.[10] This issue is not easily answered by traditional impact evaluations.

Similarly, some results from CTs may develop only over a longer time frame than that used in a typical impact evaluation; immediate or medium-term effects will not give the entire story. For instance, CTs may immediately decrease food insecurity and, as a result, also decrease malnutrition in children. However, the long-term effect of the decreased malnutrition may result in improved cognitive outcomes and performance in school and, later, increased productivity and lifetime earnings. Isolating the long-term effects of the CT may be difficult.

Likewise, CTs may have direct or indirect effects on labor supply and demand, migration and remittances, and income inequality, in both the short run and the long run. Another factor to consider is whether consistent receipt of CTs raises households' tolerance for risky investments that have higher expected returns, thus encouraging them to increase or diversify their investments and break out of low-productivity traps. Impact evaluations can answer how CTs directly affect such issues through the duration of the evaluation; however, long-term general equilibrium effects are more difficult to measure and should not be overlooked.

Concerns about the causal pathways and complementary effects of CTs present additional challenges when comparing long-term returns of a CT program and those generated by other programs. Although there is no easy solution to these issues, it is important to be aware of the multiple and often delayed effects of the programs being evaluated.

Evaluations also can determine how programs vary with beneficiary characteristics. Examining heterogeneity of impacts allows program officials to understand how the CT affects specific groups of beneficiaries and how various groups in the population might be affected if the program is expanded.

Finally, even evaluations of CTs in Sub-Saharan Africa that have not been able to isolate the CTs' causal impacts are useful in their own right. They evaluate preprogram characteristics of selected beneficiaries, thereby providing information on the quality of targeting. Such evaluations also reveal what beneficiaries report they purchased with their cash, how beneficiaries thought the programs helped them, or how they felt about receiving CTs in lieu of in-kind transfers or vouchers.

Results from Evaluations of Cash Transfer Programs in Sub-Saharan Africa

Evidence on the usefulness of CTs in Sub-Saharan Africa is clear from program evaluations and peer-reviewed literature examining program outcomes. Those results are presented here in alphabetical order, by country, because evaluation methods are often very different across programs.[11]

Davies and Davey (2008) found a multiplier of between 2.02 and 2.45 for Malawi's emergency CT program known as DECT. This result means that more than US$2 in income was generated by each US$1 transferred by the program. The multiplier effects occurred as beneficiaries stimulated the local economy by spending their transfers.

The evaluation of Malawi's SCT pilot found that after receiving transfers for six months, children and adults in beneficiary households experienced improved health, and children's self-reported school attendance and capacity to study increased. Results from the pilot showed that beneficiaries' food consumption and diversity improved over that of the comparison group. Children in beneficiary households were significantly less likely to work than those in nonbeneficiary comparison households, and household asset ownership increased as a result of the program. Results were large and often statistically significant, although differences across the treatment and comparison groups were not controlled for. Qualitative evidence from focus groups and in-depth interviews corroborated the quantitative findings (Miller, Tsoka, and Mchinji Evaluation Team 2007).

The experimental evaluation of the Zomba CT in Malawi found that CCTs improved enrollment, attendance, and test scores of adolescent girls, whereas UCTs did not have this effect on beneficiaries. However, the UCT showed better results in decreasing teen pregnancy and early marriage. The evaluation also determined that small transfers had an impact comparable to that of larger transfers in all CCT outcomes, whereas some UCT outcomes improved with increased transfer sizes. Providing a larger portion of transfers to the girls instead of parents did not improve the program outcomes (Baird, McIntosh, and Özler 2011). There was also evidence that the cash transfers were able to reduce the HIV and HSV-2 (herpes simplex virus type 2) infection rates of girls. This result appeared to be driven by the income effect of the transfers. Girls who received the transfers had less sex, and they tended to choose safer (younger) partners (World Bank 2010b).

Using propensity score matching and difference-in-difference regressions, Soares and Teixeira (2010) used data from 2008 and 2009 and found that Mozambique's PSA increased the proportion of households' expenditures on food by 22 percent. The positive impacts on food share were even larger in female-headed households. The PSA increased the likelihood that women ate additional meals daily, and marginally increased this likelihood for boys ages five to nine. Household adults increased their probability of working (by 17 percent for male adults and the elderly and 24 percent for adult women, although the increase was only marginally significant), whereas boys between five and nine were 29 percent less likely to work. Household adult hours spent in the households' own fields decreased, indicating additional labor time was being spent outside the household. One indicator showed that children's acute malnutrition decreased by 30 percent, but the study concluded that this result may have been an anomaly, given no other results supporting such strong nutritional outcomes.

Examining Namibia's grant system, Levine, van der Berg, and Yu (2009) used simulations and household survey data to determine what effects the transfers may have had on poverty and inequality in Namibia. They concluded that the transfers have significantly decreased the number of poor people, with an even stronger decrease in the number of extremely poor individuals.

A study taking advantage of variation in the rollout of the South African Child Support Grant found that exposure to the grant improved children's nutritional outcomes. The study used matching methods and regressions to determine that children who received the grant until they were three years old had greater height-for-age ratios than nonbeneficiaries. Rough calculations suggested that the rate of return to the grant ranged from 160 percent to 230 percent (Agüero, Carter, and Woolard 2007). Another study found that South Africa's Child Support Grant increased school attendance and decreased hunger in children, while it increased maternal labor force participation (Williams 2007).

South Africa's Old Age Pension is probably the most frequently studied CT program in Sub-Saharan Africa. Although the results described in these studies are not based on a specifically initiated impact evaluation, the studies used various methods to try to isolate the program's impacts on the relevant outcomes.

Case and Deaton (1998) determined that when the Old Age Pension was transferred to women, the cash had a higher likelihood of being spent in areas such as food purchases and payment of school fees, which benefited children. Duflo (2000) found that female pension receipt was associated with increases in girls' nutritional outcomes, but not boys'. Receipt by males was not associated with improvements for children of either gender. Edmonds (2006) found pension eligibility of a male in South African households was associated with increased school attendance and decreased market labor among children over age five. Impacts of the pension in households with orphans were mixed (Case and Ardington 2006).

Edmonds, Mammen, and Miller (2005) found that when South African households had a member reach pension eligibility, household composition changed, notably to add children under five years old and young women of childbearing age, while older working-age women departed. Case (2001) found that when pension income was pooled within households, health was preserved among all members, purportedly through the pension income's ability to protect members' nutrition, improve household living conditions, and decrease adult members' stress. When pension income was not pooled, the positive health changes were associated only with the health of the recipient.

Analyses of the effect of the Old Age Pension on labor supply show mixed results, with some researchers finding that pension receipt is associated with lower labor supply in certain household adults (Bertrand, Mullainathan, and Miller 2003) and others finding pensions associated with increased adult labor supply, often through migration (Ardington, Case, and Hosegood 2009; Posel, Fairburn, and Lund 2006). Jensen (2004) found that the Old Age Pension reduced private transfers made to beneficiary households by children no longer living in the household. He found no effect of the pension on labor supply, household composition, and migration.

Other evaluations of the South African Child Support Grant and Old Age Pension suggest the programs have jointly reduced the incidence of poverty by 6 percentage points, with an even greater influence on the poverty gap (European University Institute 2010). Woolard and Leibbrandt (2010) also present evidence suggesting that the South African grants have a poverty-decreasing effect.

Using data from beneficiary households only, Devereux and Jere (2008) determined that households that received cash in Swaziland's Emergency Drought Response program were better able to smooth consumption and continue investing in important activities, such as education, in spite of the drought.

Tanzania's RESPECT (Rewarding STI Prevention and Control in Tanzania) CCT, which conditions payments on the absence of curable STIs, used an experimental evaluation. After one year of implementation, the treatment group receiving the larger of two transfer sizes (US$20 three times for one year) showed a 25 percent reduction in STI prevalence. No significant impact was found among those receiving the smaller transfers (de Walque and others 2010b; see also figure 3.16). This result is important because it points to the potential for CCTs to be used to slow the spread of HIV/AIDS.

In reviewing the transfers distributed in Zambia's Kalomo SCT pilot from early 2004 through the middle of 2005, Tandeo (2005) found that a significant portion of transfers were used on food (35 percent) and livestock (22 percent). A later evaluation found that over two-thirds of transfers were spent on consumption, one-fourth were put into investment,[12] and 7 percent were put into savings (Ministry of Community Development and Social Services and German Agency for Technical Cooperation 2007). Using propensity score matching and odds-weighted regressions, an evaluation of CTs in three districts in Zambia later found positive impacts of transfers on consumption, particularly nonfood consumption. The greatest effects were seen in areas with the highest vulnerability (RHVP 2009).

Figure 3.16 Impact of Tanzania's RESPECT CCT on Prevalence of Curable STIs

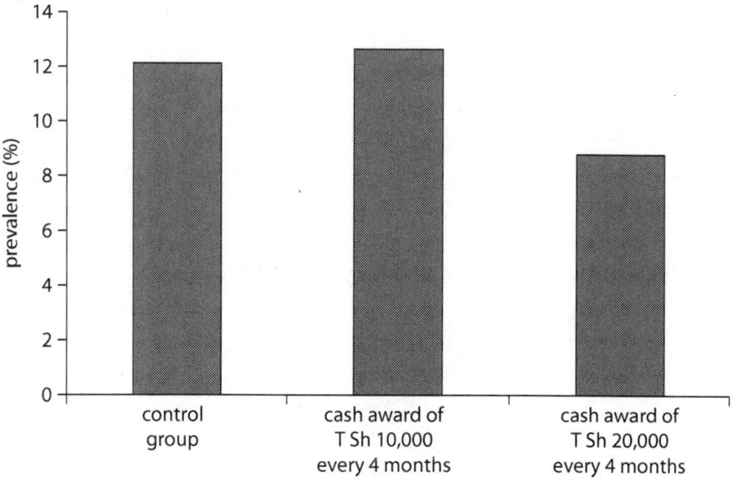

[Bar chart showing prevalence (%) on y-axis from 0 to 14. Control group: ~12%; cash award of T Sh 10,000 every 4 months: ~12.5%; cash award of T Sh 20,000 every 4 months: ~8.5%]

Source: de Walque and others 2010a.
Note: Figure shows prevalence at round 4 for combined conditioned STIs (chlamydia, gonorrhea, trichomonas, and mycoplasma genitalium).

Although these results are primarily from quantitative evaluations, results from qualitative research are also useful and should be used to drive programmatic improvements. Qualitative research of Africa's CT programs corroborates the information about households' use of transfers. Vincent and Cull (2009) assimilate evidence from evaluations of 20 CT programs in Southern Africa. In general, qualitative evidence from these reviews suggests that CTs increase the social status and self-esteem of beneficiaries, thereby increasing their independence and respect within the community.

A synopsis of additional impact evaluations that are planned, along with the outcomes that will be measured and the expected date that results will be available, is found in table 3.1.

Key Knowledge Gaps Regarding the Relative Influences of CT Components

Fiszbein and Schady (2009) discuss the knowledge gained from impact evaluations of CCTs throughout the world. They highlight that a major question not fully addressed in evaluations to date is the extent to which various components of CCTs influence their impacts. For instance, to what extent do CCTs have a positive effect on school enrollment because they transfer cash, impose conditions, use social marketing campaigns, or

Table 3.1 Experimental Impact Evaluations Planned in Selected Cash Transfer Programs

Program name	Date results expected	Key information from evaluation
Burkina Faso CCT-CT	2010	Impact of CCTs versus UCTs and payments to mothers versus fathers on education, health, and consumption outcomes
Eritrea RBF	Mid-term: 2010; final results: 2012	Impact of CCTs awarded as health conditions are fulfilled; effect of supply-side health transfers (pay for performance)
Kenya CT for OVC	2010	Impact of CCTs versus UCTs
Kenya HSNP	First results in 2010; additional results later	Impact of UCTs targeting various groups in extremely remote areas
Nigeria Kano CCT for Girls' Education	Late 2012	Impact of soft versus hard conditions; different transfer sizes; centralized versus decentralized monitoring; various communication strategies, including mobile phone technology
Rwanda VUP	2010	Impact of UCTs in a larger social protection program, which includes support for insertion into financial system and labor market when possible
Senegal CF-SCT	2011	Impact of UCTs on consumption, nutrition, and health outcomes in the presence of a successful community nutrition program
Tanzania CB-CCT	2010/11	Impact of CCT supported by communities trained in community-driven development that functions within a social fund
Tanzania RESPECT	2010/11	Impact of CCT conditioned on beneficiary's remaining free of curable STIs on STI and HIV status; initial results already available and additional results expected
Zambia Monze SCT	2010/11	Impact of UCTs on household outcomes

Source: Authors' compilation.
Note: Other programs for which experimental impact evaluations were expected to take place include Ghana's LEAP, Lesotho's CGP, and Senegal's CCT for OVC. Whether these evaluations were conducted, however, is unclear.

transfer cash to a specific household member? Only limited evidence is available on income versus substitution effects in CCTs. With UCTs, the need remains to distinguish among an income effect, impacts driven by the recipient of the cash, and the effect of social marketing.

Some CT programs in Sub-Saharan Africa are currently addressing those design questions and more, and programs in other regions also promise to inform CT design in Sub-Saharan Africa. Experiments testing whether mothers or fathers should receive CTs are being tested in Morocco's Tayssir and the Republic of Yemen's Basic Education Development Project, and Morocco is testing the value of a UCT versus a CCT (Fiszbein and Schady 2009). Monitoring intensity is also being tested in Tayssir. In that program, some schools in the education-focused CCT are lightly monitored on the basis of teachers' records of students' attendance. In another arm, schools are under a stricter monitoring protocol in which teachers report attendance but may be audited and face sanctions if they are found to misreport. A final arm of the experiment uses strict monitoring employing digital fingerprint-recognition clocks to check students' attendance (World Bank n.d.b). The above programs, among others, promise to inform CT design in Sub-Saharan Africa.

Piloting of Cash Transfers before Expansion

The very word *pilot* developed a bad reputation in many African countries as a reaction to failures of large numbers of so-called pilot programs that had been financed with fanfare by development donors in the early decades of development assistance. Such experiences notwithstanding, innovations such as CTs stand a much better chance of succeeding on a large scale if they are first tested on a small scale.

Pilot Programs Can Address Both Political and Technical Issues

Most CTs have begun with small-scale pilot programs and even occasional prepilots that test how proposed program components work in a given setting. The potential for pilots to inform later program design, as well as to generate policy support for CTs, should not be underestimated. Occasionally, sudden interest and increased political support lead to a push to expand a pilot even before an evaluation is complete (Kenya's CT for OVC) or even faster than originally planned (Rwanda's VUP). More often than not, however, results from the pilot play a major role in convincing domestic constituencies of the program's merit or lack thereof.

A crucial requirement is that pilots be designed and implemented in such a way as to achieve domestic support, provided that the program proves its merit. One way to gather necessary government support is to engage early on with the key policy and institutional stakeholders whose support will be essential to the CT's ultimate scaling up and to give them roles in the pilot that will translate into a sense of co-ownership of successes.

In Kenya, a technical working group was created to oversee the expansion of the pilot for the CT for OVC. It was charged with determining whether the program should be scaled up and, if it were expanded, what changes should be made to it (Ayala Consulting 2007). This type of group may be useful in other settings.

Pilots should test components that will be feasible as the program scales up. One approach, espoused by Senegal's CF-SCT, is as follows: start simply, build on successes, and add complexity to the design only where necessary and appropriate (World Bank 2009a). This approach allows personnel to focus their efforts on getting the basics right first, rather than diffusing energies trying to immediately implement a complicated design. The approach is particularly important for pilots that are being used to generate domestic support for a CT.

Pilots can also be used to test specific design features. In this case, the pilots have specific research objectives that will help determine the future format of the CT. Nigeria's Kano CCT for Girls' Education will test the usefulness of various technologies, distribution mechanisms, and organizational arrangements to determine how best to scale up the program. More specifically, the pilot is testing whether payments should come from a centralized system that is based on a frequently reconciled MIS or from a decentralized mechanism. The decentralized version relies on MIS data from the beginning of the school year, and school committees monitor beneficiaries without the help of the MIS throughout the year (Bouchet 2009).

Similarly, Kenya's HSNP is testing various features in its pilot phase to determine the most cost-effective and politically feasible way forward. The variations in the program are substantial. In some areas, a universal pension using categorical targeting will be given; in others, community targeting will be used to identify eligible households; in a final area, households will be targeted on the basis of their dependency ratio (HSNP n.d.). Three different NGOs will carry out the different types of targeting.

Pilot Designs: Establishing Basic Systems and Considering Strategic Issues That Aid Future Scale-Up

Certain management and design principles can increase the likelihood that pilots will succeed and eventually go to scale. The principles include (a) ensuring that pilot staff members have a relatively high capacity and the ability to pass their knowledge along to other staff members through training and example; (b) working to establish strong basic targeting, payment distribution, and monitoring systems before scale-up; (c) addressing supply-side constraints; and (d) implementing an effective evaluation design.

Other factors have been important for the success of pilots in the region. For instance, often the pilot's location is strategic. Kenya's CT for OVC originally began operating in the districts of Nairobi, Kwale, and Garissa because they were areas where UNICEF (United Nations Children's Fund) and Sida (Swedish International Development Cooperation Authority), which ran the pilot, already had ground-level knowledge and experience (World Bank 2009d). Mchinji was chosen as the district for Malawi's SCT pilot, in part because of its average poverty levels and its location, which is relatively close to the capital of Lilongwe (Schubert and Huijbregts 2006). Those features made implementation easier by facilitating access to program communities. It also made the pilot roughly representative of the conditions present in other parts of the country in terms of poverty levels. Therefore, an expanded CT program could reasonably be expected to have effects similar to those of the pilot.

Lesotho's CGP pilot selected three strategic locations to enter. Matelile in Mafeteng district, known as a soft area, is easily accessible and has most public social services available. The Semonkong in Maseru district is semi-urban, with challenging accessibility and limited availability of social services. Finally, the Lebakeng in Qacha's Nek district is very remote and difficult to access, with extremely limited availability of social services ("Q&A" 2008). Each of these locations will provide different lessons on how to reach children, given the various constraints. The idea behind Zambia's pilots in five districts is similar.

Another reason that Malawi's pilot began in Mchinji district was because of the strength of Mchinji's district assembly (Schubert and Huijbregts 2006). Officials wanted to learn whether district assemblies could implement CTs that were both cost-effective and able to reach targeted groups. Although not inappropriate, such an approach must recognize that other district assemblies may need additional capacity building before they are able to implement a CT at the level executed by the pilot district team. It also should recognize that results in the pilot district might be better than should be expected at the national level. To address those issues, Malawi's program will work to ensure that knowledge is shared between more and less experienced districts. That effort will both improve capacity and allow for more uniform program implementation.

Variations in Length of Pilot Depending on Program Context

No set amount of time is required for a pilot to proceed before it scales up. Programs that have already begun the scale-up process have taken anywhere from virtually no time as a pilot (Ethiopia's PSNP) to three years of piloting (Kenya's CT for OVC). Kenya's HSNP pilot will last for four years and reach 60,000 households; the scale-up will eventually reach a total of 300,000 households over six years (HSNP n.d.). Lesotho's CGP plans to pilot for only one year; it will then scale up to reach a total of 60,000 children within two additional years (PlusNews 2009).

Often programs attempt to conduct a self-contained pilot and expand once an evaluation has been completed. Others plan to do this but, in light of government enthusiasm for the program, begin expansion before the expected time (Kenya's CT for OVC and Rwanda's VUP). Others, such as Ghana's LEAP, take a gradual approach to incorporate a growing number of beneficiaries, aiming to reach full coverage by the end of the (somewhat misnamed) pilot.

In Sub-Saharan Africa, the tendency is for pilots to continue without evolving into larger programs as quickly as planned. Malawi and Zambia, for example, spent several years using their pilots to increase local ownership and ease concerns related to CT schemes. Before rolling out large-scale CT programs, the countries had to deal with issues not yet confronted in previous social assistance schemes and had to overcome reservations about transferring cash to the poor. This scenario is not necessarily problematic as long as stakeholders work to encourage acceptance of properly functioning programs over the long run.[13]

Expansion may also continue after a CT has reached national coverage. For example, South Africa has periodically increased the age limit for its Child Support Grant, allowing for continued gradual expansion to additional children. Obviously, expansion decisions will reflect the population's needs and fiscal space.

Some CT Programs Have Not Been Launched Using a Pilot

Notwithstanding the contributions of pilot programs, Ethiopia's PSNP stands out as a major example of a CT program in Sub-Saharan Africa for which no pilot was conducted. Previous CT programs in Ethiopia had provided the evidence necessary to assure stakeholders of the viability of such a program. The government of Ethiopia believed that the program could build on the prior experience of implementers in food distribution and other areas relevant to the PSNP. The PSNP effectively launched a simple version of the program at scale, all while under pressure to deliver in a low-capacity, high-risk environment. That large initial investment in the PSNP helped win political backing and created shared interest in its success, which were crucial, given the risks associated with launching in a time of extreme food insecurity (World Bank 2010a). Although the PSNP was able to successfully launch without a pilot, other countries interested in doing the same should not take the decision lightly.

Program Cost

An ever-present concern in designing and implementing CTs is how much the program will cost. Much of the difference in long-term cost depends on the number of beneficiaries reached by the program, the size of the transfers, and the labor intensity of administrative procedures. CCTs require additional outlay to monitor conditions. Programs with efficient MISs and targeting systems require a larger up-front investment, but they present benefits in terms of program efficiency and ability to scale up. Fortunately, small pilots may be tested to discern cost-efficiency of certain design features.[14]

Program costs are difficult to determine overall. They include the cost of targeting, transfers, transfer delivery, and monitoring, as well as costs to beneficiaries to fulfill conditions or otherwise participate in the program (Coady, Pérez, and Vera-Ilamas 2000). Start-up costs require significant initial investments, and they increase administrative costs at the outset. Those administrative costs should decrease over time, given economies of scale and the decline in required up-front investments. Their composition will also change. For example, the proportions of first-year administrative costs of Mexico's CCT Progresa[15] were 65 percent on targeting, 8 percent on monitoring of conditions, and 8 percent on delivery of transfers. Three years later, 11 percent of administrative costs were spent on targeting, 24 percent on monitoring conditions, and 41 percent on delivery of transfers (Coady, Pérez, and Vera-Ilamas 2000).

Costs of Cash Transfers in Sub-Saharan Africa: Results from Projections

Various researchers and organizations have attempted to simulate how much CT programs in Africa will cost. The International Labour Organization calculated that a universal basic child benefit would cost between 1.5 percent and 3.1 percent of GDP and a universal elderly pension would cost between 0.6 percent and 1.1 percent of GDP for a sample of Sub-Saharan African countries in 2010 (ILO 2008a).

That being said, dedicating a certain percentage of GDP to a CT program will achieve very different results, depending on the country. Stewart and Handa (2008) concluded that dedicating 0.5 percent of GDP would not cover a transfer to orphans in the poorest three deciles for Malawi, Mozambique, and Uganda, but it would cost only a little over half of the allocated budget to do so in Zambia. However, all four countries mentioned could afford transfers for labor-constrained households in the three lowest consumption deciles using this budget. (These estimates include the cost of the transfers alone.)

In a sample of West African countries,[16] Handley (2009) compiled simulated costs of a universal child transfer, a targeted child transfer, and a universal social pension. The child transfers were valued at 30 percent of the extreme food poverty line and were expected to cover children up to age 14, whereas the social pension was valued at 70 percent of the extreme poverty line. Administrative costs were estimated at 10 percent of the transfer value for the universal transfers and at 15 percent for the targeted transfers. Universal child transfers were expected to cost between 0.9 percent of GDP (in Equatorial Guinea) and 8.7 percent of GDP (in Ghana). Targeted child transfers would cost between 1.2 percent and 3.7 percent of GDP for three simulated countries, and social pensions would cost between 0.2 percent and 2.6 percent of GDP for three simulated countries.

Although analyzing the assumptions in each simulation is important, the above estimates give an idea of the varied costs estimated for potential CTs in Sub-Saharan Africa. Calculations also highlight the importance of using analytical work in determining the feasibility of CTs directed to different target populations.

Program Cost in Relation to GDP and Government Expenditures

The cost of CT programs varies widely throughout Sub-Saharan Africa. Obviously, national systems that include a wide range of cash grants for many vulnerable groups, such as those in upper-middle-income countries, are among the most expensive programs.

Botswana's pension was estimated to cost 0.4 percent of GDP annually (Samson and Kaniki 2008). Namibia's social pension was estimated to cost 1.36 percent of GDP for 2009/10,[17] and the total transfer system was estimated to cost 2 percent of the country's GDP and 6 percent of its budget (Levine, van der Berg, and Yu 2009). For 2007/08, the South African grant system cost 3.2 percent of GDP (Streak 2007). In Lesotho, a lower-middle-income country, the Old Age Pension is funded entirely through tax revenues and costs approximately 1.4 percent of

Figure 3.17 Annual Costs of CT Programs
US$ million

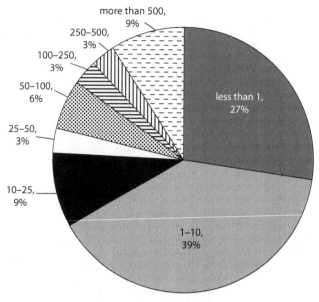

Source: Authors' representation.
Note: Sample size is 33. Analysis is limited to those programs for which specific annual cost data were available.

the country's GDP (Samson 2007). Estimated costs of reviewed CT programs are found in figure 3.17.

Given the multitude of smaller programs revealed in the review, it is not surprising that two out of three programs with available cost information had annual expenses of US$10 million or less. CT program costs are expected to increase as programs increasingly are seated in government departments and are part of a larger social protection strategy that reaches larger numbers of beneficiaries.

In the case of existing CT programs, costs are expected to reach the following amounts:

- 0.1 to 0.2 percent of government expenses for Ghana's LEAP program (IPC-IG 2008b)
- US$55 million, or 1.4 percent of GDP, annually for Malawi's SCT to reach 273,000 households (Schubert 2009)
- US$32 million to US$35 million, or 0.07 percent of nominal GDP (0.28 percent of government expenditures), for Kenya's CT for OVC to reach 100,000 households (World Bank 2009d)

Figure 3.18 Comparison of CT Cost and GNI per Capita for Programs around the World

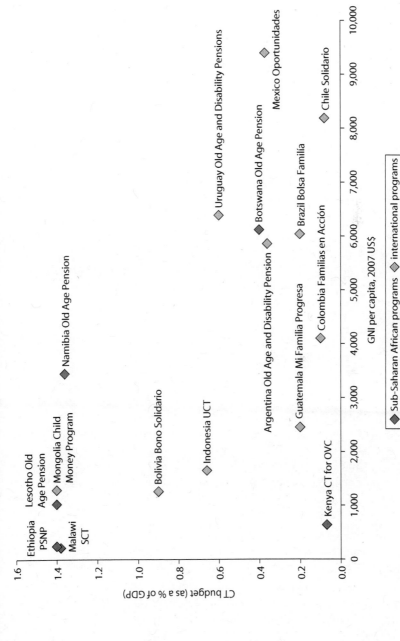

Source: Authors' representation.

- US$41.4 million for Zambia to provide CTs in 50 established districts and 22 newly operating districts by 2012, accounting for inflation (ILO 2008b)

Figure 3.18 illustrates how the costs of CT programs in Sub-Saharan African countries compare with costs of similar programs around the world in relation to countries' per capita gross national income (GNI). These other programs include CCTs, pensions, and UCTs. In general, the costs of selected CTs in wealthier countries represent a smaller percentage of their GDP. The African programs tend to cost relatively more compared to their GDP than programs in other countries. Of course, these measures are a function of the CT programs' coverage, transfer size, and efficiency.

Information is still needed on how spending on CT programs compares with governments' total social expenditures, or other types of expenditures. These data will provide insight into how CTs fit into governments' social budgets and overall spending patterns. These data were not obtained through the course of the review and are left to further studies.

Finally, analyzing CT costs in light of their potential short- and long-term benefits is important, along with a comparison of the costs and benefits of other alternatives that would be implemented in lieu of a CT program.

Who Funds Cash Transfers in Sub-Saharan Africa?

Impetus and funding for some of the early CT programs in lower-income countries in Sub-Saharan Africa came from donor groups and NGOs. However, some of the governments of some of these countries have taken leadership roles in financing their programs. Figure 3.19 provides information on the funding of identified CTs in Sub-Saharan Africa. Half of the programs were funded solely by groups outside of domestic governments. An additional third were funded only by governments, and the remaining programs were funded by both governments and outside partners.

Not surprisingly, funding for CT programs tracks closely with countries' income status. Upper-middle-income countries fund their own programs. Approximately half of the programs in lower-middle-income countries are funded solely by governments, and almost one-third are funded entirely by nongovernment sources. Two out of three CT programs in low-income countries are funded entirely by organizations outside of government. That figure is slightly higher for fragile states. Some

CT programs in fragile states are funded solely by the government, although that result is limited to Zimbabwe; programs in all other fragile states are funded in part or wholly by nongovernment sources.

The organization that most frequently funds CT programs in the reviewed Sub-Saharan African countries is the U.K. Department for International Development (DFID), with the World Bank and UNICEF following (see figure 3.20). Of those programs funded by the three organizations, the most common combination of funders was DFID and UNICEF (nine programs), followed by the World Bank and DFID (four programs). Oxfam, Save the Children, and CARE (Cooperative for Assistance and Relief Everywhere) were the most common funders from the nonprofit sector. Many other groups fund a small number of CT programs in Sub-Saharan Africa.

Relative Efficiency and the Fiscal Space Debate in Sub-Saharan Africa

Support for domestic financing of social protection also comes from within the continent. The African Union Social Policy Framework recommends that countries provide guaranteed long-term, budget-funded domestic support for social protection programs (African Union 2008). Even if governments in Sub-Saharan Africa do not spend money on CT programs, they will eventually confront the costs and consequences of growing numbers of vulnerable individuals, such as OVC, and major covariate shocks. Forward-looking countries in Sub-Saharan Africa are planning now with these medium- and long-term social changes and risks in mind.

Domestic fiscal space for CT programs. The programs that Sub-Saharan African countries can afford will vary depending on the countries' financial environment. That being said, African members that participated in the Livingstone meetings agreed that countries and development partners together could support a minimum package of social transfers (Taylor 2010). Market-based growth and appropriate management of the macroeconomy, revenue from natural resources, improved governance and tax collection, debt relief, and support from donors will continue to allow many Sub-Saharan African countries to access additional financing for social protection programs.

Some countries in the region, including the middle-income countries of Botswana, Lesotho, and South Africa, have clearly recognized their responsibility to support social protection. They have taken the initiative

Figure 3.19 Funding of Cash Transfers in Sub-Saharan Africa, by Country Income Status

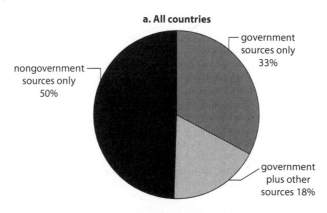

a. All countries
- government sources only 33%
- government plus other sources 18%
- nongovernment sources only 50%

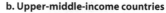

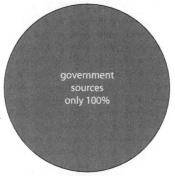

b. Upper-middle-income countries
- government sources only 100%

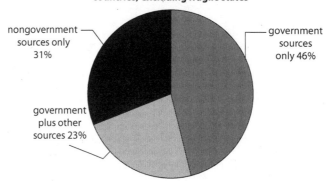

c. Lower-middle-income countries, excluding fragile states
- government sources only 46%
- government plus other sources 23%
- nongovernment sources only 31%

(continued next page)

Figure 3.19 *(continued)*

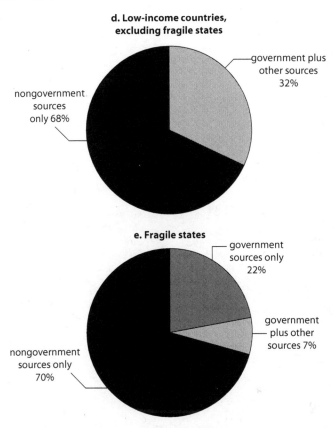

Source: Authors' representation.
Note: Sample size is 107 for panel a, 23 for panel b, 13 for panel c, 44 for panel d, and 27 for panel e. Analysis is limited to those programs with clear information on funding sources. Categories are mutually exclusive. Difference in total percentage of government-funded programs with percentage shown in panel a is due to rounding.

to implement CT programs funded through their own budgets. Given the strong GDP growth seen throughout much of Sub-Saharan Africa before the recent global economic crisis and the expected continued growth in the region, this budget support looks increasingly possible for many countries.

A number of other Sub-Saharan African countries have looked into options that would allow them to finance CT programs using funds that have already been allocated. For instance, Ghana is using HIPC (Heavily Indebted Poor Countries) Initiative funds for its CT program. Malawi's SCT has been able to use National AIDS Commission funds, since

Figure 3.20 Specific Funders of Cash Transfers

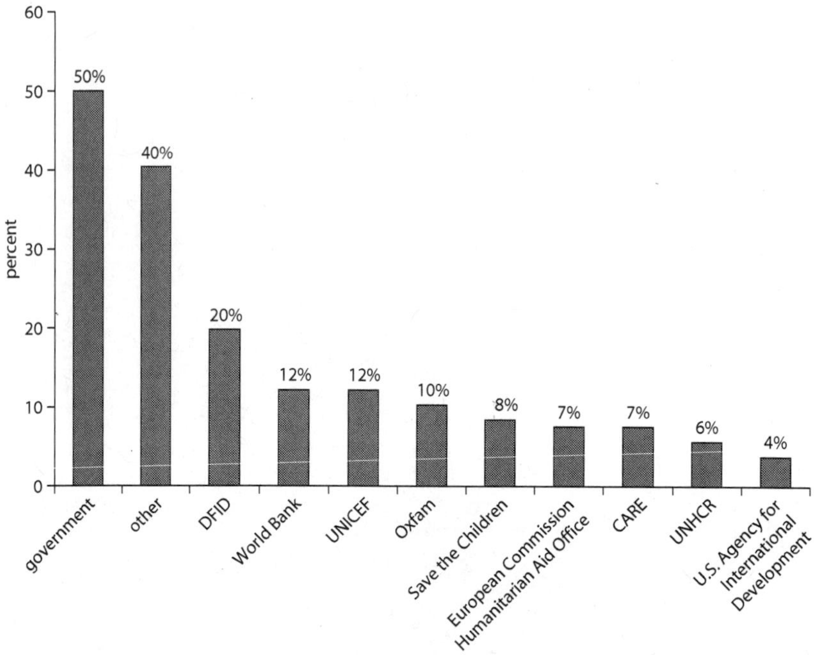

Funder	percent
government	50%
other	40%
DFID	20%
World Bank	12%
UNICEF	12%
Oxfam	10%
Save the Children	8%
European Commission Humanitarian Aid Office	7%
CARE	7%
UNHCR	6%
U.S. Agency for International Development	4%

Source: Authors' representation.
Note: Sample size is 107. Analysis is limited to those programs with clear information on funding sources. Total is greater than 100 percent because multiple organizations fund many programs. Although programs may be funded by multiple organizations classified in the "other" category, each program is included only once in "other." "Other" includes, among others, Canadian International Development Agency; Concern Universal; Concern Worldwide; Danish International Development Agency; Danish Refugee Council; Development Cooperation Ireland; Food and Agriculture Organization of the United Nations; German Agency for Technical Cooperation; Global Fund to Fight AIDS, Tuberculosis, and Malaria; HelpAge International; Horn Relief; ILO; Japan Social Development Fund; Royal Netherlands Embassy; Red Cross; Swedish International Development Cooperation Authority; World Food Programme; and World Vision International.

approximately 70 percent of beneficiary households have been affected by HIV/AIDS (Schubert 2007b).

Other funding sources have been advanced. One suggestion is that properly managed oil revenues in certain countries, such as Ghana, could be used to fund the countries' CT programs (Jones 2009). However, the often-cited negative correlation between oil revenues and institutional capacity must be considered (Handley 2009). Hanlon, Barrientos, and Hulme (2010) suggest that low-income countries consider funding CT programs by implementing a financial transaction tax. Countries that currently collect a small percentage of GDP as taxes may be able to fund programs through increases in tax collection (Niño-Zarazúa and others 2010). Barrientos (2007) argues that the cost of improving tax collection might be offset by the long-term social benefits provided by social protection programs.

Given the various demands on budgets throughout the continent, no one-size-fits-all approach can be used to find fiscal space for CT programs. In some cases, countries clearly should be able to allocate greater spending to social protection programs. For instance, a UNICEF study of fiscal space in West and Central Africa found that some countries with relatively small populations and high oil revenues would be able to afford social pensions and universal benefits for children. At the same time, the study found that more limited (targeted) CT programs could still provide significant benefits to key populations in countries with tighter fiscal limits. As an example, the study recommended expanding Ghana's LEAP program to cover all extremely poor households at a cost of less than 1 percent of the country's GDP (Handley 2009).

Countries with less immediate budgeting room for social protection would have to build fiscal space for programs over the medium term while making difficult decisions about how to prioritize spending on social protection. Vital to those decisions is political will, good governance, and the technical capacity to implement programs (Handley 2009).

Efficiency of cash transfers may create fiscal space. Properly designed and administered CT programs offer important potential cost savings over some of the past responses that governments have adopted to reduce vulnerabilities in times of economic crises and natural disasters.

The removal of certain generalized and ineffective food subsidies has the potential to open up fiscal space for more effective strategies of social protection targeted to the most vulnerable groups. Countries that introduce CTs in place of food subsidies may increase the efficiency of spending on social protection while removing the moral force of arguments coming from interest groups opposed to phasing out certain subsidies. Such a phase-out of expensive subsidies occurred as CTs were initiated in Indonesia, Mexico, Mozambique, and other countries.

This phasing out of ineffective programs continues to occur in Sub-Saharan Africa. Senegal provided tax relief and food subsidies in reaction to rising food prices in 2007. Policy makers quickly recognized that these programs were very expensive, costing between 3 and 4 percent of GDP. They also were not pro-poor (World Bank 2009a). The government abandoned the subsidies at the end of 2008, but the experience led it to search for ways to implement better safety net programs and well-targeted CTs.

Cash transfers that are part of national social protection programs may also be more efficient than small-scale programs implemented by multiple providers. A study in Kenya found that civil society organizations spent between 30 and 60 percent of program funding on administrative or overhead costs (Devereux and Pelham 2005). This percentage was significantly higher than that found in Kenya's CT for OVC, where administrative costs were expected to be approximately 25 percent in 2012 and were projected to drop (World Bank 2009d).

Administrative costs of other programs are estimated to be lower than those of Kenya's program. For Rwanda's VUP, administrative costs were estimated to be approximately 8 percent of total expenses (DFID 2009). In Zambia's five pilot SCTs, expected administrative costs did not exceed 20 percent, and they were substantially lower in four of the five pilots (RNA 2007). In the Zambian scale-up plan, administrative costs were expected to be 15.2 percent in 2009 and to decrease to 13.6 percent by 2012, provided that the same types of costs were incurred as in Kalomo district (Republic of Zambia 2007). As of 2009, administrative costs of Ghana's LEAP were relatively high at 30 percent; policy makers hope that number will decrease to 20 percent by 2015/16 (World Bank 2010c).

CTs also can be inefficient. In 2007, Mozambique's PSA was estimated to spend US$1.55 for every dollar of benefits delivered. This difference was attributed to the program's inefficient structure and administration (Ellis 2007). This statistic highlights that CT programs are not automatically more efficient than other programs; however, evidence suggests that they can achieve high levels of cost-efficiency when they are designed and executed well. In cases where CT programs are not relatively cost-efficient, the source of the inefficiencies should be examined to determine how to improve program execution.

Figure 3.21 shows CT programs' administrative costs as a percentage of total program costs and the number of households covered in the programs. The African programs with available data tend to have higher administrative costs and lower coverage when compared with transfer programs in other regions. The chart illustrates potential efficiency gains that can be achieved as African programs increase in scale. Administrative costs are also expected to decline as programs improve their basic systems

Figure 3.21 Comparison of Programs' Administrative Costs and Program Coverage

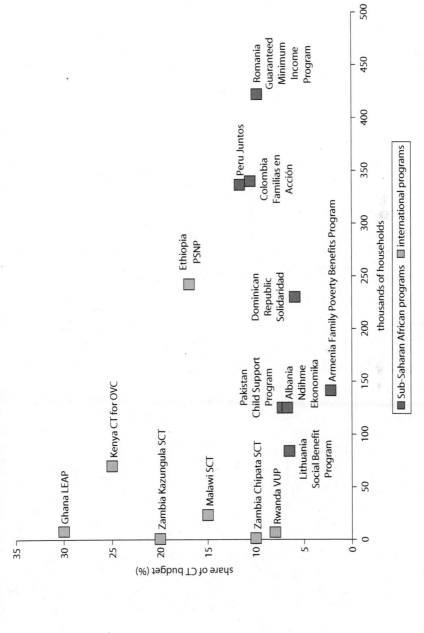

Source: Authors' representation.

and capacities and capitalize on synergies with other social protection programs.

Incremental development of CT (and broader social protection) programs can help reduce the immediate fiscal pressure on governments, as well as generate evidence and political support for successful programs (O'Cleirigh 2009). Budget reallocation toward CTs and away from inefficient or regressive programs is a medium- or long-term endeavor (Barrientos 2007), and incremental shifts in budgets will be the norm across the region. Fiscal allocation to social protection programs and CT programs in particular requires both political will and a long-term framework. It also may involve the use of civil society to help develop an understanding of the state's social contract with the individual (Barrientos 2007).

Countries are planning for the future cost of social protection. Even when programs are efficient, many CT programs face rising costs as a result of obligations to a growing eligible population. Those programs must anticipate the fundamental changes and plan accordingly. Although its economic and demographic makeup is somewhat different from that of most other African countries, Mauritius provides an example of a country that is addressing current and future social protection costs. Faced with an aging population and already spending 2.0 percent of GDP and 8.7 percent of government expenditures on its basic (and enhanced) retirement pension (Government of Mauritius 2008), the country has been forced to reformulate the pension to maintain its affordability. The size of the population eligible for the pension is expected to triple by 2050, which would increase the pension's cost to approximately 5.7 percent of GDP. To address this rise in cost, the retirement age has been gradually increasing toward 65 since late 2008, and yearly increases in the basic retirement pension will be limited (Government of Mauritius 2009).

For other countries, medium- to long-term costs of their cash grant systems are expected to be more affordable. Under two different scenarios, costs for Namibia's grant system are not expected to increase much beyond 3 percent of GDP. With GDP growth similar to that in the country's recent history, the costs are expected to be less than 2 percent of GDP by 2030. These calculations allow for program expansion and increased grant values (Levine, van der Berg, and Yu 2009).

Donor funding for CT programs. In addition to the domestic funding that most programs ideally use, a major potential funding source for CT programs is donor financing. Several Sub-Saharan African countries have begun CT programs using only funds from development partners. Stakeholders hope that once a small pilot has proved its merit, government support will be gained. Donor funding for CTs is expected to eventually transition to funding from domestic revenues, with sensitivity toward national conditions and issues (Blank and Handa 2008).

Malawi and Zambia have both attempted this approach, with limited success in gaining the necessary government backing to meet program goals of scaling up. For 2010/11, Malawi's Ministry of Finance committed US$1 million for the country's SCT, indicating an increasing willingness to support the program. In 2007/08, the government of Zambia allotted its own funds to its CT programs for the first time, budgeting US$350,000 after the Ministry of Community Development and Social Services extensively lobbied the Ministry of Finance (German Agency for Technical Cooperation 2007). Since then, the government's contributions have continued to increase, and political support for Zambia's CTs has grown significantly. The Ministry of Finance has also shown its support for the CTs by signing an agreement to continue expanding the program for 10 years.

Ethiopia and Sierra Leone both worked using already-allocated emergency resources to initially fund their CT programs. This required the countries to provide part of the transfers in food and the rest in cash, but it enabled them to establish programs, nonetheless. Both countries have searched for additional financiers to allow them to distribute cash rather than only food aid.

Legitimate Concerns of Policy Makers That Call for Long-Term Donor Commitment to Cash Transfers

A concern articulated by a number of leaders in Sub-Saharan Africa is that they do not want to allow a CT program to begin if it will be supported by a development partner only for a limited time. When donor funds disappear, such leaders argue, the program will be at risk of doing the same. The more successful the CT has been, the more problems domestic politicians will be left with in trying to close a popular program.

Some donors are recognizing the legitimacy of these concerns, and they have begun to outline longer-term frameworks for their support for social protection and CTs. Planning for the programs has also begun to include estimates of how long it would take countries to be able to fund CT programs entirely through domestic funds, based on assumptions of GDP growth and increases in the tax base as well as declines in poverty. Africans involved in CTs often voice hopes that their donors will evolve such longer-term frameworks and commitments for consistent support for the programs. In Ethiopia, great strides have been made toward donor harmonization and the use of longer-term financing and planning frameworks to ensure that program funds are predictable and operations remain consistent. Use of a rolling Medium-Term Expenditure and Financing Framework has allowed Ethiopia to assimilate government and donor resources in cash and food to implement a wide-scale, stable program (World Bank 2010a).

Whether or not such support is forthcoming, Sub-Saharan African governments face urgent social protection issues. Waiting on longer-term commitments from donors is potentially dangerous, with the risk that "he who pays the piper calls the tune." Some countries, recognizing the importance of a strong social protection strategy to their own national security and economic growth, are moving to create budget lines for new programs such as CTs and are recognizing that they should support the programs with their own funds to the greatest extent possible. One strategy that some programs have taken is to allow governments to fund all or part of the cost of the actual transfers, while development partner funds are used primarily for initial program investments (such as for a strong MIS), evaluations, capacity building, and institutional strengthening. This approach is being used in Ghana's LEAP and Lesotho's CGP, among others.

Building the Constituency for Domestic Support: Easing the Path to Scaling Up Cash Transfers

Increasing international experience and well-documented positive evaluations have whetted Sub-Saharan African countries' interest in CTs, but the path from interest to implementation opens up fully only with the emergence of a domestic constituency that is ready to support the programs.

In an environment of limited resources, some of the opposition to CTs may come from groups with a special interest in continuing less effective but politically popular programs. Other opposition stems from genuine questions and valid concerns that need to be clearly addressed before programs can move forward. CT program advocates and planners need to acknowledge and understand those issues and purposefully develop constituencies of support.

Strong, transparent systems with robust controls are crucial for gaining and retaining domestic support. A pilot that includes a rigorous monitoring system and impact evaluation can go a long way in generating support. Regular outputs from monitoring systems can provide information on the quality of implementation. Evaluations can provide evidence of the CT's impacts, and they can show nonbeneficiaries that the program is unbiased and targets the poor well. They can help convince the public that targeting does not depend on households' or communities' political preferences or other special relationships. The payment system can control against significant fraud and corruption, and the controls and results can be systematically communicated to the public.

Domestic support for CTs will be more forthcoming as it becomes clear that the CT program is feasible and that departments will be appropriately supported as they carry out their duties. Adequate investments must be planned and made in supply-side infrastructure so that the CT does not gain a reputation for burdening already-taxed systems.

Support for CTs may also be gained as policy makers are given information on the role of social protection in economic growth, an issue of obvious concern to African policy makers. Connections need to be drawn between social protection programs and their potential to affect economic growth and increase productivity, in addition to assisting the destitute (Niño-Zarazúa and others 2010).

Support for good governance may also play a role in generating demand for CT programs in Sub-Saharan Africa. In Namibia and South Africa, where the programs and platforms of strong, centralized political parties were able to eclipse traditional patronage systems, social protection has received broad-based support and has been expanded to cover large portions of vulnerable groups (Niño-Zarazúa and others 2010).

A Good Advocacy Strategy: Taking a Systematic Approach

Information about CT systems and results, along with basic messages about the program's objectives and expected outcomes, should be intentionally communicated. Communication should be tailored to the listening audience, and it should extend to domestic politicians, nonbeneficiaries, and beneficiaries alike.

Program champions may generate support for cash transfers. Often, one or several program champions can be instrumental in generating widespread support for a CT. In Ghana, for example, popular opinion held that LEAP would be a handout to the poor and that HIPC Initiative funds should be used for other programs that would generate employment or more direct economic growth. Ghana's Ministry of Employment and

Social Welfare was proactive in communicating the purpose of the National Social Protection Strategy and LEAP to the public.[18] The ministry took a strong stance and launched its own campaign to explain why LEAP was necessary. The campaign was successful in communicating to the public that some of the most vulnerable groups, such as children or the elderly, could not benefit from other programs. Advocacy led by the deputy minister of employment and social welfare was a key force in obtaining political support in the Ministry of Finance and the cabinet (Sultan and Schrofer 2008).

Champions of CT programs have been important in several other countries throughout the region. Support from Ethiopia's prime minister and deputy prime minister influenced the development of Ethiopia's PSNP (Ashley, Brown, and Gibson 2007). Support by Kenya's vice president helped pave the way for Kenya's CT for OVC (World Bank 2005), which was also encouraged by initial political advocacy work by UNICEF (Pearson and Alviar 2009). Government approval of the concept convinced UNICEF to fund a prepilot CT program.

Program advocates and planners should identify potential champions early on in the CT's development. People who can be champions often already have some understanding of or at least sympathy for social protection, and they either have influence over domestic policy or are in direct contact with those who do. Such individuals, if kept abreast of the program's operations, may be very helpful in obtaining support for the program at key points in its evolution. Organizations such as NGOs are also often crucial players in advocacy work for social protection and cash transfers.

Other activities may increase support for cash transfers: South-South learning and exchange and community of practice. In countries with no existing CT programs, the first challenge is to obtain enough interest and support to initiate a pilot. Some countries, including Ghana, Kenya, and Zambia, have used a very small pilot, or what has been called a prepilot, to test the feasibility of cash transfers. A very small program may improve program viability and generate interest.

"Experience exchange" and "community of practice" initiatives can also spark interest in CTs. Groups may invite and host experts (preferably advocate-communicators) who have previous experience with CTs to discuss social protection with key domestic constituents. Sending domestic policy makers to visit functioning programs in other countries may also be useful. Brazil, for instance, has been a key player in South-South learning experiences that help African policy makers better envision how CTs might work in their countries.

Another helpful activity was undertaken in Ghana, where the Ministry of Employment and Social Welfare provided the Ministry of Finance with a document that included a detailed design and budget for LEAP. The quality of this work convinced the Ministry of Finance that LEAP would have the necessary capacity to execute a well-planned program (Sultan and Schrofer 2008). In addition to being a helpful exercise, this type of activity may be useful in countries where the capacity of the ministry in charge of a CT program is questioned.

Capturing political support may have unintended consequences. Programs must make efforts to gain political support, but they must also prepare themselves to deal with that support once it is received. Program officials must be careful to avoid becoming captives of that support, which might compromise the program. Maintaining autonomy is not always easy to do, but Kenya's CT for OVC provides an example of a program that has successfully done so.

Political enthusiasm for Kenya's pilot CT for OVC complicated, and yet advanced, the program. Funds were allocated to the program from the national budget, but they were awarded only under the condition that the program be expanded to new districts. CT officials felt pressure to spend the money within the year to show they could use the funds and to ensure that they would receive money in subsequent years. Despite limited capacity for scaling up, the Central Program Unit decided to implement the CT in new districts using the government money. This decision led to the development of parallel programs that used separate funds from the domestic and external sources. In some cases, different protocols developed in the separately funded programs. Although this experience has been challenging, program officials have embraced the challenge, and the two programs are currently being assimilated as capacity continues to grow.

Programs must avoid becoming overly politicized. An important factor in CTs' long-term sustainability is their level of politicization. Although political buy-in is extremely important, excessive politicization of domestic support can threaten a CT program's longer-term existence. A program is overpoliticized, for instance, if its association with a certain political party is so strong that the CT is eliminated as soon as the party is no longer in power. Sultan and Schrofer (2008) noted the need for

Ghana's LEAP program to become institutionalized so that it can continue regardless of the election cycle or political winners. Too close an embrace between a political party and a CT can also lead to compromises of integrity and transparency and to the misdirection of benefits for political purposes. Ensuring that programs do not become overly politicized is key to their long-term sustainability.

Although no foolproof strategy exists that will avoid overpoliticization, steps may be taken to prevent it. From the outset, program officials should be selected for their technical expertise and capabilities rather than their political affiliation. Program managers must stand up for the transparency and objectivity of targeting and the integrity of the MIS and fiduciary controls. Strict standards relating to processes, protocol, and evaluations should be maintained and widely communicated in messages about the program. Controls should be in place to make corruption difficult.

Most Sub-Saharan African countries have strong civil service structures whose career personnel will be in charge of providing orientation to the changing cast of ministers who take over the political leadership of the ministries. This group includes mid-level personnel who do much of the day-to-day work that ultimately leads to policy and budget decisions. Those personnel, in particular, need to be cultivated to ensure that they understand the program. The best of them will be allies in efforts to avoid overly politicizing programs.

That being said, political support is obviously extremely important to CTs' success and institutionalization. Each country is unique and will face its own challenges in gaining government buy-in for programs. Much progress in these areas has been made for the countries of Sub-Saharan Africa, but much is still to be gained.

The Role of Cash Transfers within a Social Protection Strategy: Gaining National Support and Building Up Social Protection Systems

CT designs also need to take into account the role the CT programs are to play in a country's overall social protection strategy—assuming, of course, that such a strategy has been outlined. A social protection strategy creates an umbrella of support for CTs, justifying their existence and providing support for their inclusion in the national budget.

When programs are not aligned under a social protection strategy, they tend to be fragmented and less efficient. Their objectives are often less clear, and duplication and power struggles may weaken them. In an overly complex, uncoordinated system, CT and other social protection programs tend to overlap and compete for resources, mutually undermining political support and decreasing the effectiveness of all such programs.

Cash transfers may grow out of a social protection strategy. Ghana's National Social Protection Strategy provides a good example of how a government has outlined specific goals for the country's social protection system. The government has used the strategy to integrate social protection programs in a manner that can be sustained and achieve long-term impacts. The strategy addressed existing weaknesses in social protection by establishing three main priorities: (a) providing a basic, dependable income source for households considered most vulnerable (through LEAP); (b) improving targeting of existing programs to better reach the poorest people; and (c) using multiple complementary and coordinated interventions to fight poverty. The processes used to formulate the strategy helped uncover gaps in government programming, paving the way for the LEAP CT (Sultan and Schrofer 2008).

Cash transfer implementation can advance a broader social protection agenda. The absence of a national social protection strategy does not necessarily negate the usefulness of establishing a CT. Where policy development processes are overly slow or constrained by political obstacles, successes of a well-designed and credibly evaluated CT may spur the development of a broader social protection agenda. The program's analytical work and documentation of experiences and of the scope of unaddressed difficulties faced by vulnerable groups can highlight the need for a social protection strategy for the country, demonstrate the feasibility of practical action, and generate necessary political support.

For instance, Malawi's government has had an ongoing interest in developing a national social protection strategy, but such a strategy has not been adopted quickly. The experiences of Malawi's SCT will certainly help guide the formulation of this strategy, and its very existence makes the need for such a strategy that much greater. In Kenya, the success of a CT program for orphans (the CT for OVC), combined with increasing government support for social protection programs, undoubtedly encouraged the development of a subsequent CT program intended to address a much different need in another part of the country: the chronic food insecurity of people living in arid lands (HSNP).

Growing capacity in a CT program can also make the road easier for other social protection programs. Ghana's LEAP plans to move to a computerized single registry system that will allow it to link to other social protection programs in the country (World Bank 2010c), enabling the other programs to make use of LEAP's already-existing system.

The Role of Development Partners in Program Initiation and Scale-Up

Development partners, including donors, NGOs, think tanks, or other groups interested in social protection, have important roles to play in supporting Sub-Saharan African countries that are developing CTs. They can support individuals on the ground involved in advocacy work, and they can encourage and provide guidance to governments when requested, always with the country's culture, history, and politics in mind.

Partners' Role in Encouraging Knowledge Exchange

Some donors, such as DFID, have been instrumental in raising awareness about social protection within countries. This work requires patience, but it pays off over the longer term in government ownership, which is essential to CT programs' success. Other donors, including the World Bank, have been instrumental in gathering regional experts on social protection for meetings and dialogue about CTs. These experiences facilitate South-South learning and dialogue.

Other groups, such as the Brazilian government and the United Nations Development Programme's International Policy Centre for Inclusive Growth (IPC-IG),[19] have also encouraged South-South learning by arranging trips for African policy makers to visit Brazil's successful Bolsa Família program. Brazil's Ministry of Social Development and Fight Against Hunger has cooperated with Ghana, Mozambique, Senegal, and South Africa in the area of social protection (IPC-IG 2008a). This arrangement has been particularly helpful for Africa's lusophone countries, which now have substantial resources about CTs available to them in Portuguese. In addition, the Information and Exchange Centre for the Extension of Social Protection in Portuguese-Speaking Countries was recently created to support lusophone countries interested in social protection.

Similar resources are notably lacking for francophone countries, and this gap may be affecting CT programming in these countries in Sub-Saharan Africa. With the exception of Rwanda and Senegal, francophone countries are lagging others on the continent in their use of CTs. Many individuals in the region have voiced the need for written and oral support for French-speaking countries—a need that development partners could help address.

A number of countries are leading in social protection and CT programs throughout the region, and they can be used as examples for other Sub-Saharan African countries that want to develop cash transfers. Development partners can provide support for such intercountry learning, including for capacity building within social ministries, to ensure that capacity constraints in those institutions do not hold back urgently needed progress in social protection.

Support for national or regional African-based research on CTs and for the development of this research capacity in the region would also be helpful. Such research can generate greater insight into issues specific to Sub-Saharan Africa, lend additional credibility to research results, and help speed the communication of results (European University Institute 2010).

Development Partners Can Capitalize on Their Strengths When Supporting Cash Transfers

Development partners can also use their expertise and experience with CT programs to encourage improvements in CT design, although they must be careful not to force a one-size-fits-all model on countries. Organizations such as DFID, UNICEF, and the World Bank have extensive experience helping low-income countries design and implement CTs. In its work for children, UNICEF has used its advocacy, together with the flexibility that its government-UNICEF programming structure allows, to help CT programs move quickly into prepilot and pilot stages with government support. DFID's constant advocacy for the development of social protection and cash transfers and its support for such programs have been crucial to countries in Sub-Saharan Africa.

The technical expertise that development partners can provide—and ideally pass along to domestic partners—is invaluable. The World Bank provides excellent support for countries interested in ensuring that they have strong program fundamentals (targeting, MIS, evaluation, and so forth). Also crucial for CT programs is other technical support, capacity building, and institutional strengthening that development partners can provide. Most, if not all, programs need this type of support and find it to be very useful.

NGOs also have important skills to offer to countries interested in implementing CTs. Often, their on-the-ground knowledge is excellent, and they can provide insight into programs' day-to-day functioning. Some

NGOs have extensive experience with providing CTs in emergency situations. These groups include, but are not limited to, Concern Worldwide, Save the Children, and Oxfam. Other NGOs are involved in implementing key components, such as targeting, in nonemergency transfer schemes. Many international NGOs are increasingly interested in using CTs as part of their portfolio, and they are often interested in implementing strong evaluations and generating evidence related to CTs. Finally, some NGOs have played a vital role as vocal advocates of social protection throughout the region.

Although development partners have a role to play in CT programs, they should be careful not to force a particular favorite agenda on countries or even to selectively ignore evidence supporting another intervention or target group. They should view their role as that of a partner that supports governments rather than as a donor that has the final word. Their assistance should be in line with domestic priorities and strategies. As development partners support evidence-based debates rather than dictate answers, progress will be made toward increasing government ownership of CT programs.

Donor Involvement in Fragile States

Donors must also be sensitive to the timeline for social protection in fragile, postconflict countries. Most countries will want to transition from emergency aid to state-led social protection and possibly CT programs, but donors must be sensitive to when and how this transition should occur. They need to carefully negotiate their dealings with domestic actors (European University Institute 2010), as tensions and power struggles likely remain that could be affected by which actors donors choose to work with.

Long-Term Funding and Support from Development Partners

Obviously, development partners can also provide funding for CTs. Those funds should be directed and controlled appropriately, and they should be given in a longer-term framework rather than through short-term projects, when possible. Many of the reviewed CT programs in Sub-Saharan Africa were funded as one-off projects by donors, without an explicit attempt to develop institutionalized, domestically driven CTs with the systems necessary to achieve crucial scale effects. This type of funding increasingly needs to become the exception rather than the rule. The increased use of sector and general budget support may facilitate the financing of CTs through longer-term donor aid linked to national strategies (European University Institute 2010; O'Cleirigh 2009).

As mentioned earlier, long-term funding for programs is a key part of securing domestic support for CTs. Zambia is a case in point. The government has been hesitant to fund its CT pilots. However, a commitment by donors (DFID and Irish Aid) to finance the country's CT programs for 10 years led the government to draw up its own plan for financing in the mid term. It plans to increase its support for the programs to cover most of their cost by the end of the 10 years (European University Institute 2010).

A key role for donors may be to provide funds for initial investments and fixed-cost items. This funding could include investments in monitoring systems, identification and registration systems or expansion of national identification systems, evaluations, and more. Funding for capacity building in those areas would also be helpful. Support from development partners for program evaluations, both within and across countries,[20] would also provide a valuable source of information throughout the region.

Donor Coordination and Support for Domestic Priorities

A concern with programs that are funded by multiple donors is the inefficiencies that will be present if donors do not coordinate their efforts. These inefficiencies include, but are not limited to, differential reporting, procedural, and financing practices and requirements. Although harmonizing donor involvement will require significant time, funding, and effort, this coordination is imperative to limit burdens placed on domestic partners and maximize a CT's potential effects. The responsibility for such harmonization belongs to the donor group.

When possible, donor financing should be pooled and agreements should be established through a memorandum of understanding. Basket mechanisms are used for CTs in Ethiopia, Kenya, Mozambique, Rwanda, and other countries. Pooling of finances will reduce the administrative burden on domestic counterparts, and it can encourage donors to provide long-term resourcing as they jointly commit to a CT. By pooling financing and relying on a longer-term financing framework, Ethiopia's PSNP has been able to secure predictable long-term funding while allowing donors to comply with their own internal financing cycles (World Bank 2010a).

Ethiopia's experience provides an example of the benefits of donor coordination. As a pilot country in the Paris Declaration on Aid

Harmonization, Ethiopia and its donors made major efforts to harmonize aid and increase domestic ownership of the PSNP. It established a donor coordination team that helped to coordinate and encourage involvement of donors in the PSNP's Donor Working Group. The working group has agreed on policy positions, and it works with common financial and procurement processes and a common monitoring framework to limit burdens placed on the government. The group works from one principal program document for implementation. Funding for these efforts has come from the World Bank's Multi-donor Trust Fund. Technical advice is harmonized through another similar fund (World Bank 2010a).

Just as donors should work together, they should make sure that they are working to achieve domestic objectives. If donors are not in agreement with domestic priorities, there is room for discussion, but the state is the ultimate authority on how programs should progress. Rwanda takes a proactive approach to ensure that donors support domestic priorities by requiring them to report their work in social protection to district officials to confirm that activities mesh with district priorities. Donor funds for social protection also have to be channeled through sector funding to ensure that they align with the government's priority of developing a national social protection system (European University Institute 2010).

Countries that depend heavily on donors face a special challenge because it is difficult to determine the extent to which domestic constituents truly espouse a program favored by donors. Attention must be paid to garnering authentic support for CTs from key officials. The support should come from a strong understanding of the relationships between social protection, growth, and stability.

Working from Consensus

An important role for development partners is to support consensus building around CT programs. Donors and domestic partners will inevitably have different visions. However, overlapping priorities often can form a foundation on which to build.

Once again, the experience of Ethiopia's PSNP sheds light on these issues. Disagreements between PSNP donors were prevalent: some favored conditional transfers while other wanted unconditional transfers, some preferred transferring food while others wanted cash, and some advocated transfers while others preferred a focus on productivity. Donors worked through their disagreements and approached the government with their own consensus. Then the government and donor group had to work through their own significant differences, including conflicting opinions over why emergency food aid had become a chronic necessity and how a program like the PSNP should work. However, both groups were concerned with decreasing Ethiopia's reliance on emergency food aid (World Bank 2010a).

Working from the consensus belief that the system needed to change, stakeholders eventually agreed on key principles that could direct their work. The principles included the reliability and appropriate timing of transfers, the preference for cash transfers over food aid, the need to positively influence local development, the necessity of long-term financing, the importance of government ownership, and the need to use domestic officials and systems. Although these principles were agreed on, not all questions were solved by the time the program was launched (World Bank 2010a). Ultimately, the government launched the program at scale using its own systems (the government's preference). The program included a condition of public works for some beneficiaries (the government's preference) but was unconditional for the remaining Direct Support recipients (a donor preference). The decisions ultimately made were the result of bargaining among the partners, and politics played a role in the outcomes (European University Institute 2010).

A key to building and maintaining this consensus was the establishment of a logical framework to which all partners agreed. The framework established the program's objectives and listed key monitoring and evaluation outcomes that were to be measured. Program execution was measured against the framework. Although the establishment of the logical framework involved intense debates on the nature and implementation of the PSNP, those initial discussions eventually put program stakeholders on the same page. It allowed the government to work from a single model and left donors to balance their own institutional demands with the requirements of the agreed-on framework (World Bank 2010a).

The program has since worked from a pragmatic stance, confronting issues related to implementation and policy as needed. This approach has engendered a spirit of compromise and has allowed the involved partners to respond quickly to problems as they arise, even in light of limited information (World Bank 2010a).

Conclusions

The cash transfers identified through the recent desk review provide significant insights into CT programs in Sub-Saharan Africa. The programs exhibit a broad range of characteristics covering both cut-and-dried issues as well as softer issues related to political will and donor involvement. The summary and analysis presented in this chapter provide a rich source of information about the state of CTs throughout the region. The information gained from these programs can inform the design and execution of other CT programs in the region and contribute to the evolving body of global knowledge and experience.

Although this chapter has provided detailed information about trends in CT programs and their implementation, more analysis of those trends is important and is provided in chapter 4.

Notes

1. Sometimes the term *proxy means* includes only indicators related to household income, and indexes related to household well-being are known as multidimensional indexes. Here, both of these types of targeting are included in the definition of proxy means tests.
2. *Ubudehe* is a program that unites community members in a traditional decision-making process by targeting local households to receive support. Households are ranked by a committee, and a public meeting is held to validate the outcomes. Benefits are given to households on the basis of the ranking (DFID 2009).
3. They also retrieve their salaries through this method. The extent to which retrieving the transfers causes schools and health posts to be closed for longer than normal periods is unclear (Ministry of Community Development and Social Services and German Agency for Technical Cooperation 2007).
4. This number was out of 7,500 accounts (1 per household) that were anticipated to be opened (Beswick 2008).
5. The plan to enforce conditions in Monze district was not fully implemented.
6. Fiszbein and Schady (2009) also suggest that constraints within households that are affected by conditions, such as parenting practices or limited information, may depress final health and education outcomes.
7. This type of setup was used, for instance, in Nicaragua's Red de Protección Social CCT, in which NGOs provided health care in program areas that the Ministry of Health could not reach.
8. The reference quintile in Soares and Teixeira's (2010) study is based on a well-being index for rural households, calculated using Mozambique's 2008 Multiple Indicator Cluster Survey.
9. The authors are grateful to the book's reviewers, who provided several important suggestions to substantially improve the discussion of program evaluations.

10. O'Cleirigh (2009) discusses several ways to go about analyzing the role of CTs in terms of their trade-offs with other programs.
11. Results from additional evaluations are summarized in the book's appendixes.
12. These investments included activities that did not necessarily generate much profit but that enhanced households' capacity for income smoothing.
13. Malawi planned to begin designing a National Social Support Program once the cabinet passed its social support policy. The program includes plans for national scale-up of the country's SCT. Zambia, too, saw marked improvements in domestic support for CTs by early to mid-2010.
14. When one is analyzing the cost-efficiency of pilots, the larger up-front investments required to begin programs must be considered.
15. Progresa was later renamed Oportunidades.
16. Countries in the sample varied by simulation, but for at least one of the simulations they included the Republic of Congo, Equatorial Guinea, Ghana, Mali, and Senegal.
17. The number from Levine, van der Berg, and Yu (2009) does not include administrative costs. It is based on official budget data.
18. Ghana's Ministry of Employment and Social Welfare was known as the Ministry of Manpower, Youth, and Employment until January 2009.
19. The IPC-IG was formerly known as the International Poverty Centre.
20. Multicountry studies are already taking place. UNICEF and Save the Children are studying the effects and cost-effectiveness of transfer programs on children's well-being in a five-year study of six countries in Eastern and Southern Africa. The countries involved in the study are Ethiopia, Kenya, Malawi, Mozambique, Rwanda, and Tanzania (Save the Children and UNICEF 2009).

References

African Union. 2008. "Social Policy Framework for Africa." First Session of the African Union Conference of Ministers in Charge of Social Development, Windhoek, October 27–31.

Agüero, Jorge, Michael Carter, and Ingrid Woolard. 2007. "The Impact of Unconditional Cash Transfers on Nutrition: The South African Child Support Grant." Working Paper 39, International Poverty Centre, Brasília.

Andrade, Melissa. 2008. "Social Protection in Africa: A Mapping of the Growing Cash Transfer Experiences in the Region." Presented at the International Poverty Centre, Brasília, May 20.

Ardington, Cally, Anne Case, and Victoria Hosegood. 2009. "Labor Supply Responses to Large Social Transfers: Longitudinal Evidence from South Africa." *American Economic Journal: Applied Economics* 1 (1): 22–48.

Ashley, Steve, Taylor Brown, and Sam Gibson. 2007. "Building Consensus for Social Protection: Insights from Ethiopia's Productive Safety Net Programme." IDL Group, Bristol, U.K.

Attanasio, Orazio, Erich Battistin, Emla Fitzsimmons, Alice Mesnard, and Marcos Vera-Hernández. 2005. "How Effective Are Conditional Cash Transfers? Evidence from Colombia." Briefing Note 54, Institute for Fiscal Studies, London.

Attanasio, Orazio, and Alice Mesnard. 2006. "The Impact of a Conditional Cash Transfer Programme on Consumption in Colombia." *Fiscal Studies* 27 (4): 421–42.

Ayala, Francisco. 2009. "Design Proposal for a Kano State Pilot CCT for Girls' Education." Federal Republic of Nigeria, Nairobi.

Ayala Consulting. 2007. "Cash Transfer Programme for Orphans and Vulnerable Children (CT for OVC), Version 2.0." Office of the Vice President and Ministry of Home Affairs, Nairobi.

———. 2008. "Community-Based Cash Transfer Pilot CB-CCT: Operational Manual, Version 1.0." Prepared for the Republic of Tanzania. Ayala Consulting, Quito.

———. 2009. "Eritrea Results Based Financing (RBF) Pilot, Version 1.0." Prepared for the Government of Eritrea and Ministry of Health. Ayala Consulting, Quito.

Baird, Sarah, Ephraim Chirwa, Craig McIntosh, and Berk Özler. 2010. "The Short-Term Impacts of a Schooling Conditional Cash Transfer Program on the Sexual Behavior of Young Women." *Health Economics* 19 (S1): 55–68.

Baird, Sarah, Craig McIntosh, and Berk Özler. 2010. "Cash or Condition? Evidence from a Randomized Cash Transfer Program." Policy Research Working Paper 5259, World Bank, Washington, DC.

———. 2011. "Cash or Condition? Evidence from a Cash Transfer Experiment." World Bank, Washington, DC. http://ipl.econ.duke.edu/bread/papers/0511 conf/Baird.pdf.

Barrett, Christopher B., and Daniel G. Maxwell. 2005. *Food Aid after Fifty Years: Recasting Its Role.* London: Routledge.

Barrientos, Armando. 2007. "Financing Social Protection." Brooks World Poverty Institute Working Paper 5, School of Environment and Development, University of Manchester, U.K.

Basic Training Course. 2009. "Introduction to Social Safety Nets and Their Development in Senegal." Draft 4.1, Senegal National Social Protection Strategy, Dakar.

Bertrand, Marianne, Sendhil Mullainathan, and Douglas Miller. 2003. "Public Policy and Extended Families: Evidence from Pensions in South Africa." *World Bank Economic Review* 17 (1): 27–50.

Beswick, Claire. 2008. "Distributing Cash through Bank Accounts: Save the Children's Drought Response in Swaziland." FinMark Trust and Save the Children, Marshalltown, South Africa.

BFTU (Botswana Federation of Trade Unions). 2007. "Policy Position Paper on Social Security and Social Protection in Botswana." BFTU, Gaborone.

Blank, Lorraine. 2008. "Lesotho Child Grant Pilot Operating Manual." United Nations Children's Fund, New York.

Blank, Lorraine, and Sudhanshu Handa. 2008. "Social Protection in Eastern and Southern Africa: A Framework and Strategy for UNICEF." United Nations Children's Fund, New York.

Bouchet, Brigitte. 2009. "Kano State Pilot CCT for Girls' Education: Operations Manual, Version 1.0." Federal Republic of Nigeria, Nairobi.

Burt, Martha, and Harry Hatry. 2005. "Monitoring Program Performance." Presented at the Training Course on Monitoring and Evaluating Social Programs, World Bank, Washington, DC, July 26.

Case, Anne. 2001. "Does Money Protect Health Status? Evidence from South African Pensions." NBER Working Paper 8495, National Bureau of Economic Research, Cambridge, MA.

Case, Anne, and Cally Ardington. 2006. "The Impact of Parental Death on School Outcomes: Longitudinal Evidence from South Africa." *Demography* 43 (3): 401–20.

Case, Anne, and Angus Deaton. 1998. "Large Cash Transfers to the Elderly in South Africa." *Economic Journal* 108 (450): 1330–61.

Central Statistics Office. 2007. *Social Security Statistics, 2000/2000–2005/2006.* Port Louis: Ministry of Finance and Economic Development.

CNLS (Conseil National de Lutte contre le SIDA et les IST). 2008. "Recherche Action sur la Prise en Charge Communautaire des Orphelins et Enfants Vulnérables du VIH/SIDA dans les Provinces du Nahouri et du Sanmatenga." CNLS, Ouagadougou.

CNLS (Conseil National de Lutte contre le SIDA et les IST) and World Bank. n.d. "Projet de Transfert Conditionné de Fonds pour la Scolarisation de 5,000 Orphelins et Enfants Vulnérables (OEV) du Sénégal." PowerPoint presentation.

Coady, David P., Margaret Grosh, and John Hoddinott. 2004a. "Targeting Outcomes Redux." *World Bank Research Observer* 19 (1): 61–85.

———. 2004b. *Targeting of Transfers in Developing Countries: Review of Lessons and Experience.* Washington, DC: World Bank.

Coady, David, Raúl Pérez, and Hadid Vera-Ilamas. 2000. "A Cost Analysis of Progresa." In *The Application of Social Cost-Benefit Analysis to the Evaluation of Progresa*, ed. David P. Coady, 21–30. Washington, DC: International Food Policy Research Institute.

Croome, David, Andrew Nyanguru, and M. Molisana. 2007. "The Impact of the Old Age Pension on Hunger Vulnerability: A Case-Study from the Mountain Zone of Lesotho." Prepared for the Regional Hunger Vulnerability Programme, Institute of Southern African Studies and National University of Lesotho, Roma.

Das, Jishnu, Quy-Toan Do, and Berk Özler. 2005. "Reassessing Conditional Cash Transfer Programs." *World Bank Research Observer* 20 (1): 57–80.

Datt, Gaurav, Ellen Payongayong, James L. Garrett, and Marie Ruel. 1997. "The GAPVU Cash Transfer Program in Mozambique: An Assessment." FCND Discussion Paper 36, Food Consumption and Nutrition Division, International Food Policy Research Institute, Washington, DC.

Davey, James. 2007. "Concern Worldwide's Food and Cash Transfer (FACT) Programme." Wahenga Brief 10, Regional Hunger and Vulnerability Programme and Concern, Wahenga Institute, Johannesburg.

Davies, Simon, and James Davey. 2008. "A Regional Multiplier Approach to Estimating the Impact of Cash Transfers on the Market: The Case of Cash Transfers in Rural Malawi." *Development Policy Review* 26 (1): 91–111.

del Ninno, Carlo. 2009. "Payment Systems." PowerPoint presentation at World Bank Institute's Training Session on Designing and Implementing CCTs in Nigeria, Washington, DC, April 20.

Devereux, Stephen, Frank Ellis, and Philip White. 2008. "Coordination and Coverage." REBA Thematic Brief 4, Regional Hunger and Vulnerability Programme, Johannesburg.

Devereux, Stephen, and Paul Jere. 2008. "Choice, Dignity, and Empowerment: Cash and Food Transfers in Swaziland." Centre for Social Protection, Institute of Development Studies, Brighton, U.K., and PJ Development Consulting, Lilongwe.

Devereux, Stephen, and Michael Mhlanga. 2008. "Cash Transfers in Lesotho: An Evaluation of World Vision's Cash and Food Transfers Pilot Project." Centre for Social Protection, Institute for Development Studies, Brighton, U.K., and Mhlanga Consulting Services, Maseru, Lesotho.

Devereux, Stephen, and Larissa Pelham. 2005. "Making Cash Count: Lessons from Cash Transfer Schemes in East and Southern Africa for Supporting the Most Vulnerable Children and Households." Save the Children UK, HelpAge International, and Institute of Development Studies, London. http://www.ids.ac.uk/go/idsproject/making-cash-count.

Devereux, Stephen, Rachel Sabates-Wheeler, Rachel Slater, Mulugeta Tefera, Taylor Brown, and Amdissa Teshome. 2008. *Ethiopia's Productive Safety Net Programme (PSNP): 2008 Assessment Report*. Sussex, U.K.: Institute of Development Studies, Overseas Development Institute, Dadimos Development Consultants, IDL Group, and A–Z Consult.

Devereux, Stephen, Rachel Sabates-Wheeler, Mulugeta Tefera, and Hailemichael Taye. 2006. "Ethiopia's Productive Safety Net Programme (PSNP): Trends in PSNP Transfers within Targeted Households—Final Report." Institute of Development Studies, Sussex, U.K., and Indak International, Addis Ababa.

de Walque, Damien. 2009. "Evaluating the Impact of Conditional and Unconditional Cash Transfers in Rural Burkina Faso." PowerPoint presentation, Development Economics Research Group, World Bank, Washington, DC, January 12.

de Walque, Damien, William H. Dow, Rose Nathan, Carol Medlin, and RESPECT Study Team. 2010a. "Evaluating Conditional Cash Transfers to Prevent HIV and Other STIs in Tanzania." Poster #MOPE0835, presented at the International AIDS Conference, Vienna, Austria, July 19.

———. 2010b. "The RESPECT Study: Evaluating Conditional Cash Transfers for HIV/STI Prevention in Tanzania." World Bank, Washington, DC.

DFID (U.K. Department for International Development). 2006. "Managing the Fiduciary Risk Associated with Social Cash Transfer Programmes." Policy Division Info 98, DFID, London.

———. 2009. "Vision 2020 Umurenge Programme (2009–2013)." Project document, DFID, Kigali.

Dlamini, Armstrong. 2007. "A Review of Social Assistance Grants in Swaziland: A CANGO/RHVP Case Study on Public Assistance in Swaziland." Regional Hunger Vulnerability Programme, Johannesburg.

Document de Cadrage Technique. 2009. "Project de Transfert de Fonds Conditionné pour la Scolarisation et la Formation Professionnelle de 5,000 OEV au Sénégal."

Duflo, Esther. 2000. "Child Health and Household Resources in South Africa: Evidence from the Old Age Pension Program." *American Economic Review* 90 (2): 393–98.

Edmonds, Eric. 2006. "Child Labor and Schooling Responses to Anticipated Income in South Africa." *Journal of Development Economics* 81 (2): 386–414.

Edmonds, Eric, Kristen Mammen, and Douglas Miller. 2005. "Rearranging the Family? Income Support and Elderly Living Arrangements in a Low-Income Country." *Journal of Human Resources* 40 (1): 186–207.

ELCRN (Evangelical Lutheran Church in the Republic of Namibia). 2007. "Access to Government Grants." Desk for Social Development, ELCRN, Windhoek.

Ellis, Frank. 2007. "Food Subsidy Programme, Mozambique." REBA Case Study Brief 7, Regional Evidence Building Agenda, Regional Hunger Vulnerability Programme, Johannesburg.

———. 2008. "'We Are All Poor Here': Economic Difference, Social Divisiveness, and Targeting Cash Transfers in Sub-Saharan Africa." Paper presented at the conference on Social Protection for the Poorest in Africa: Learning from Experience, Entebbe, Uganda, September 8–10.

European University Institute. 2010. *Social Protection for Inclusive Development: A New Perspective in EU Cooperation with Africa*. San Domenico di Fiesole, Italy: Robert Schuman Centre for Advanced Studies, European University Institute.

Evans, David. 2008. "Tanzania Community-Based Conditional Cash Transfer (CB-CCT) Pilot." PowerPoint presentation, World Bank, Washington, DC, November 12.

Ferreira, Francisco H. G., Deon Filmer, and Norbert Schady. 2009. "Own and Sibling Effects of Conditional Cash Transfer Programs: Theory and Evidence from Cambodia." Policy Research Working Paper 5001, Development Research Group, Poverty and Inequality Team, and Human Development and Public Services Team, World Bank, Washington, DC.

Fiszbein, Ariel, and Norbert Schady, with Francisco H. G. Ferreira, Margaret Grosh, Nial Kelleher, Pedro Olinto, and Emmanuel Skoufias. 2009. *Conditional Cash Transfers: Reducing Present and Future Poverty*. Washington, DC: World Bank.

Gentilini, Ugo. 2007. "Cash and Food Transfers: A Primer." Occasional Paper 18, World Food Programme, Rome.

Gerelle, Eric. 2009. "Mobile-CCT: Requirements for a Mobile Information System to Support an Educational CCT Program in Northern Nigeria." Consultant Report to the World Bank, Washington, DC.

German Agency for Technical Cooperation. 2007. "Social Cash Transfers in Zambia: Setup, Lessons Learned, and Challenges." PowerPoint presentation at the Africa Regional Workshop on Cash Transfer (CT) Programmes for Vulnerable Groups, Mombasa, Kenya, February 26–28.

Gertler, Paul, Sebastián Martínez, and Marta Rubio-Codina. 2006. "Investing Cash Transfers to Raise Long-Term Living Standards." Policy Research Working Paper 3994, World Bank, Washington, DC.

Gilligan, Daniel O., John Hoddinott, Neha Rati Kumar, and Alemayehu Seyoum Taffesse. 2009a. *An Impact Evaluation of Ethiopia's Productive Safety Nets Program*. Washington, DC: International Food Policy Research Institute.

Gilligan, Daniel O., John Hoddinott, Neha Rati Kumar, Alemayehu Seyoum Taffesse, Samson Dejene, Fikru Gezahegn, and Yisehac Yohannes. 2009b. *Ethiopia Food Security Program: Report on 2008 Survey*. Washington, DC: International Food Policy Research Institute.

Government of Kenya. 2005. "Rapid Assessment, Analysis, and Action Planning Process (RAAAPP) for Orphans and Other Children Made Vulnerable by HIV/AIDS in Kenya (Kenya RAAAPP)." Office of the Vice President and Ministry of Home Affairs, Nairobi.

———. 2006. "Cash Transfers for Orphan and Vulnerable Children (OVC)." Cash Transfer Pilot Project, Office of the Vice President and Ministry of Home Affairs, Nairobi.

———. 2007. "OVC in Kenya." 2007. PowerPoint presentation by the Ministry of Home Affairs at the Africa Regional Workshop on Cash Transfer Programmes for Vulnerable Groups, Mombasa, Kenya, February 26–28.

Government of Mauritius. 2008. "Mauritius: Ageing in Place." Presented by the Ministry of Social Security, National Solidarity, and Senior Citizens Welfare and Reform Institutions at the International Federation of Ageing's Ninth Global Conference, Montreal, Canada, September 4–7.

———. 2009. "Mauritius Pension System Ahead of World Bank Model, Says Minister Bappoo." Government Information Service, Prime Minister's Office, Port Louis. http://www.gov.mu/.

Grosh, Margaret, Carlo del Ninno, Emil Tesliuc, and Azedine Ouerghi. 2008. *For Protection and Promotion: The Design and Implementation of Effective Safety Nets*. Washington, DC: World Bank.

Hamonga, Jean. 2006. "Community-Based Targeting Case Study: Zambia." Presented at the Third International Conference on Conditional Cash Transfers, Istanbul, June 29.

Handley, Geoff. 2009. "Fiscal Space for Strengthened Social Protection in West and Central Africa." United Nations Children's Fund, Dakar.

Hanlon, Joseph, Armando Barrientos, and David Hulme. 2010. *Just Give Money to the Poor: The Development Revolution from the Global South*. Sterling, VA: Kumarian.

Hoddinott, John, Emmanuel Skoufias, and Ryan Washburn. 2000. "The Impact of PROGRESA on Consumption: A Final Report." International Food Policy Research Institute, Washington, DC.

HSNP (Hunger Safety Net Programme). n.d. "Welcome to Hunger Safety Net Programme." HSNP, Nairobi.

———. 2008. "Know Hunger Safety Net Programme: Delivering Payments." HSNP, Nairobi. http://www.hungersafetynet.org/index2.htm.

Hurrell, Alex, Patrick Ward, and Fred Merttens. 2008. *Kenya OVC-CT Programme Operational and Impact Evaluation: Baseline Survey Report.* Oxford Policy Management, Oxford, U.K.

IFPRI (International Food Policy Research Institute). 2005. *Sistema de Evaluación de la Red de Protección Social (RPS): Mi Familia, Nicaragua—Evaluación del Impacto, 2000–04.* Washington, DC: IFPRI.

ILO (International Labour Organization). 2008a. "Can Low-Income Countries Afford Basic Social Security?" Social Security Policy Briefing Paper 3, ILO Social Security Department, Geneva.

———. 2008b. *Zambia Social Protection Expenditure and Performance Review and Social Budget.* Geneva: ILO Social Security Department.

IPC-IG (International Policy Centre for Inclusive Growth). 2008a. "International Cooperation on Social Protection." *Brasil and Africa Newsletter* 2: 3.

———. 2008b. "Social Protection in Ghana: The Livelihood Empowerment against Poverty (LEAP)." *Brasil and Africa Newsletter* 1: 1–2.

Jensen, Robert. 2004. "Do Private Transfers 'Displace' the Benefits of Public Transfers? Evidence from South Africa." *Journal of Public Economics* 88 (1–2): 89–112.

Jones, Nicola, with William Ahadzie and Daniel Doh. 2009. *Social Protection for Children: Opportunities and Challenges in Ghana.* London: Overseas Development Institute.

Langhan, Sarah, Gordon Mackay, and Craig Kilfoil. 2008. "Distribution Mechanism Scoping Study." Quindiem Consulting, Johannesburg.

Levine, Sebastian, Servaas van der Berg, and Derek Yu. 2009. "Measuring the Impact of Social Cash Transfers on Poverty and Inequality in Namibia." Stellenbosch Economic Working Paper 25/09, Department of Economics and Bureau for Economic Research, University of Stellenbosch, Stellenbosch, South Africa.

Macours, Karen, Norbert Schady, and Renos Vakis. 2008. "Cash Transfers, Behavioral Changes, and the Cognitive Development of Young Children: Evidence from a Randomized Experiment." Policy Research Working Paper 4759, World Bank, Washington, DC.

Maluccio, John A. 2005. "Coping with the 'Coffee Crisis' in Central America: The Role of the Nicaraguan *Red de Protección Social.*" Discussion Paper 188, Food Consumption and Nutrition Division, International Food Policy Research Institute, Washington, DC.

———. 2010. "The Impact of Conditional Cash Transfers in Nicaragua on Consumption, Productive Investments, and Labor Allocation." *Journal of Development Studies* 46 (1): 14–38.

Maluccio, John, and Rafael Flores. 2005. "Impact Evaluation of a Conditional Cash Transfer Program: The Nicaraguan Red de Protección Social." Research Report 141, International Food Policy Research Institute, Washington, DC.

Miller, Candace, Maxton Tsoka, and Mchinji Evaluation Team. 2007. "Evaluation of the Mchinji Cash Transfer: Report II—Targeting and Impact." Center for International Health and Development, Boston University, Boston, and Centre for Social Research, University of Malawi, Zomba.

Miller, Candace, Maxton Tsoka, and Kathryn Reichert. 2008. "Targeting Report: External Evaluation of the Mchinji Social Cash Transfer Pilot." Center for International Health and Development, Boston University, Boston, and Centre for Social Research, University of Malawi, Zomba.

———. 2010. "Targeting Cash to Malawi's Ultra-Poor: A Mixed Methods Evaluation." *Development Policy Review* 28 (4): 481–502.

Ministry of Community Development and Social Services. 2008. *Manual of Operations for the Social Cash Transfer Scheme.* Lusaka: Ministry of Community Development and Social Services.

Ministry of Community Development and Social Services and German Agency for Technical Cooperation. 2007. "Final Evaluation Report: Kalomo Social Cash Transfer Scheme." Ministry of Community Development and Social Services, Lusaka.

Mobenzi Researcher. 2011a. "Beneficiary Registration and Attendance Monitoring: Kano, Nigeria." Mobenzi Researcher, KwaZulu-Natal, South Africa. http://www.mobenzi.com/researcher/Case-Studies/KanoCCT.

———. 2011b. "Mobile Data Collection for the Real World." PowerPoint presentation for the Lesotho Ministry of Health and Social Welfare, Mobenzi Researcher, KwaZulu-Natal, South Africa.

Mvula, Peter. 2007. "The Dowa Emergency Cash Transfer (DECT) Project: A Study of the Social Impacts." Background study, Regional Hunger and Vulnerability Programme, Johannesburg.

Niño-Zarazúa, Miguel, Armando Barrientos, David Hulme, and Sam Hickey. 2010. "Social Protection in Sub-Saharan Africa: Will the Green Shoots Blossom?" Brooks World Poverty Institute Working Paper 116, University of Manchester, Manchester, U.K.

O'Cleirigh, Earnán. 2009. "Affordability of Social Protection Measures in Poor Developing Countries." In *Promoting Pro-Poor Growth: Social Protection*, 111–25. Paris: OECD.

Pearson, Roger, and Carlos Alviar. 2009. "Cash Transfers for Vulnerable Children in Kenya: From Political Choice to Scale Up." Social and Economic Policy Working Paper, United Nations Children's Fund, New York.

Plaatjies, Daniel. 2006. "Conditional Cash Transfer Programs in South Africa." Presented at the Third International Conference on Conditional Cash Transfers, Istanbul, June 26–30.

PlusNews. 2009. "Lesotho: Cash for Kids." Integrated Regional Information Network, May 3. http://www.irinnews.org/report.aspx?ReportId=83855.

Posel, Dori, James Fairburn, and Frances Lund. 2006. "Labour Migration and Households: A Reconsideration of the Effects of the Social Pension on Labour Supply in South Africa." *Economic Modelling* 23 (5): 836–53.

"Productive Safety Nets Programme in Ethiopia: The Public Works Component." n.d. PowerPoint presentation, World Bank, Washington, DC.

"Q&A: Child Cash Grants Programme." 2008. UNICEF, Lesotho.

Ravallion, Martin. 1999. "The Mystery of the Vanishing Benefits: Ms. Speedy Analyst's Introduction to Evaluation." Policy Research Working Paper 2153, World Bank, Washington, DC.

———. 2005. "Evaluating Anti-poverty Programs." Policy Research Working Paper 3625, World Bank, Washington, DC.

———. 2007. "How Relevant Is Targeting to the Success of an Antipoverty Program?" Policy Research Working Paper 4385, World Bank, Washington, DC.

Rawlings, Laura, and Gloria Rubio. 2005. "Evaluating the Impact of Conditional Cash Transfer Programs." *World Bank Economic Observer* 20 (1): 29–55.

Regalia, Fernando. 2006. "Some Thoughts about 'Conditionalities' in Cash Transfer Programs: Lessons from Latin America and the Caribbean." Presented at the Learning Workshop on Orphans and Vulnerable Children and Conditional Cash Transfers, Nairobi, February 20–21.

Republic of Namibia. 2007. *Namibia National Plan of Action for Orphans and Vulnerable Children*. Vol. 1. Windhoek: Ministry of Gender Equality and Child Welfare.

Republic of Rwanda. 2009. "Vision 2020 Umurenge Programme (VUP): Direct Support Operational Framework and Procedure Manual." Ministry of Local Government, Good Governance, Community Development, and Social Affairs, Kigali.

Republic of Zambia. 2007. *Implementation Framework for Scaling Up to a National System of Social Transfers in Zambia*. Lusaka: Ministry of Community Development and Social Services.

RHVP (Regional Hunger and Vulnerability Programme). 2007. "Old Age and Public Assistance Grants, Swaziland." REBA Case Study Brief 6, Regional Evidence Building Agenda, RHVP, Johannesburg.

———. 2009. "Impact of Social Cash Transfers on Household Welfare, Investment, and Education in Zambia." Wahenga Brief 17, RHVP, Johannnesburg. http://www.wahenga.net/node/223.

RNA (RuralNet Associates). 2007. "Case Study on the Chipata and Kazungula Social Cash Transfer Schemes by CARE International." Regional Hunger and Vulnerability Programme, Johannesburg.

Sabates-Wheeler, Rachel, and Stephen Devereux. 2010. "Cash Transfers and High Food Prices: Explaining Outcomes on Ethiopia's Productive Safety Net Programme." *Food Policy* 35 (4): 274–85.

Sabates-Wheeler, Rachel, Stephen Devereux, and Bruce Guenther. 2009. "Building Synergies between Social Protection and Smallholder Agricultural Policies." FAC Working Paper SP01, Future Agricultures Consortium Secretariat, Institute of Development Studies, University of Sussex, Brighton, U.K.

Samson, Michael. 2007. "African Perspectives on Cash Transfers: The Developmental Impact of Social Transfers." PowerPoint presentation at the Africa Regional Workshop on Cash Transfer Programmes for Vulnerable Groups, Mombasa, Kenya, February 26–28.

Samson, Michael, and Shesangai Kaniki. 2008. "Social Pensions as Developmental Social Security for Africa." *Poverty in Focus* 15: 22–23.

Save the Children and UNICEF (United Nations Children's Fund). 2009. "Regional Research Programme to Strengthen the Evidence Base on the Impact of Social Transfers on Child Development." Concept Note, Save the Children, Westport, CT.

Schubert, Bernd. 2007a. "Manual of Operations for the Malawi Pilot Social Cash Transfer Scheme." United Nations Children's Fund, Lilongwe.

———. 2007b. "Piloting the Scale Up of the Malawi Social Cash Transfer Scheme (Fifth Report: January–June 2007)." United Nations Children's Fund, Lilongwe.

———. 2009. "Targeting Social Cash Transfers: The Process of Defining Target Groups and the Targeting Mechanism for the Malawi Social Cash Transfer Scheme." Regional Hunger and Vulnerability Programme, Johannesburg.

Schubert, Bernd, and Mayke Huijbregts. 2006. "The Malawi Social Cash Transfer Pilot Scheme, Preliminary Lessons Learned." Presented at the conference on Social Protection Initiatives for Children, Women, and Families: An Analysis of Recent Experiences, New York, October 30–31.

Schultz, T. Paul. 2004. "School Subsidies for the Poor: Evaluating the Mexican PROGRESA Poverty Program." *Journal of Development Economics* 74 (1): 199–250.

Schüring, Esther. 2010a. "Conditions, Conditionality, Conditionalities, Responsibilities: Finding Common Ground." Working Paper 2010WP014, Maastrict Graduate School of Governance, Maastrict, Netherlands.

———. 2010b. "Strings Attached or Loose Ends? The Role of Conditionality in Zambia's Social Cash Transfer Scheme." Maastricht Graduate School of Governance, Maastricht, Netherlands.

Slater, Rachel, Steve Ashley, Mulugeta Tefera, Mengistu Buta, and Delelegne Esubalew. 2006. "PSNP Policy, Programme, and Institutional Linkages."

Overseas Development Institute, IDL Group UK, and Indak International, London.

Slater, Rachel, and John Farrington, with Marcella Vigneri, Mike Samson, and Shaheen Akter. 2009. "Targeting of Social Transfers: A Review for DFID." Final report. Overseas Development Institute, London.

Slater, Rachel, and John Farrington. 2010. "Appropriate, Achievable, Acceptable: A Practical Tool for *Good* Targeting." Social Protection Toolsheet: Targeting Social Transfers. Overseas Development Institute, London.

Soares, Fábio Veras, Guilherme Issamu Hirata, and Rafael Rivas. n.d. "The Programa Subsidio de Alimentos in Mozambique: Baseline Evaluation." International Policy Centre for Inclusive Growth, Brasília.

Soares, Fábio Veras, and Clarissa Teixeira. 2010. "Impact Evaluation of the Expansion of the Food Subsidy Programme in Mozambique." Research Brief 17, International Policy Centre for Inclusive Growth, Brasília.

Stewart, Scott R., and Sudhanshu Handa. 2008. "Reaching OVC through Cash Transfers in Sub-Saharan Africa: Simulation Results from Alternative Targeting Schemes." United Nations Children's Fund, Nairobi.

Streak, Judith. 2007. "Brief Overview of Cash Transfer System in South Africa and Introduction to HSRC Going to Scale Research Project." PowerPoint presentation at the Africa Regional Workshop on Cash Transfer Programmes for Vulnerable Groups, Mombasa, Kenya, February 26–28.

Sultan, Sonya M., and Tamar T. Schrofer. 2008. "Building Support to Have Targeted Social Protection Interventions for the Poorest: The Case of Ghana." Presented at the Conference on Social Protection for the Poorest in Africa: Learning from Experience, Kampala, September 8–10.

Tandeo, Andrew. 2005. "Internal Monitoring System: Summary Report on the Use of Transfers."

TASAF (Tanzania Social Action Fund). 2008. "Tanzania Community-Based Conditional Cash Transfer Pilot." TASAF, Dar es Salaam.

Taylor, Viviene. 2010. *Social Protection in Africa: An Overview of the Challenges.* Addis Ababa: African Union.

Urban Institute and Birhan Research and Development Consultancy. 2008. *The Ethiopia Productive Safety Net Program, in the Financial Transparency and Accountability Perception Survey.* Washington, DC: Urban Institute; Addis Ababa: Birhan Research and Development Consultancy.

Van Domelen, Julie. 2010. *The 2001 Africa Social Protection Strategy: Review of Implementation FY01 to FY10.* Washington, DC: World Bank.

Vincent, Katharine, and Tracy Cull. 2009. "Impacts of Social Cash Transfers: Case Study Evidence from across Southern Africa." II Conferência do IESE, "Dinâmicas da Pobreza e Padrões de Acumulação Económica em Moçambique, Maputo, April 22–23.

Waterhouse, Rachel. 2007. "Briefing Paper: Coordination and Coverage of Social Protection Initiatives in Mozambique." International Policy Centre for Inclusive Growth, Brasília. http://www.ipc-undp.org/.

White, Philip, Frank Ellis, Stephen Devereux, and Katharine Vincent. 2009. "Poverty Targeting: New Evidence on Spatial and Distributional Impacts." Frontiers of Social Protection Brief 2, Regional Hunger and Vulnerability Programme, Johannesburg.

Williams, Martin J. 2007. "The Social and Economic Impacts of South Africa's Child Support Grant." Working Paper 39, Economic Policy Research Institute, Cape Town, South Africa.

Woolard, Ingrid, Kenneth Harttgen, and Stephan Klasen. 2010. "The Evolution and Impact of Social Security in South Africa." Background note for *European Report on Development 2010*. San Domenico di Fiesole, Italy, European University Institute.

Woolard, Ingrid, and Murray Leibbrandt. 2010. "The Evolution and Impact of Unconditional Cash Transfers in South Africa." Southern Africa Labour and Development Research Unit, University of Cape Town, Cape Town, South Africa.

World Bank. n.d.a. "CCT in Nigeria: Preliminary Concept Note." World Bank, Washington, DC.

———. n.d.b. "Morocco: Conditional Cash Transfers and Education." World Bank, Washington, DC.

———. 2005. "Conditional Cash Transfers for Vulnerable Children in Kenya: Frequently Asked Questions." World Bank, Washington, DC.

———. 2008. "Joint World Bank–DFID–ESSPIN–UNICEF Partners Mission on Girls' Education Conditional Cash Transfers Pilot Programme for Northern Nigeria (Kano and Bauchi States)." World Bank, Washington, DC.

———. 2009a. "Emergency Project Paper under the Global Food Crisis Response Program on a Proposed Grant from the Multi-Donor Trust Fund in the Amount of US$8 Million and a Proposed Credit in the Amount of SDR 6.8 Million (US$10 Million Equivalent) to the Republic of Senegal for a Rapid Response Child-Focused Social Cash Transfer and Nutrition Security Project." Human Development II, Country Department AFCF1, Africa Region, World Bank, Washington, DC.

———. 2009b. "Nigeria: Conditional Grant and Cash Transfer Project." Project Concept Note, Social Protection, Africa Region, World Bank, Washington, DC.

———. 2009c. "Program Document on a Proposed Grant in the Amount of SDR 4 Million (US$6 Million Equivalent) Funding to the Republic of Rwanda for a First Community Living Standards Grant (CLSG-1)." Human Development III, Eastern Africa Country Cluster II, Africa Region, World Bank, Washington, DC.

———. 2009d. "Project Appraisal Document for a Cash Transfer for Orphans and Vulnerable Children Project." World Bank, Washington, DC.

———. 2010a. *Designing and Implementing a Rural Safety Net in a Low Income Setting: Lessons Learned from Ethiopia's Productive Safety Net Program 2005–2009*. Washington, DC: World Bank.

———. 2010b. "Malawi and Tanzania Research Shows Promise in Preventing HIV and Sexually Transmitted Infections." World Bank, Washington, DC. http://web.worldbank.org/WBSITE/EXTERNAL/COUNTRIES/AFRICAEXT/EXTAFRHEANUTPOP/EXTAFRREGTOPHIVAIDS/0,,contentMDK:22649337~menuPK:717155~pagePK:34004173~piPK:34003707~theSitePK:717148,00.html.

———. 2010c. "Project Appraisal Document on a Proposed Credit in the Amount of SDR 58.4 Million (US$88.6 Million Equivalent) in the Amount of SDR 31.3 Million (US$47.6 Million Equivalent) in Pilot CRW Resources to the Republic of Ghana for a Social Opportunities Project." Western Africa I, Social Protection, Africa Region, World Bank, Washington, DC.

———. 2011. "Managing Risk, Promoting Growth: Developing Systems for Social Protection in Africa—Africa Social Protection Strategy 2011–2021." Concept Note, World Bank, Washington, DC.

CHAPTER 4

Synthesis, Conclusions, and the Way Forward

The previous two chapters have provided a broad framework through which one can understand the rise and general characteristics of Sub-Saharan Africa's cash transfer (CT) programs, and they have discussed specific trends in the identified programs. This chapter examines how the region's CT programs stand apart from other programs around the world. It also discusses how the programs are expected to evolve, outlines knowledge gaps and areas for research, and presents conclusions.

Unique Program Characteristics of Cash Transfers in Sub-Saharan Africa

The purpose of this review was to obtain information about CTs in Sub-Saharan Africa; however, this information is perhaps more interesting when compared with general trends in CTs in other regions. There are a wide variety of CTs around the world, and this discussion does not intend to subsume program differences. Instead, it is meant to contrast general trends in Sub-Saharan African CT programs with trends in CTs in other regions. This section highlights some of the characteristics of Sub-Saharan Africa's CTs that stood out as relatively unique to the region. The discussion, though not exhaustive, highlights how the region's unique challenges have driven program variations.

Some of the explored variations, such as the range of program objectives, reflect the unique environment in Sub-Saharan Africa. Other variations, such as the level of community involvement in CTs, are not inherently positive or negative. Community involvement reflects the traditional role that communities have played in individuals' lives and their potential to assist with CTs. However, this variation and others should not be used without concern for program integrity or implementation.

Still other characteristics unique to Sub-Saharan Africa have arisen because CTs have been used to confront challenges of greater frequency or depth than those seen in programs in other regions. Such components may not be a first-best approach in most situations. They are a best response, or at least an attempted best response, given the challenges of the specific context. As parameters change and constraints relax, the responses may no longer be the best solution.

CT Objectives as a Reflection of the Region's Unique Challenges: Food Insecurity, HIV/AIDS, and Orphans

The divergence of Sub-Saharan African program objectives from the human capital objectives commonly seen in programs—especially conditional cash transfers (CCTs)—in other regions reflects some of the most pressing social assistance needs in the region. Provided that those objectives have a solid empirical basis, their unique characteristics are appropriate to the region. Although traditional CCT programs often address households' lack of human capital as a source of poverty, programs in Sub-Saharan Africa recognize that even more basic issues, such as food security and survival, must be addressed. Therefore, their objectives often focus more directly on households' immediate needs than do some of the long-term objectives in other programs.[1] One tendency of some programs in the region is to address emergency food shortages with CTs, in lieu of previously received food transfers. Although the CT programs are necessary in the short term, the evolution of programs to work as preventive mechanisms, rather than emergency stopgap responses, will be welcome.

Some programs in Sub-Saharan Africa also focus on sexual activities and outcomes, such as early marriage and sexually transmitted infection status. Those types of objectives, while similar in part to some programs in South Asia, are relatively unique, and they reflect a programmatic variation that can address Sub-Saharan Africa's challenges in those areas. Programs that focus on supporting orphans and vulnerable children (OVC) also help to systematically deal with the OVC crisis affecting many countries in the region.

Community Involvement: A Hallmark of African Cash Transfer Programs

Although many CT programs around the world require communities to support their activities to a certain extent, the programs in Sub-Saharan Africa often rely on communities in ways beyond those found in other regions. The communities are involved in identifying potential beneficiaries, targeting, collecting data, verifying information about beneficiaries, distributing cash, monitoring beneficiaries' use of cash (even in unconditional transfers), and addressing grievances. This extensive community involvement sometimes reflects capacity limitations within implementing bodies.

In addition, communities in Sub-Saharan Africa sometimes have claims on transfers. For instance, in some villages in Niger, local leaders taxed CT beneficiaries. In other cases, communities pooled transfers and redistributed them, although some program beneficiaries were awarded larger amounts than nonbeneficiaries (Save the Children UK 2009). Some community groups have also imposed restrictions on how beneficiaries may use cash, thereby limiting the fungibility of transfers.

Although community involvement can raise new concerns about CTs and their management, that involvement has been indispensable to programs' implementation in Sub-Saharan Africa. When correctly managed, community involvement can lower costs, improve implementation, and provide support to traditional support systems that have been weakened by constant pressure and a changing environment. Community targeting that builds on existing local capacity for such exercises can speed program implementation and improve targeting outcomes, as in Ethiopia's Productive Safety Net Programme (PSNP) and Rwanda's Vision 2020 Umurenge Programme (VUP). Community involvement needs to be appropriately monitored to ensure that abuses do not occur, because communities can both help protect vulnerable individuals and groups and be a source of exclusion and discrimination to those not favored by traditional authorities or majority ethnic or clan powers.

The usefulness of the community involvement depends in part on its motivation and on its implementation. Programs that use communities simply as a stopgap solution for weak institutional capacity may have difficulty effectively implementing CTs at scale. In CT programs that rely on well-trained communities with support from institutions with adequate capacity, community involvement may facilitate an effective program rollout.

No Gender Preference for Payments

In contrast to many other CT programs around the world, some programs in Sub-Saharan Africa do not specify that a female should be the recipient of cash transfers. Fewer than half of the reviewed CCT programs, and approximately 1 in 10 unconditional CT (UCT) programs, specified that transfers be distributed to females. The trend is partially driven by the number of programs that transfer cash to individuals rather than to households (that is, social pensions). Even so, that factor does not fully explain this tendency, and it is not clear that this programmatic variation is a first-best approach.

Empirical work and anecdotal evidence have pointed to the benefits that can accrue to children as women's control of household resources increases; this result has appeared across multiple cultures and regions, including in Sub-Saharan Africa. For instance, Duflo (2003) and Quisumbing and Maluccio (2000) found qualified evidence of such benefits in South Africa and Ethiopia, respectively. However, assuming that all recipients of cash transfers in Sub-Saharan African households should be women could be naive. Households may redistribute resources to negotiate the increase in women's cash, and household roles may be affected. Even if women receive and control cash, another consideration to be made is whether their control of cash affects their male and female children differently.

Fortunately, programs are testing how results differ when transfers are distributed to males rather than females in Burkina Faso. CTs are examining this question outside of the region in Morocco and the Republic of Yemen, which have some similar gender dynamics with parts of Sub-Saharan Africa. Results from these programs will be able to inform CT design in Sub-Saharan Africa to determine whether this program characteristic is appropriate and aligns with existing evidence about females' control of resources and household outcomes. Qualitative analysis of the effect of providing transfers to females also should be conducted to determine whether this feature affects household violence and how it affects females' bargaining power.

Conditions in Cash Transfer Programs: Less Prevalent in Sub-Saharan Africa, but Rising

For the most part, the reviewed CCTs had conditions similar to those in other regions. Most conditions were based on activities, such as school enrollment or attendance, rather than outcomes, such as school achievement. In contrast, CCTs in other regions sometimes have conditions attached to beneficiary outcomes, such as students' maintaining certain grades or passing exams and parents' being involved in children's schooling. This difference is most noticeable in education-related conditions.

The tendency for conditions to focus on activities rather than outcomes may reflect the difficulty associated with monitoring conditions in Sub-Saharan Africa. It may also reflect concerns over the burdens that conditions place on households or the quality of supply-side services, which may limit final outcomes. Whatever the motivation, any conditions required of CT beneficiaries in Sub-Saharan Africa should be chosen with these concerns in mind. Capacity constraints and the depth of poverty in the region must be carefully considered before any conditions are decided on, and those decisions should be informed by quantitative and qualitative research, as well as by a thorough analysis of the costs and benefits of applying conditions, both for program officials and for beneficiaries.

Another unique aspect of CT programs in Sub-Saharan Africa is the flexibility with which conditions are applied.[2] Many CCTs in Sub-Saharan Africa use soft conditions that impose no penalties for noncompliance. Even in programs with hard conditions, most CCTs apply conditions flexibly. For example, they may be applied only in areas with adequate supply-side infrastructure or in areas that receive additional supply-side investments. In some cases, only households that are judged capable of fulfilling conditions are required to abide by them. Conditions are often monitored less frequently than they are in other regions, and warnings and partial payment penalties are often applied when beneficiaries do not comply with conditions to ensure that benefits are not inappropriately kept from needy households.

This hesitancy to apply cut-and-dried conditions reflects valid concerns about beneficiaries' ability to fulfill conditions, the capacity of supply-side institutions to handle increased demand, and the CT programs' capacity to monitor conditions. Programs that apply soft conditions should consider the possible direct and indirect effects of this feature. Once again, these issues are being tested by evaluations in the region, and they deserve further analysis.

A Variety of Cash Transfer Methods

Although some CT programs in other regions use more than one method of cash distribution, programs in Sub-Saharan Africa consistently use multiple payment methods to deliver CTs to beneficiaries. This design variation reflects the difficulty associated with serving hard-to-reach clients; therefore, whatever methods work best in a given area are used there. Although using multiple payment methods may be effective at reaching beneficiaries, it can decrease scale effects and increase costs of payment distributions. However, this solution may be the most effective way to reach beneficiaries in remote areas and serve beneficiaries in ways that suit them.

Leapfrog Technology: Transfer by Mobile Phones, Point-of-Sale Devices, and Web-Based Monitoring

CTs in Sub-Saharan Africa are investigating the use of advanced technologies to overcome traditional capacity constraints. Some of the technologies address characteristics unique to the region. Biometric identification can overcome traditional difficulties in identifying beneficiaries who lack appropriate documentation; point-of-sale devices or mobile phones can be used to transfer cash to nomadic or hard-to-reach beneficiaries; mobile phones can be used for social marketing, communication, or monitoring; and web-based management information systems may be able to integrate program databases across remote locations.

The possibility for technology to address capacity constraints in the region is still being investigated, and it may be capable of overcoming additional challenges, such as collecting data about beneficiaries. Although there is excitement about the possibility of using advanced technologies in the region, this excitement should be tempered with a realistic understanding of whether these technologies can deliver all that they promise and how they can best be leveraged. New technologies should be thoroughly tested before being rolled out. Training should be completed to ensure that program officials and beneficiaries are capable of, and comfortable with, using the technologies.

Institutional Location and Funding of Cash Transfer Programs: Both Government and Donor Based

Unlike the vanguard CT programs in other regions, almost half of the identified programs in Sub-Saharan Africa were seated outside of government institutions, and one in two were funded entirely using nongovernmental funds. This trend was especially prominent in low-income countries. In part, it reflects the nascent stage of CTs and social protection in many Sub-Saharan African countries. It also reflects the role that short-term, externally funded CTs have played in addressing emergencies in the region.

Although such programs have provided useful assistance and generated important information, continuing this trend in the long run would

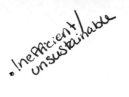
Inefficient, unsustainable

be inefficient. Programs located outside the government often fail to capitalize on potential economies of scale needed to effectively implement a CT program. These programs often lack the strong targeting, monitoring, and evaluation systems needed to achieve cost-efficiencies in implementation. Meanwhile, duplication of effort occurs across programs because each CT program establishes its own systems and procedures. These inefficiencies limit impacts and waste resources.

In addition, multiple small CT programs often are characterized by patchy, uncoordinated coverage of the population. Large swaths of the potential beneficiary population may remain unsupported. Meanwhile, in areas where multiple small programs overlap, coverage of different beneficiaries with varying benefit levels can cause confusion among beneficiaries (O'Cleirigh 2009).

Because many programs operate almost entirely outside of the state system, they fail to develop capacity within government institutions and fail to encourage development of the social contract.

CTs that rely almost exclusively on donor funding also are subject to the whims of donors and to short funding cycles. They face challenges of balancing domestic and external priorities, and they are vulnerable to being driven by donor preferences. Therefore, greater domestic investment in programs promises to provide important benefits to the region.

A fortunate trend in Sub-Saharan Africa is the tendency toward greater institutionalization and domestic funding of CT programs. Programs in Ethiopia, Ghana, Kenya, Rwanda, and other countries enjoy strong domestic support and leadership, and they promise to reap the benefits of more cost-effective programs. That being said, many programs will continue to need external financing and support, and development partners can make important contributions by adopting long-term, coordinated approaches to funding CT programs and by supporting long-term capacity building and technical support for CTs.

Knowledge Gaps and Areas for Future Research

Although the review uncovered substantial data about many programs, it also highlighted knowledge gaps about the region's CTs. Information about collecting data in settings with limited financial and human resource capacity, targeting individuals who may not be easily identified because of stigma or inaccessibility, improving the implementation of targeting at the community level, and effectively communicating targeting criteria to program beneficiaries and nonbeneficiaries will be helpful.

Care should also be taken to understand how receipt of CTs, especially by females, affects intrahousehold relationships in the varied cultural settings in Sub-Saharan Africa.

Many programs in Sub-Saharan Africa are experimenting with novel means of delivering cash to beneficiaries, and those experiences will help others seeking to implement programs, particularly in remote rural settings. Continued analysis of optimal transfer size with respect to program goals is an area in which further study will be useful as programs gauge how to maximize their impacts with limited budgets. Although the optimal frequency of cash distribution merits further analysis, much of this decision rests on pragmatic questions of human resource availability and program capacity to process payments. Therefore, case studies and other information related to improving on-time delivery of transfers may be more useful.

Given the challenges inherent in applying conditions in many Sub-Saharan African countries, an important element of program planning involves testing this design feature in a variety of contexts in the region. Although traditional impact evaluations are important for learning the effectiveness of CCTs and UCTs on specific outcomes, other studies are also important. For instance, process evaluations will provide information about compliance with conditions. Other studies could cover soft issues related to conditions, including beneficiary and public perception of conditions, challenges in applying conditions, the potential exclusionary roles of conditions, and political economy dynamics that affect the usefulness of conditions. Another area of study that may prove fruitful concerns which conditions should be applied and how often conditions should be monitored in Sub-Saharan Africa's CCTs.

Information on how to effectively implement monitoring systems in a limited-capacity setting will also be helpful. Some information exists on this topic, but additional information from established programs may be helpful as new programs begin and attempt to scale up. Case studies that illustrate how some programs have overcome technological constraints in monitoring, as well as how they have increased capacity of program personnel for monitoring, will be important.

Information for programs that use community members for targeting, distribution, and program monitoring will also be helpful. When community members are involved in these processes, they must be monitored to avoid abuses. Cost-effective methods of monitoring communities involved in CTs, especially given capacity constraints, need to be identified.

A final issue that needs to be addressed is how to monitor who actually is residing in beneficiary households. Such information is particularly important when benefits are tied to household size.

Additional information on how programs coordinate roles depending on their political structures will also be useful, particularly for countries with a federal system (such as Ethiopia and Nigeria) that allow lower-level autonomous units considerable power to plan and execute their CT programs.

Given the major role of donors in many CT programs in Sub-Saharan Africa, additional case studies and information on how donors can coordinate their efforts and funding, all while supporting government priorities and systems, will be illustrative for the region and beyond.

Interest remains in learning how CTs affect informal risk-coping mechanisms, such as migration and remittances, and informal insurance arrangements at the local level. Immediate effects of programs will be of interest, but their long-term influence on these structures is also important. Issues to consider are whether CTs might erode or support informal safety nets (whether they be burial societies, child-fostering practices, simple norms of reciprocity, or others) and what the consequences of those changes would be. Although CTs have responded to a weakening in traditional support systems, these systems still play an important role in the lives of many Africans. Therefore, formal programs should understand how they affect informal protection mechanisms and should ensure that they do not have unintended adverse impacts (European University Institute 2010).

Also, the potential effect of CTs on traditional local hierarchies is of interest. Cash for the poor may reorient relationships with local traditional authorities and disband entrenched patronage systems (European University Institute 2010), or traditional systems may place additional demands on CT beneficiaries. Social dynamics continue to be important.

The role of CTs in settings where governance, accountability, and political freedoms are still nascent is also of interest. Cash transfers in Sub-Saharan Africa are thought to be helping to enfranchise marginalized groups in the state system for the first time, possibly engendering greater political accountability and representation (European University Institute 2010). If CTs really affect these areas, the transition from emergency to predictable transfers in fragile or postconflict environments may have a positive influence on citizen-state relations. This potential should be understood and capitalized on.

Conclusions and the Road Ahead

This book has argued that CTs can be very valuable. However, CTs are not a panacea or a silver bullet. They are not always an appropriate tool, nor can they address all vulnerabilities or problems. However, if correctly designed and implemented, CT programs have the potential to positively affect the lives of many individuals in Sub-Saharan Africa.

This book has provided general observations and summary information about CTs throughout Sub-Saharan Africa, giving a broad view of the past, current state, and future direction of CTs. Perhaps the most remarkable outcome of the review is its exposure of the large number and wide variety of CT programs that have functioned or currently exist throughout Sub-Saharan Africa. The review also brings to light the fragmented state of cash transfers and social protection within most countries, with the noted exception of some of the middle-income countries. The majority of identified programs have been short term and limited in coverage, and many are donor driven and project based. Because this fragmentation fails to capitalize on potential efficiencies, countries and donors should work toward developing longer-term, coordinated, government-led programs that can achieve maximal results.

The success of CTs in Sub-Saharan Africa hinges on several factors: the transfers must be evidence driven, and they must have solid fundamentals. CT programs should be built on strong analytical work and defensible quantitative and qualitative research. Also, they should use properly designed and tested systems of targeting, payments, monitoring, and appeals. These building blocks are crucial to CTs' success.

However, even programs that have strong fundamentals and are based on solid analytical work may not be successful. CTs must be designed with the program's specific context in mind. Cash transfers, though often supported by donors in Sub-Saharan Africa, should not be designed in a one-size-fits-all manner. The more they are designed with the specific culture and constraints in mind, the greater their chance of success and longevity.

Despite these caveats and others mentioned throughout the book, experience has shown that implementing effective, state-led CT programs for large populations in Sub-Saharan Africa is possible, even in low-income countries. Several programs described in this book provide examples of programs with strong fundamental systems that are being implemented using government agencies, relying on domestic leadership and buy-in, all with long-term funding and support from multiple development partners.

Excitement around the potential use of CTs in Sub-Saharan Africa is not unmerited. Experiences, many relatively successful, reveal that the question is not whether cash transfers *can* be used in Sub-Saharan Africa, but rather *how* they should be used, and how they can be adapted and developed to meet social protection and development goals. Cash transfers may well prove to be an important tool for addressing the region's development, poverty alleviation, and human rights aspirations.

Clearly, CTs in Sub-Saharan Africa have reached a tipping point; their presence in the region is expected to multiply rapidly within the next few years. Fortunately, the way ahead is not without direction. It can draw from the rich lessons already learned through existing CTs in the region.

Notes

1. However, an inherent tension exists in program objectives of many traditional CCTs that aim to both decrease short-term poverty and increase long-term human capital accumulation. See Soares and Britto (2007) for examples of this tension in Latin America. Some interpret CCTs as antipoverty programs with conditions attached for (typically) political reasons, rather than as programs with human capital objectives that use cash as an incentive.
2. Although conditions are applied more flexibly in Sub-Saharan Africa than in other regions, this difference does not mean that conditions are always applied strictly in CCTs in other regions.

References

Duflo, Esther. 2003. "Grandmothers and Granddaughters: Old-Age Pensions and Intrahousehold Allocation in South Africa." *World Bank Economic Review* 17 (1): 1–25.

European University Institute. 2010. *Social Protection for Inclusive Development: A New Perspective in EU Cooperation with Africa*. San Domenico di Fiesole, Italy: Robert Schuman Centre for Advanced Studies, European University Institute.

O'Cleirigh, Earnán. 2009. "Affordability of Social Protection Measures in Poor Developing Countries." In *Promoting Pro-Poor Growth: Social Protection*, 111–25. Paris: OECD.

Quisumbing, Agnes R., and John A. Maluccio. 2000. "Intrahousehold Allocation and Gender Relations: New Empirical Evidence from Four Developing Countries." FCND Discussion Paper 84, Food, Consumption, and Nutrition Division, International Food Policy Research Institute, Washington, DC.

Save the Children UK. 2009. *How Cash Transfers Can Improve the Nutrition of the Poorest Children: Evaluation of a Pilot Safety Net Project in Southern Niger.* London: Save the Children.

Soares, Fábio Veras, and Tatiana Britto. 2007. "Confronting Capacity Constraints on Conditional Cash Transfers in Latin America: The Cases of El Salvador and Paraguay." Working Paper 38, International Poverty Centre for Inclusive Growth, Brasília.

APPENDIX A

Detailed Reviews of Sub-Saharan Africa's Cash Transfer Programs
Country-by-Country Information on Design and Implementation

This appendix provides additional information about the major CT programs that were examined in the desk review. Reviewers attempted to obtain standardized information on each program to allow for presentation in a systematic and consistent format. Unfortunately, desired data have not always been readily available; moreover, it was not always clear whether such information was describing current, past, or some anticipated future status of the program. The text in this appendix reflects this uncertainty when it has arisen and been recognized.

The information provided in this appendix should not take the place of more in-depth assessments, such as country visits and reviews to investigate the individual programs and to understand their implementation dynamics. At the very least, however, this information can provide a useful starting point for understanding key issues and can direct further inquiry on a country-by-country basis.

Botswana

Botswana has one of the most extensive social grant systems in the region, including separate programs for elderly people, orphans, and people living with disabilities.

Old Age Pension

The Old Age Pension reaches a large proportion of Botswana's population. Launched in 1996 after its announcement in the annual budget speech (Devereux and Pelham 2005), the Old Age Pension has the objective of financially assisting elderly people who do not have other support. The pension was necessitated by deterioration of informal support systems such as the extended family (Gaolathe 2009). The pension is a universal, noncontributory pension for individuals over age 65. Benefits are distributed through post offices, where beneficiaries must present their national registration card. If an alternate receives the cash in the beneficiary's name, the pensioner must sign a life certificate every quarter to prove he or she is still living. The number of beneficiaries grew from approximately 70,000 in 2000 to 89,471 in early 2009. Benefits indirectly reach approximately 42 percent of the population (Devereux and Pelham 2005).

Samson and Kaniki (2008) estimate that Botswana's Old Age Pension costs 0.4 percent of gross domestic product (GDP) annually. The original transfer value was P 100 (US$30),[1,2] and it was indexed to civil servants' pay levels. By 2007, the monthly transfer was P 166 (US$26)[3] per month (BFTU 2007). In general, the transfer's real value, adjusted annually for inflation, has hovered between US$27 and US$30.

The commissioner for social benefits, an official in the Ministry of Local Government, manages the pension (Gaolathe 2009).

Orphan Care Program

Botswana's Orphan Care Program is open to all orphans, who are registered when community members identify them and a social worker has assessed their case (BFTU 2007). The Orphan Care Program reached approximately 25,000 beneficiaries by 2005, and the number approximately doubled by 2009 (Devereux and Pelham 2005; Gaolathe 2009). The number of beneficiaries is expected to rise as more children are orphaned because of AIDS, although the introduction of widespread access to antiretroviral therapy has at least temporarily lowered the very high rates of adult mortality. The orphan care benefit mainly provides in-kind transfers, but it is supplemented with an additional cash transfer of P 400 (approximately US$60)[4] once a year (Bar-On 2002). Orphans are also provided psychosocial support. Stigma attached to AIDS hinders children from being registered for the program, leaving orphans underserved (BFTU 2007).

Program for Destitute Persons

Besides an additional transfer to veterans of World War II, a transfer known as the Program for Destitute Persons was begun in 1980. The program's objective is to provide minimum social assistance to ensure that the destitute maintain their health and welfare (BFTU 2007). The Program for Destitute Persons targets individuals with fewer than four units of livestock, individuals who earn less than P 120 (US$24),[5] people living with disabilities, minors not receiving other support, and individuals affected by systemic shocks. Also covered are children under 18 years of age with terminally ill parents who cannot care for them. Beneficiaries must apply or be nominated for the program, and a social worker must assess their status before they can receive benefits.

In 2005, the program provided transfers of P 61 (US$12) monthly. Other in-kind benefits, ranging from P 181 to P 256 (US$36 to US$51), were given to beneficiaries, and fees for education, health, and utility services were waived (Devereux and Pelham 2005). Beneficiaries are also supposed to receive psychosocial support (BFTU 2007). Benefit levels differ depending on whether beneficiaries live in urban or rural areas and whether the beneficiary is designated as a temporarily or permanently destitute person. As of February 2009, the Program for Destitute Persons reached 40,525 beneficiaries (Gaolathe 2009).

Burkina Faso

Pilot Conditional Cash Transfer–Cash Transfer Program

Pilot program tests how UCTs and CCTs can support OVC. The Burkina Faso government and the World Bank support a CT as part of a broader project created to help orphans and vulnerable children (OVC) in the provinces of Nahouri and Sanmatenga. The CT component operates in Nahouri province in south-central Burkina Faso, bordering Ghana. Burkina Faso's permanent secretary of the National Council against AIDS and STI and the University of Ouagadougou, at the national level, have worked with the World Bank's Africa Region to design and implement the program.

The CT was designed and is being evaluated to test whether successes of CTs seen outside the region can be transferred to rural areas of Sub-Saharan Africa. Also being tested is the value of conditional cash transfers (CCTs) versus unconditional cash transfers (UCTs) and the value of distributing transfers to mothers versus fathers in this setting.

Program has an experimental research design. The study includes 75 villages with approximately 3,250 households. As part of the program's experimental design, villages were randomly selected to receive one of four possible interventions or to belong to a control group. Poor households and households with OVC within those villages were eligible to receive program benefits. Households were classified as poor depending on their ownership of durable assets that were known to be correlated with consumption levels (proxy means). Within the group of eligible households, beneficiary households were randomly selected to be a part of the program (de Walque 2009).

Baseline data were collected in mid-2008, and follow-up surveys were planned for March 2009 and 2010. Data were collected by the economics department of the University of Ouagadougou, the Institute of Health Science Research, and the World Bank's Economic and Development Research Group, in collaboration with the Center for Global Development, the University of Illinois, and the University of Oklahoma. The evaluations measure school enrollment, attendance, performance, and grade progression; children's health and development; anthropometric indicators; household consumption; and other human capital indicators (CNLS 2008).

Transfer amounts, conditions, and coordination. The program began awarding quarterly transfers in October and November 2008 and planned to continue for two years. Households receive transfers for children under age 15. Both CCTs and UCTs were CFAF 1,000 (US$2) per quarter for children ages 6 and under, CFAF 2,000 (US$4) per quarter for children ages 7 through 10, and CFAF 4,000 (US$8) per quarter for children ages 11 through 15. Given Burkina Faso's GDP per capita of approximately CFAF 220,000, or US$440 (de Walque 2009), the transfer amounts do not surpass 7.5 percent of GDP per capita in a household with one child in the oldest group.

Program conditions require that children ages 6 and under visit the local health center at a rate determined by local health providers, and that children ages 7 through 15 enroll in school and attend at least 90 percent of the time (de Walque 2009). Eligible children are given a booklet that is color coded by whether the mother or father should receive the transfers. Health service workers record when the child visits the clinic. Likewise, education workers help verify fulfillment of educational conditions (CNLS 2008). Spot-checks are conducted at the centers to ensure that monitoring proceeds correctly.

Funds are remitted from the National Committee against AIDS to provincial and then village committees, which oversee community committees that deliver payments. Village committees against AIDS and decentralized line services also monitor the fulfillment of conditions. Coordination is required between provincial and regional committees against AIDS, local committees, and representatives of the line ministries. Village committees and other community-level organizations and associations are charged with executing the project (CNLS 2008).

World Bank funding comes from the World Bank's Multi-country HIV/AIDS Program. Other groups granted research funding (de Walque 2009). Costs were expected to be US$732,000 for the government of Burkina Faso and US$512,500 for the World Bank's research costs (CNLS 2008, exchange rate standardized).

Burundi

Cash Transfers for Repatriation

The Office of the United Nations High Commissioner for Refugees (UNHCR) has been providing CTs to Burundians who were displaced and living in western Tanzania to encourage their return to Burundi. The CTs are valued at FBu 50,000 (US$41). Beneficiaries receive 20 percent of the transfer when they arrive in Burundi; the rest is given later. The cash is granted along with in-kind assistance. The first UNHCR cash grants were given in mid-2007. Although not all details of the scheme are clear, the transfers assisted more than 30,000 refugees in 2007 alone (UNHCR 2007). The operation was suspended in December 2008 but resumed in late April 2009, with another 25,000 refugees expected to return by the end of the year (IRIN 2009).

UNHCR contracted local groups to distribute the CTs, and females were encouraged to manage the funds. The results of this advice were not monitored. To ensure that beneficiaries did not claim benefits more than once, the program maintained a database of registered refugees, which was checked when beneficiaries claimed funds (Troger and Tennant 2008). An evaluation of the transfers showed that they had been used to buy land and build houses, as well as to purchase health care and to support income-generating activities. UNHCR determined that the grant sped up the repatriation process and encouraged development.

Cape Verde

Minimum Social Pension

Cape Verde's noncontributory Minimum Social Protection Program began in 1995. In 2006, it was combined with the Social Solidarity Pension, a pension for former members of the military (Government of Cape Verde 2011). The consolidated pension is known as the Minimum Social Pension and is based in the National Social Pension Center, also created in 2006.

The Minimum Social Pension provides monthly transfers to the temporarily and permanently labor-incapacitated, in addition to former military members. Targeting of labor-incapacitated individuals implies that many beneficiaries are elderly. By 2006, the consolidated program reached slightly more than 21,000 beneficiaries, of which a little more than 8,000 were nonmilitary recipients. Local authorities distribute the transfers (Government of Cape Verde 2011).

In 2008, the transfers were worth CVEsc 3,500 (US$43) monthly, although plans were to increase the benefit to CVEsc 5,000 (US$61) by 2011. The total annual cost of the Minimum Social Pension was reported to exceed CVEsc 289 million (US$3.6 million) (Government of Cape Verde 2011).

Significant improvements made to Cape Verde's noncontributory system have been the completion of a reregistration process, creation of a database of beneficiaries, adoption of a beneficiary identification card, unification of the noncontributory pensions, and creation of the National Pension Center. The World Bank provided some support in the improvement process (IMF 2006).

Democratic Republic of Congo

Emergency Cash Grants for Reintegration of Ex-combatants

Emergency CTs were used in 2004 to help reintegrate up to 120,000 ex-combatants in the Democratic Republic of Congo. Beneficiaries received an initial payment of US$110 and then received monthly cash transfers of US$25 for one year. Transfers were distributed via mobile phones through FirstRand Banking's Celpay program. Beneficiaries received an identification number, which they provided at a Celpay station. There, the number was sent through the cell phone network and linked with a central information system. Cash from the Celpay station, acquired through the station's sales, funded the transfers. The National

Commission for Demobilization and Reintegration administered the program. Transfers were supported by the Multi-country Demobilization and Reintegration Program, which is supported by many partners, particularly the World Bank (MDRP 2006).

Eritrea

Results-Based Financing

Eritrea has completed extensive planning and is now initiating a program known as the Results-Based Financing (RBF) CCT for Maternal and Child Health and Nutrition. RBF's goal is to improve health outcomes of mothers and children in targeted rural areas of Eritrea. Specifically, it aims to boost the use of health facilities and services, improve children's health outcomes, and improve the coverage and quality of health services. The program is more comprehensive than many CCTs in that it specifically seeks to address both supply and demand of health services, it relies on vouchers as well as transfers, and it gives systematic attention to issues of community awareness and engagement. The three-year pilot will run from mid-2009 through mid-2012. It will roll out in a gradual manner to allow for learning throughout the project cycle, to ensure supply-side supports are in place, and to accommodate budget limitations. The demand side of the program is expected to cost US$4 million, and supply-side components are estimated at US$3 million (Ayala Consulting 2009).

Benefits are structured to achieve better health outcomes. Beneficiaries eligible to receive a CCT are pregnant women and mothers with children under two years of age who live in selected subregional rural areas in Eritrea. To increase institutional deliveries, especially when women live in remote areas with poor access to health centers, transportation vouchers will be given to individuals who transport a woman from her home to an eligible institution for delivery (Ayala Consulting 2009).

Payments will be made to women once they meet certain criteria. After attending three prenatal visits, they will receive US$5, followed by another US$5 when the fourth prenatal visit is complete. If they have an institutional birth, they will receive a one-time payment of US$20. When a child between one and two years of age completes his or her first growth checkup and has met international height and weight criteria, the mother will receive a US$6 payment. She will earn an additional US$5 after a second checkup in the same year. Children under two before the program began may receive benefits if they fulfill the program's relevant criteria, and women may receive payments for more than one birth, as long as they space births apart by two years or more (Ayala Consulting 2009).

Women may receive the benefits for prenatal checkups regardless of how far along they are in the pregnancy when they are enrolled, provided that they complete the required checkups before giving birth. After fulfilling the conditions, women have health or growth monitoring cards marked by local health officials. The women take these cards to local or subregional administrative offices to receive their payments (Ayala Consulting 2009).

Transportation vouchers will be paid after an eligible driver, enrolled through subregional coordinating officials, transports an eligible woman to a health center. Communities will hold meetings to inform members about the program and the transportation voucher component, and drivers must be agreed on by the group. Drivers are required to transport pregnant women who are in labor or are experiencing complications to health centers, regardless of the time of day, and to treat the occasion as an emergency. Drivers registered in the community are to set up schedules so that women always have available transportation to a health center (Ayala Consulting 2009).

Although drivers located in communities use formal enrollment and payment procedures, a woman living in a remote area may use the vouchers to travel to a health center with the help of an available driver not from her community. After delivering the woman to the health center, the driver will receive a voucher from the center, which is redeemable at the subregional or local administrative office (Ayala Consulting 2009).

The transportation vouchers range from US$5 to US$15, depending on the type of terrain covered. Per-kilometer compensation may vary when the beneficiary comes from an area with a challenging topography. Communities may also help decide on the payment levels, but the amounts should not be above the market amounts charged (Ayala Consulting 2009).

The project also addresses supply-side service delivery bottlenecks. Subregions are eligible for the program only after they meet certain supply-side criteria. They must have at least one qualified health center, determined by a health supply capacity evaluation. Qualified health centers must have proper sanitation practices, a clean water source, proper lighting, a qualified vehicle, and minimally qualified health personnel.

They must be located outside of any main urban areas. *Kebabis* (the smallest administrative unit in Eritrea) were randomly selected as treatment locations in the pilot, provided that the closest health facility passed the supply capacity assessment for health facilities (Ayala Consulting 2009).

Most of the supply-side financing will go to provide payments to regional or lower-level health officials on the basis of their achievement of mutually agreed-on health targets. Payments are based on a simple formula that uses the population and maternal mortality rates in each region. The World Bank will give another US$500,000 to the Ministry of Health when the country meets certain agreed-on aggregate health outcomes. The payments are supposed to occur every 6 months at the regional and subregional levels and once every 18 months within the Ministry of Health (Ayala Consulting 2009).

If the unit's goals are not met, reduced payments may be made to the Ministry of Health if it has achieved at least 75 percent of its goal. Payments are to be made only after performance has been verified. The cash incentives lost during a period in which the unit did not meet its goals may be disbursed at a later time if the goals are met. The funds may be used however the region decides, taking the input of the Ministry of Health into consideration (Ayala Consulting 2009).

The RBF program, funded by the World Bank, is expected to complement a pilot program funded by the World Bank known as the HAMSET II (Second HIV/AIDS/STI, Tuberculosis, Malaria and Reproductive Health Project). The HAMSET II supports the health sector by training health employees, providing necessary supplies, and promoting appropriate behavioral changes (Ayala Consulting 2009).

Communication and awareness raising are a necessary step. The RBF CCT is to begin only after awareness of the program has been raised through national and local promotional activities. Communities, in meetings coordinated by village health committees, are to locate potential eligible beneficiaries and invite them to enrollment meetings. Village health committees will also explain the program to individual women who do not attend the enrollment meeting. Beneficiaries are then enrolled, and their information is passed up through the coordinating bodies and is entered into the management information system (MIS) (Ayala Consulting 2009).

An innovative information, education, and communication component of the project will seek to increase households' demand for services through an initiative linked to a larger nationwide program for National Women's Day. This component is open to both treatment and control locations of the RBF. Pregnant Eritrean women who have attended at least four prenatal visits and given birth in an eligible institution will be entered to win prizes in the "Spin the Wheel for Healthy Mothers" game on National Women's Day. This component was created to raise awareness about maternal and children's health and to improve outcomes. The prizes from the Healthy Mothers Campaign will be distributed depending on the number of pregnant women in a region and a hardship adjustment associated with the region's terrain. Each of the 22 prizes given annually has an approximate value of ERN 10,000, or US$667 (Ayala Consulting 2009).

Separate program management unit operates under Ministry of Health. The RBF CCT's institutional arrangement allows it to complement the work of the Ministry of Health, where it is seated under the direction of the Family and Community Health Division's Family and Reproductive Health Unit. The program will operate out of a separate program management unit that reports to the Ministry of Health. In addition to these organizational units, the project's coordinator and project management unit, as well as regional health officials, are closely involved in the project (Ayala Consulting 2009).

At the regional level, health administrative officials will coordinate with local health centers, including hospitals and health stations, and regional RBF officials. The regional officials will be in charge of subregional officials, who will provide oversight to local-level administrators. The local officials will provide transfers to beneficiaries in some cases; in other cases, subregional officials will provide the transfers. A capacity assessment at the local level determines whether local offices have the ability to make payments (Ayala Consulting 2009).

Monitoring, evaluation, and research designs link to three-year rollout. The program will be subject to internal monitoring by a data entry official, as well as to externally based spot-checks and financial audits. Information on health facilities will be entered into the project's MIS and a broader health MIS that follows the health facilities. In addition to monitoring the health supply to which payments are linked, the supply side of the program will monitor other aspects of health service performance and outcomes that are not tied to payments, such as the percentage of stillbirths and children receiving supplements (Ayala Consulting 2009).

The project will be rolled out over three years. In the first year, the CCTs will be available in only 30 percent of eligible kebabis. Coverage will expand to 60 percent of eligible kebabis in the second year and to 100 percent in the third. The eligible but untreated groups will serve as control groups for the program. The transportation vouchers will be rolled out more quickly. They will initially be given in two states, and two more states will be covered in subsequent quarters until the country's six states are covered (Ayala Consulting 2009).

An impact evaluation will use data collected from a nationally representative baseline of 12,000 households in late 2009. Follow-up surveys will take place halfway through the program and at the close of the project. The evaluation will exploit the program's gradual rollout (Ayala Consulting 2009).

Ethiopia

The Direct Support Component of the Ethiopian Productive Safety Net Programme

The Direct Support component of the Ethiopian Productive Safety Net Programme (PSNP-DS) is one of the better-known examples of a CT in Sub-Saharan Africa. The PSNP is notable for its flexible use of food and cash transfers, its use of public works and direct cash grants, and its ability to rapidly scale up during a crisis, making it one of the leading social protection programs in the region. For 2009, the PSNP had an annual budget of US$414 million, of which US$360 million went directly to the program and US$54 million went to government-based staff time (World Bank 2010a). The Direct Support component alone provides approximately US$33 million in transfers annually. Administrative costs were 16.9 percent of total costs in 2009 (World Bank 2010a).[6] Next to South Africa's grants system, the PSNP is the largest social protection program in the region.

The program's annual budget of 1.38 percent of GDP[7] includes the costs of several major components that reach 10 percent of Ethiopian households living in food insecurity. In 2009, the Direct Support component (a UCT) reached 242,383 households, or approximately 1.2 million individuals (World Bank 2010a). The PSNP is based in the government of Ethiopia's Office of Food Security, under the Ministry of Agriculture and Rural Development, and it has received support from the World Bank, U.S. Agency for International Development (USAID), Canadian International Development Agency (CIDA), U.K. Department for

International Development (DFID), Development Cooperation Ireland, the European Commission, and the World Food Programme (WFP), among others (World Bank 2010a).

Changing perspectives of governments and donors regarding the methods that should be used to provide aid to areas with recurrent food crises were catalysts for the creation of the PSNP. Food aid in Ethiopia had cost US$265 million from 1997 through 2002, and it had been given to more than 5 million people annually (Hoddinott n.d.). Nevertheless, households were still being depleted of assets, and their supposed acute food insecurity was increasingly recognized as chronic food insecurity. The PSNP was developed after it became clear that food aid, despite the funds devoted to it, was failing to protect Ethiopians from future food crises.

Rationale and objectives tackle poverty traps and crises. The PSNP was created to help households break out of existing poverty traps. It began in early 2005 with the objective of providing households with cash or food transfers to help meet their food needs and protect them from depleting their assets. The program is also intended to build productive assets in communities to decrease the causes of chronic food insecurity. The PSNP is one of the few Sub-Saharan Africa CTs that have launched at full scale without a pilot.

The PSNP explicitly wanted to combine programs that provided relief, protection of assets, and development into one program. For that reason, the program was designed with both a public works component and a direct cash transfer for those unable to participate in public works.

The first program phase was planned to last five years, and a second phase followed the first. The program's reach is extensive. In 2005, the PSNP targeted 5 million chronically food-insecure individuals, a number chosen on the basis of the average number of individuals who needed food aid in the previous five years (World Bank 2010a); this figure was increased to 8 million people in 262 *woredas* (districts) in 2006 (Devereux and others 2006). The first two years of the program were used to help the government transition from its traditional emergency response to a focus on development and nonemergency support. In 2009, the PSNP provided transfers to 7.6 million beneficiaries and worked in 290 woredas in 8 out of a possible 10 regions; however, most of those beneficiaries participated in the public works program (World Bank 2010a).

In the event of an emergency, the PSNP can grow to reach 15 million beneficiaries. An expansion took place to address the crisis of 2008, when Ethiopian food price inflation reached 91.7 percent for the 12 months prior to August. The PSNP grew to cover an additional 947,000 beneficiaries, and it adjusted wages up to Br 10 (from the original Br 6) by the beginning of 2009. It also attempted to provide more transfers in food rather than in cash to address concerns over eroding transfer values (World Bank 2011). The PSNP played a role in mitigating the effects of the food price crisis, but the extremely high inflation still affected transfer values and helped drive beneficiaries' preferences for food aid over cash transfers (Sabates-Wheeler and Devereux 2010).

The PSNP has also had pilots in pastoral and agropastoral areas. These pilots have shown that the program can assist pastoral households in chronic food insecurity, but certain mechanisms, such as targeting, should be tailored to the dynamics of various pastoral groups (World Bank 2010a). An additional pilot is investigating whether to link the Direct Support component with Ethiopia's national nutrition program (World Bank 2010a).

PSNP design and targeting mix public works and unconditional cash transfers. The PSNP is composed of a public works component and Direct Support, which is provided as a UCT. Although the majority of program resources go toward cash-for-work or food-for-work projects, the Direct Support component provides transfers to households with no member capable of participating in the public works. These households include elderly people, people with disabilities, orphans, people who are ill, and pregnant or lactating mothers (Ashley, Brown, and Gibson 2007). The program was designed to allow 20 percent of beneficiaries to receive Direct Support, but this number is determined at the local level, without reference to quotas. In practice, the number of Direct Support beneficiaries varies over time and location, with approximately 15 percent of beneficiaries of the PSNP receiving the transfers. The PSNP has linked lists of public works and Direct Support beneficiaries, so it can respond to changes in a household's vulnerability and ability to participate in public works (World Bank 2010a).

Targeting of the PSNP is based first on geographic criteria. Areas with high chronic food insecurity were identified down to the smallest enumeration level (about 1,000 households). Localities used their own community Food Security Task Forces to select program beneficiaries. These task forces are made up of a local development agent, an official from the kebele (the municipal level below the woreda), and elected individuals who represent various demographic groups. In an effort to empower rural Ethiopian women, the program requires this group to have representatives at the woreda, kebele, and community levels. Initially, households were eligible for selection if they had received emergency food relief and experienced at least three months of food shortages for the past three years, were vulnerable because of a major asset loss within the past one or two years, or did not have informal support (World Bank 2010a). A community assembly is held to review, amend, and approve the list of selected beneficiaries. Previous community experience targeting households for food aid facilitates this activity. Appeals of these decisions can be considered at the locality and district levels through appeal committees, which were established in 2007 as a separate system from the targeting and graduation systems. Further redress is provided through the kebele council or woreda council, if the case is still not resolved satisfactorily (World Bank 2010a).

The value of the Direct Support transfer is typically equal to the amount earned in the public works component ("Productive Safety Nets Programme in Ethiopia" n.d.). If households cannot provide all labor necessary to fulfill public works requirements, they receive part of the transfer as Direct Support beneficiaries (World Bank 2010a). Transfer values are supposed to let households smooth their consumption or cover their food gap.

Transfers of food or cash are provided for only part of the year. One major feature of the PSNP is that it may provide either cash or food transfers, depending on the local needs of the community and the availability of food. For 2009, the estimated mean annual transfer was valued at US$137 per household, which was equal to approximately 10 percent of the basket corresponding to the national poverty line for 2007/08. Given the poverty in PSNP households, this value is actually closer to 40 percent of annual food requirements (World Bank 2010a). The cash is distributed to beneficiaries in communities by woreda-level cashiers of the Ministry of Finance and Economic Development. Food transfers may be retrieved from woreda-level locations. Community members supervise payments.

Transfers occur monthly for six successive months. The lean season is April through September, and public works are undertaken from January through June, when recipients have few agricultural labor demands on them. The goal is to provide transfers (including the PSNP-DS transfers) within six weeks after the end of the month in which public works are undertaken, which allows transfers to coincide more closely with the lean season (World Bank 2010a).

The program's use of both food and cash transfers was found to be extremely helpful in adapting to the needs of specific locations. Over time, the program has tried to transition more transfers from food to cash (Wiseman and Hess 2008). However, in localities experiencing acute food scarcity, the cash value in relation to local food prices has decreased significantly (Devereux and others 2006), making cash less desirable to households in those circumstances. The declining value of transfers was a major issue in some areas during the food price crisis in 2008 (Sabates-Wheeler and Devereux 2010).

Payment levels for the PSNP-DS generally corresponded to amounts received by public works participants. However, local flexibility in implementation generated spatial and temporal variation in payment levels. Some woredas decided to provide Direct Support transfers of a smaller size to a greater number of individuals, whereas others provided larger transfers to fewer beneficiaries (Gilligan and others 2009b).

Households are supposed to graduate from the PSNP when they are able to obtain all necessary food for one year without having to rely on the transfers, and they are able to survive moderate shocks. Criteria used to determine food security status, which is collected by development agents, vary regionally. Officials at the kebele and woreda levels validate the information, and it is also discussed in community-level meetings. Appeals of graduation decisions may be made to kebele appeal committees, similar to other grievances (World Bank 2010a).

PSNP monitoring and implementation use multiple systems and take advantage of decentralized organizational structures. A monitoring system known as the Payroll and Attendance Sheet System is used to mark attendance and transfer payments. Rather than create a separate MIS, officials decided that the monitoring systems for Ethiopia's overall Food Security Program, of which the PSNP is a part, should be improved and used for the PSNP. Data are captured at regular intervals through the government systems, which tend to be low capacity and often manual. A plan for improving the systems was developed early on. Because the PSNP was launched very quickly, government monitoring and evaluation systems were not yet at their required capacity. Monitoring reports were often late, patchy, and not followed up on (World Bank 2010a).

Major concerns of whether the PSNP was addressing acute food insecurity during a humanitarian crisis led the program to set up the PSNP Information Center, which continues to supplement government monitoring reports, whose quality still suffers. The PSNP Information Center, which is seated in the Food Security Coordination Directorate, captures data on food prices and transfer status every two weeks in 81 selected woredas. When problems have been uncovered by the PSNP Information Center, higher-level groups have worked with local officials to fix them (World Bank 2010a).

The PSNP is managed by the Ministry of Agriculture and Rural Development. It is coordinated by the Disaster Risk Management and Food Security Sector, whose Food Security Coordination Directorate administers the program's activities (transfers, public works); provides oversight to the PSNP and links it to other productivity-generating programs, especially other Food Security Programs; submits the overall budget, allocating funding to the country's eight program regions; supports regional food security offices; and monitors and evaluates the program and implementation capacity. Within the same sector office is the Early Warning and Response Directorate, which delivers food transfers and links the PSNP with emergency activities and the early warning system for the risk financing facility. Other responsible bodies include the National Resource Management Directorate in the Ministry of Agriculture and Rural Development, which is in charge of the public works component, and the Ministry of Finance and Economic Development, which is in charge of the program's finances and disbursement (World Bank 2010a).

The program's decentralized structure and the need to harmonize both the nine donors' aid requirements and various local-level arrangements have resulted in differential implementation at the woreda level. The responsibility mix between woredas and nongovernmental organizations (NGOs) varies geographically (World Bank 2010a). Similarly, the program has allowed significant local autonomy to fix criteria for payment at the woreda level, if not lower.

The decentralized organization of the PSNP is based on woreda, kebele, and community-level food security task forces. The kebele task forces are supposed to work with the woreda committee to implement the program, use community targeting to identify public works and Direct Support beneficiaries, prepare safety net plans for the kebele, and set up and instruct community food security task forces. The task forces are charged with identifying potential beneficiaries, conducting assessments to determine whether the household should receive direct or public works support, allowing the community to discuss the list, and ultimately supporting the list of selected beneficiaries in a village meeting. The task forces have additional duties related to public works projects (Gilligan and others 2009b).

Contingency financing gives the PSNP needed flexibility. Because the PSNP benefits households that experience both chronic and transitory food insecurity, the program has been designed to meet both of those needs, or at the very least to coordinate with programs that can meet transitory needs. Therefore, the PSNP has developed rolling contingency funding that decentralized authorities can use to meet transitory food insecurity. The budget allocation (20 percent of the program's base cost), as well as a risk financing mechanism that frees additional financing in emergency situations for contingency transfers, allows the program to cover new households that have fallen into chronic food insecurity, as well as to scale up in case of additional transitory food insecurity.

The risk financing facility is funded by a grant from the World Bank and assurances from other donors. It is triggered by an early warning system that provides alerts of possible food emergencies. Woredas have plans and have been trained to be able to quickly release the funds during an emergency scale-up. The system also is linked to emergency response systems in case they are needed (World Bank 2010a).

Three-fourths of the contingency budget is allocated at the regional level, and the final one-fourth is allocated to woredas. This additional funding allows woredas to provide transfers to those who successfully appeal their exclusion from the program and to provide additional transfers for households in transitory food insecurity (World Bank 2010a).

The PSNP enjoys coordinated support from the government and donors. The PSNP is supported in Ethiopia's 2002 Sustainable Development and Poverty Reduction Program and its 2007 Plan for Accelerated and Sustained Development to End Poverty. The government pays for 8 percent of the PSNP budget, and the nine donors pay for the remaining amount (European University Institute 2010). However, this percentage may not fully illustrate the government's commitment to the PSNP, because much of the work for the PSNP is integrated into the daily duties of domestic officials, who devote significant time to the PSNP (World Bank 2010a).

The PSNP plays a major role in a broader Food Security Program implemented by the government (Hoddinott n.d.). The other food security programs that are linked to the PSNP include programs that provide subsidized productive inputs and subsidized credit. These programs aim to increase productivity and asset accumulation. Some households have also been resettled to areas where the land is more conducive to productive activities. Coverage of the other Food Security Programs within PSNP areas has improved over time. Slater and others (2006) report that the PSNP has improved at linking beneficiaries to itself and other Food Security Programs that can help them to generate productive income or assets.

The government is expected to create a national social protection policy in which the PSNP will play a role. Oversight of social protection is expected to be placed in the Ministry of Labour and Social Affairs (World Bank 2010a).

Coordination among donors and the government has been vital to the success of the PSNP. The group had to establish a uniform set of monitoring criteria, evaluation methods, outcomes to measure, and timelines. Donors have had to make significant efforts to ensure that the PSNP achieves its goal of accessing regular, anticipated funding. Although annual budgets are used, the government and donors plan for multiple years at once through the Medium-Term Expenditure and Financing Framework, which allows funding and programming to maintain predictability (World Bank 2010a).

Many PSNP results have improved with time. Multiple evaluation instruments are in place for the PSNP, including an evaluation of the public works component, qualitative assessments, and a small household survey. A long-term impact evaluation is also set up, which surveys a panel of regionally representative households every two years (World Bank 2010a).

Early evaluations of the PSNP found that it did not cover all eligible beneficiaries in communities, which led it to expand significantly. Bottlenecks were found that resulted from limited capacity, which led the program to classify districts on the basis of their ability to implement the program and to work within those parameters. Regional budgets were also increased to support capacity building and strengthening at the district level ("Productive Safety Nets Programme in Ethiopia" n.d.).

A thorough review of the program was undertaken in 2006. Results guided the second part of the first phase of the PSNP, which began in 2007. At that time, the review determined that the PSNP was well targeted, particularly in terms of selection of households for public works versus Direct Support (Devereux and others 2006).[8] Almost 60 percent of surveyed households that received Direct Support could not work, and 25 percent of those surveyed were elderly. PSNP-DS beneficiaries had lower incomes, fewer assets, and less land than the public works households. Likewise, public works beneficiaries were well targeted out of the rest of the population.

A number of problems with the PSNP's initial implementation were discovered using qualitative research combined with a household survey conducted in 2006. At that point, approximately 25 percent of surveyed beneficiary households received Direct Support, while the rest of the households participated in the public works program (Devereux and others 2006). Some key issues uncovered by the evaluation were as follows:

- Projections of local rations needed, which were based on estimates of possible Direct Support beneficiaries, were inaccurate.
- Transfers were unreliable because of semiannual retargeting, which undermined the security households needed for their own planning and production decisions.
- Some households were being pushed out of the program if they had acquired significant assets during the period, even if those assets were acquired on credit.

Additional areas that the evaluation found needed improvement were appeals and grievance processes, other monitoring processes, targeting practices at the woreda level and lower, and sensitivity to female-specific concerns (Sharp, Brown, and Teshome 2006).

According to this first major round of evaluations, close to 70 percent of surveyed beneficiary households received a combination of cash and food transfers, although in a specific month, the transfers were typically either all food or all cash. Approximately 15 percent of households received only food and 15 percent received only cash (Devereux and others 2006).

A follow-up evaluation of the PSNP was conducted in mid-2008, which found that targeting had improved in many areas. This improvement was attributed to the program's linking lists of beneficiaries and moving pregnant women from public works to Direct Support (Devereux and others 2008).

The 2008 follow-up evaluation found that between 50 percent and 65 percent of households thought the community targeting was fair (Gilligan and others 2009b). Another report from a 2008 survey found that more than 85 percent of survey respondents thought the process for selection into the PSNP was fair (World Bank 2010a). Public understanding of the targeting for the cash transfer was found to have improved over time. In practice, the Direct Support was typically provided to households headed by elderly females.

A process evaluation conducted in 2008 found that PSNP cash and food transfers were being used to fund food consumption, as well as to purchase nonfood items. Recipients of PSNP cash used 84 percent of their money to purchase staple foods; 74 percent of food transfer recipients consumed all of the food (Devereux and others 2008). Households also reported using cash to invest in education, agriculture, debt repayment, health care, and small businesses.

The program's official impact evaluation found significant variation in beneficiaries' ease of access to their payments. In some localities, most people were paid close to their homes. In others, up to a third of households had to spend the night away from home when they retrieved the transfers (Gilligan and others 2009b).

Matching methods combined with difference-in-difference regressions revealed that the PSNP increased households' months of food security by 11 percent, increased livestock ownership by 7 percent, and improved self-reported welfare. PSNP households affected by drought achieved a 30 percent larger increase in caloric acquisition than non-PSNP households (Gilligan and others 2009a). PSNP households reported greater use of health care services, and they were able to keep children in school longer than they had in the prior year, with 47 percent and 43 percent of respondents, respectively, saying that this increase was due to the PSNP (World Bank 2010a).

Remaining challenges must be addressed. Many of the positive effects found in the 2008 PSNP impact evaluation were severely dampened in those households that received either low or irregular transfers. Results were also muted if households did not have access to other Food Security Programs, which still occurred too often, but which also highlighted the potential synergies between the programs (Gilligan and others 2009a).

An additional concern was that the program gave insufficient attention to the needs of those eligible for the Direct Support component. The beneficiaries of Direct Support were found to be less informed than other beneficiaries about how much and what type of transfer they were supposed to receive (World Bank 2010a). The PSNP's focus was on connecting households to the public works programs and on links to other Food Security Programs that would allow beneficiaries to graduate from the PSNP. More recently, client cards and a charter of clients' rights and responsibilities have been used to help beneficiaries better understand the appeals process and their entitlements (World Bank 2010a). This problem has lessened in some, but not all, studied areas (Gilligan and others 2009b).

Similarly, some former beneficiaries appeared to have been pushed out of the program before they were able to survive without the transfers (Devereux and others 2008). The evaluation noted the need to clarify the PSNP's roles as a development program (for those able to work) and as a welfare program (for the PSNP-DS beneficiaries). Although the PSNP has received positive recognition for its combined public works program and UCTs, a program review suggested that the PSNP-DS should be developed on its own, apart from the public works component, to better assist those in chronic poverty (World Bank 2010a).

Finally, annual audits have found that the PSNP suffers from expenditure miscoding and poor maintenance of records. Those issues have been ascribed to capacity constraints rather than to widespread corruption (World Bank 2010a).

Ghana

Livelihood Empowerment Against Poverty

Ghana's Livelihood Empowerment Against Poverty (LEAP) is a pioneer CT in West Africa. LEAP combats poverty in children and vulnerable groups. It was developed with technical support from the Brazilian government's Ministry of Social Development and Fight Against Hunger, DFID, and the United Nations Children's Fund (UNICEF). As of 2008, the Ghanaian government funded transfers of US$4.2 million out of its own budget, drawn from Heavily Indebted Poor Countries (HIPC) Initiative funds (Sultan and Schrofer 2008). DFID has provided funding for South-South learning from the Brazilian government and capacity building in the Ministry of Employment and Social Welfare to support LEAP.

Structure and scale do not attempt to reach all extremely poor households. A large-scale pilot planned to last five years, LEAP is a central component of the government's national social protection strategy (World Bank 2010c). LEAP is run through the government's Department of Social Welfare within the Ministry of Employment and Social Welfare, although there are plans to eventually establish the Ministry of Social Development. This ministry would evolve from the Directorate of Social Protection, also envisioned by the program. In the meantime, the Ministry of Employment and Social Welfare has worked to expand both its staff and technical skills to accommodate the program's needs.

At its planned scale, the pilot program will reach 160,000 extremely poor households, equal to one in six extremely poor Ghanaians. Transfers began in March 2008. Plans called for covering 15,000 households in 15 districts by year-end 2008; a little more than 8,000 households were actually covered in May 2009. In response to food and fuel price hikes in 2008, as well as flooding, combined with concerns that LEAP was poorly targeted at the regional level (Jones 2009), the World Bank provided funds for transfers for 28,000 additional households in northern Ghana for six months (Sultan and Schrofer 2008).[9] The program's coverage was reduced again after the temporary expansion.

LEAP plans to "graduate" beneficiaries after they have received transfers for three years; hence, its aim is to increase the productivity of Ghanaians and not to directly reduce poverty or vulnerability (Jones 2009).

There have been challenges to keeping targeting transparent. Plans call for beneficiaries to be selected through geographic targeting of districts via poverty maps (World Bank 2010c), further refined through proxy means tests and community verification (IPC-IG 2008).[10] Criteria for the proxy means test include indicators of infrastructure, exposure to shocks, human capital investment, and supply-side availability of services, among other variables. Targeting at the community level is completed by community LEAP implementation committees, which are composed of volunteers (Jones 2009). Community leaders, such as chiefs and elders, act as key informants to the Ministry of Employment and Social Welfare's district social welfare officials to help them identify households in extreme poverty (World Bank 2010c). The program's beneficiaries were initially limited to OVC, elderly people (over 65 years old), and people with major disabilities (Sultan and Schrofer 2008). Plans for expansion would cover the labor constrained, those sick with HIV/AIDS (IPC-IG 2008), and pregnant and lactating women (World Bank 2010c).[11]

Ideally, targeting is implemented as follows. Districts allow communities to select a given number of beneficiaries on the basis of the program's targeting criteria. The eligibility of beneficiaries nominated by the community is verified by field visits. Beneficiaries are registered through completing application forms, which are used to rank households electronically and generate a list of eligible beneficiaries. The district LEAP implementation committee verifies the beneficiary list, and the community then endorses it. Households are informed of their selection and the benefits they will receive, and they are given a program identification card that should contain a photograph and biometric data. Surveyors hired at the national level independently verify the eligibility of beneficiary households (World Bank 2010c).

During LEAP's initial implementation, questions arose regarding the transparency of targeting decisions, the linkage of poverty indicators to beneficiary selection, and the possibility that political motives and political expediency may influence selection processes (Jones 2009).

Alignment of LEAP plans and implementation are still improving. Transfers are given to caregivers in beneficiary households. Anywhere from 10 percent to 15 percent of initial transfers are given to male household members (Jones 2009), suggesting that over 85 percent go to females. Benefits are supposed to range from ₵8 (about US$8) to ₵15, depending on household composition. Up to four beneficiaries per household may receive benefits, which are given on a bimonthly basis (IPC-IG 2008). Transfers are slated to end after a household has been in the program for three years, at which point beneficiaries are expected to be able to sustain themselves. In practice, households with OVC receive ₵16, and no graduation strategies have been planned (Jones 2009). Another report suggests average LEAP transfers are approximately ₵14 monthly, which is equal to 20 percent of the bottom quintile of Ghanaian households' average consumption. Reviews of the LEAP pilot suggest that most of the grants were used to increase food consumption (World Bank 2010c).

Payments are distributed through Ghana Post, which coordinates with district social welfare officials and community LEAP implementation committees to identify and pay beneficiaries. Mobile paypoints have been set up for remote areas. On payment days, a meeting is held with beneficiaries, during which time they may provide feedback to community LEAP implementation committees and obtain program-related information, including information on their rights and responsibilities (Jones 2009). After paydays, reports are sent from paypoints to higher-level program representatives for reconciliation.

The CTs are linked to conditions in some cases, but those conditions are largely unenforced, and some suggest the conditions do not seem to be central to the program's current focus. However, Jones (2009) says that beneficiaries are informed about the importance of making the conditioned investments.[12] The conditions outlined in program manuals require that households make sure their children enroll in and attend school, register all household members in Ghana's National Health Insurance Scheme, register children under 18 months old in the national registry, take children under 18 months old to medical checkups, register children in the country's expanded immunization program, and keep all children from being trafficked or forced to participate in the most exploitative types of child labor (IPC-IG 2008). Communities are supposed to ensure that households fulfill conditions and are adequately connected to complementary programs (World Bank 2010c). In 2008, the only condition that was actually enforced was birth registration of children at the time of enrollment (Jones 2009).

The program's budget has varied from US$8 million to US$26 million annually, depending on the stage of the pilot. Infrastructure development needed in the first year was expected to keep transfers at 22 percent of LEAP's budget. Plans for later years estimate that transfer payments will make up between 58 percent and 75 percent of the budget. The program is expected to cost somewhere between 0.1 percent and 0.2 percent of the government's total expenditures (IPC-IG 2008). As of 2009, LEAP's administrative costs were relatively high at 30 percent; it is hoped that this number will decrease to 20 percent by 2015/16. Transfer costs were 1 percent of the transfer quantity plus ₵1,500 (US$1,000) per transfer round (World Bank 2010c).

LEAP is administered through the Department of Social Welfare in the Ministry of Employment and Social Welfare. Its project coordinating unit works with relevant line ministries and has a memorandum of understanding with them for this purpose. Within the country's 10 regions, regional LEAP steering committees help implement the CT and coordinate with complementary programs (World Bank 2010c). As of 2009, links to complementary programs have been limited and require more attention (Jones 2009).

Within these committees are the regional social services subcommittees of the regional coordinating councils. Civil society representatives and officials from relevant line ministries serve on the subcommittees. The subcommittees must monitor, evaluate, coordinate, research, and perform advocacy work related to social services. District LEAP implementation committees are composed of representatives from civil society and the National Disaster Management Agency, and they represent social service committees at the district level. They help implement, monitor conditions, and communicate information about LEAP. These district committees work with the Department of Social Welfare and the Department of Community Development to form community LEAP implementation committees. The community committees are composed of local leaders, nurses, teachers, NGO representatives, and five community representatives who are tasked with addressing appeals and increasing program awareness (World Bank 2010c).

Additional plans to improve LEAP include continuing the program's rollout, extending the program's reach in areas where LEAP is already operating, improving the proxy means test, connecting beneficiaries to the Labor-Intensive Public Works program and studying how the two programs could complement each other, moving to a single computerized registry with biometric identification for social protection programs in Ghana, using more advanced distribution methods (such as mobile phones), using LEAP to potentially replace less effective safety net programs, encouraging successful graduation into other social programs, and improving capacity at all levels of program management and implementation (World Bank 2010c).

Kenya

Over a five-year period, Kenya has systematically built up two major CTs: the Cash Transfer for Orphans and Vulnerable Children and the Hunger Safety Net Programme.

Cash Transfer for Orphans and Vulnerable Children

The Cash Transfer for Orphans and Vulnerable Children (known as the CT for OVC) began as a prepilot in 2004. It has since gone through a five-year pilot project and has been scaled up from a very small budget to a projected US$26 million budget for 2010 (World Bank 2009e). The program is extensively documented and has provided valuable experience in advocacy, design, and implementation of CTs in Sub-Saharan African settings. It is a key component of Kenya's broader social protection strategy because it addresses risks to children in communities where increasing numbers of OVC are overwhelming informal safety net systems. In addition to attracting donor interest, the CT for OVC has received strong domestic political support, including pressure to scale up the program quickly.

CT for OVC prepilot tests how CTs can support OVC in their communities. Kenya's CT for OVC was begun as the government searched for ways to systematically support Kenya's OVC and prevent their institutionalization. The prepilot's goal was to generate evidence regarding the applicability of a CT to support OVC in Kenya. The prepilot phase (phase 1) began in December 2004, initially reaching 500 children. It was later expanded to reach at least 5,000 children. The prepilot was supported through UNICEF and the Swedish International

Development Cooperation Authority (Sida) and administered from the Department of Children Services (World Bank 2009e).

The program's initial districts—Nairobi, Kwale, and Garissa—were selected because they were areas where UNICEF and Sida already had ground-level knowledge and experience. The prepilot targeted poor households and households with OVC that did not receive other formal support. Prepilot targeting was based on agreed-on standards, though no actual indicators of poverty were used in the targeting process. Actual targeting practices and results likely varied by district (World Bank 2009e).

Beneficiaries received K Sh 500 (US$6.25) monthly per child (Devereux and Pelham 2005). Technically, the prepilot transfers had conditions attached, but noncompliance had no consequences (World Bank 2009e). The prepilot did not enforce conditions because of concerns that children would be separated from their households to meet program requirements (World Bank 2005). However, communities and some donors requested that the transfers be conditioned, particularly as the program expanded to areas in the west that had higher HIV levels.

The prepilot functioned using a manual filing system. Evaluation of the prepilot found its communication strategies to be weak and its transfer size inadequate to achieve the program's goals (World Bank 2009e). Additionally, the enrollment process needed to be more informative.

The CT for OVC was redesigned for a full pilot. Drawing on prepilot experiences, the official pilot of the CT for OVC program (phase 2) began in 2005 and ran through mid-2009. The program specifically focused on households with OVC, with the goal of keeping children within families and encouraging investment in their human capital. The specific program goals—improving health (reducing morbidity and mortality of children under age 5 years); nutrition (encouraging food security and improving household nutrition); education (school enrollment of children ages 6 to 17 years); birth, death, and identity registration; and awareness of these issues (that is, health and nutrition)—are very similar to those seen in other well-known CCT programs in Latin America (Government of Kenya 2007; Hussein 2006).

Plans for the pilot program envisaged reaching seven districts with support from the government of Kenya, DFID, UNICEF, and Sida (World Bank 2009e). Funds from development partners in the pilot reached 17,500 households, which were still receiving benefits at the time of writing. Between 1,000 and 4,600 beneficiary households are covered in each of the districts. By the end of phase 2 (June 2009), benefits were expected to reach 70,000 households.

Targeting takes a complex five-step approach that includes community committees. Targeting in the pilot was refined from prepilot methods. It is completed in five steps (World Bank 2009e). Geographic targeting selects program districts on the basis of poverty and HIV/AIDS levels. The districts are ranked depending on the number of extremely poor households with OVC in the district. Within the districts, the number of households with OVC is calculated. Communities are selected to belong to the program provided that they have more than 5,000 members, of which at least 60 percent must live below the poverty line (Hussein 2006).

Community committees (local OVC committees) were created to select households eligible for the transfers. The households must be unable to meet all of their basic needs, and they must have a permanent OVC member less than 17 years of age in the household who is not receiving benefits from another CT (Government of Kenya 2006).

Within this group of eligible households, local OVC committees decide whether households meet criteria related to poverty (for example, the household has no access to a safe water source, members are in poor health, or members eat one or fewer meals per day). Households meeting at least 3 of the more than 10 criteria listed are considered poor (World Bank 2009e).

Trained enumeration teams visit identified households and verify this information, which is then put into the MIS. A priority list of identified households is created using proxy means tests to generate a ranking of households (Government of Kenya 2006). Greatest priority is given to households with heads over age 65 and under age 24. The community confirms this list in a *baraza* meeting (a type of awareness-raising gathering), where participants receive information about the program (World Bank 2009e). Although the targeting may be more efficient than the simpler methods of the prepilot, some confusion has arisen among households regarding why some households are selected as beneficiaries and others are not.

Eligible households are invited to enroll in the program, preferably during a special enrollment window. At that time, they receive information about the program and sign a contract. Their rights and responsibilities in the program are outlined, and they are informed of school and health center locations. Households may also enroll at the District Children's Office if they go within a given time frame (Government of Kenya 2006).

The households are encouraged to acquire identification cards within the next six months, and registration for cards is available at enrollment. The program provides photo identification cards at enrollment for the beneficiary and designated alternate caretakers (World Bank 2009e). The enrollment process relies significantly on community volunteers (Government of Kenya 2006). During enrollment, households must also specify the education and health centers that their children use so that monitoring can take place. Reregistration is expected to occur every five years (World Bank 2009e).

Transfer values are graduated, and the post office is used for transfer delivery. The government of Kenya discussed transfer size with the World Bank, DFID, economists from the University of Cape Town, and others. Transfers were ultimately set at a level that was believed to cover enough needs of OVC to help keep them within their households. Transfer values vary by the number of OVC in the household. Households with up to two OVC receive K Sh 1,000 (US$14), those with three or four OVC receive K Sh 2,000 (US$28), and those with five or more OVC receive K Sh 3,000 (US$42) (World Bank 2009e).

If K Sh 1,500 (US$20) is used as a reference transfer value, the transfer is sizable compared to the average per adult equivalent for consumption (K Sh 1,800), as shown in the baseline study. The transfer is equal to approximately 20 percent of poor Kenyan households' expenditures (World Bank 2009e). However, transfers have not been indexed to inflation, so their value has eroded as food prices have risen.

Transfers in the pilot districts are delivered using the Postal Cooperation of Kenya—a method that was found to function well. Some expansion program districts used a different payment mechanism. Payments are awarded once every two months (Government of Kenya 2007). Transfers are supplied along with a receipt outlining whether the household received the full possible payment and, if not, why (Government of Kenya 2006). Transfers are given to a female member of the household—the mother or other household head or caretaker—whenever possible.

Soft enforcement of conditions is used. Similar to conditions in CCTs in Latin America, Kenya's CT for OVC beneficiaries have responsibilities related to child health and education: children under 1 year old must attend a local clinic six times within their first year to be immunized, receive vitamin A supplements, and have their growth monitored; children between 1 and 3 years must have a growth-monitoring checkup and receive vitamin A supplements twice a year; children between 6 and 17 years must enroll in school and maintain attendance for 80 percent of school days; and caretakers must attend educational seminars at least once annually (World Bank 2009e).

All the children in the household are supposed to fulfill the relevant conditions, even if they are not the designated beneficiary (Government of Kenya 2006). However, the program's intention is to enforce conditions only in locations with adequate supply-side support within a certain distance from the household (Government of Kenya 2007). Conditions are not intended to be used to punish households but to encourage households to invest in human capital. Households that do not comply with conditions are supposed to receive warnings before any payments are reduced.

Until very recently, these conditions have not been applied in the program; the transfer has been essentially unconditional. Part of the program's design was intended to compare the effects of a CCT with those a UCT, but this design component was not tested until late 2008. Thus far, confusion has existed over how to apply health conditions, and only education conditions have been applied. In areas where conditions are applied, the reduction in transfer for noncompliance is K Sh 400 per child or adult who does not comply with co-responsibilities (World Bank 2009e).

Even though only some households were placed in a program with conditions, all households are supposed to be given training through awareness-raising sessions (Government of Kenya 2006). As of April 2009, such training was not being fully implemented.

The pilot has attempted to improve the program's transparency and enhance understanding of the CT through a strong communication plan. The campaign provides information about the program to participating communities, lets communities know which households belong in the program (for validation purposes), and holds meetings for all relevant stakeholders in program areas. Some of the strategies used in the communication plan have been taken from lessons learned from other programs, especially Kenya's Free Primary Education Programme (World Bank 2009e).

Households exit the program if there is no longer an OVC in the household under 18 years old or if the household is reassessed and no longer deemed to be poor. Households that migrate from the program area, voluntarily withdraw, or are found to have falsified information are also no longer in the program (World Bank 2009e). Finally, after three consecutive periods of failing to fulfill co-responsibilities, households are supposed to exit the program.

The organization and management systems require intersectoral coordination. The pilot's Central Program Unit, composed of units for operations, monitoring and evaluation, administration and finance, and information systems, was originally situated within the Department of Children Services in Kenya's Ministry of Home Affairs (Government of Kenya 2006). The country's vice president holds ultimate control over the program (Hussein 2006).

The Department of Children Services (and consequently the Central Program Unit) was moved from the Ministry of Home Affairs to the new Ministry of Gender, Children, and Social Development in April 2008 (World Bank 2009e). This ministry is growing in its capacity, and a permanent secretary under the minister has been supportive of the CT for OVC.

Enforcement of conditions requires close coordination by line ministries with the program, because the education objectives are executed by the Ministry of Education and the health objectives by the Ministry of Public Health and Sanitation. Coordination with the Ministry of Medical Services and Ministry of Immigration and Registration of Persons is also supported (World Bank 2009e).

All participating districts should have one or two officials in the District Children Office (DCO) who are fully dedicated to the CCT. DCO officials are charged with monitoring the fulfillment of conditions and sending this information to the main offices. An advisory area council is composed of district-level officials involved in activities helping children. It is also in charge of creating a district OVC subcommittee, which is in charge of executing the program (Government of Kenya 2006).

The district OVC subcommittee, local OVC committee, and volunteer children officers support the DCO (Government of Kenya 2006). The district OVC subcommittee is in charge of the local OVC committees, which play a major role in program execution at the local level. They receive program training and also supervise data collection used in targeting, program enrollment, and transfer distribution, among other things (Hussein 2006). They also must sensitize communities to the situation of OVC and people with HIV/AIDS, support program goals in the community (such as a birth and death registry), and find OVC in their communities and support the progress of OVC in the program.

These local committees are also in charge of carrying out the initial targeting—that is, finding enumerators and supervisors, training them, conducting household surveys, and transferring this information to the district OVC subcommittee (Government of Kenya 2006). Although local OVC committee members did not originally receive remuneration, now they are given small monetary incentives to compensate them for the expenses associated with fulfilling committee duties. These payments help to maintain morale in the committees.

The pilot has taken significant measures to maintain adequate controls, including the use of an extensive MIS. The MIS is centered at the national level, but it will later be decentralized to the districts (World Bank 2009e).

When conditions are enforced, teachers and health care workers fill out forms reporting school attendance and health center visits. Volunteers collect the forms. District officials then collect the records and pass them on to the DCO, which either sends the information to the Central Program Unit of the MIS or enters it online (Government of Kenya 2007). The central MIS tracks information by district.

Conditions are supposed to be monitored every two months for children up to age one, every six months for children ages one through five, every three months for the education conditions, and once per year for the adult training sessions. Compliance with program conditions is supposed to be spot-checked through visits to beneficiary households and other measures.

After the Postal Cooperation of Kenya delivers payments, it sends lists of those who received payments to the Department of Children Services, which checks the lists against the MIS. The transfers distributed by 2009 were reported to have gone smoothly and on schedule, despite violence in the country (World Bank 2009e).

Appeals may be submitted to the DCO, which also accepts complaints concerning payment quantities and quality of supply-side services. The DCO also must be informed of changes in the household, the supply-side facility used, and other issues (Government of Kenya 2007). In practice, the process for appeals and complaints is not fully developed.

Results from the experimental evaluation design will be useful. The pilot program in the original seven districts is subject to an impact evaluation. Conducted by Oxford Policy Management, the evaluation includes qualitative and quantitative components. The evaluation design is experimental (although significant differences existed across the treatment and control groups in the baseline). Two treatment locations and two control locations were randomly selected within each of the seven districts. The unconditional and conditional design was also randomly assigned to allow the evaluation to determine which design had a greater impact on key indicators (Hurrell, Ward, and Merttens 2008).

The study will follow nonrecipient households in treatment and control areas to examine issues of dynamic exclusion. It will also cross-validate household reports of school registration and attendance with school data. Baseline data from OVC households and community surveys were collected from March through August 2007 (Hurrell, Ward, and Merttens 2008), and a follow-up survey was conducted in mid-2009 (Oxford Policy Management 2009). The evaluation also performed checks on the program's financial components (Hurrell, Ward, and Merttens 2008).

The baseline sample included 2,759 households. Its analysis of targeting revealed that most selected households did have at least one orphan or vulnerable child (98 percent) and that most of those households were poor. However, the extremely poor were underrepresented in the program (Hurrell, Ward, and Merttens 2008).

Funding and expansion are included in the Medium-Term Plan. The CT for OVC is included in Kenya's Medium-Term Plan and Vision 2030. The Kenyan government funded the CT for OVC program in 2005–06 using K Sh 48 million (US$675,000) (Hussein 2006). Because of its expansion, the program is expected to cost US$26 million in fiscal year 2010. This figure is 0.08 percent of nominal GDP and 0.31 percent of government expenditures. When the program reaches 100,000 households, it is expected to cost between US$32 million and US$35 million, or approximately 0.07 percent of nominal GDP and 0.28 percent of government expenditures at that time (World Bank 2009e). Administrative costs are expected to be approximately 25 percent by 2012, and they are expected to continue to drop. This percentage is much lower than the 40 percent administrative costs in the prepilot.

A technical working group was created to oversee the pilot's expansion. The group was supposed to evaluate the program to date and determine what changes should be made. It also was charged with determining whether the program should be scaled up, and if so, how (Ayala Consulting 2007). However, results from the pilot were not gathered before the program began a rapid expansion.

Enthusiasm for the program led the government to allocate significant funding to the CT for OVC from the national budget. To receive the money, the program had to spend it in new districts, despite limited capacity for scaling up. The program was quickly expanded to 33 additional districts, with a goal of reaching 30,000 additional households (World Bank 2009e). External and domestic funds combined were expected to support a total of approximately 70,000 households by July 2009.

The program's rapid expansion spread program management capacities thin. In areas funded by the domestic budget, initially fewer than 300 households were enrolled in the CT program per district. The pressure for a rapid scale-up in these districts caused different protocols to be used in the donor-funded and nationally funded districts. Although there is only one office and staff, the CT has been operating two parallel programs, with differences in targeting, payment systems, and so on. For example, the domestic program pays benefits through the district treasury, and benefits have sometimes been delayed beyond their two-month schedule. During the initial expansion period, DCO officials were expected to deliver transfers to all households, which will not be feasible as the coverage per district increases.

Adaptations will be made to the CT for OVC in phase 3. The political pressures for more rapid expansion of the CT for OVC pilot into additional districts have resulted in the development of two parallel programs. A third program phase now seeks to harmonize those programs and build capacity for their effective implementation. The government's goal is to cover 100,000 households by 2012 (approximately 2,000 households per district), thereby reaching approximately half of the 600,000 extremely poor OVC in the country (World Bank 2009e).

World Bank International Development Association (IDA) funds will support program expansion in 25 of the 47 districts that already have the CT in place. By the end of fiscal year 2013, the IDA loans are expected to support up to 56,000 OVC households, DFID and UNICEF will support up to 37,000 households, and the government of Kenya will fund another 30,000 households, totaling approximately 123,000 OVC households. The districts supported by national funds are expected to scale up from approximately 800 households per district to more than 2,000 households. A major part of the IDA funds for phase 3 will also go toward standardizing program targeting, benefits, payment mechanisms, and monitoring between the two systems (World Bank 2009e).

Improvements will be made to the standardized program on the basis of issues noted in phase 2. The targeting mechanism will be adjusted in accordance with results from evaluations, Kenya's Integrated Household Budget Survey, MIS data, and baseline data. Because distance to the Postal Cooperation of Kenya's sites and security issues can be problematic, phase 3 will link the postal system to a new financial MIS module. It will also procure an alternative payment mechanism (World Bank 2009e).

The MIS will be upgraded to enable it to efficiently handle the increased demands placed on it due to the rapid scale-up, and an organization will be contracted to provide external monitoring. The external monitoring will spot-check the program, conduct community censuses to evaluate the quality of local OVC committees, and use "citizen report cards" to ascertain beneficiary and nonbeneficiary opinions and satisfaction with the program. This improved accountability is particularly important in light of concerns over governance and corruption in Kenya (World Bank 2009e).

Extensive effort will be made to improve communication about the program to both beneficiaries and nonbeneficiaries. Monitoring of the conditions is expected to improve. The communication campaign will support a program website, pamphlets, posters, and more. Part of the IDA loan will also support educational seminars for caretakers in beneficiary households. Those sessions (which were planned for prior versions of the CT but not implemented) will cover immunization, health, nutrition, HIV/AIDS, and more (World Bank 2009e).

By mid-to late 2010, testing regarding the use of penalties in response to noncompliance with co-responsibilities was expected to be complete (World Bank 2009e). Another evaluation, both of operations and program impacts, is due to start in fiscal year 2009 and will provide early feedback on progress made in harmonizing different program components and systems.

IDA funds will also support institutional strengthening in the Ministry of Gender, Children, and Social Development to better coordinate Kenyan social protection programs and more effectively manage the CT for OVC program. Enhanced coordination will be supported both by relevant line ministries and by programs that provide income generation and skills training to caretakers of OVC. Evaluations of supply-side capacity will also be conducted. This capacity building is crucial; program officials have made notable achievements in implementing the program and improving capacity already, but more must be done to meet the challenges of continued scaling up (World Bank 2009e).

The third phase of the CT for OVC will rely on a new World Bank loan of US$50 million from fiscal year 2010 through fiscal year 2013. DFID and UNICEF will provide US$34 million and US$12 million, respectively. Some additional funds come from Sida and the Danish International Development Agency (DANIDA); they will mainly support transfer payments in non-IDA-funded districts. DFID also has pledged funds for 2014 through 2017 (World Bank 2009e). The total expected cost for fiscal year 2010 through fiscal year 2013 is expected to be US$126 million. The government of Kenya will provide US$30 million over that period. The IDA money will also support an institutional strengthening component to help the government coordinate and improve execution of social protection programs through the national level.

Hunger Safety Net Programme
The HSNP pilot will test various design components to address food insecurity in arid and semiarid lands. The popularity and relative success achieved by the CT for OVC helped create a receptive environment for a second potentially large-scale CT initiative, the Hunger Safety Net Programme (HSNP). The HSNP provides regular cash transfers to households living in chronic food instability and poverty in the arid and semi-arid lands of northern Kenya. Its objective is to decrease hunger and vulnerability in targeted households through the provision of CTs and to contribute to the formation of Kenya's national social protection strategy and policies (HSNP n.d.).

The HSNP is supported by DFID. The program began in 2009, and many onlookers are interested in it because of its use of innovative technology to deliver CTs to extremely remote areas. The program's first phase will use substantial flexibility in targeting, payment mechanisms, and other components to determine the most cost-effective and politically feasible methods to move forward. Substantial coordination between major NGOs will be used in the HSNP.

The motivation for the HSNP was similar to that for the PSNP in Ethiopia: what was initially thought to be acute food insecurity was eventually recognized as chronic. Past food transfers had not prevented asset depletion among vulnerable groups. In targeted areas, more than 70 percent of people are poor, and 60 percent have relied on emergency food aid for their survival for longer than 10 years. Acute malnutrition is consistently as high as 30 percent. The hunger is predictable, and regular CTs were thought to be a possible solution (HSNP n.d.).

The HSNP is expected to cover a large number of beneficiaries. Phase 1 will last for four years and reach 60,000 households. Phase 2, the scale-up, will last for six years and target 300,000 households, using support from the government of Kenya. The program hopes to reach approximately 40 percent of the poorest households in targeted districts (HSNP n.d.).

Cash distributions began in early 2009. The program's pilot phase covers the four districts of Turkana (24,000 beneficiaries), Mander (8,000 beneficiaries), Marsabit (16,000 beneficiaries), and Wajir (12,000 beneficiaries) (World Bank 2009e). The locations chosen for phase 1 within the selected districts depend on their levels of poverty and security, availability of cash in the economy, and presence of needed infrastructure (HSNP n.d.).

The program's targeting and enrollment are being carried out by a group led primarily by Oxfam. Initially, several types of targeted transfers will be used. In some areas a universal pension will be given to individuals over 55 years old, which will reach an estimated one in three households in the districts. In other areas, transfers based on community targeting will be used. A final area will use dependency ratio criteria for targeting. Only one targeting method will be used in each subdistrict (HSNP n.d.). Each of the targeting methods will be carried out by one of three NGOs: Oxfam, CARE (Cooperative for Assistance and Relief Everywhere), or Save the Children UK.

The monthly amount of the transfer is K Sh 2,150 (US$26.88),[13] which covers approximately 30 to 40 percent of beneficiary households' food expenditures. This transfer value is based on the five-year average price of cereals (HSNP 2008). The transfers are supposed to be adjusted to account for inflation (5 percent) each year, although such adjustments will probably not occur in phase 1 because of budget constraints. Beneficiaries are encouraged to use the money to support productive activities and to purchase livestock insurance when it becomes available. Beneficiary households are still eligible to receive other types of aid and relief.

After the HSNP has been explained to beneficiaries, registration centers will be set up to help eligible households enroll. Households are registered in the HSNP using biometric technology, which will help identify them later when they retrieve transfers (HSNP n.d.).

The HSNP uses innovative methods to provide transfers to hard-to-reach groups. Another innovative aspect of the HSNP is its partnership with Equity Bank, which operates in Kenya's poorest areas. Equity Bank will distribute the transfers. The bank has opened seven additional branches to support the HSNP. In areas where bank branches are unavailable, payments will be made through point-of-service locations in local stores (HSNP n.d.).

The point-of-service devices rely on smart cards and fingerprint verification to securely identify beneficiaries. They are portable and work offline, but they must occasionally be connected to a mobile network to update financial records (HSNP n.d.). The point-of-service agents, selected by Equity Bank, will be local shopkeepers with a trusted record and the necessary liquidity to finance CTs for approximately 100 individuals each month. When the point-of-service agents pay cash to beneficiaries, a bank account for the agents is automatically paid the amount of the transfer plus a fee. The agents may then retrieve cash as needed from an Equity Bank branch. The point-of-service machines are also able to function as miniature automated teller machines (ATMs) for beneficiaries and nonbeneficiaries alike. No fee is charged to beneficiaries for their first four cash withdrawals per month.

The MIS for the HSNP will be web-based and capable of coordinating with databases from other programs, which will encourage coherent coverage of social protection programs in the future (HSNP n.d.). The MIS will integrate information from the point-of-service devices into the system. Internal monitoring will be complemented by HelpAge International, which is charged with protecting beneficiaries' rights.

Oxford Policy Management and Research Solutions will conduct an experimental impact evaluation that includes three survey waves. Selection of treatment sublocations will be random, based on a larger list. The control households may later be enrolled in the HSNP as it gradually rolls out (HSNP n.d.). Other evaluations of targeting, operational performance, and cost-effectiveness will take place.

The HSNP will be administered from the Ministry for the Development of Northern Kenya and Other Arid Lands, using extensive horizontal and vertical coordination (HSNP 2008). The five program components (administration, payments, social protection rights, monitoring and evaluation, and MIS), all led by consultants, will be coordinated by the HSNP secretariat, located within the ministry. A steering committee composed of government, donor, and civil society representatives will also provide leadership to the program (HSNP n.d.). Finally, a management consultants' forum composed of the consultant groups will meet regularly to guide program execution.

DFID is the primary financial supporter of the HSNP, providing £80 million (US$148 million) over a 10-year period.[14] DFID will collaborate with the WFP, the European Community Disaster Management Initiative,

USAID, the Food and Agriculture Organization of the United Nations (FAO), and others also at work in the districts (HSNP n.d.). District steering groups will manage and plan the program's execution (HSNP 2008).

Part of the HSNP phase 1 funding will also be used to coordinate Kenya's social protection programming, as well as to generate evidence on the need for better social protection in Kenya. The phase 1 social protection component will support the development of a social protection strategy and policy, and it will support harmonization of donor support for the HSNP (HSNP 2008). The government is expected to take a stronger role in the second phase, provided that the first phase is successful (HSNP n.d.).

Lesotho

Lesotho has two CTs: an Old Age Pension and the Lesotho Child Grants Programme (CGP). The pension for the elderly has been in operation since 2004. By March 2009, it had 78,064 registered beneficiaries (African Peer Review Mechanism 2010, as cited in European University Institute 2010). As of 2005, 60 percent of beneficiaries were women (Devereux and Pelham 2005). The CGP, beginning in 2009, seeks to enhance income in poor households with OVC. It plans to scale up through 2010 and 2011 to eventually reach 60,000 children, or approximately one-third of Lesotho's orphans (PlusNews 2009).

Old Age Pension

The Old Age Pension began smoothly without a pilot. The government of Lesotho's noncontributory pension program for the elderly, with the objective of reducing poverty, was announced in a budget speech in April 2004. The transfers began in November of that year. They are available to all citizens of Lesotho age 70 and older who do not receive other government retirement benefits (Croome, Nyanguru, and Molisana 2007).

Registration of recipients has largely relied on voter registration cards distributed during the 2002 elections. The Ministry of Finance registers pension recipients with the help of local chiefs, who identify and verify the ages of potential recipients. Recently organized community councils may now take a stronger role in the process (Croome, Nyanguru, and Molisana 2007).

The transfer was equal to M 150 (US$25) monthly until May 2007, when it was increased to M 200 (US$29) per month.[15] The increase coincided with the reelection of the Lesotho Congress for Democracy in the 2007 general elections. In April 2009, the pension was increased once again to M 300 (US$35).[16] The original value of the transfer covered the cost required to meet 75 percent of the minimal caloric needs of a household of five (Croome, Nyanguru, and Molisana 2007). The Ministry of Finance administers the transfer, which beneficiaries retrieve from the post office. When transfers are distributed, security forces are also hired if needed.

In 2007, the Old Age Pension cost approximately M 125 million annually (US$17.44 million)[17] (RHVP 2007a), amounting to 1.4 percent of the country's GDP (Samson 2007). The pension is funded solely by tax revenues (Croome, Nyanguru, and Molisana 2007). The cost of delivering transfers was estimated to be 6 percent of the pension amount. The government of Lesotho tried to keep costs low by making use of existing infrastructure, such as the postal system. The Ministry of Finance, which administers and maintains information regarding the pension, was already experienced in managing similar pension programs for veterans and retired civil servants.

As of 2007, the government of Lesotho had not evaluated the pension, although another group, which included Save the Children, HelpAge International, and the United Nations Educational, Scientific, and Cultural Organization (UNESCO), had completed an evaluation. A pension impact group based in Lesotho has also performed an external evaluation (Croome, Nyanguru, and Molisana 2007). The pension was found to have been delivered on time practically since inception, even though there had been no pilot.

Child Grants Programme

Lesotho's other major CT is the Lesotho CGP, which was publicly introduced by the finance minister in February 2009. The idea of a CT for children gained support following a 2008 World Vision transfer program in the country (PlusNews 2009). The pilot is part of phase 1 (lasting from 2007 through 2011) of a plan to develop a replicable and scalable model of a social CT program under the broader agenda of a child- and gender-sensitive social protection system for Lesotho.

The CGP addresses major vulnerabilities attributable to the HIV/AIDS crisis and to poverty. The objective of the Lesotho CGP is to enhance income in poor households with OVC. More specifically, it will use a predictable cash grant to supplement the income of poor households caring for OVC, including child-headed households. The grant is to be used for the high-priority needs of beneficiary children, such as to improve access to health care and nutritious food, increase school enrollment and attendance, and protect children from abuse and exploitation ("Q&A" 2008).

In April 2009, the CGP pilot began disbursing cash transfers in three community councils: the Matelile, Semonkong, and Lebakeng councils. The selection of community councils was based on the accessibility and availability of social services. Matelile, in Mafeteng district, considered a soft area, is easily accessible and has most public social services available. Semonkong, in Maseru district, is semiurban with challenging accessibility and limited availability of social services. Finally, Lebakeng, in Qacha's Nek district, is a hard-to-reach area; it is highly remote, is difficult to access, and has very limited availability of social services. The pilot will develop and test systems for targeting, enrollment, payments, monitoring, procurement and financial management, training of stakeholders, and public information and education. Lessons learned will guide refinement of the CGP in preparation for the program's rollout ("Q&A" 2008).

After receiving information from an initial awareness-raising campaign, households must apply for the program and then be ranked, if deemed eligible, by a village verification committee (Blank 2008). Eligible households must have resided in the community for the past 12 months and have a permanent household member under 18 years old. Targeted households contain or are headed by OVC, though other poor, vulnerable households may also be eligible.

Beneficiary applications may be received for up to two weeks, and during that time village leaders and social or child welfare officers are supposed to locate eligible households that have not applied for the program. Information about households will be verified by visits of the auxiliary social welfare officers to applicant households, and the district child welfare officer will coordinate activities at the district level. Lists of eligible households are supposed to be posted in public places for two weeks, and then public notices of group enrollment sessions are posted. Chiefs are responsible for communicating this information to eligible households. Despite these initial plans, the process is expected to be reviewed and further improved under the design completion phase (Blank 2008).

According to the operations manual, household representatives were to provide birth certificates for caretakers and eligible children (or a letter signed by the chief) during registration. They were then to fill out a registration form and obtain a photo identification card for the household representative and an alternate. At that time, they also were to receive a child grant coupon book and information about the program (Blank 2008). Following disbursement of the transfer, a payment coupon and receipt was supposed to be stamped from the child grant coupon book, which has a unique household identifying number. As is common in many pilots, a number of adjustments had to be made to the procedures outlined in the operations manual. These adjustments allowed for accelerated implementation of the pilot. These procedures are expected to be critically analyzed in the near future to ensure their efficiency and effectiveness.

Expectations are in place regarding the use of unconditional transfers. The UCT will be awarded to households on a quarterly basis. The grant is M 360 (US$38) for the current number of 1,250 beneficiary households. This coverage translates into benefits for approximately 5,000 OVC (UNICEF n.d.a). The relatively small size of the transfer was decided on in response to concerns about encouraging dependency in households and in consideration of the capacity of the government of Lesotho to finance the grant in the future (PlusNews 2009).

Although the transfers are unconditional, beneficiary households are expected to apply for birth certificates for children and the household caretaker or representative, attend educational and training seminars, and collect and use payments for the best interest of children—which should include investing in children's human capital (Blank 2008). Community committees will monitor the use of the transfers (PlusNews 2009).

Households exit the program if they have no children under 18 years old, if they fail to collect benefits for two quarters, if they fail to present a request for birth certificates for all children and the representative within six months of program enrollment, or if they migrate out of a pilot community (Blank 2008).

Organization and monitoring involve all levels. The Child Welfare Division of the Department of Social Welfare within the Ministry of Health and Social Welfare will coordinate and implement the CGP. A child grants technical team will report to the National Coordinating Committee for Orphans and Vulnerable Children. The Ministry of Finance and Development Planning will handle budget considerations. Future beneficiaries are required to hold birth certificates, which the Registry of Births and Deaths will help them obtain (Blank 2008).

The District Child Welfare Services, chieftains, and committees of community volunteers will provide substantial support for targeting, enrollment, questions and complaints, and payment of beneficiaries (UNICEF n.d.a). Local-level committees include village verification committees, caregiver support groups, community appeals and complaints committees, and community committees. Community committees are composed of the chief, a councilor, a social welfare officer, and two other members of the village caregiver group (Blank 2008). They are supposed to verify household information and confirm beneficiary eligibility. Caregiver support groups will participate in the village verification committee, supervise child-headed households, and identify social welfare needs of households. A district child protection team will work with community committees to implement the child grants and coordinate other child social services across the district. Annual meetings of the beneficiaries and the district child welfare officer are to be held to obtain feedback and determine how to improve the program (Blank 2008).

Targeting and creation of the MIS will be contracted out to consultants procured by UNICEF (UNICEF n.d.a). Both an internal audit and an impact evaluation are planned. Technical support will come from UNICEF through an agreement with the European Commission. The pilot will receive European Union funds of €5 million (US$7 million)[18] until December 2011. Other support will come from the European Commission financing agreement with Lesotho's government. Some of this financing will support capacity building in the Ministry of Health and Social Welfare, a secondary goal of the program (Blank 2008). The government of Lesotho has already been financing certain aspects of the program, including some staff and office costs.

Malawi

Malawi has had two major CTs. One, the Social Cash Transfer (SCT) program, began with UNICEF support as a pilot in Mchinji district in 2006, with goals to scale up eventually to a national program. Its objective is to decrease poverty, hunger, and starvation of the extremely poor and households without an eligible member able to participate in the labor force, which includes many households with OVC. The second program, a World Bank initiative, is the Zomba CT program, which is an experimental program started in January 2008 in Zomba district, targeting 1,320 unmarried women ages 13 to 22, to examine questions of interest to policy makers designing CTs.

Social Cash Transfer Program

SCT pilot tackles extreme poverty. Schubert and Huijbregts (2006) report that about 10 percent of all Malawian households (250,000) are extremely poor and incapable of work (that is, they are labor constrained or labor incapacitated). In the 10 years preceding 2006, the extreme poverty rate had not decreased in Malawi. Some officials suggested that if 10 percent of households received CTs, the country's extreme poverty rate would decrease from 22 percent to 12 percent at a cost of US$41 million per year. This analysis contributed to the decision to target 10 percent of households, limited to the extremely poor and labor-constrained households in the initial pilot area of Mchinji. This equaled approximately 15,000 individuals in 3,000 households (Chipeta and Mwamlima 2007). In addition to its poverty-related objective, the program seeks to improve beneficiary children's enrollment and attendance at schools, provide information about how well a CT could fit into Malawi's social protection agenda, and test whether district assemblies can implement decentralized CTs that are both cost-effective and able to reach targeted household groups (Schubert and Huijbregts 2006). Mchinji was chosen for the pilot because of its strong district assembly, average poverty levels, and relatively close location to the capital of Lilongwe.

Targeting of the pilot uses elected village committees. Eligible households must reside in the bottom expenditure quintile and below the national extreme poverty line. Given this stipulation, beneficiary households should be unable to purchase needed nonfood goods. They should also be labor constrained, meaning that they have no household member age 19 to 59 capable of working or they have a dependency ratio higher than three.

To select the households, locally elected committees known as *community social protection committees* first create a list of all households that they think may fulfill the program's poverty- and labor-related requirements. The committees are selected through elections during the initial program meeting (Schubert 2007a). Village heads are not allowed to be on the committees, although they still appeared to have influence in some cases (Miller, Tsoka, and Reichert 2010). The committees must then call on and interview all potential beneficiary households, and the village head verifies the information gathered (Miller and Tsoka n.d.). Next, committees rank identified households according to their level of neediness. The ranking is discussed and approved or changed in a community meeting. The information is passed to a secretariat and a social protection subcommittee, which must approve or disapprove the list.

Transfers are graduated and distributed at local paypoints. Monthly transfers in Mchinji, all unconditional, are graduated by household size and the number of children in school. One-person households receive MK 600 (about US$4.00), two-person households receive MK 1,000 (US$6.67), three-person households receive MK 1,400 (US$9.33), and four-person households (or larger) receive MK 1,800 (US$12.00) (Schubert and Huijbregts 2006).

Households with children in primary school receive an additional MK 200 (US$1.33) per child, and households with children in secondary school earn an additional MK 400 (US$2.67) per child. This bonus is not tied to school attendance. It is simply given when school-age children reside in the household. The average monthly transfer value was found to be MK 1,700 (US$11.33)[19] per household, which was deemed large enough to fill the extreme poverty gap in targeted households (Schubert and Huijbregts 2006).

Transfers are given at local paypoints, such as schools. When beneficiaries receive their transfers, the payment is recorded on the back of a program-issued photo identification card. The cards also contain information regarding household composition and transfer size (Schubert 2007a).

The first transfers of the pilot program were distributed in late 2006. The pilot was expected to cost US$371,000 annually, amounting to US$144 per household plus US$20 per household for administrative costs. Original plans for expansion envisioned reaching three other districts by late 2008, with a total of 32,000 households and an annual cost of US$5.2 million. Coverage was expected to roll out gradually to eventually reach 250,000 households in all districts by 2014 or 2015 (Schubert and Huijbregts 2006). Later reports suggest the program will reach approximately 300,000 households by 2015. By the beginning of 2008, 3,000 households were receiving transfers in Mchinji district, and monthly program expenditures were US$43,000 (Miller, Tsoka, and Reichert 2008b). The pilot scale-up was postponed because of funding delays; however, it was able to reach seven districts by the end of 2008 (Horvath, Huijbregts, and Webb 2008). As of April 2009, the pilot reached 92,786 beneficiaries in 23,561 households in seven districts (UNICEF and Government of Malawi 2009).

The Social Cash Transfer program is implemented locally and funded jointly. The Department of Child Development Affairs in the Ministry of Gender, Children, and Community Development and the Department of Poverty Reduction and Social Protection in the Ministry of Development, Planning, and Cooperation coordinated the pilot with help from UNICEF (Chipeta and Mwamlima 2007). Additional support has come from the Ministry of Economic Planning and Development (Miller, Tsoka, and Reichert 2008a). The Mchinji pilot was implemented by the local assembly, whose district executive committee had a subcommittee on social protection with line ministry representatives. This subcommittee approved applications to the program. The Malawi district structure has officers that come from various departments and are able to support the program, although capacity is still limited at the district level (Schubert and Huijbregts 2006).

Below the subcommittee is the SCT program secretariat, with personnel who implement the program, control the budget, and perform periodic monitoring. Below the secretariat, the village development committee is in charge of the community social protection committee, which both targets and tracks beneficiaries (Schubert and Huijbregts 2006). Community social protection committee teams receive remuneration to compensate them for some activities performed (Schubert 2007a).

For the pilot, UNICEF provided technical assistance, supported program setup, funded the transfers until December 2006 (Miller and Tsoka n.d.), and supported advocacy and capacity building in Malawi. Its activities included funding visits of government representatives to Brazil and Zambia, holding workshops, and conducting field trips to Mchinji (Schubert and Huijbregts 2006).

Additional funding to finish the pilot and to scale up in 2008 and 2009 came from the Global Fund to Fight AIDS, Tuberculosis, and Malaria (GFATM) through the National AIDS Commission. The GFATM's contributions to the scale-up were supposed to exceed US$12 million (European Commission 2009) and to begin in mid-2007 (Miller and Tsoka n.d.). GFATM's support was expected to continue through September 2010 (European Commission 2009). National AIDS Commission funds were used because approximately 70 percent of beneficiary households were affected by HIV/AIDS (Schubert 2007b).

The European Commission conducted an external program review and found implementation capacity and bottlenecks to vary significantly by district. It suggested several major improvements be made prior to scaling up, especially better control of data and internal monitoring, improvements in management structure, use of other payment mechanisms, and revision of targeting methods (European Commission 2009). Some of the recommendations apparently will be used.

The country has expressed interest in obtaining further financing from development partners through a basket fund after the SCT has been incorporated into the national social protection strategy and has received full cabinet support (Schubert and Huijbregts 2006). Other donors in a pool fund were expected to be the World Bank, DFID, CIDA, and the Norwegian Agency for Development Cooperation (Horvath, Huijbregts, and Webb 2008).

Challenges arose in the evaluation design. Internal monitoring is completed through the production of monthly reports on costs, activities, outputs, and more. Boston University's Center for International Health and Development performed external program monitoring in 2007 and 2008. UNICEF and USAID supported a joint external program evaluation conducted by Boston University and the Centre for Social Research in Malawi (Miller, Tsoka, and Reichert 2008b).

Targeting evaluations were completed in March and June 2007, and a process evaluation was conducted in October 2007 (Miller, Tsoka, and Mchinji Evaluation Team 2007a). The baseline household survey was conducted in treatment and comparison village groups in March 2007 before treatment households received a grant. Follow-up surveys were carried out in August and September 2007 and March 2008. Qualitative data were collected from October to November 2007. Experimental methods appear to have been compromised in the evaluation. For instance, comparison households did not understand that the research was unrelated to their grant receipt. The extent to which this issue may have affected results is unclear.

The targeting evaluation of the Mchinji program concluded that almost one-third of community members in program areas thought targeting was not fair. This result could reflect a need to improve targeting methods or communication of targeting methods. The evaluation suggested that targeting should be more objective, standardized, and transparent (Miller, Tsoka, and Reichert 2008b). Depending on definitions of eligibility, exclusion errors in communities ranged from 37 percent through 68 percent. However, this range reflects the size of the budget as well as the quality of targeting. Estimates of inclusion errors ranged from

16 percent to 34 percent, depending on definitions of eligibility. Specific targeting difficulties were related to differentiating between poor and ultrapoor households and establishing clear criteria for consistent beneficiary selection (Miller, Tsoka, and Reichert 2010).

The evaluation found that beneficiaries' food consumption and diversity had improved over those of the comparison group. In addition, children's and adults' health had improved, and children's self-reported school attendance and capacity to study increased. Child labor also decreased significantly in the treatment group, whereas the comparison group's labor participation did not change. The evaluation also concluded that beneficiary households' productivity had increased because of the transfers (Miller, Tsoka, and Mchinji Evaluation Team 2007b). Although the glitches in the experimental design should be taken seriously and the evaluation did not control for these differences, the results point to potentially positive program effects.

The expected cost of scaling up the program nationally to 273,000 households (1.2 million individuals, of which 60 percent are expected to be OVC) is approximately US$55 million annually, or 1.4 percent of GDP (Schubert 2009).[20] In June 2007, delivery of the transfers cost less than 2.5 percent of program costs, and administrative costs were less than 15 percent of program costs (Horvath, Huijbregts, and Webb 2008).

Malawi's SCT has faced significant challenges, which include the need for more, better-trained district-level staff members and lower turnover of government employees (Horvath, Huijbregts, and Webb 2008). At the time of writing, the program needed improved financial mechanisms to transfer funds at high levels and an improved MIS that could connect district- and national-level data. It also needed to put a complaints and appeals procedure in place (UNICEF and Government of Malawi 2009). Increased government commitment, particularly from the Ministry of Finance, and additional capacity building, collaboration, and technical assistance at all levels of government will be necessary if scaling up is to succeed. Revisions of the management structure, automation of records, and implementation of rolling enrollment are also expected to be important in improving performance before a larger-scale rollout (Miller, Tsoka, and Reichert 2008a).

More recently, the program has been adapted so that it can improve its targeting, monitoring, and performance even as it continues to scale up. In particular, targeting must now go through a round of verification by extension workers in communities, and proxy means targeting will soon be piloted.

Zomba CT Project

The World Bank–supported Zomba CT program, implemented in Malawi's southern region, had an experimental evaluation design. The program's objective was to better understand questions of interest to policy makers designing CTs. The project aimed to test the extent to which unconditional cash transfers and conditional cash transfers affect outcomes, to understand the elasticity of outcomes with respect to transfer size, to learn how results change when portions of transfers are given to parents and adolescents, and to study effects of CTs on sexual behavior and risk for HIV. Secondary areas examined included spillover effects of transfers and the impact of the CT on teenage girls' labor market participation and economic independence (Baird and others 2009). Results from the Zomba CT experiment will inform the design of CTs in the region and beyond.

Zomba research intervention focuses on young women. Eligible beneficiaries of the Zomba CT were 13- to 22-year-old unmarried women. In the baseline survey, some girls had already dropped out of school and others still attended. The 1,230 beneficiaries received a household transfer and a girl-level transfer of varying amounts. The program also paid secondary school fees for girls receiving conditional transfers. (Most girls were in Standard 7, Form 4.) Some girls' transfers were conditional on 80 percent or higher secondary school attendance, whereas other girls' transfers were unconditional. Program conditionality, transfer size, and proportion of the transfer given directly to the girl varied randomly. The total transfer size ranged from US$5 through US$15 monthly (Baird and others 2009), and transfers were given for the 10 months of the school year. The average transfer value of US$10 per month equaled approximately 15 percent of the studied households' total consumption per month (Baird and others 2010).

A Malawian NGO located in Zomba district administered the program. The NGO monitored conditions when appropriate and distributed the CTs, which were given each month at various paypoints. Conditions were monitored using school visits, calls to principals, school records, and random spot-checks (Baird and others 2009). Because the Zomba CT was project based, it was not seated within a government ministry.

The Zomba CT began in January 2008 and ended in November 2009. Baseline data were collected in the fall of 2007 through early 2008. Follow-up collection occurred in the fall of 2008 and fall of 2009. Plans include conducting another follow-up survey in 2011 (Baird and others 2009).

Insights were gained for improving enrollments and reducing risks for girls. The main results of the program evaluation found the CCT arm to be effective at increasing school enrollment, attendance, and test scores. Although the UCT was able to increase school enrollment, its impact was only 43 percent of that obtained by the CCT. In terms of these schooling outcomes, the CCT also promised to be more cost-effective, since it could achieve with a US$5 transfer what a UCT could with a US$10 transfer. When this cost savings was combined with the reduced payments for noncompliance, the savings associated with enforcing conditions was expected to be greater than its cost (Baird, McIntosh, and Özler 2011).

Although the CCT had a significant positive effect on educational outcomes, the UCT was more effective in decreasing the likelihood of teenage pregnancy and early marriage. This result was driven by the income effects of the UCT and by the nature of the beneficiary groups. Although the CCT was able to discourage early marriage and pregnancy by inducing some girls to remain in school, a remaining group of potential beneficiaries (known as *noncompliers*) would drop out of school whether they received a CCT (thus forfeiting payment) or a UCT. Dropouts were more vulnerable to marriage and pregnancy, and income from a UCT was able to help them delay those actions. The substantial size of the group of so-called noncompliers led to the large effect of the UCT on those outcomes.

The results highlighted the ability of the CCT to achieve condition-related goals while it risked excluding vulnerable girls from the program (that is, those vulnerable to early marriage and pregnancy who would not remain in school with either type of transfer).

Other variation in the experimental treatment showed that small transfers could achieve results similar to those of larger transfers (that is, elasticity of outcomes with respect to transfer size was small) for CCTs, while some UCT outcomes improved with increased transfer size. Additional benefits did not generally accrue when part of transfers were given to the adolescent beneficiaries instead of their parents (Baird, McIntosh, and Özler 2011).

Finally, evidence showed that the CTs were able to reduce the HIV and HSV-2 (herpes simplex virus type 2) infection rates of the girls.

This result appeared to be driven by the income effect of the transfers. Girls who received the CTs had less sex, and they tended to choose safer (younger) partners (World Bank 2010b).

Mali

Bourse Maman

UNICEF funded an extremely small CT pilot program in Mali known as Bourse Maman. Its objective was to improve school attendance in the targeted area through mothers' participation in the program (Bourse Maman n.d.). The program began in 2002 and ended in 2007. It provided CCTs to women in the regions of Mopti and Kayes, areas where the Millennium Development Goal (MDG) for primary school enrollment was failing.

Bourse Maman was inspired by Brazil's Bolsa Família. It provided conditional transfers to mothers in 430 to 500 households annually. The households contained children in nine different schools. Transfers were conditioned on the children's school enrollment and attendance on 80 percent or more of school days. Larger transfers were given for female students than for males. The monthly transfer was approximately CFAF 5,000 (US$12), paid to mothers for the eight months of the school year. NGOs and school authorities verified school attendance (UNICEF 2009).

One NGO in each region worked with UNICEF to help communities identify beneficiary households. Households with the highest poverty levels and highest numbers of eligible primary school children were selected. Other groups involved in beneficiary selection included local councils, groups of women, school directors, school management committees, and local education authorities. Both community targeting and proxy means testing appear to have been used (UNICEF 2009).

UNICEF Mali commissioned an external evaluation of Bourse Maman in 2005. It concluded that the program significantly increased both school enrollment and attendance. Major issues arose because of confusion over targeting, coordination failures with NGOs, and opposition from local Muslim leaders. Significant payment delays also occurred. Program expansion and increased communication helped to resolve some of those issues (UNICEF 2009). UNICEF suggested that the program be expanded, given the high poverty levels and low school attendance prevailing in the area.

Bourse Maman was administered and coordinated by UNICEF, participating schools, and the Centres d'Animation Pédagogique in the

Mopti and Kayes regions, along with implementing NGOs and communities. It cost approximately US$36,800 annually (UNICEF 2009).

Mauritius

Universal Old Age Pension

Mauritius has a universal Old Age Pension (Croome, Nyanguru, and Molisana 2007) that was created in 1951 and is paid to all citizens 60 years and older (Lallmahomed 2008). The pension was means tested until 1958, when it transitioned to a universal pension. Later, it transitioned back to a means-tested program, until the pension once again became a universal transfer in 1977 (Willmore 2003). It has remained a universal transfer since 1977, except during a brief six-month period from 2004 through 2005 (Central Statistics Office 2007).

The pension's absolute purchasing power has increased over time, although its relative value in terms of GDP per capita has not kept pace. In 2008, the transfer was worth US$100 monthly (Government of Mauritius 2008), or approximately 20 percent of the average wage (Central Statistics Office 2007). Significantly higher amounts are given to individuals who are 90 and 100 years or older. Individuals who are blind or paralyzed and other dependent individuals receive the Enhanced Retirement Pension, which provides an additional US$54 (Government of Mauritius 2008). Recipients must reside in Mauritius for at least 12 to 15 years to be eligible to receive the pension, which is part of a larger social security system (Lallmahomed 2008). In 2007, the basic and enhanced pensions had 148,800 beneficiaries.

In 2007, spending on the basic and enhanced pensions was US$159 million, equal to 8.7 percent of government expenditures and 2.0 percent of GDP (Government of Mauritius 2008). Increased aging in the most recent demographic transition has led to higher pension spending. The government of Mauritius has been forced to reformulate the pension to maintain its affordability. The size of the population eligible for the pension is expected to triple by 2050, causing the pension's cost to grow to 5.7 percent of GDP. To address these issues, the retirement age has been gradually increasing toward 65 since late 2008, and annual increases in the basic pension will be restricted (Government of Mauritius 2009).

Other Pensions and Allowances

The government of Mauritius also funds a Basic Widow's Pension, which as of June 2006 reached almost 23,000 beneficiaries; a Basic Invalid's

Pension for approximately 27,600 beneficiaries; a Carer's Allowance for caregivers of people who are severely disabled, which reached almost 8,000 individuals; and a Basic Orphan's Pension, which reached only slightly more than 400 beneficiaries (Central Statistics Office 2007). When children live in a pensioner's household, transfers are increased by a Child's Allowance. The allowance is given in households with children under 15 years (or under 20 if the child is a full-time student). Up to three children per household may receive the Child's Allowance, and benefits continue even if the parent's pension is no longer granted. In June 2006, approximately 19,500 children received the Child's Allowance.

A grant known as Social Aid is paid to poor households with a head who cannot earn money for the household. The grant is means tested, and it is frequently given to households in which a breadwinner is in jail or a spouse has been abandoned and has to care for children. The grant value equals the difference between the household's income and its expected expenditure needs. In June 2006, approximately 17,200 households were receiving this benefit (Central Statistics Office 2007).

An additional monthly grant of US$3.50 per household member is provided to beneficiaries of Social Aid, recipients of Unemployment Hardship Relief, and recipients of other grants whose income levels would have qualified them for Social Aid if they had not received another grant (Government of Mauritius 2008). This transfer, called Food Aid, began in 1993 and was given so that beneficiaries could purchase food staples. As of June 2006, there were 53,000 beneficiaries of the Food Aid CTs (Central Statistics Office 2007).

Mauritius's social protection programs are administered by the Ministry of Social Security, National Solidarity, and Senior Citizens Welfare and Reform Institutions.

Mozambique

Food Subsidy Program

Mozambique's Food Subsidy Program (Programa de Subsidio de Alimentos, or PSA) is one of the earliest-established CTs in a low-income country in Africa. It began in 1993 as an emergency program to aid poor urban dwellers after subsidies for commodities were removed (World Bank 2009a).[21] The PSA was created to ensure that consumption did not fall to levels insufficient for survival. Its original goal was to ensure that beneficiaries' caloric intake reached 1,700 kilocalories daily (Datt and others 1997). These objectives are reflected in the program's name, despite major changes in program management and design over the years. The Office for Assistance to the Vulnerable Population (Gabinete de Apoio à População Vulnerável, or GAPVU), under the Ministry of Finance (Waterhouse 2007), ran the program until 1997, when concerns about corruption led to closure of GAPVU. The program was taken over by the National Institute for Social Action (Devereux and Pelham 2005). Unlike many CTs in the region that focused on the rural poor, the PSA originally was limited to the urban poor, though changes in the past decade have seen a broadening of the program's targeting.

PSA phase 1 created an urban safety net program. The PSA initially targeted those living in urban areas, as it was thought that many city dwellers lacked the informal community and family safety nets thought to be available to rural Mozambicans. The transfer size was initially a set amount for each beneficiary, but it was soon replaced with a benefit that varied with household size. Strict targeting limited transfers to 1 percent of the country's population, but within this limitation, coverage reached 16 percent of urban households in 1997 (Devereux and Pelham 2005).

To qualify for the PSA, households could not contain an able-bodied adult between 18 and 59 years old, and they had to contain a child under 5 years old with diagnosed risks related to malnutrition or a pregnant female with identified risks (Datt and others 1997). The program provided transfers to more than 80,000 households by the end of 1995. In mid-1995, it was expanded to cover (a) households headed by females with at least five children that had no other adult members between ages 18 and 59 and (b) households headed by a chronically ill person. As of 1997, the PSA was functioning in 13 urban areas.

To be eligible for benefits, households had to prove that they had lived in their urban area for more than 12 months and that they did not have a migrant household member between the ages of 18 and 59. A means test was supposedly applied, which required that households earn under Mt 24,000 monthly (US$4.80) per capita in 1995.[22] This amount was adjusted to Mt 32,000 (US$2.88) monthly in 1997.[23] Women headed almost one in two beneficiary households. Datt and others' (1997) study revealed that many of the eligibility criteria, such as the maximum income stipulation and the requirement that elderly households could not have working-age household members, were not strictly enforced.

Elderly individuals and people with disabilities were informed about the PSA at community meetings, and they had to apply for the program through a local neighborhood secretary. Leaders of small neighborhood groups also supported the application process. Pregnant women and children were located through local maternal-child health clinics, which identified potential beneficiaries and passed the information to the city's GAPVU office. Households were visited by city GAPVU officials to verify the information submitted (Datt and others 1997). Both nurses and local secretaries received incentives for recommending applicants to the program.

Benefits were paid every month for one year for elderly people, people with disabilities, and children. After one year, beneficiaries were reevaluated and could have their status renewed. Children could have their status renewed annually until they were five years old, and pregnant women could receive benefits until six months after their babies were born (Datt and others 1997).

Leakages and corruption undermined GAPVU implementation. An International Food Policy Research Institute study of GAPVU in 1997 suggested that two-thirds of the individuals reached by the program were poor and lived in worse conditions than other urban households. At that time, the monthly transfer value was approximately US$1 per capita, which was 13 percent of the per capita consumption value of beneficiaries. Beneficiary households often did not know how much their transfers should be, however, and many households received transfer amounts lower than the amounts they qualified for. On average, transfers amounted to approximately two-thirds of the value for which households were qualified to receive. This underpayment was due to low household awareness of benefit eligibility and to payment interruptions (Datt and others 1997).

The program was housed within the Ministry for Coordination of Social Action, which has traditionally been closely tied to the Ministry of Finance. Program administration was carried out at the provincial level, and provincial GAPVU teams were led by provincial leaders in the Ministry of Planning and Finance (Datt and others 1997). GAPVU was closed because of corruption in 1997, and the National Institute for Social Action took over responsibility for PSA implementation (Devereux and Pelham 2005).

The reorganized PSA expands. The PSA has experienced some changes since it was placed under the jurisdiction of the National Institute for Social Action. In 2006, the PSA covered 96,600 beneficiaries. Despite its increased coverage, it was estimated to reach only 15 percent of poor, elderly Mozambicans in 2006 (Ellis 2007). Since then, it has been expanding rapidly. Benefits reached 101,800 beneficiaries in March 2007 (Ellis 2007) and 287,454 beneficiaries by the end of 2008 (Soares, Hirata, and Rivas n.d.).

By 2007, program targeting primarily reached women over age 55 and men over age 60 who were incapable of participating in the labor force and who lived alone or headed a destitute household. In March 2007, 93 percent of beneficiaries were elderly and 66 percent were females. Many beneficiaries cared for OVC. The program's recent baseline evaluation found that approximately half of the sample households had children less than 18 years of age in the household; slightly under two-thirds of those children were grandchildren of the household head (Soares, Hirata, and Rivas n.d.). The program also reached people living with disabilities, malnourished pregnant women, and the chronically ill (Ellis 2007; Waterhouse 2007). By 2007, the means criteria had been set at Mtn 70 (US$2.70) per capita monthly.[24]

The monthly payment levels of the PSA in 2007 were as follows: Mtn 70 (US$2.70) for a one-member household; Mtn 100 (US$3.80) for a household with one dependent; Mtn 120 (US$4.60) for a household with two dependents; Mtn 130 (US$5.00) for a household with three dependents; and Mtn 140 (US$5.40) for a household with four or more dependents (Ellis 2007). The levels were reportedly enough for households to buy food for up to two days. Although the PSA was originally set at one-third of the country's minimum salary, it was worth only between 4 percent and 6 percent of the minimum wage in 2007.

By 2009, the government of Mozambique had raised the transfer value to range from Mtn 100 to Mtn 300, or from US$3.71 to US$11.13 (World Bank 2009a).[25] Note that Mtn 100 is less than 10 percent of the minimum wage. Despite the apparent low value of the transfer, a 2008 evaluation found that the average benefit received by beneficiary households equaled about 22 percent of the households' current consumption levels, a number comparable to that found in similar programs. However, the benefit is still considered low in relation to the minimum value of the monthly food basket outlined by the government of Mozambique. Households also tend to receive a transfer that is smaller than the amount to which they are entitled.

People living with HIV/AIDS or tuberculosis were not included as eligible beneficiaries, since the National Institute of Social Action is unable to provide benefits for everyone suffering from those illnesses.

They were also excluded, in part, because of the difficulty in identifying those individuals (World Bank 2009a). In practice, some people living with HIV/AIDS are covered (Waterhouse 2007).

Child dependents in beneficiary households are not supposed to receive benefits unless they are double orphans (Soares, Hirata, and Rivas n.d.; Soares and Teixeira 2010). This rule limits transfers to many households despite their size. In a survey of beneficiaries in 2008, only 11 percent of the beneficiary households were awarded more than the basic transfer of Mtn 100, although 40 percent of the sample included children (Soares and Teixeira 2010).

The application process is slow and administrative processes incur high costs. The self-application process was still used in 2007. A decision regarding the application was supposed to be made within 15 days of application, and applicants received a reference number. If accepted, they received a beneficiary identity card. The enrollment process in 2007 was reported to take months and to be limited by the requirement that the applicant have an identification card (Ellis 2007).[26]

Paid individuals known as *permanentes* provide vital auxiliary support for the PSA at the community level. Selected by their communities, these individuals each serve at least 15 beneficiaries in rural areas and 25 in urban areas (Ellis 2007). As of 2007, the permanentes received Mtn 300 monthly. The permanentes' duties include providing the community with information regarding the PSA, visiting beneficiaries at their homes, assisting at the paydays, and verifying the list of payment recipients. The quality of their support varies greatly (Waterhouse 2007). Supposedly, permanentes' low salaries affect their job performance, leading to increased delays in identifying eligible beneficiaries and distributing payments (World Bank 2009a).

Transfer payments occur as follows. The Ministry of Finance transfers money directly to the bank accounts of the 19 delegations of the National Institute for Social Action. The cash is securely transported to local delegations. The delegations determine the date for payment, which often changes monthly. The permanentes inform beneficiaries of the pay date. On that date, National Institute for Social Action cashiers arrive, accompanied by paid police, and pay the PSA transfers with the permanentes' help. The only automated portion of this process occurs when the money is initially transferred to the delegations' bank accounts. Permanentes are allowed to collect and sign for beneficiaries who are unable to retrieve their money on the pay date (World Bank 2009a).

Beneficiaries are automatically removed from the information system if they miss three consecutive transfer months. The computer system at the National Institute for Social Action, LINDEX, is not networked, and the various delegations run their own version of the program (Ellis 2007).

The PSA's home, the National Institute for Social Action, is a semiautonomous body in the Ministry of Women and Social Action (Ellis 2007), and it obtains its budget directly from the Ministry of Finance. The institute's budget was Mtn 164.2 million (US$6.3 million) in 2006 and Mtn 188.6 million (US$7.3 million) in 2007. Only 11 percent of the Ministry of Women and Social Action's budget is from donors. The organization is allocated 0.3 percent of the national budget (World Bank 2009a), a relatively low proportion compared to allocations received by national programs elsewhere.

The 2008 budget allocation for the PSA was Mtn 198.7 million (US$8.3 million).[27] Administrative costs were said to equal 15 percent of the National Institute for Social Action's budget, but this percentage is probably too low (Ellis 2007). Costs remain high because of the complex arrangements for payment distribution and because payments or allowances are provided to many involved parties. In 2006, 1,000 permanentes, 250 local activist employees, and police forces were paid in addition to the institute's staff. Extra per diem allowances of Mtn 1,500 were given to staff members who visited program locations for business. These visits numbered in the thousands each month. In 2006, the estimated return for US$1.41 in program expenditures translated to only US$1.00 in delivered benefits.

Despite mentioned weaknesses, PSA has a significant, positive influence on beneficiaries' lives. An evaluation of the PSA's targeting using 2008 data suggested that treatment localities were better off than nontreatment localities and highlighted that geographic targeting of localities could be improved. Although that result may be partially driven by nonrandom selection of comparison households in nontreatment localities (Soares and Teixeira 2010), Massingarela and Nhate (2006) suggested that targeting of funds for the PSA has tended to align with provinces associated with political winners.

Targeting within localities was successful at selecting the worst-off households. Soares and Teixeira (2010) used a targeting index created by Coady, Grosh, and Hoddinott (2004), in which the percentage of the beneficiary population that falls in the bottom quintile of a reference distribution is divided by 20. Higher numbers of this calculation indicate the program is more pro-poor. Using a reference quintile based on a well-being index calculated for rural households from the 2008 Multiple Indicator Cluster Survey, the PSA was found to be relatively well targeted. The index calculated for PSA-treated households was 2.69. When the sample was limited only to potentially eligible rural households, the index was still 1.88. In comparison, Coady, Grosh, and Hoddinott (2004) calculated an index of 1.80 for the CT programs they reviewed.

Using propensity score matching (PSM) and difference-in-difference regressions, Soares and Teixeira (2010) used data from 2008 and 2009 to find that the PSA increased the proportion of expenditures on food by 22 percent. The positive impacts on food share, as well as the probability of consuming flour, were even larger in female-headed households. The PSA increased the likelihood that women ate additional meals daily (and marginally increased this probability for boys ages five to nine). Household adults increased their probability of working (by 17 percent for male adults and the elderly and 24 percent for adult women, although this finding was only marginally significant), whereas boys between five and nine years old were 29 percent less likely to work. Hours spent by household adults in their own fields decreased, indicating additional labor time was being spent outside the household. One indicator showed that children's acute malnutrition decreased by 30 percent, but the study concluded that this result may have been an anomaly, given no other results supporting such strong nutritional effects.

Discussions to strengthen and expand the PSA are under way. Efforts to increase the PSA's scope and build its capacity have been going on since 2007, both through the government and with the help of development partners. Efforts have been made to ensure that benefits are given to cover dependents within beneficiary households (Soares, Hirata, and Rivas n.d.), and the National Institute for Social Action has worked with NGOs and other donors to pilot different forms of the PSA to rural locations (Ellis 2007). Other partnerships have been discussed with UNICEF, CARE, and Caritas (Waterhouse 2007). Along with this expansion came the initiation of an impact evaluation supported by the United Nations Development Programme (UNDP) International Policy Centre for Inclusive Growth (Soares, Hirata, and Rivas n.d.).

The Ministry of Women and Social Action, National Institute for Social Action, and donors have been trying to develop a more coherent, coordinated, and comprehensive set of social protection programs for Mozambique. The Ministry of Planning and Development began investigating the cost-effectiveness of increasing social protection, and others have been in contact with the International Labour Organization (ILO) about modeling the effects of social protection programs. The Ministry of Women and Social Action, DFID, Royal Netherlands Embassy, and UNICEF undertook a study to examine whether a targeted transfer for the elderly could be used to reach OVC (Waterhouse 2007). The National Institute for Social Action was working with support from HelpAge International and the Netherlands to test how to decrease costs and increase the transfer value, partially through relying on greater community involvement. The National Institute for Social Action was also looking into how to link the PSA to its other programs, both programmatically and in its information systems (Ellis 2007).

Multiple studies have been commissioned to evaluate the state of the PSA's parent institute and ministry. These studies have exposed weak capacity and the need for major institutional strengthening. Weaknesses uncovered by the evaluations include the large percentage of unfilled positions and the lack of needed equipment, training, and systems in the ministry (World Bank 2009a). The Ministry of Women and Social Action's political influence is also weak, and there have been conversations about returning the ministry to the Ministry of Health, where its departments used to reside (Waterhouse 2007).

Namibia

The Namibian and South African social welfare systems were linked prior to Namibian independence in 1990 (Levine, van der Berg, and Yu 2009). All citizens, regardless of ethnicity, were eligible to receive grants from 1973 onward, although significant racial discrimination was present in transfer levels. Once it was independent of South Africa, Namibia provided increasingly equitable transfers, including old age and disability pensions and a variety of grants for children. Namibia's long-established legal support and extensive administrative experience with the CTs have contributed to a fairly efficient system, which in 2009 reached 250,000 beneficiaries, or about 12 percent of the country's estimated population.[28] However, there are some indications that a comprehensive policy framework put in place in recent years to deal with burgeoning numbers of OVC still has weaknesses that affect coverage of these children.

Old Age and Disability Pensions

Namibia's Old Age Pension is a universal grant of N$450 monthly (US$57)[29] for Namibian citizens or permanent residents 60 years of age or older (Levine, van der Berg, and Yu 2009). The pension technically began with the Old Age Pensions Act of 1928 but was legally established in an independent Namibia in 1992 through the country's National Pension Act. Support for means testing of the Old Age Pension has been officially enacted, but it remains a universal pension in practice. Nevertheless, it appears to be relatively well targeted to the poor, in part as a result of the poverty of the elderly and in part as a result of low uptake by the wealthier elderly. At the end of 2008, the country had slightly more than 130,500 beneficiaries of the Old Age Pension (Levine, van der Berg, and Yu 2009).

All applicants for the pension must prove Namibian citizenship or permanent residency. Applicants submit various documents, including birth, identification, and proof of marriage (required of women only). Applications are submitted to the Ministry of Health and Social Service's regional pension office (ELCRN 2007).

Old Age Pension payments are made through bank deposits, post offices, or mobile banking units that use smart cards (outsourced through United Cash Pay Masters). Two-thirds of beneficiaries currently receive their payments through mobile banking units and smart cards. Beneficiaries may select an alternate to collect their payments. Distribution days are announced over the radio. If payments are not collected once every three months, the grant is suspended (ELCRN 2007; Levine, van der Berg, and Yu 2009).

The Disability Pension is paid to recipients age 16 or older who have been clinically diagnosed as temporarily or permanently disabled. This diagnosis must be supported by an official medical report from a Namibian state doctor. Coverage includes people with symptomatic, diagnosed AIDS. The applicant applies for and receives the money in the same way as the other grants (ELCRN 2007). The Disability Pension is equal to N$450 (US$57) monthly (Levine, van der Berg, and Yu 2009). In December 2008, approximately 20,400 beneficiaries received the grant.

Recipients of the Old Age and Disability Pensions are required to purchase a life insurance policy as an additional mandatory benefit. The policy covers funeral costs of up to N$2,200. The policy not only helps households after a member has died, but also reduces the likelihood that benefits will continue to be collected for deceased individuals (Levine, van der Berg, and Yu 2009).

Both the Old Age and Disability Pensions were housed in the Ministry of Health and Social Welfare until 2004, when they were moved to the Ministry of Labour and Social Services (Levine, van der Berg, and Yu 2009). Since 1990, coverage of the Old Age and Disability Pensions has increased by 184 percent, primarily owing to an increase in coverage of the Old Age Pension (Levine, van der Berg, and Yu 2009).[30]

Postindependence Policy Framework for Children's Grants
The Children's Act of 1960 was applied in preindependent Namibia, but children's grants were not actually put into place until 1977. Some areas of Namibia were not covered by the children's grants until independence in 1990 (Levine, van der Berg, and Yu 2009). These transfers were also highly discriminatory until 1997, when levels were equalized across races. The formal legal framework for Namibia's child grant system became fully established in 2000 (McGrath 2006). The system includes the Child Maintenance Grant, Special Maintenance Grant, Foster Care Grant, and Place of Safety Allowance (McGrath 2006). In all cases, households apply for children's grants in the same way that other pension and disability grants are applied for, and transfers are distributed through the same system.

The Ministry of Gender Equality and Child Welfare took over the administration of the children's grants from the Ministry of Health and Social Services in 2004 (Republic of Namibia 2007).

Child Maintenance Grant
The Child Maintenance Grant provides regular CTs to low-income households. Benefits are paid to eligible households with children under 18, though the age limit is extended to 21 if the child is a student. Beneficiary households must be headed by a single parent or a married woman whose husband is incapable of work, is incarcerated, has deserted the family, or receives a Disability or Old Age Pension (UNICEF n.d.b). As of 2000, households must earn less than N$1,000 (US$126.20) monthly to qualify for the grant, although this means test appears not to have been applied in many cases, and errors of both inclusion and exclusion have been found to be high (Levine, van der Berg, and Yu 2009). In practice, the grant tends to focus on supporting single and double orphans.

Beneficiaries of the Child Maintenance Grant must apply through pension offices, social workers, or local authorities (UNICEF n.d.b). Social workers provide assistance to households as they apply for the program, in addition to psychosocial support. The documents required for enrollment are the same as those listed for the Old Age Pension, in addition to the child's birth documentation, proof of the household's income, status of the husband, and child's latest school report (ELCRN 2007). At year-end 2008, approximately 86,100 beneficiaries received the Child Maintenance Grant (Levine, van der Berg, and Yu 2009).

Transfers are N$200 (US$25) monthly for the first child and N$100 (US$13) per additional child for up to six children (ELCRN 2007).[31] Although the transfer is considered unconditional, children over seven years old are required to attend school, which must be verified when they apply for the grant, and they must turn in their most recent school report. However, a social worker's report is accepted in lieu of the school documents. In reality, this requirement is used simply as a means to verify that the child is alive.

Other Grants That Support Children

The Foster Care Grant, which is provided to caretakers of foster children, was legally established by the Children's Act of 1960. Similar to the case in South Africa, the Children's Court has to have ordered that the child be placed in foster care, and a social worker has to have examined the case for a child to be eligible for the grant. The applicant's foster parent must submit a court order, the child's birth documentation, and proof of the child's school attendance or progression (or a social worker's report) in addition to the basic required documentation (ELCRN 2007; UNICEF n.d.b). In 2009, the monthly grant was N$200 (US$25) for the first child and N$100 (US$13) for each additional child (UNICEF n.d.b). The Foster Care Grant is paid from the application date until the social assistance clerk recommends that it be terminated (ELCRN 2007). Approximately 13,400 beneficiaries were receiving the Foster Care Grant at the end of 2008 (Levine, van der Berg, and Yu 2009).

The Place of Safety Allowance also provides N$10 daily for each child under 21 years taken in by a household or institution for the short term (Levine, van der Berg, and Yu 2009; Republic of Namibia 2007).

There is also a disability grant for children known as the Special Maintenance Grant. The grant is N$200 (US$25) monthly for children under age 16.[32] All procedures are the same as those of other grants (ELCRN 2007). When the child turns 16, this grant converts to the Disability Pension.

Cash grants have replaced emergency food aid. Coverage of the Child Maintenance and Foster Care Grants has increased 10 times over, from fewer than 10,000 children at the beginning of 2003 to approximately 99,500 at the end of 2008. This increase has occurred in response to the rapid growth in the OVC population, which is attributable to the HIV/AIDS epidemic. The vulnerability of OVC was increasingly recognized during the drought and food security crisis that hit southern Africa in 2002 and 2003 and overwhelmed the capacity of informal safety net systems. In the emergency response to that crisis, large numbers of OVC were identified and enrolled for emergency food aid through a joint WFP-FAO program that distributed food to 110,000 OVC in six northern regions with extremely high HIV seroprevalence levels. Those poor and relatively more isolated areas of the country previously had a relatively low level of child grant coverage.

The WFP's food aid was originally intended to last for only six months, but it was later extended until 2005. It soon became clear that the food aid was addressing chronic, rather than acute, food insecurity, and a longer-term transition to cash grants was required. The Ministry of Gender, Equality, and Child Welfare set out to transition children receiving WFP food aid to cash grant support, thereby significantly increasing coverage of the child grants in those regions (Levine, van der Berg, and Yu 2009). That transition was scheduled to last from January 2006 through December 2007. In 2006, it was estimated that 156,000 OVC would ultimately be targeted for the transition to cash grants (McGrath 2006). The national plan aimed to cover 80 percent of those OVC by 2008.

Targeting of the OVC was carried out with the help of local leaders. At locations where food was distributed, information was provided to potential cash recipients on how to apply for the grants (McGrath 2006). After the children successfully applied for a grant, they received food transfers for one additional transition month.

McGrath (2006) reports that almost 52,000 OVC were registered for a government cash grant by July 2006. However, the WFP reports that when food support ended in April 2008, only 25,000 OVC had transferred from the food aid to the government grant system (WFP 2009).

Delays in transfers to the grant system arose because of many children's lack of formal vital registration records and parentage information and the dearth of social workers needed to carry out eligibility checks. In these regions, which have high migration levels, many children have a non-Namibian parent, and children whose fathers are not Namibian may not be eligible for the grants. In addition, the Foster Care Grant can be given only when a court has approved the child's placement in a foster home. Human resource capacity is low in the court system, creating a major bottleneck (McGrath 2006).

In general, implementation of the Namibian grants for children has been weaker than descriptions in the policy framework would suggest (Nekundi 2007). In many cases, registration takes up to three months to complete. Nevertheless, the government has worked to strengthen its capacity to administer the grants. Expansion of the grant was minimal until 2003, but coverage has increased substantially since then because of an awareness campaign that informed the public about grant eligibility (Republic of Namibia 2007). Community child care workers have also been recruited to facilitate the application process and provide other support.

Major barriers still exist, especially for individuals living in isolated areas. Those individuals may still not be aware of their eligibility, or they may have trouble obtaining the correct documentation to apply for grants. The Ministry of Gender Equality and Child Welfare made a goal of reaching 50 percent of registered OVC with some form of support, including grants, by 2010 (Republic of Namibia 2007). Grant criteria are being revised to ensure that all OVC have access to this support.

Overall costs and effectiveness have been examined. Excluding administration costs, Namibia's social pension system was estimated to cost approximately 1.36 percent of GDP in 2009/10, and the uptake rate for the pension is 81.7 percent. The total transfer system costs approximately 2 percent of Namibia's GDP and 6 percent of the country's budget (Levine, van der Berg, and Yu 2009).[33] Under two different scenarios, the costs are not expected to ever rise much higher than 3 percent of GDP. If GDP growth similar to that in Namibia's recent history can be assumed, the costs will be under 2 percent of GDP by 2030. These calculations allow for program expansion and increased grant values.

The system's administrative costs have been difficult to estimate, although the cost to deliver N$300 via mobile banking units is known to be approximately 3.25 percent of the transfer costs (Levine, van der Berg, and Yu 2009).

Levine, van der Berg, and Yu (2009) used simulations and household survey data to determine what effect the transfers may have on poverty and inequality in Namibia. They conclude that the transfers have decreased the number of poor people by a significant amount, with an even stronger decrease in the number of very poor individuals. Probit regressions led Levine, van der Berg, and Yu to conclude that the Old Age Pension had the greatest overall effect on decreasing poverty. According to their analysis, both the Old Age Pension and Child Maintenance Grant are associated with smaller poverty gaps and squared poverty gaps. Targeting used by the Old Age Pension appears to be better (that is, more pro-poor) than that used by the Child Maintenance Grant.

Niger

Cash Transfers in Response to the Food Crisis

Save the Children UK began a CT program in Tessaoua district of Niger's Maradi region in 2008. The subregional committee for prevention and management of food crisis helped to design and implement the CT. Funded by the European Commission Humanitarian Aid Office, the project sought to combat rising malnutrition levels caused by increasing food prices. The government had declared the targeted areas to be severely food insecure. Targeting covered 1,500 extremely poor households, households with widows, and households with members with disabilities, representing approximately one-third of the population in targeted areas (Save the Children UK 2009). Households with children under five were also favored in the targeting.

Targeting was completed using the household economy analysis approach, which analyzes various aspects of the livelihoods of households within a community to determine who should be targeted for social programs. Controversy surrounded the targeting, and in some villages, beneficiaries were taxed by local leaders. In other cases, benefits were pooled by the community and redistributed, although official beneficiaries received larger amounts than other community members (Save the Children UK 2009).

Three transfers of CFAF 20,000 (US$40) were given to a female household representative. The only condition tied to the transfers was that households must attend educational seminars teaching them about nutrition and health issues. The households were also supposed to form community committees that monitored health and participated in activities each week to improve community sanitation (Save the Children UK 2009). Save the Children conducted the project evaluation using household economy analysis techniques. It determined that the project had a positive effect on households. No control or comparison group was used in the analysis. Save the Children UK suggested that the transfers be complemented with micronutrient supplementation and techniques to control diseases to maximize the effect on children's nutrition levels (Save the Children UK 2009).

Nigeria

Nigeria has two known CCT programs—In Care of the Poor (COPE) and the Kano CCT for Girls' Education—which were started only recently as pilots to guide possible future expansion of the CT concept in this large-population country. The evolution of the Nigerian programs will be of interest to policy makers. The large size of the Nigerian population and the potential reach of the country's CCTs will interest many onlookers, who are eager to see how a CCT functions in this diverse country.

COPE

COPE began in 2007 with pilot activities slated for 12 states with some of the lowest human capital investments in the country (World Bank 2009c). COPE addresses poverty by combining a temporary CT redistributive element with conditions to strengthen human capital in beneficiaries. COPE also links beneficiaries to other programs that provide skills, vocational training, and microcredit to enable them to achieve a higher level of self-sufficiency when the monthly CTs cease. Additional support is included in a lump-sum payment that is intended to be used for major household investments. Although the number of COPE beneficiaries is small at only 1,000 households per state, the program has been conceived as a way to test how a national CCT program might be designed and ultimately scaled up within a federal system that encompasses great diversity across different states.

COPE targets short-term poverty and longer-term human capital investment. COPE began implementation in early 2008 in 12 states, although progress has been slow. The timelines for COPE rollout differ by state; some programs are still being designed, while others have begun small pilots.

The transfers include two components. The Basic Income Guarantee provides a monthly transfer of ₦1,500 (US$13) for a household with one child, ₦3,000 (US$26) for a household with two or three children, and ₦5,000 (US$43) for a household with four or more children. The Poverty Reduction Accelerator Investment is a compulsory savings component of ₦7,000 monthly (US$60) that is transferred as an annual payment of ₦84,000 (US$717). It is supposed to be given only after households receive training to create a microenterprise. Transfers are distributed by microfinance organizations or local banks to an adult female household member. They are supposed to be given to households monthly for one year, although their actual distribution has often been delayed (World Bank 2009c).

COPE CTs have conditions related to education, health, and skill acquisition for productive activities. Mothers must attend prenatal checkups, children must enroll in and attend primary and junior secondary education at least 80 percent of the time, and households must have a member participating in life skills and vocational training. Households must turn in forms signed by the relevant institutions to local program offices to prove that they fulfilled conditions (World Bank n.d.).

Targeting uses a combination of community and proxy means methods. Targeted households include those in extreme poverty, those with children under 15, those with a member with physical disabilities, those containing orphans or street children, those with pregnant women, seasonally poor households, and those affected by HIV/AIDS. The exact targeted groups vary by state (World Bank 2009c).

Federal, state, and local differences require ongoing attention to prepare for COPE scale-up. The Ministry of Poverty Eradication and Value Reorientation and the National Poverty Eradication Program are in charge of COPE (World Bank 2009c). The National Poverty Eradication Program, and therefore COPE, is also linked to microfinance programs, which program officials hope will increase productive activities among poor beneficiaries. The National Poverty Eradication Program's national and state offices work with state CCT offices and local government social assistance committees to implement COPE (World Bank n.d.).

Nigeria's federal structure allows programs to differ significantly by state, and the potential use of national-level requirements is limited by state-level variations in levels of supply-side support (World Bank n.d.). The CCTs are being built on successful community-driven development projects already undertaken in Nigeria (World Bank n.d.). The foundation of those projects is expected to improve program implementation. Funding for COPE has come from the MDG Debt Relief Fund and lower-level counterpart funds. The World Bank has provided some technical assistance to the program. The World Bank, DFID, UNICEF, and the UNDP International Policy Centre for Inclusive Growth are expected to provide funding and technical support to COPE. Donor funding is expected to support program implementation and expansion to cover approximately 1 in 10 eligible vulnerable households within a given state (World Bank 2009c). Domestic funding is expected to run through the government's successful conditional grants scheme, which has encouraged investment in supply-side infrastructure required to support human capital investments.

Targeting and design improvements are needed for scaling up. Weaknesses emerging in the state-level pilots have led to recognition that designs need to be revised before any scale-up is feasible. Some states have approached the World Bank to receive technical assistance related to program design. The designs in those states will reflect technical input from the World Bank. Specific problems encountered by COPE include the scarcity of data for targeting purposes and obstacles to monitoring conditions when the supply side is under the jurisdiction of other institutions. Other challenges have arisen in payment distribution and monitoring and evaluation. Unclear delineation of the respective roles and responsibilities of state and federal stakeholders also remains an issue, which is now being reviewed through an examination of how Brazil's Bolsa Família functions within its federal structure. Development partners are expected to support efforts to improve systems at both the federal and the state levels (World Bank 2009c).

Kano CCT for Girls' Education

Nigeria's other CCT program, the Kano CCT for Girls' Education, is limited to the state of Kano in northwest Nigeria. The program's three-year pilot phase, which began in early 2010, uses a robust evaluation component to test various design features. The components are intended to encourage households to keep girls in school; they include conditional cash grants to households and communication initiatives to address cultural norms that discourage female education. Funds for Kano will come from the federal MDG fund and potential local counterpart funds, and the CCT will function under the State Education Sector Project in Kano. In addition to supporting 12,000 beneficiaries in 10,000 households with a three-year budget of US$9 million, the program is expected to provide guidance to Kano and neighboring states regarding how to move more effectively toward achieving MDGs related to universal primary education and gender equality.

MDG challenges lead to Kano CCT for Girls' Education. Planning for Kano state's CCT began after the state's education ministry requested assistance from development partners to confront low female school enrollment (Ayala 2009). In the northwest region of Nigeria, 50 percent of males and 72 percent of females have no education. At the secondary level in Kano state, slightly over two-thirds of eligible boys attend secondary school, whereas just under one-third of girls attend secondary school.

The pilot CCT aims to improve girls' primary and secondary school enrollment and to reduce gender inequities and poverty in the program area, thereby improving progression toward the MDGs of universal primary education and gender equality (Ayala 2009). More specifically, the pilot hopes to increase enrollment and attendance rates and reduce girls' dropout rates from upper primary and junior secondary school by 10 to 15 percent over baseline numbers. Depending on the local availability of junior secondary schools, the program will focus either on primary school completion or on the transition of girls to junior secondary school.

To ensure that program schools are capable of keeping pace with the increased demand resulting from the CCT, other programs that support improved school quality are expected to work with the CCT and complement its efforts (World Bank 2008). Schools that are not receiving supply-side support under the national and state education plans are not eligible to belong to the CCT (Ayala 2009), and capacity assessments will be conducted to reveal supply-side limitations (Bouchet 2009).

Pilot will test the impact of conditions, transfer levels, and payment mechanisms. The Kano CCT pilot phase is expected to run for three years beginning in late 2009. The program will be implemented in rural parts of 12 local government areas in Kano state. The CCT is expected to rely on schools and communities to implement targeting and other components. Targeting will use both community and proxy means tests for verification. Eligible girls must be enrolled in grades 4 through 7 (or have already completed school through grade 6), belong to a household with a daily income lower than US$1 per capita, have lived within the program area for one year or longer, and receive no other CCT benefits. Girls who have dropped out of school are eligible to return and enroll in the CCT if they are not more than four years older than the expected age for someone in the grade at which they will begin (Ayala 2009). Girls living in female-headed households, girls with disabilities, orphans, households without an adult male able to participate in the labor force, and households with multiple beneficiaries are prioritized in targeting.

School-based management committees will identify potential beneficiaries and collect information to be used in a proxy means test. This information will allow the project management unit to generate a list of eligible households, which must be verified at a community council meeting (Bouchet 2009). The project management unit also ranks households for program eligibility on the basis of their estimated poverty levels (Ayala 2009). An enrollment meeting occurs at schools, where households receive information about the program and sign agreements to participate.

Two levels of benefits will be tested in the pilot: one of US$140 per year for each girl, and another of US$70 per year for each girl (Ayala 2009). The larger transfer of US$140 (₦20,000) is approximately 20 percent of GDP per capita in 2007.[34] No limit is imposed on the number of children within a household who are eligible for transfers.

Conditions tested are divided into hard and soft conditions. Noncompliance with the hard condition of 80 percent school attendance results in loss of benefits, with school attendance monitored quarterly. Soft conditions, which will be monitored, are whether girls pass their classes and obtain birth certificates, whether siblings under five attend medical checkups and receive immunizations, whether mothers attend pre- and postnatal classes, and whether mothers and their partners attend seminars intended to raise awareness on important issues. Girls not fulfilling the school registration requirement (for the first payment) and the attendance requirements (for the second through fourth payments in the year) will forfeit any transfer for that period (Bouchet 2009).

Given the pilot's limited duration, households leave the project if they voluntarily withdraw, provide false information, no longer have an eligible girl attending grades 4 through 9, or do not collect benefits for three pay periods in a row. Individual girls must exit the program if they do not fulfill conditions three periods in a row or if they turn 18, move out of the program area, or participate in the program for three years (Bouchet 2009).

The program will also test the use of mobile phone technology to support processes such as targeting, payments, monitoring and evaluation, data collection, and communication. Several payment mechanisms will be tested, including distribution through banks, through a payment agency with mobile phones, and through school-based management committees. These committees will also be important for targeting, registration, monitoring of conditions, training of other locally involved individuals, and case management (Ayala 2009). Payments through banks and school committees will be made to a household head or alternate member on a designated payment day, whereas payments through the information technology company will be made to a household member's mobile phone (Bouchet 2009).

Plans for the Kano CCT also include a strong communication strategy to combat cultural norms opposed to girls' education (World Bank 2008). Details of the communication design and approach were not yet available at the time of writing.

Monitoring systems will differ depending on whether payments are centralized or decentralized, although teachers will fill out forms to monitor school attendance in all cases (Bouchet 2009). Centralized payments will be made through the MIS and reconciled frequently. The decentralized payment system relies on MIS data at the beginning of the school year, but transfers through the remainder of the year are made on the basis of the school committees' monitoring activities without relying on the centralized MIS. If households miss collecting prior payments, they may retrieve them at a later payment date if they are working with the centralized system, but this policy is not available to those under the decentralized system.

Decentralized data will be entered into the MIS at the end of the school year (Bouchet 2009). Local government education authorities will oversee the activities of the school-based management committees, and the committees are expected to provide information on their financial management each quarter.

Experimental evaluation design promises lessons for wider application.
The Kano CCT pilot program uses an experimental evaluation to examine program impacts. Kano's CCT is expected to serve as an example to other Nigerian states interested in implementing CTs and to inform their designs. The pilot is also designed to allow the program to scale up without problems if the evaluation shows that it has been successful (Bouchet 2009).

Rwanda

Vision 2020 Umurenge Programme

In an effort to speed up poverty reduction, spark growth in rural areas, and strengthen social protection, the Rwandan cabinet officially approved and began implementing VUP in 2007 (Republic of Rwanda 2009). Rwanda's Vision 2020 Umurenge Programme (VUP) combines a public works program, a direct support CT, and a financial services (microcredit) component into a major national initiative aimed at decreasing extreme poverty. The program enjoys strong support from the Rwandan government, which has encouraged donors to harmonize their aid and coordinate their actions with the government's goals (European University Institute 2010).

Rwanda adopts a comprehensive, policy-driven approach to poverty. In 2007, Rwandan leadership noted that the pace of poverty reduction was too slow to reach the government's goal of eliminating extreme poverty. It had also concluded that social protection programs were fragmented, often worked outside of the national budget, and did not achieve their full potential (World Bank 2009d).

VUP is a leading program in the government's National Economic Development and Poverty Reduction Strategy for 2008 through 2012. The program's objectives are to decrease extreme poverty from almost 37 percent in 2005 and 2006 to 24 percent in 2012, and to more effectively fight poverty by helping people achieve greater productivity, by increasing capacity for sustainable production, and by improving targeting of social protection to vulnerable groups. Specific objectives include increasing opportunities for nonfarm labor force participation, developing more formal financial markets and labor markets in rural areas, and improving targeting of assistance to those without land and those unable to participate in the labor force (Republic of Rwanda 2009).

The goal of VUP's direct support component is to improve living standards among targeted households through the provision of regular CTs (Republic of Rwanda 2009). VUP also hopes to increase households' productive capacity when possible. More specifically, protective aims of the CTs are to increase incomes, to help households maintain minimal standards of living, and to help households maintain productive assets and increase their ability to confront adverse shocks. The transfers' productive aims are to encourage households to take appropriate risks, to help capable individuals create improved livelihoods, to encourage the poor to participate in formal markets and entrepreneurial activities, and to increase social solidarity by helping marginalized groups integrate into the economy.

Approximately 24,400 households were enrolled in VUP by early 2009, almost 7,000 (28 percent) of which receive the direct support UCTs (DFID 2009). Total program costs are projected to be US$16.7 million in 2012, with the scaled-up program reaching about 42,000 households (11,500 on direct support, at 20 percent of total program costs).

Decentralized engagement involves communities in targeting cash transfers. Villages use the *Ubudehe* method, which uses community decision making to target poor households, to qualitatively identify and classify households in one of six poverty groups. This method is already being used in many locations in Rwanda for various purposes, and it has helped the program to function more efficiently (European University Institute 2010). To be eligible for direct support CTs, households must be extremely poor, own less than 0.25 hectares of land, and have no household member 18 or older able to participate in the labor force (Republic of Rwanda 2009). Community Ubudehe committees create lists of potential beneficiaries, which communities jointly verify. The Ubudehe committees must consider any appeals made by local households concerning their status on the list. Final lists of beneficiaries are posted in VUP offices.

There is an expectation that some beneficiaries will graduate to productive activities or into the public works component. For that reason, targeting is to be reviewed at the local level every six months, at which point new lists of beneficiary households are submitted. However, some beneficiaries will remain long-term recipients of the transfers because of their inability to graduate (Republic of Rwanda 2009).

The household head receives a cash transfer of RF 250 (US$0.45) per day.[35] A transfer of RF 150 (US$0.27) daily is given for a second household member, and RF 100 (US$0.18) is given for up to three additional household members (Republic of Rwanda 2009). In cases where households are already receiving similar transfers, their grant value will be reduced by the amount of the offsetting transfer. Households will be encouraged to participate in savings schemes and to graduate from direct support whenever possible. Training will help them integrate more effectively into formal markets and financial systems.

CTs are distributed monthly, with lists posted in public places in communities to let households know what they will receive (Republic of Rwanda 2009). Payments will be made to bank accounts for recipients when possible. Beneficiaries will be encouraged to save part of their transfers in the accounts. To receive their payments, beneficiaries must attend a payment distribution meeting each month to sign or fingerprint a form verifying that they have received funds either in cash or in their bank account.

VUP organization seeks efficiency by building on existing decentralized structures. VUP builds on achievements of the country's existing Decentralization and Community Development Project to achieve efficiencies and transparency in implementation (World Bank 2009d).

Districts are responsible for financial administration of VUP, including contracting with partners and making payments (Republic of Rwanda 2009). The sector and lower-level units carry out targeting and daily implementation and administration of VUP. Villages monitor distribution of payments and ensure that community members receive the correct mix of benefits. Problems are resolved at the lowest levels possible, and comprehensive planning and involvement are expected at the village, cell, and sector levels within each district.

VUP is under the jurisdiction of the Ministry of Local Government, Good Governance, Community Development, and Social Affairs, along with a steering committee composed of several major ministries, including the Ministry of Finance and Economic Planning (Republic of Rwanda 2009). Coordination at all levels will ensure that households' needs are met and programs are efficiently coordinated to help households move out of poverty.

VUP was being expanded to the most disadvantaged *Umurenge* (sector) in each district in 2008 and 2009 (Republic of Rwanda 2009). The Umurenge was selected on the basis of its access to water, food security, and distance from the closest school and health center, among other criteria (Musoni n.d.). National scale-up is supposed to begin in July 2009 and be completed within three years (DFID 2009). The public works component began in July 2008, and direct support began in February 2009.

Because it uses existing decentralized structures, VUP's administrative costs are expected to be kept to approximately 8 percent of program costs (DFID 2009). As of February 2009, total costs for VUP were expected to be US$15.5 million for 2009/10, US$14.8 million for 2010/11, and US$16.7 million for 2011/12 and 2012/13. The scaled-up program is expected to reach approximately 42,000 households by 2012. The direct support component is currently budgeted at 20 percent of total VUP expenses, although coverage of direct support will vary depending on conditions in communities. The government plans to support all households eligible for direct support rather than limiting these numbers (Republic of Rwanda 2009).

DFID will provide £20 million (US$31.3 million)[36] to fund the program, and it will supply technical assistance to VUP in the five years running from 2009 to 2013. Its technical support will cover monitoring and evaluation, financial and program management, and program development. The World Bank is also supporting VUP through the First Community Living Standards Project with funds of US$6 million. The government of Norway plans to provide US$4 million more to support capacity building and program improvement (World Bank 2009d).

A review of VUP[37] conducted at the end of 2009 found that much of the transferred cash helped beneficiaries fill basic consumption needs (Devereux and Ndejuru 2009, as cited in European University Institute 2010). Other reviews have found that 55 percent of beneficiaries put some of their transfers in savings, 53 percent purchased food, almost 25 percent bought livestock, 18 percent bought farm inputs, and 13 percent invested in education. The percentage of beneficiary households that were previously classified as most vulnerable (41 percent) dropped to 9 percent. The official program evaluation, released in late 2010, found that extreme poverty had decreased from 39.0 percent in 2006 to 34.5 percent in 2009, although this reduction was basically found in male-headed households. Poverty in female-headed households decreased by only 0.4 percent (Hartwig 2010, as cited in European University Institute 2010).

São Tomé and Príncipe

Success of the Brazilian Bolsa Família program generated interest in CTs in other lusophone countries. São Tomé and Príncipe implemented its own version of this CCT from 2002 through 2005. The program reached 2,000 individuals in approximately 400 households but was subsequently closed because of a lack of funds.

Senegal

Senegal has two major CTs in operation. One, the CCT for OVC, is a conditional cash transfer program for orphans and vulnerable children that seeks to address vulnerabilities and developmental needs related to all stages of the childhood life cycle. It targets its interventions to orphaned children and those affected by HIV and AIDS. The other program, the Child-Focused Social Cash Transfer (CF-SCT) and Nutrition Security Project, aims to increase human capital development in children under age five by improving nutrition and fighting vulnerability to risk. Both programs are well rooted in national policy, growing out of the country's national social protection strategy for 2005 through 2015, which emphasizes, among other things, the need to increase social protection and protect individuals and groups at risk of systemic shocks. The 2006 Poverty Reduction Strategy Paper II also calls for better social protection for the poor and vulnerable, and for increased connection of vulnerable groups to social services, risk-protection services, and income-generating activities (Basic Training Course 2009).

Senegal also has a means-tested noncontributory old age pension (Croome, Nyanguru, and Molisana 2007). However, the pension is given only to individuals born before 1922 who have been employed for at least five years as domestic workers and do not receive benefits from a contributory pension (U.S. Social Security Administration 2009). In practice, this pension reaches only a very small and rapidly declining number of beneficiaries.

CCT for OVC

Senegal's CCT for OVC encourages community engagement. USAID–Family Health International, the World Bank (through the Multi-country HIV/AIDS Program), UNICEF, and the National Committee against AIDS undertook a study to understand the plight of OVC in Senegal. The executive secretary of the National Committee against AIDS began the CCT for OVC in 2008 in response to report recommendations that community groups be provided support to improve education and vocational training for OVC (Document de Cadrage Technique 2009).

Senegal's CCT for OVC started at the beginning of the 2008/09 school year (Document de Cadrage Technique 2009). Its general objective is to support education and vocational training of 5,000 OVC. The specific program objectives are to ensure access to education and vocational training; to support OVC's financial needs (for transportation, uniforms, and so forth); and to support OVC's psychosocial, family, educational, and professional sustenance (CNLS and World Bank n.d.). The first phase of the CCT for OVC runs through the 2008/09 school year, at which time lessons were to be assimilated (Document de Cadrage Technique 2009).

Before the project makes any payments, a responsible adult must sign a commitment form stating that he or she will provide proof that the beneficiary has fulfilled the CCT conditions. The adult in charge of the child will receive a savings booklet to take to a local postal bank to withdraw cash during an allotted time frame. The post location closest to where the beneficiary lives will provide the funds to the designated beneficiary through a secure payment method. The postal bank will receive the funds from the National Committee against AIDS and regional support committees, and it must inform the national group of funds dispersed (CNLS and World Bank n.d.).

The adult in charge of the child must provide proof that the child has been enrolled in school or training, has paid school or vocational fees, has attended school or vocational training regularly, and has received adequate medical care (CNLS and World Bank n.d.). The schools also must provide proof of the student's enrollment and payment of fees (Document de Cadrage Technique 2009). NGOs may also be contracted to support monitoring activities. Any continual failures to fulfill conditions could lead to expulsion from the program (Document de Cadrage Technique 2009). OVC will continue to receive transfers for the following year if they have fulfilled the program's conditions.

The CCT for OVC relies on the decentralized Ministry of Education and other groups that support OVC (for example, community associations and NGOs working for OVC), as well as on decentralized units of the National Committee against AIDS and the Multisectoral Thematic Group. Other support is provided by the Ministry of the Family, Ministry of Female Entrepreneurship and Microfinance, and Ministry of Health (Document de Cadrage Technique 2009). Operations are decentralized to the lower levels of the educational system and to the community level for social services. Regional pilot committees will provide additional support.

The CCT for OVC targets multiple stages of OVC's life cycle. Senegal's program targets children ages 2 through 18 affected by HIV/AIDS, children living in households affected by HIV/AIDS, and other poor orphans who need schooling or vocational training or who are at risk of dropping out of school (Document de Cadrage Technique 2009). Children across all regions of the country will be covered. Targeting makes use of NGOs and other groups that normally are in contact with OVC, such as district-level social service delivery organizations and associations for people living with HIV/AIDS.

Once a potential beneficiary is identified, a home visit is conducted to evaluate the child's eligibility and schooling-related risks. Visits to classrooms may also identify children vulnerable to school dropout. Children sometimes are not identified or do not enroll immediately because of stigma associated with HIV/AIDS; therefore, continuous registration will be practiced so that OVC who are not immediately located can be registered in the future (Document de Cadrage Technique 2009).

Transfers, paid quarterly, are given to a parent, guardian, or institution in charge of the child. In practice, the most effective adult for this role has proved to be the mother figure in the household. Six transfer levels were created. They vary depending on the costs of the different levels of schooling and training. Total annual transfers are CFAF 108,000 (US$225) for children in kindergarten,[38] CFAF 125,000 (US$260) for those in first-level primary school, CFAF 135,000 (US$281) for those in second-level primary school, CFAF 145,000 (US$302) for children in the first level of secondary school, and CFAF 165,000 (US$343) for those in the second level of secondary school. For beneficiaries in professional training courses, CFAF 280,000 (US$582) is provided for a two-year course (Document de Cadrage Technique 2009). The transfer amount per household depends on the number of eligible children in the household (CNLS and World Bank n.d.).

Early lessons learned are that coordination among decentralized authorities is essential, psychosocial support increases the program's effect, and the productivity of cash is increased by providing regular transfers. The program officials also recognized that sensitization and communication measures should be undertaken to increase support for the program (CNLS and World Bank n.d.). A formal evaluation of the CCT was planned for the end of 2009.

Child-Focused Social Cash Transfer and Nutrition Security Project

CF-SCT and Nutrition Security Project tests emergency response to protect at-risk children under the age of five. Senegal's CF-SCT, supported by World Bank funds, was created as a temporary response to sharp increases in food staple prices caused by decreased domestic supply and rising world prices. Even though prices have dropped from their highest levels, they are still structurally higher than they were previously, and a CT is seen as an appropriate instrument to address those changes.

The CF-SCT's goal is to decrease food and nutritional insecurity in children under age five living in poor areas by providing transfers to their mothers. The focus on children under five arose because of the longer-term negative impact that even a temporary period of malnutrition can have on the development of children in this age group. In addition to improvements in health and nutrition, the project also seeks to increase birth registration (World Bank 2009b).

The transfer amount was set at CFAF 7,000 (US$14) monthly, or approximately 14 percent of the value of the average food basket for households with four adults. The transfer does not change on the basis of household size, although the amount may be adjusted by the program as needed (World Bank 2009b). The transfers are given to mothers every two months for six months, although this period may be extended to last for one year. Transfers are supposed to be given to new communities after the first six months. This design feature was created to increase food consumption but not dependency.

Transfers will originally be distributed through local paypoints, where adults may arrive to retrieve the cash within a given time frame. If the transfer is not retrieved within a 15-day window, the payment is forfeited. The woman is identified at the paypoint using her identification card or fingerprint (World Bank 2009b).

Support for the CF-SCT is expected to come from the National Executive Bureau, which has three regional bureaus. Community executing agencies and local governments will also be important at the local level. NGOs are supposed to be contracted through local governments, which have to support nutrition in their (typically) infrastructure-focused local development plans. Clearly outlined tasks are defined for local groups. The Coordination Unit for the Fight against Malnutrition in the Nutrition Enhancement Program will decide on local transfer providers depending on the location. The community executing agency determines cash needed, and the district monitoring committee verifies the amount. The community executing agency makes a request for the funding to the coordination unit, which transfers the money and a list of beneficiaries to the requisite payment provider (World Bank 2009b).

The CF-SCT is an example of a cash transfer that is being used to complement other programs with similar goals. The pilot is housed within the Coordination Unit for the Fight against Malnutrition in the Nutrition Enhancement Program (Basic Training Course 2009).[39] The CF-SCT will draw on the success of the Nutrition Enhancement Program by using the monitoring and evaluation system already developed for that project (World Bank 2009b). In addition, targeting will identify potential beneficiaries using the project's existing structure.

CF-SCT *examines boundaries between acute and chronic food insecurity.* The pilot CF-SCT was scheduled to start in June 2009 in 10 districts with high malnutrition, as identified by the Ministry of Health (World Bank 2009b). To capitalize on potential program synergies, the first community groups phased in have been exposed to the Nutrition Enhancement Program for six months or more. For comparison purposes, later recipients will belong to both project and nonproject locations.

Initial targeting will decide on the number of beneficiaries allowed per district. The selection involves the Coordination Unit for the Fight against

Malnutrition, a monitoring committee, a local selection committee, and a community executing agency (World Bank 2009b). The local selection committees include village chiefs and health and religious leaders, who select households with children up to age five who do not have adequate household food stocks or who consume too few meals per day. The households should also have limited assets. The community executing agency may be an NGO, civil society organization, or other group that implements the community-level nutrition program and verifies the local list of beneficiaries. Community targeting criteria may vary by location (World Bank 2009b).

It is assumed that if the targeting correctly identifies vulnerable households, the transfer will be used appropriately. Proper targeting, combined with a strong communication strategy, support for health and nutrition activities, and extensive beneficiary involvement, is expected to negate the need for conditions. An unconditional transfer is also justified, given that the transfer is created to deal with an acute crisis (World Bank 2009b).

The program's communication strategy is a priority, in terms of both communicating procedures and processes and sensitizing beneficiaries about the program's anticipated benefits (World Bank 2009b). The communication strategy includes orientation meetings at multiple levels. A major component of the strategy will highlight nutrition for mothers and children.

The CF-SCT will be funded using US$1.4 million from IDA and US$4.9 million from the Multi-Donor Trust Fund supporting the Global Food Price Crisis Response Program. The CT component is expected to receive US$1.0 million in 2009, US$3.7 million in 2010, and US$1.6 million in 2011 (World Bank 2009b).

The CF-SCT purposefully starts with a somewhat simple design that can be adapted as needed, and it recognizes the tendency to encounter problems when designs are too complicated (World Bank 2009b). The pilot will examine program design issues, including the use of different payment mechanisms, designation of alternate beneficiary recipients, transfer sizes and durations, supplemental payments to beneficiaries to cover incurred transportation costs, and methods to improve targeting. It will also analyze the usefulness of stricter beneficiary identification criteria for payments through a single registry or biometric identification system. The possibility of imposing soft conditions will also be considered (World Bank 2009b). Payment mechanisms that will be tested include central payments in villages and payments through smart cards or cell phones. The pilot will also be used to examine whether a national strategy is best or whether payment processes should vary by location.

An evaluation is planned that will make use of the gradual program rollout. The evaluation will focus on inclusion errors (which should be kept at 20 percent or lower), the percentage of planned transfers made to pay providers (goals are 70 percent in the first year and 80 percent subsequently), and placement of the CF-SCT within the national social protection strategy (World Bank 2009b).

The Seychelles

In the Seychelles, an Old Age Pension, which is universal, is given to individuals age 63 and older. The country also has a grant for orphans amounting to US$115.60 monthly (Miller 2006). A larger CT is reportedly under consideration to replace other programs.

Somalia

CTs have been used as a common response in emergency situations in Somalia. With vulnerabilities high in the country, some groups have sought to address emergency needs using fairly small-scale, short-term CTs. No large-scale, long-term CTs are known of in Somalia.

Sierra Leone

Unconditional Cash Transfer for the Old and Needy
Sierra Leone has had a UCT in place for elderly and poor people since 2007. The Unconditional Cash Transfer for the Old and Needy began after chiefs requested support for vulnerable populations in their communities. The CT mechanism was deemed the quickest, easiest way to reach the targeted populations (International Poverty Centre n.d.).

Community transparency sought for benefit targeting and distribution. Benefits of the UCT for the Old and Needy are targeted to individuals at the chief or section levels. Transfers have been given in the entire northern region at different times, and in selected communities of the southern and eastern regions. The UCT for the Old and Needy provides a one-time transfer of Le 200,000 (US$68), which is intended to last a beneficiary for six months. Beneficiaries have caretakers who are given the transfers and who assist them in spending the cash appropriately over the six-month time frame. Benefits are supposed to be spent on food. Beneficiaries are typically elderly and lack a stable income source. They should be incapable of work and lack the support of a family or community (International Poverty Centre n.d.). The program appears to have favored women for transfers, who have been thought to use transfers responsibly, including for the care of their grandchildren.

Transfers are distributed publicly at a community meeting. The entire community is involved to ensure that the beneficiary receives the money safely. Identity is verified through a photo card. If a beneficiary dies, a family member will still receive a final transfer to cover the costs of the funeral (International Poverty Centre n.d.). Anecdotally, the program increased community cohesiveness and the sense of responsibility for the elderly and vulnerable populations. Such cohesiveness is particularly important in Sierra Leone, given the previous violence in the country.

Communities organize social safety net chiefdom committees, which are composed of representatives from civil society and the Ministries of Health and of Employment, a designated leader of youth, a leader of women, and a religious leader. The committees select beneficiaries. Program officials must verify the committee's selection, through either a visual inspection or a short survey of about 15 questions. At the central level, the National Social Safety Net Program in the Ministry of Employment and Social Security administers the program.

In 2007, the program had 38,000 applicants, but only 16,890 people were registered after the verification process. The program was reportedly popular, and people were demanding that it expand to cover new regions and age ranges (International Poverty Centre n.d.). It was expected to reach 35,000 beneficiaries in 2009.

The program's original funding came through food aid from China and Italy. The government sold the food and used the funds to create the social safety net. During initial distributions they also gave beneficiaries a bag of rice to ensure that the aid increased beneficiaries' food consumption as intended by the food aid. The government has continued to fund the program at its current scale, but the Ministry of Finance has expressed concerns that it will increase dependency. If the UCT for the Old and Needy were to be scaled up, the cost would be about US$23 million each year to reach the 170,000 potential program beneficiaries. In light of Sierra Leone's current economy and budget, a larger program would have to be financed at least in part by donors.

South Africa

The long-running South African CT system is well developed and far reaching, covering the largest number of beneficiaries of any program in Sub-Saharan Africa. South Africa has legal protections for the programs it has implemented, including the Aged Persons Act of 1967, the Child Care Act of 1983, and the Social Assistance Act of 2004. These acts cover the Old Age Pension, the Disability Grant, the Child Support Grant, the Foster Care Grant, and the Care Dependency Grant (Plaatjies 2006), which make up the five main noncontributory transfers in the South African system. Additional grants in the country are the War Veterans Grant, the Grant for Carers of the Aged, and Social Relief of Distress Grant (U.S. Social Security Administration 2009).[40] The grant system was characterized by racial discrimination until the end of apartheid, but policy changes, combined with recent expansion of coverage, have moved the country toward a more equitable system. Recent scaling up of the grants system was purposefully undertaken, in part to address these historical injustices and coverage inequalities (European University Institute 2010).

Policy Framework and Implementation System of the South African Cash Grants

The current structure of South Africa's social welfare and grant system was outlined in the country's White Paper on Social Welfare, made available in 1997 by the Department of Welfare. In 2004, the Social Assistance Act was passed, which put the national government in charge of social protection. The Department of Welfare was converted into the Department of Social Development, which outlines the policies to be used in grants and is in charge of the South African Social Security Agency (SASSA). The previous South African system operated at the provincial level, whereas the new arrangement operates on a national level (Pauw and Mncube 2007). SASSA, which was created in 2005 but began operations in 2006, is in charge of implementing the grants.

Individuals who think they are eligible for a grant must apply and present identifying materials to a SASSA office. If the application is rejected, an appeal may be presented through a formal system (South African Government Services 2009). Despite the large number of grant recipients, undercoverage remains a concern for grants directed to children (Lund 2007).

Transfers are delivered through multiple methods, such as through paypoints at a specified time and location, via direct deposit to a bank account, through a postal bank account (South African Government Services 2009), or through the private company Net1. Net1 is in charge of transfer distribution in five of the nine South African provinces. Using the Net1 method, beneficiaries receive their transfers from mobile ATMs that function both online and offline. They use smart cards and fingerprints to prove their identity. The smart card system can be used to receive transfers, make payments, and transfer funds, among other things (del Ninno 2009). Several regions also distribute vouchers (SASSA 2009).

Cash Grant Program Coverage and Cost

The total number of cash grant beneficiaries has increased from approximately 3.0 million beneficiaries in 1997 to 13.2 million in April 2009 (SASSA 2009). Grant coverage has increased as benefits have been expanded to cover additional groups, transfer values have increased, and awareness of the grants has grown. The effects of the HIV/AIDS crisis probably are also increasing grant uptake.

The cost of the cash grant system has also increased over time. In 2001/02, all transfers equaled 2 percent of South Africa's GDP (Pauw and Mncube 2007); in 2007/08, they cost 3.2 percent of GDP (Streak 2007). HelpAge International (n.d.) estimates that the South African pension alone costs approximately 1.4 percent of GDP annually. Spending on child transfers has increased relative to spending on other grants over time. For instance, elderly grant–related expenditures increased by 6.3 percent between 2001/02 and 2005/06, whereas the increase for child grants ranged from 36.1 percent for the Care Dependency Grant to 49.4 percent for the Child Support Grant (Pauw and Mncube 2007).

Old Age Pension

The longest-running major grant in South Africa is the Old Age Pension, also known as the Old Age Grant. The first law related to the Old Age Grant was established in 1928. The pension uses a formula based on the beneficiary's marital status and income to determine the grant amount (Pauw and Mncube 2007). It is a means- and asset-tested program for women over 60 and men over 65, with means tests varying by marital status (Devereux and Pelham 2005; Plaatjies 2006). The age threshold was expected to decrease to age 60 for men by 2010 (South African Government Services 2009). To receive the grant, beneficiaries must not receive other grants or belong to a state institution that cares for them. Coverage of the grant grew from 1.7 million beneficiaries in 1997 to 2.4 million beneficiaries in April 2009 (SASSA 2009). The grant reaches 5 percent of all South Africans and 70 percent of all South Africans eligible for the pension.

The Old Age Pension was set at R 1,010 (US$112)[41] monthly in April 2009 (South African Government Services 2009). The pension's real value increased about 2.1 percent annually from 2000 to 2006, and it equaled approximately 1.75 times the median per capita income in 2010 (Woolard and Leibbrandt 2010). The tendency for recipients to live in households that are larger than normal indicates that the grant improves more lives than simply the pensioner's (Pauw and Mncube 2007), which is particularly important because increases in mortality among prime-age adults have passed greater burdens of care for grandchildren to the elderly.

Evidence related to the effects of the Old Age Pension is relatively abundant. Woolard and Leibbrandt (2010) presented suggestive evidence of a poverty-decreasing effect of the South African grants. Case and Deaton (1998) determined that when the Old Age Pension was transferred to women, the cash had a higher likelihood of being spent in areas that benefited children, such as to pay for food or school fees. Duflo (2000) found that pension receipt by women is associated with increases in girls' nutritional outcomes, but not boys'. Receipt by men was not associated with these improvements for either gender. Edmonds (2006) found pension eligibility of a man in South African households was associated with increased school attendance and decreased market labor among children over five. Effects of the pension in households with orphans were mixed (Case and Ardington 2006).

Case (2001) found that when pension income was pooled within households, health was preserved among all members, purportedly through the pensions' ability to protect members' nutrition, improve household living conditions, and decrease adult members' stress. When the income was not pooled, the positive health changes were associated only with health of the recipient.

Analysis of the effect of the Old Age Pension on labor supply has produced mixed results, with some studies finding that pension receipt is associated with lower labor supply in certain household adults (Bertrand, Mullainathan, and Miller 2003) and others finding that pension receipt is associated with increased adult labor supply, often through migration (Ardington, Case, and Hosegood 2009; Posel, Fairburn, and Lund 2006).

Jensen (2004) found that the Old Age Pension reduced private transfers from children no longer living in the household.

Jensen (2004) also found no effect of the pension on labor supply, household composition, and migration. In contrast, Edmonds, Mammen, and Miller (2005) found that when South African households had a member reach pension eligibility, household composition changed, notably to add children under five and young women of childbearing age, while older working-age women departed.

Disability Grant

The Disability Grant, established in 1946, is also means and asset tested, with thresholds varying by marital status (Plaatjies 2006; U.S. Social Security Administration 2009). The means test requires that recipients earn less than R 29,112 (US$3,358) annually if they are single or R 58,224 (US$6,716) if they are married (South African Government Services 2009).

To be eligible for the Disability Grant, beneficiaries must be between 18 and pension-eligible ages and be classified as disabled by a doctor. They cannot be cared for in a state institution or receive any other state grants (Pauw and Mncube 2007). The maximum monthly benefit in 2009 was R 1,010 (US$112) (South African Government Services 2009). The grant equaled approximately 1.75 times the median per capita income in 2010 (Woolard and Leibbrandt 2010). In 1997, about 750,000 beneficiaries received the Disability Grant. By April of 2009, this number was 1.3 million (South African Government Services 2009), or about 3 percent of all South Africans.

Child Support Grant

The three major grants intended to benefit children in South Africa are the Child Support Grant, the Foster Care Grant, and the Care Dependency Grant. The grant with the most beneficiaries by far is the Child Support Grant. It was created in 1998 to replace the State Maintenance Grant (Streak 2007).[42] The Child Support Grant is child focused, so it follows children who move to a different household. The grant is given to a biological parent or other caretaker who has legally affirmed his or her status as the child's caretaker. Most primary caretakers are women. When the Child Support Grant was established, it targeted the poorest 30 percent of children and relied on household-level means tests to determine eligibility. The means test in 2009 was set at R 28,800 (US$3,322) annually for a single person and R 57,600

(US$6,644) annually for a married couple (South African Government Services 2009).

In 1999, the Department of Welfare changed the household-based means test to one that counted income of the designated primary caretaker and his or her spouse, less other transfers received by the state. This measure was taken to increase program uptake. The value of the grant increased from R 100 (US$14) in 2000 to R 142 (US$21) in 2006 (Pauw and Mncube 2007) and increased further to R 240 (US$27) by April 2009 (South African Government Services 2009). The grant equaled approximately 40 percent of median per capita income in 2010 (Woolard and Leibbrandt 2010). The upper age limit for recipients of the Child Support Grant has also changed over time, increasing from 7 years to 9 years in April 2003, to 11 years in 2004 (Agüero, Carter, and Woolard 2007), and 14 years in January 2009 (UNICEF 2008). In 2010, the upper age limit was expected to increase to 18 years (Woolard and Leibbrandt 2010).

Changes in eligibility, as well as growing knowledge of the program, have significantly increased uptake of the Child Support Grant. In 2001, less than 1 million children benefited from the grant. This number increased to 6.8 million by 2006 (Pauw and Mncube 2007) and 8.8 million by April 2009 (SASSA 2009). The targeting criteria are not always strictly enforced because of the great need for the transfers; undercoverage of the Child Support Grant was still viewed as a serious problem as late as 2005 (Streak 2007). The program's budget increased greatly from US$173 million in 2003/04 to US$1 billion in 2005/06.

The Child Support Grant was initially established as a transfer conditioned on children's involvement in development programs, up-to-date immunizations, and households' proof of making a good faith effort to obtain employment and child support, when relevant. These conditions were soon dropped, in part because of the recognition that many children did not have access to development programs, and the worst-off children were most likely to forfeit transfers on the basis of the immunization criteria (Woolard and Leibbrandt 2010). An assessment was proposed to examine application of both soft and hard conditions to the Child Support Grant, with plans for a randomized evaluation (Streak 2007). Beginning in 2010, social workers were supposed to meet with children receiving the grant who did not enroll in school to correct the problem (Woolard and Leibbrandt 2010). However, opinions are mixed in South Africa regarding fully conditional transfers in South Africa, and incorporating true conditions is not expected in the near term.

A process evaluation of the Child Support Grant, completed in 2008 by the Community Agency for Social Enquiry, found that the program was well targeted in the low-income areas covered by the review, with inclusion errors of 13 percent and exclusion errors of 21 percent. Most recipients of the transfers (that is, the children's caregivers) were females. Recipients often encountered obstacles to grant registration and receipt because of costs associated with obtaining required documentation for registration. This issue was particularly salient for nonbiological caregivers. Evidence indicated that more efforts should be made to connect grant recipients with other social protection programs and services. Evaluations also highlighted the need to review the means test to ensure that eligible households were not excluded from the grant and to increase communication about the grant to improve uptake (Community Agency for Social Enquiry 2008).

Evaluations of the Child Support Grant have primarily relied on variations in grant eligibility and uptake to achieve identification. An evaluation by Samson and others (2004), who used instrumental variables for identification, found that the grant decreased poverty and child hunger and increased food consumption and school attendance. Other evaluations also found the grant improved school attendance, labor force participation, self-reported measures of children's hunger (Williams 2007, as cited in EPRI 2008), and children's height-for-age ratio (Agüero, Carter, and Woolard 2007).

A later evaluation, which used propensity score matching and difference-in-difference regressions, found that the Child Support Grant decreased children's hunger by 4 to 7 percentage points and increased school attendance by 6 to 8 percentage points. The grant was also found to help beneficiary households continue agricultural activities and to increase mobile phone penetration among beneficiary households. In this case, the grant was not found to affect children's labor activities, household employment, or likelihood of using a social worker (EPRI 2008).

Other Grants

The Care Dependency Grant is given to households with children between 1 and 18 years with physical or mental disabilities who are cared for in their homes. It is means tested, with annual income thresholds in 2009 at R 121,200 (US$13,980) for a single person and R 242,200 (US$27,938) for a married couple (South African Government Services 2009). Benefits in 2009 were R 1,010 (US$117) monthly. The grant covered approximately 107,134 beneficiaries in April 2009 (SASSA 2009).

The Foster Care Grant is given when children are placed in foster care by the court system. The grant was R 680 (US$76) monthly in April 2009 (South African Government Services 2009). The grant equaled approximately 1.15 times median per capita income in 2010 (Woolard and Leibbrandt 2010). The benefit does not rely on a means test for caregivers, but rather provides grants to state-approved foster parents. A means test is applied to the child's annual income, limiting it to R 14,880 (US$1,716) in 2009. The fostered child must be orphaned; abandoned; or deemed neglected, abused, or at risk. Caretakers are often children's grandparents. Eligibility for the Foster Care Grant is reviewed every two years by social workers (Plaatjies 2006). In 1997, approximately 43,000 grants were awarded; by April of 2009, approximately 484,000 were awarded (SASSA 2009). Eligible children are covered through age 18; students are eligible through age 21 (U.S. Social Security Administration 2009).

The Social Relief of Distress Grant is provided to households that are temporarily unable to cover basic living expenses. It is means tested and provided each month for up to three months (U.S. Social Security Administration 2009). Finally, information about the Grant for Carers of the Aged is limited.

Swaziland

Swaziland has an Old Age Grant for poor people over 60 years old and a Public Assistance Grant for individuals younger than 60 who do not receive income or other grants. The transfers are provided for in the Swazi bill of rights, which requires the government to protect the welfare of children, people with disabilities, and the elderly (Dlamini 2007). Both the Old Age Grant and Public Assistance Grant programs are seated in the Department of Social Welfare in the Ministry of Health and Social Welfare (RHVP 2007a). Potential beneficiaries must enroll to receive a transfer, and community leaders provide support in identifying those who are eligible (Dlamini 2007).

Old Age Grant

The government officially launched the Old Age Grant in October 2005, only afterward conducting a national survey to learn more about the country's elderly. The grant was created to address the growing vulnerability of poor, elderly Swazis, particularly in light of the negative effects of the country's high HIV/AIDS rates on informal support systems (Dlamini 2007). The Old Age Grant is awarded to Swazi citizens over age 60 who have proof of identity, do not receive other grants, and have no other reliable source of income (RHVP 2007a). Beneficiaries must meet certain requirements regarding poverty and vulnerability, although the requirements are not well enforced. The monthly value of the grant was raised from E 80 (US$12) to E 100 (US$15) in 2007. Transfers, distributed quarterly, were originally paid through post offices. Distribution quickly shifted to be paid through the Department of Social Welfare. Transfers are given in both cash and check form; short-term workers are hired to distribute the transfers at selected paypoints.

The Old Age Grant is funded by the budget, and the government has an obligation to provide transfers to all registered beneficiaries. The government was expected to spend approximately E 60 million (US$8.6 million)[43] for 2006/07 for the Old Age Grant, twice that of the 2005/06 budget. In 2007/08, the budget for the Old Age Grant was set to increase to E 65 million (US$9.2 million).[44] For each dollar transferred to beneficiaries, the Old Age Grant cost US$1.11 (RHVP 2007a).

In 2005/06, approximately 28,000 Swazis received the Old Age Grant. This number increased to 49,000 in 2006/07, a little less than 5.5 percent of the Swazi population. During 2007/08, the program was expected to cover approximately 60,000 beneficiaries. This figure is above the estimated number of eligible Swazis, suggesting that significant errors of inclusion have occurred in the grant targeting and registration (RHVP 2007a).

Public Assistance Grant Coverage

The Public Assistance Grant, in existence since 1985, targets vulnerable groups in acute distress who do not receive the Old Age Grant or have another source of income. Beneficiaries include people with disabilities, the extremely poor, and those affected by crises (RHVP 2007a). Social workers and other community officials assess the vulnerability status of potential beneficiaries and determine their grant eligibility after they apply at one of four regional offices of Swaziland's Department for Social Welfare (Dlamini 2007). Eligible beneficiaries also must pass a means test. However, both the administrative and outreach capacity of the Department for Social Welfare within the Ministry of Health and Social Welfare are severely limited, so access to the grant is limited. Transfers are given only as checks, and they are distributed from one of the four social welfare offices (RHVP 2007a), which further restricts access to the grant.

The transfers are given quarterly. Their value in 2007 was E 80 (US$12) per month. Support is also provided to help beneficiaries purchase medical equipment to deal with disabilities. The Public Assistance Grant was estimated to reach only 5,000 beneficiaries in 2005/06. Only 2,260 beneficiaries were reported in 2006/07, when the budget for the Public Assistance Grant was E 2,165,000 (US$306,737). The grant's coverage is limited to funds allocated to it within the budget, which vary by year (Dlamini 2007).

The Public Assistance Grant is plagued by severe undercoverage, which is extremely problematic, given the major AIDS epidemic in Swaziland.

Administrative Problems

Several problems are known to exist with the Old Age and Public Assistance Grants. The Old Age Grant has high transfer and disbursement costs, and there have been indications of ongoing fraud. Although benefits are distributed using electronic identification and personal identification numbers, the initial enrollment allowed multiple documents to be used to prove identity, creating a problem of double registration by beneficiaries, as well as other opportunities for fraud (RHVP 2007a).

Using checks to distribute grants is also not ideal since beneficiaries must travel to a bank to cash them (RHVP 2007a). Distribution is somewhat irregular, and announcements about distributions do not always reach beneficiaries. The government also is in need of capacity building within the Ministry of Health and Social Welfare to establish stronger procedures and create a unit dedicated to the transfer schemes. Alternative payment mechanisms were being considered in 2007, with the hope that they would decrease fraud and increase cost-effectiveness. An additional known problem with the Public Assistance Grant is its lack of links to productive programs that could help capable beneficiaries, such as youth, exit the program (Dlamini 2007).

Tanzania

Tanzania has two recently developed conditional cash transfer pilot initiatives, both of which have unique characteristics that promise to inform the body of research on CCTs in Sub-Saharan Africa and beyond. They are the Community-Based Conditional Cash Transfer (CB-CCT) and Rewarding STI Prevention and Control in Tanzania (RESPECT).

Community-Based Conditional Cash Transfer

Structure of CB-CCT is unique among African CCTs and builds on existing community development work. The CB-CCT pilot will test the effectiveness of CCT components in a community-driven development program that functions within a social fund. Its programmatic goal is to increase the access of the poor and vulnerable to basic services. More specifically, it aims to increase beneficiaries' school attendance and health care visits (Ayala Consulting 2008b). Functioning in 40 villages of three rural districts (Kibaha, Bagamoyo, and Chamwino districts), it will target 6,000 beneficiaries in 2,000 households over a three-year period. Its rigorous definition of targeting, ongoing monitoring, collection of baseline and annual data, and experimental impact evaluation design are expected to yield valuable information and lessons to inform broader government social protection policies. It is also expected to cast light on how a CCT that relies on community-driven development and functions within a social fund could be effectively implemented, and to demonstrate how such a CCT might be used to lessen the impact of AIDS in communities (TASAF 2008).

The Tanzania Social Action Fund (TASAF), begun in 2000, is currently in its second phase (2005–10). The goal of TASAF II is to help local groups effectively implement small projects that will improve their livelihoods and contribute to national poverty reduction. It includes grants for vulnerable groups and a cash-for-work component. TASAF II extends the program's reach to a national level. It receives support from the government of Tanzania, the World Bank, local government authorities, and community and faith-based organizations (Tanzania Team 2007).

TASAF II has started a pilot CCT, which will be the first CCT in the region funded through a social fund. It is being implemented using a community-based approach and thus is known as a community-based CCT, or CB-CCT (Evans 2008). The pilot, financed by the Japanese Social Development Fund, was set to begin providing transfers in January 2010 (World Bank 2010d).

To be eligible for the CB-CCT, a community must have successfully implemented a TASAF subproject, and it must have a functioning community management committee. The rigorous targeting process already used to select villages for TASAF will ensure that targeted communities are some of the poorest and most vulnerable in the country (Evans 2008).

Targeting methodologies combine rigorous data analysis with community involvement. Targeting is completed after training and sensitization exercises have been undertaken (World Bank 2010d). Targeted households must have a member over age 60 or an orphan or vulnerable child; they must not receive similar benefits from another program; and they must meet three of six listed household characteristics associated with extreme poverty, which include homelessness, difficulty in consuming two or more meals daily, unemployment of household adults for at least the previous month, poor condition of children's clothes and shoes, and lack of own livestock or land (Evans 2008). Priority is given to orphans age 12 or younger (Ayala Consulting 2008a).

Existing community management committees will first collect information on all households in the village through a scheduled voluntary enrollment session and through visits by the committees to households of nonattendees (World Bank 2010d). Committees send this information, along with recommendations of which households should receive benefits, to the central program office (Ayala Consulting 2008a). This information, once entered into the MIS, is part of the selection process. The MIS generates lists of eligible households using the age category eligibility criteria, results of the community targeting, data consistency checks, and a proxy means test. Provided that most households are easily classified as eligible or ineligible, communities proceed to validate the list of targeted households generated by the MIS. When eligibility boundaries are less clear, a second process will be completed. This process requires the community management committees to collect more data; then a second, different proxy means test is applied to determine which households are eligible for the program. The list of eligible beneficiaries is ultimately sent to the villages. The MIS also generates a priority ranking of eligible households, which is used if not enough benefits are available to cover all eligible households (Evans 2008).

Once the list of eligible households is generated and ranked, a village assembly must validate the list. The village assembly is composed of two members from the central pilot unit or the local government authority, as well as two or more members of the community management committee. Communities are invited to participate in a validation meeting and to submit appeals at that time (Ayala Consulting 2008a). Approximately 2,060 households were registered and confirmed for the program through this process (World Bank 2010d).

Conditions are not enforced in all cases. Benefits are given bimonthly, and they range from US$12 to US$36 per pay period. Despite this stated range, benefits per child are US$6 every two months, which is half of the food poverty line based on the household budget survey from 2000/01,

(World Bank 2010d).[45] Benefits per elderly person are US$12 every two months, equal to the food poverty line (Evans 2008).

Funds are transferred from TASAF to a local government authority bank account and then to accounts managed by the community management committees. Then community management committee members distribute the payments to beneficiaries (Evans 2008). Transfers through mobile phones were also being considered. An additional community banking component will also be a part of the CB-CCT.

Transfers are conditional on children's school attendance and fulfillment of health-related conditions. Children up to age 5 must attend medical checkups three times per year, and children up to age 2 must attend three medical checkups and receive required vaccinations. Children ages 7 through 15 must enroll in and attend primary school at least 80 percent of the time. Elderly beneficiaries must attend one medical checkup per year (Ayala Consulting 2008b).

Health centers and schools complete monitoring forms, which community management committees collect and give to TASAF. TASAF then enters them in the MIS (TASAF 2008).[46] Conditions are monitored once annually for school enrollment and checkups of elderly people; they are monitored three times annually for the other conditions (Ayala Consulting 2008b).

Conditions will not be enforced when education and health centers are located far from communities, when a beneficiary is chronically ill, or when a child is the household head (Ayala Consulting 2008b). Noncompliance with conditions initially results in a warning. A second consecutive four-month period of noncompliance results in a reduction of payments by 25 percent and another warning (Evans 2008).[47] Additional penalties may eventually be applied, with the highest penalty allowed for the maximum payment of US$36 equal to US$18. Further noncompliance results in suspension from the program, although beneficiaries may return at a later date.[48]

The household will exit the program if it no longer has a member who meets program eligibility criteria, if it does not comply with the program rules, if it migrates, or if the program no longer considers the household poor (Ayala Consulting 2008b). All households are supposed to exit at the end of three years regardless of their status.

Management is integrated into existing TASAF structures. To execute the CB-CCT, a pilot unit has been formed within TASAF. This office will have a coordinator and officials in charge of operations, monitoring and evaluation, finances and administration, MIS engineering, and data entry. Below the pilot unit, local government authority focal point officers will be in charge of coordinating the program at the decentralized level. District-level education and health officers are to support the program and provide the necessary training and monitoring of services (Ayala Consulting 2008b).

Existing TASAF community management committees carry out many of the local-level duties as already described, and village councils supervise their work. These committees are elected by their communities (Ayala Consulting 2008b), and they have already received training from TASAF. Their responsibilities include assisting in targeting, distributing payments, communicating the program to beneficiaries, encouraging beneficiaries to comply with conditions, monitoring, and meeting with households (Ayala Consulting 2008b; TASAF 2008).

Extensive monitoring is planned for the CB-CCT. In addition to process audits and other requisite monitoring activities, a community scorecard component will be used. The scorecard will help to track inputs, and it will use community focus groups to evaluate the program. Self-assessments will also be completed by community management committees, and meetings will be held with stakeholders to discuss program improvement (TASAF 2008). Supply-side capacity assessments will be conducted to understand where households should be required to fulfill conditions (Ayala Consulting 2008b).

Baseline data for an experimental impact evaluation were collected in late 2008 and early 2009, and follow-up data were to be collected in December 2009 and December 2010 (Evans 2008). Early assessments of the program found it to be functioning well and capable of scaling up, provided that some adjustments are made (World Bank 2010d).

Rewarding STI Prevention and Control in Tanzania (RESPECT)

Based in the rural southern region of Morogoro's Ifakara Health and Demographic Surveillance Site, the RESPECT CCT is given to individuals between the ages of 18 and 30 and their spouses over age 16. The CCT is part of a larger experimental research program examining how to prevent STIs and HIV in the region. The treatment and control groups received counseling pre- and post-STI testing, and individuals were invited to participate in group counseling on relationships, gender issues, and other topics. Both groups also benefited from free testing for STIs, a small payment for their participation, and treatment of any STIs detected throughout the life of the program. The treatment group also received cash conditional on maintaining a negative test result for a number of curable STIs. Transfers were equal to either US$30 or US$60 total, given as US$10 or US$20 every four months. This amount was substantial in relation to the reference earnings per year of US$250 for the studied group. The CCT has approximately 1,500 beneficiaries in total (de Walque and others 2010).

After one year of implementation, the treatment group receiving the larger transfer size showed over a 25 percent reduction in STI prevalence. No impact was found among those receiving the smaller transfers. The CCT's impacts were strongest among those with the lowest socioeconomic status, and they did not differ by gender. Impacts will also be tested a year after the CCT is discontinued (de Walque and others 2010).

The pilot is expected to last two years. Institutions supporting the program include the University of California at Berkeley, the University of California at San Francisco, the Ifakara Health Research and Development Centre, and the World Bank. The program cost US$1.8 million (de Walque and others 2010).

Zambia

Zambia has CT programs in five districts. The programs are implementing various designs with the intention of incorporating lessons learned from the programs into a scaled-up national program.

Social Cash Transfer Pilots

SCT pilots build on the Kalomo district pilot. Zambia's Kalomo SCT pilot began in 2003 and expanded into four additional pilot districts (Chipata, Katete, Kazungula, and Monze) from 2005 to 2007. Motivation for the programs came from the increasing number of households affected by HIV/AIDS that lacked a head of household capable of benefiting from work-based assistance programs or microcredit (Schüring 2010). The program has gradually amassed knowledge and experience regarding the design and potential effects of CTs in Zambia. The group of five pilots was expected to finish a final period of learning and adjustment by the end of 2008. Plans for the program's scale-up began in mid-2008. By the end of 2009, a 10-year plan was completed.[49] National rollout has begun.

Political support for CTs in Zambia has been slowly increasing, and the programs have recently enjoyed much greater domestic ownership, having received greatly increased support from the Ministry of Finance as the pilots have continued. At the time of writing, the government of Zambia supplied approximately 20 percent of program funds. Obtaining this much domestic financial support, even for the pilot operations, took time to achieve, but the efforts appear to be paying off. That being said, a long-term challenge for the Zambian SCTs is the need to continue to expand political support for CTs in the country. Programs are still primarily donor funded, with cautious support from the Ministry of Finance.

Scale-up costs for Zambia's SCTs are expected to reach US$41.4 million by 2012, when transfers will be given in 50 well-established and 22 newly opened districts (ILO 2008). The scale-up has relied on significant efforts to build institutional capacity to improve program implementation.

The lead donors for Zambia's SCTs are currently DFID and UNICEF. A basket mechanism was established for the pilot schemes in recent years, and it has been further formalized for the expanded schemes. DFID, UNICEF, and Irish Aid are supporting the program's standardization through financial and technical support. The ILO has helped determine the long-term cost and effects of benefits, and it has tested a costing tool for CTs that can inform the debate on how to move forward (ILO 2008). Other groups interested in supporting the transfers at various points have included Concern Worldwide, the Norwegian Agency for Development Cooperation, and the World Bank.

Experience is being built through on-the-ground implementation. The Kalomo SCT began in 2003 with a small pilot in Kalomo district. Its objectives are to decrease poverty, starvation, and hunger of targeted households and to generate information about the viability of a social cash transfer program in Zambia (Ministry of Community Development and Social Services and German Agency for Technical Cooperation 2005). It began with a six-month test phase that provided benefits to about 100 beneficiaries from November 2003 to April 2004 (Ministry of Community Development and Social Services and German Agency for Technical Cooperation 2005; Schubert 2003). It then expanded to 1,027 households (3,856 beneficiaries) in 2004 and to 3,575 households by January 2008 (Mukuka 2008).

The Kalomo SCT provides transfers to households in two agricultural blocks, one entirely rural and the other a mixture of urban and rural areas (Ministry of Community Development and Social Services and German Agency for Technical Cooperation 2007a). Targeting aims to reach the 10 percent of the population deemed most needy and unable to provide for themselves. This percentage was decided on after a preliminary report by the German Agency for Technical Cooperation stated that approximately 1 in 10 households were in urgent need of social assistance, given that they were very poor and could not participate in productive activities. AIDS is one of the main causes of their destitution and limited labor force participation (Ministry of Community Development and Social Services and German Agency for Technical Cooperation 2007b).

In general, the targeting is supposed to select households in which no adults ages 18 to 60 are able to work. Selected households included many female-headed households and skipped-generation households with OVC (Ministry of Community Development and Social Services and German Agency for Technical Cooperation 2005). Community welfare assistance committees play a major role in targeting. They locate the most incapacitated households in their communities, interview them, and rank them according to their vulnerability. Village heads then validate the information on every household's application, and the community meets to discuss the rankings, suggest changes to the list, and finally approve it (Hamonga 2006). The list is given to the district social welfare officer, who presents the verdict on the list to the district welfare assistance committee. The committee determines the final list of households (Ministry of Community Development and Social Services and German Agency for Technical Cooperation 2005). Households may have their acceptance into the program privately challenged, in which case a home visit is paid to verify the household's eligibility (Hamonga 2006).

The unconditional cash transfers were equal to K 30,000 per month (US$6) in 2005 (Ministry of Community Development and Social Services and German Agency for Technical Cooperation 2007b). Households with children were supposed to begin receiving US$2 extra after retargeting was implemented (German Agency for Technical Cooperation 2007). The payments are made at banks for those within 15 kilometers of Kalomo; otherwise, coordinated paypoints are used. In 2003 and 2004, total Kalomo SCT costs amounted to US$168,000 (Ministry of Community Development and Social Services and German Agency for Technical Cooperation 2005).

The Kalomo pilot functions under the Public Welfare Assistance Scheme, which supervises the district welfare assistance committees, area coordinating committees, and community welfare assistance committees (Ministry of Community Development and Social Services and German Agency for Technical Cooperation 2005). The Public Welfare Assistance Scheme, located in the Department of Social Welfare, has existed for many years in Zambia, although its decentralized format was not introduced until 2000. It relies on community volunteers and existing organizations to implement its programs.

An evaluation of the Kalomo pilot consisted of a baseline and follow-up quantitative survey and qualitative research. The evaluation did not include a control group, nor did it control for important factors in program districts, which limits any conclusions that can be drawn. However, reports based on the evaluation claim that the Kalomo SCT has improved health, nutrition, education (to a limited degree), asset ownership, and local economic activity (German Agency for Technical Cooperation 2007). A review of the use of the transfers distributed from early 2004 through mid-2005 found that a significant portion of transfers was used on food (35 percent) and livestock (22 percent) (Tandeo 2005). Much of the spending varied with the seasonal variation in food availability. A later evaluation found that more than two-thirds of transfers were spent on consumption, one-quarter were put into investment, and 7 percent were put into savings (Ministry of Community Development and Social Services 2007).

Initial challenges encountered in the Kalomo SCT pilot were low capacity of involved parties and nepotism in targeting. Administrative capacity within the Public Welfare Assistance Scheme was limited by low literacy and the need for better equipment and training. The pilot attempted to confront these issues by providing better training and information to communities, involving local leaders in targeting but allowing for confidential appeals processes, holding community meetings in which villages had to approve of the list of beneficiaries, and providing incentives to the community welfare assistance committees to ensure that they fulfilled their duties (Hamonga 2006). The incentives to the committees were eventually discontinued.

Four more pilot areas seek to increase political support and inform design. The Kalomo SCT pilot showed that social cash transfers were possible in Zambia, but the impact evaluation was not rigorous enough to guide new national policy initiatives. Therefore, an extended pilot was planned to test for the most appropriate targeting, transfer conditions, payment distribution, and other components. The evaluation of the extended pilot would also determine where the transfer program should be seated and how to capitalize on other social protection and development programs. It also would increase understanding related to how the transfers affected informal safety nets (Ministry of Community Development and Social Services 2007). It was hoped that piloting over a longer period and a wider geographic area would allow the time to build up further political support for the program. The extension provided time to improve communication through a documentary and website and to conduct site visits by key ministry officials.

The additional pilots began in Kazungula district in 2005, in Chipata district in February 2006, and in Monze and Katete districts in 2007. In all districts except Katete, the pilots retained the Kalomo pilot goal of reducing starvation and poverty in the 10 percent of households that were most destitute and incapacitated (Ministry of Community Development and Social Services 2007).

The new pilot district CTs share many characteristics with the Kalomo CT. Targeting in all the pilot areas is still carried out by community welfare assistance committees. Retargeting is supposed to be completed every three years, but community committees may also identify households to fill newly emptied positions twice per year (Ministry of Community Development and Social Services 2008). If retargeting determines that a household is no longer extremely poor and labor constrained, the household is paid a graduation bonus and exits the program. To receive the bonus of K 500,000 (US$125), the household must fulfill a business training requirement, although it is not clear whether this aspect of the program has been implemented.

In most districts, payments are picked up every two months in the district capital by a designated paypoint manager. The paypoint manager is usually a local teacher or health care worker (Ministry of Community Development and Social Services 2008). The paypoint managers are supposed to collect the cash at the same time they collect their paychecks. They must also turn in financial records at that time (Ministry of Community Development and Social Services and German Agency for Technical Cooperation 2007b). Paypoints vary by month for security purposes.[50]

If a beneficiary cannot retrieve his or her transfer from the paypoint manager, a designated alternate may retrieve it in the beneficiary's name. Alternatively, the beneficiary or alternate can receive the cash from the paypoint manager before the official has gone to the district capital the next month. Community welfare assistance committees monitor the distribution process (Ministry of Community Development and Social Services and German Agency for Technical Cooperation 2007b).

Most documentation for the pilot SCTs is kept in manual files. However, a beneficiary database and payment registrar are completed on computers. This information is transported to and from districts and headquarters using CDs (Ministry of Community Development and Social Services 2008).

The Ministry of Community Development and Social Services remains the government-implementing counterpart in all five districts. It was assisted in Kalomo and Monze districts by the German Agency for Technical Cooperation until 2007 and in the other three districts by CARE until the end of 2008. Since then, the ministry has taken on full responsibility for the programs, although it has still received support in monitoring, evaluation, and capacity building. A technical working group on social assistance exists and is seated under a sector advisory group on social protection. The technical working group is composed of members from the Ministry of Community Development and Social Services' Planning Unit, the Department of Social Welfare, and other partners. The working group is expected to provide direction for the scaled-up national program (Ministry of Community Development and Social Services 2008).

Ongoing capacity challenges affect the Ministry of Community Development and Social Services. The ministry's one or two social workers in rural districts are already overloaded. Use of teachers and health workers as paypoint managers has also placed demands on them, taking time away from their respective activities in health or education.

Pilots jointly reach more than 12,000 households. Coverage of the CTs began expanding throughout all of Kalomo district in 2006 and was completed in January 2008. The Kalomo program revised transfer levels to equal K 40,000 (US$10.00) per household, along with a K 10,000 (US$2.50) child bonus (Ministry of Community Development and Social Services 2007). The transfers covered the price of a 50-kilogram bag of maize, which would allow a household of six individuals to consume an additional meal per day, presumably their second (Schüring 2010). Although not enough to cover the poverty gap, this amount was supposed to pull people from extreme poverty (Ministry of Community Development and Social Services and German Agency for Technical Cooperation 2007b). Kalomo households continued to receive their transfers through distribution at paypoints. Total annual costs per household are equal to K 660,000 (US$165) on average. Transfers are given on a bimonthly basis, and they are supposed to be increased by 10 percent every two years to account for inflation (Ministry of Community Development and Social Services 2007). As of mid-2009, the Kalomo SCT reached 3,573 households.

In Kazungula district, higher transfers of K 50,000 (US$12.50) and K 20,000 (US$5.00) for each child were provided (Ministry of Community Development and Social Services and German Agency for Technical Cooperation 2007b). This area is very rural and difficult to access, which has raised administrative costs to approximately 20 percent of total expenses, significantly higher than in other pilot areas (RNA 2007).[51] In this region affected by climate change, soil depletion, and devastating livestock diseases, 735 households benefited from the transfers as of mid-2009.

In Katete district, an old age transfer of K 60,000 (US$15) per month was distributed to individuals rather than households. The transfer is universal and given to all adults age 60 and older (Ministry of Community Development and Social Services and German Agency for Technical Cooperation 2007b). Beneficiaries are paid every two months (Mboozi n.d.). In mid-2009, approximately 4,500 beneficiaries received the CT in Katete.

Chipata district was chosen to test the effectiveness of providing CTs in more urban areas. Household benefits are K 50,000 (US$12.50). A flat bonus of K 10,000 (US$2.50) is given to households with two or more individuals. If households have a child enrolled in primary school, they earn K 10,000 (US$2.50) extra, and children enrolled in secondary school entitle the household to K 20,000 (US$5.00) extra (Ministry of Community Development and Social Services and German Agency for Technical Cooperation 2007b). The program is testing how providing a bonus conditional on children's school attendance affects outcomes. Administrative costs for Chipata were estimated at 10 percent of total costs (RNA 2007). As of mid-2009, 1,163 households were receiving transfers in Chipata.

The pilot in Monze district also provides K 40,000 (US$10.00) and a bonus of K 10,000 (US$2.50) for children (Ministry of Community Development and Social Services and German Agency for Technical Cooperation 2007b).[52] This pilot was designed to test soft conditions that called on households to invest in education and health care to receive transfers. The household was supposed to agree either in writing or verbally to send children over five years old to school and to maintain a health card for children under five (Ministry of Community Development and Social Services 2007). No penalty would be charged for noncompliance. However, these agreements were not signed, and plans for the soft conditions have not been implemented (Ministry of Community

Development and Social Services and German Agency for Technical Cooperation 2007b). DFID and UNICEF have funded an experimental evaluation in Monze that will test whether the CTs improve beneficiaries' welfare. By mid-2010, transfers were scheduled to be given to 2,069 households.

Additional evaluations uncover positive results and further room for improvement. A joint evaluation of several pilots was completed for Chipata, Kalomo, and Kazungula districts. The study examined the program's targeting and tried to identify impacts on households' well-being, investment activities, education outcomes, and asset ownership (RHVP 2009).

Targeting objectives were satisfied to a certain extent, but significant problems were uncovered. In some areas, older households were less likely to be part of the program, male-headed prime-age households were more likely to be beneficiaries, and more remote households were less likely to be beneficiaries. Targeting was especially problematic outside of Kalomo (RHVP 2009). Another analysis by Watkins (2008a) discussed how Kalomo's community-based targeting had various checks in it that allowed it to perform relatively better than targeting in other districts. Targeting was also less effective when it rationed program households to equal 10 percent of the population in all areas; it would work better if budget allocations varied with local poverty levels (Watkins 2008b). The benefits of enhanced targeting will have to be carefully weighed against the additional costs and capacity required to implement such a scheme, particularly as the program aims for cost-effective expansion.

The evaluation of program impacts in the three districts primarily used weighted regressions after applying propensity score matching methods in a cross-sectional dataset. Although certain caveats are still in order, this method was an improvement over prior, less rigorous evaluations of the SCTs. The study found positive impacts on consumption—especially nonfood consumption—in beneficiary households. The greatest effects were seen in areas with the highest vulnerability. Impacts varied by district and between households, depending on their asset ownership levels. The impact on education was mixed; school enrollment improved in Kalomo district only for boys. School attendance increased across the board only in the urban location of Chipata, which had imposed a premium payment for school attendance (RHVP 2009) and presented relatively few obstacles to accessing the educational system.

Zimbabwe

Zimbabwe has experience with multiple CTs, many of which have been government sponsored.

Government-Supported Cash Transfers

Zimbabwe has had a range of CTs, including a program known as the Public Assistance Program dating back before independence. The Public Assistance Program was given legal support in the Welfare Assistance Act of 1988. A review of its performance was completed in the 1990s (Munro 2005). Although the scope of the Public Assistance Program was limited, it did pay regular maintenance allowances. Its coverage peaked at 69,308 individual beneficiaries in 1994, and declined to 20,562 by 1998. The government spent approximately one-hundredth of a percent of national income on the program, which was situated in the Department of Social Welfare. The grants were primarily given to destitute elderly individuals who could not work and did not have families to support them, although others, such as children in dire circumstances, people with disabilities, and the chronically sick, were also eligible. The program was not well advertised, potential beneficiaries had to travel to district offices to apply, and transfer sizes, which were relatively small to begin with, did not keep up with the high inflation in Zimbabwe. It is not clear whether the program still exists.

Other government-supported CTs that functioned, at least from 2005 through 2007, include the Care for the Elderly Program, Support to Families in Distress, Maintenance of Disabled Persons, Support to Children in Difficult Circumstances, Maintenance of Hero's Dependents, and Drought Relief and Public Works Program. All of the programs were operated by the Department of Social Services within Zimbabwe's Ministry of Public Service, Labour, and Social Welfare, and all except the Maintenance of Hero's Dependents and the Drought Relief and Public Works Program are self-targeted (RHVP 2007b).

Eligible groups for transfers include destitute people over 60 (Care for the Elderly), poor households (Support to Families in Distress), people living with disabilities (Maintenance of Disabled Persons), vulnerable children (Support to Children in Difficult Circumstances), and wives and children of Zimbabwean heroes (Maintenance of Hero's Dependents). Beneficiaries of these grants received monthly checks from the Zimbabwean government until January 2007, when they began to receive cash transfers through post office savings books.

In 2005, the Care for the Elderly program had 39,468 beneficiaries, Support to Families in Distress had 39,278 beneficiaries, and Maintenance of Disabled Persons had 21,535 beneficiaries. Transfer values ranged from Z$445,720 (US$45) through Z$528,571 (US$53).[53] By early 2007, transfers were typically new Z$8,000 (US$23)[54] for adults and new Z$4,000 (US$12) for children (RHVP 2007b). It is not clear how these grants have changed following recent economic hardships.

The Drought Relief and Public Works Program aims to help vulnerable households during times of chronic drought. It is administered by the Department of Social Welfare in the Ministry of Public Service, Labour, and Social Welfare. It is targeted using local leaders and district drought relief committees. From September 2005 to May 2006, 2.9 million beneficiaries received transfers through this program. For individuals able to participate in the labor force, the program is a public works program. Elderly people, people with disabilities, and chronically ill individuals received unconditional cash transfers (RHVP 2007b).

Protracted Relief Programme

DFID has supported the Protracted Relief Programme (PRP) in Zimbabwe. The program began in 2004 and is ongoing. The program's second five-year phase, funded by more than US$130 million, began in mid-2008 (PRP 2011). Contributing partners include 28 international organizations, NGOs, and technical partners that implement the program through 30 local organizations under the responsibility of a consulting firm (GRM International), which manages and coordinates the project (PRP 2011).

The PRP targets extremely poor households that are vulnerable to adverse shocks. The program's goals are to decrease the reliance of households on food aid by increasing their food production, to increase access to basic water and sanitation services, and to care for the chronically ill (DFID 2008). Later reports suggest that the programmatic goals were to decrease extreme poverty by improving social protection and food security to keep the poor and vulnerable from becoming destitute and to protect and promote livelihoods (PRP 2011).

The program provides in-kind transfers of farming inputs, training in agricultural activities, and home care for the chronically ill. It also provides cash and vouchers to some households that normally receive in-kind assistance. Early work with cash was halted in 2007 because of hyperinflation, low food supplies, and the collapse of the financial sector. The program began to distribute cash in foreign currencies in March 2009. Households receive US$20 monthly.

The PRP is estimated to reach approximately 2 million individuals, between 15 percent and 20 percent of the country's population (European University Institute 2010). Coverage of CTs in the PRP is much more limited. In 2009/10, six NGOs implemented CTs in two rural and eight urban districts, reaching 3,425 households. The various organizations provided transfers through a range of methods, including through banks and supermarkets (PRP 2011).

Supporting organizations for the CTs in the PRP include ActionAid International, Farm Community Trust of Zimbabwe, Joint Initiative, and Zimbabwe Community Development Trust, among others. Most of these organizations have ties to home-based care organizations, and many beneficiaries are victims of HIV/AIDS. Although cash was distributed by hand as of 2009, program officials have discussed setting up bank accounts for beneficiaries.

The program operates outside of the Zimbabwean government, although it hopes to eventually transition into the system. A working group on cash transfers meets every two months to share information and learning about CTs.

Notes

1. In this appendix, all values in U.S. dollars are stated as reported in original documents. When original documents do not specify a given exchange rate or dollar value, average exchange rates for the reference period were used.
2. This calculation uses an average 1996 exchange rate of P 3.33 per US$1.
3. This calculation uses an average 2007 exchange rate of P 6.30 per US$1.
4. The result is US$60 using the 2008 average exchange rate of P 6.68 per US$1. It is US$65 using the 2002 average exchange rate of P 6.20 per US$1.
5. This calculation uses an average 2005 exchange rate of P 5.05 per US$1, the year in which relevant documentation provided the means test level.
6. Costs were 17.2 percent when capacity building costs were included (World Bank 2010a).
7. This figure is 1.2 percent of GDP when the estimated cost of staff time is excluded (World Bank 2010a).
8. This study lacks a control group, which it mentions as an inherent weakness (Devereux and others 2006).
9. Jones (2009) reported that by May 2009, LEAP had reached 26,200 households and 131,000 beneficiaries, and the program's goal was to cover 165,000 households in the five-year time frame. This number appears to include some

of the beneficiaries covered by the six months of transfers provided by the World Bank.
10. Plans for support from the World Bank to create a proxy means test for beneficiary selection were in place in early 2010.
11. Some sources suggest fisherpeople and subsistence farmers will also be covered; other sources exclude these groups.
12. It is not clear whether beneficiaries believe they must comply with the conditions to receive program benefits, so the conditions cannot be classified as soft conditions, although Jones (2009) suggests that the conditions are soft.
13. This figures uses an average 2009 exchange rate of 1 K Sh = US$0.0125.
14. This figure is based on an average 2008 exchange rate of £1 = US$1.86.
15. The plural for Lesotho's currency, the loti (L), is maloti (M). The average exchange rate for May 2007 was L 1 = US$0.14485.
16. The European University Institute (2010) shows this value as US$42; however, the average exchange rate for April 2009, L 1 = US$0.1165, yields the result reported in the text.
17. This figure uses an average 2007 exchange rate of L 1 = US$0.1395.
18. This figure uses an average 2009 exchange rate of €1 = US$1.39463.
19. This number standardizes the exchange rate to that used in the previous reference to Malawi's transfers. It is slightly different from that given by Schubert and Huijbregts (2006).
20. At the time of writing, the program expected to scale up to approximately 300,000 households, reaching about 1.3 million individuals at an annual cost of US$68.5 million.
21. Other reports suggest that in 1991 transfers were already being distributed to 2,000 households, while Soares, Hirata, and Rivas (n.d.) say it was started in 1990.
22. This figure uses an average 1995 exchange rate of Mt 1 = US$0.00020.
23. This figure uses an average 1997 exchange rate of Mt 1 = US$0.00009.
24. The Mtn is the new metical.
25. This figure uses an average 2009 exchange rate of Mtn 1 = US$0.0371. In 2008, transfers to the first household beneficiary increased from Mtn 70 to Mtn 100, and transfers for up to four additional beneficiaries within a household went from Mtn 10 to Mtn 50 per person (Soares, Hirata, and Rivas n.d.).
26. The PSA has been working with Civil Identification Services to help individuals obtain their cards, and card applications are also accepted in lieu of actual identity cards. More recently, voting cards are also accepted.
27. This figure uses an average 2008 exchange rate of Mtn 1 = US$0.04160.

28. This figure is based on the population estimate for 2008 (Levine, van der Berg, and Yu 2009).
29. This figure uses an average June 2009 exchange rate of N$1 = US$0.12620.
30. In addition, a War Veterans Subvention was established by the War Veterans Subvention Act of 1999 and was updated in 2008 in the Veterans Act (Levine, van der Berg, and Yu 2009). By early 2009, the pension was given to approximately 1,800 individuals, though it was estimated that as many as 30,000 beneficiaries were eligible to receive the transfers. The Ministry of Veterans Affairs has managed the pension since the ministry's creation in 2006.
31. Nekundi (2007) reports that the limit is three children.
32. ELCRN (2007) reported this amount to be N$300 (about US$39) monthly.
33. This estimate is based on official budget data for 2009/10.
34. This statistic is reported in the proposal by Ayala (2009), which does not clarify whether this figure is for national or local GDP. The figure uses an exchange rate of ₦145 = US$1.
35. This figure uses an average 2009 exchange rate of RF 1 = US$0.00179.
36. This figure uses an average 2009 exchange rate of £1.56593 = US$1.
37. This evaluation covered all three components of VUP and not simply the direct support component.
38. This figure uses the average exchange rate for October 2008, the first month of the 2008/09 school year: CFAF 1 = US$0.00208.
39. The Nutrition Enhancement Program receives funding and technical support from UNICEF and the WFP and funding from the World Health Organization, USAID, African Development Bank, and Micronutrient Initiative. Its first phase ran from 2002 to 2006; phase 2 runs from 2007 to 2011 and extends the project's mandate and reach to cover half of Senegalese children. Phase 3 is expected to run from 2012 to 2015 and will strengthen and integrate the project. The first phase reached approximately 200,000 children under age two, along with their mothers, and it helped NGOs set up more than 900 community health sites and train more than 2,500 nutritional aides. The project has been associated with large, strong impacts on children's health and nutrition (World Bank 2009b).
40. For the War Veterans Grant, beneficiaries must have served in World War II or the Korean War to receive the benefits. This grant reached fewer than 1,500 beneficiaries in April of 2009 (SASSA 2009). Pauw and Mncube (2007) note that the War Veterans Grant will probably be phased out soon because of natural attrition. The grant is also means and asset tested; the maximum value in 2007 was R 1,010 (US$143.78) (South African Government Services 2009).

41. This figure uses the average exchange rate for April 2009 of R 1 = US$0.11110.
42. The State Maintenance Grant reached approximately 300,000 households, but its coverage of black South Africans was limited.
43. This figure uses the average exchange rate for April 1 through March 31 of 2006/07 of E 1 = US$0.14355.
44. This figure uses the average exchange rate for April 1 through March 31 2007/08 of E 1 = US$0.14168.
45. The information provided in the program documentation does not clearly state whether the US$12 is a minimum transfer value, regardless of household composition, or whether there is a discrepancy in the specified minimum transfer value and the child-level benefits.
46. Ayala Consulting (2008b) says the forms are given to local government authority officials by the community management committees. The local authorities pass the forms on to TASAF.
47. The operational manual, dated March 2008, suggests penalties are 50 percent of the payment for a child beneficiary and 25 percent for an elderly beneficiary (Ayala 2008b).
48. The March 2008 manual also suggests that households will be removed from the program if children have not complied for three consecutive monitoring periods or elderly members have not complied for two consecutive monitoring periods (Ayala 2008b).
49. In early 2010, the 10-year arrangement was signed by the government of Zambia and relevant development partners.
50. In Chipata and Kazungula, some beneficiaries received payments through bank accounts rather than through paypoints (RNA 2007).
51. Other less official estimates suggest that the amounts cited here as the administrative costs for the districts are underestimated.
52. A report finished after the review was completed says that the transfers were increased to K 80,000 (US$16) for households without children and K 100,000 (US$20) for recipients with children in their household (Schüring 2010).
53. This figure uses an average 2005 exchange rate of Z$1 = US$0.00010.
54. This figure uses an average 2007 exchange rate of new Z$1 = US$0.00288.

References

African Peer Review Mechanism. 2010. *Country Report: Kingdom of Lesotho*. Addis Ababa: African Union.

Agüero, Jorge, Michael Carter, and Ingrid Woolard. 2007. "The Impact of Unconditional Cash Transfers on Nutrition: The South African Child Support Grant." Working Paper 39, International Poverty Centre, Brasília.

Ardington, Cally, Anne Case, and Victoria Hosegood. 2009. "Labor Supply Responses to Large Social Transfers: Longitudinal Evidence from South Africa." *American Economic Journal: Applied Economics* 1 (1): 22–48.

Ashley, Steve, Taylor Brown, and Sam Gibson. 2007. "Building Consensus for Social Protection: Insights from Ethiopia's Productive Safety Net Programme." IDL Group, Bristol, U.K.

Ayala, Francisco. 2009. "Design Proposal for a Kano State Pilot CCT for Girls' Education." Federal Republic of Nigeria, Nairobi.

Ayala Consulting. 2007. "Cash Transfer Programme for Orphans and Vulnerable Children (CT for OVC), Version 2.0." Office of the Vice President and Ministry of Home Affairs, Nairobi.

———. 2008a. "Annex B: Targeting Manual for the Community-Based Cash Transfer Pilot (CB-CCT)." Prepared for the Republic of Tanzania, Ayala Consulting, Quito.

———. 2008b. "Community-Based Cash Transfer Pilot CB-CCT: Operational Manual, Version 1.0." Prepared for the Republic of Tanzania, Ayala Consulting, Quito.

———. 2009. "Eritrea Results Based Financing (RBF) Pilot, Version 1.0." Prepared for the Government of Eritrea and Ministry of Health, Ayala Consulting, Quito.

Baird, Sarah, Ephraim Chirwa, Craig McIntosh, and Berk Özler. 2009. "Unpacking the Impacts of a Randomized CCT Program in Sub-Saharan Africa." Research proposal, University of California–San Diego and World Bank, Washington, DC.

———. 2010. "The Short-Term Impacts of a Schooling Conditional Cash Transfer Program on the Sexual Behavior of Young Women." *Health Economics* 19 (S1): 55–68.

Baird, Sarah, Craig McIntosh, and Berk Özler. 2011. "Cash or Condition? Evidence from a Cash Transfer Experiment." World Bank, Washington, DC. http://ipl.econ.duke.edu/bread/papers/0511conf/Baird.pdf.

Bar-On, Arnon. 2002. "Going against World Trends: Social Protection in Botswana." *Social Policy Journal* 1 (4): 23–41.

Basic Training Course. 2009. "Introduction to Social Safety Nets and Their Development in Senegal." Draft 4.1, Senegal National Social Protection Strategy, Dakar.

Bertrand, Marianne, Sendhil Mullainathan, and Douglas Miller. 2003. "Public Policy and Extended Families: Evidence from Pensions in South Africa." *World Bank Economic Review* 17 (1): 27–50.

BFTU (Botswana Federation of Trade Unions). 2007. "Policy Position Paper on Social Security and Social Protection in Botswana." BFTU, Gaborone.

Blank, Lorraine. 2008. "Lesotho Child Grant Pilot Operating Manual." United Nations Children's Fund, New York.

Bouchet, Brigitte. 2009. "Kano State Pilot CCT for Girls' Education: Operations Manual, Version 1.0." Federal Republic of Nigeria, Nairobi.

Bourse Maman. n.d. "Evaluation de l'Initiative Bourse-Maman dans 09 Écoles de Kayes et de Mopti." Bourse Maman, Bamako.

Case, Anne. 2001. "Does Money Protect Health Status? Evidence from South African Pensions." NBER Working Paper 8495, National Bureau of Economic Research, Cambridge, MA.

Case, Anne, and Cally Ardington. 2006. "The Impact of Parental Death on School Outcomes: Longitudinal Evidence from South Africa." *Demography* 43 (3): 401–20.

Case, Anne, and Angus Deaton. 1998. "Large Cash Transfers to the Elderly in South Africa." *Economic Journal* 108 (450): 1330–61.

Central Statistics Office. 2007. *Social Security Statistics, 2000/2000–2005/2006*. Port Louis: Ministry of Finance and Economic Development.

Chipeta, Paul, and Harry Mwamlima. 2007. "Malawi Social Protection Programme." PowerPoint presentation at the Africa Regional Workshop on Cash Transfer Programmes for Vulnerable Groups, Mombasa, Kenya, February 26–28.

CNLS (Conseil National de Lutte contre le SIDA et les IST). 2008. "Recherche Action sur la Prise en Charge Communautaire des Orphelins et Enfants Vulnérables du VIH/SIDA dans les Provinces du Nahouri et du Sanmatenga." CNLS, Ouagadougou.

CNLS (Conseil National de Lutte contre le SIDA et les IST) and World Bank. n.d. "Projet de Transfert Conditionné de Fonds pour la Scolarisation de 5,000 Orphelins et Enfants Vulnérables (OEV) du Sénégal." PowerPoint presentation.

Coady, David P., Margaret Grosh, and John Hoddinott. 2004. "Targeting Outcomes Redux." *World Bank Research Observer* 19 (1): 61–85.

Community Agency for Social Enquiry. 2008. "Review of the Child Support Grant: Uses, Implementation, and Obstacles." Report for the Department of Social Development, the South African Social Security Agency, and the United Nations Children's Fund, Johannesburg.

Croome, David, Andrew Nyanguru, and M. Molisana. 2007. "The Impact of the Old Age Pension on Hunger Vulnerability: A Case-Study from the Mountain Zone of Lesotho." Prepared for the Regional Hunger Vulnerability Programme, Institute of Southern African Studies and National University of Lesotho, Roma.

Datt, Gaurav, Ellen Payongayong, James L. Garrett, and Marie Ruel. 1997. "The GAPVU Cash Transfer Program in Mozambique: An Assessment." FCND Discussion Paper 36, Food Consumption and Nutrition Division, International Food Policy Research Institute, Washington, DC.

del Ninno, Carlo. 2009. "Payment Systems." PowerPoint presentation at World Bank Institute's Training Session on Designing and Implementing CCTs in Nigeria, Washington, DC, April 20.

Devereux, Stephen, and A. Ndejuru. 2009. "Annual Review of DFID Support to the Vision 2020 Umurenge Programme (VUP)." U.K. Department for International Development, Kigali.

Devereux, Stephen, and Larissa Pelham. 2005. "Making Cash Count: Lessons from Cash Transfer Schemes in East and Southern Africa for Supporting the Most Vulnerable Children and Households." Save the Children UK, HelpAge International, and Institute of Development Studies, London. http://www.ids.ac.uk/go/idsproject/making-cash-count.

Devereux, Stephen, Rachel Sabates-Wheeler, Rachel Slater, Mulugeta Tefera, Taylor Brown, and Amdissa Teshome. 2008. *Ethiopia's Productive Safety Net Programme (PSNP): 2008 Assessment Report*. Sussex, U.K.: Institute of Development Studies, Overseas Development Institute, Dadimos Development Consultants, IDL Group, and A–Z Consult.

Devereux, Stephen, Rachel Sabates-Wheeler, Mulugeta Tefera, and Hailemichael Taye. 2006. "Ethiopia's Productive Safety Net Programme (PSNP): Trends in PSNP Transfers within Targeted Households—Final Report." Institute of Development Studies, Sussex, U.K., and Indak International, Addis Ababa.

de Walque, Damien. 2009. "Evaluating the Impact of Conditional and Unconditional Cash Transfers in Rural Burkina Faso." PowerPoint presentation, Development Economics Research Group, World Bank, Washington, DC, January 12.

de Walque, Damien, William H. Dow, Rose Nathan, Carol Medlin, and RESPECT Study Team. 2010. "The RESPECT Study: Evaluating Conditional Cash Transfers for HIV/STI Prevention in Tanzania." World Bank, Washington, DC.

DFID (U.K. Department for International Development). 2008. "DFID Programmes in Zimbabwe." DFID, London.

———. 2009. "Vision 2020 Umurenge Programme (2009–2013)." Project document, DFID, Kigali.

Dlamini, Armstrong. 2007. "A Review of Social Assistance Grants in Swaziland: A CANGO/RHVP Case Study on Public Assistance in Swaziland." Regional Hunger Vulnerability Programme, Johannesburg.

Document de Cadrage Technique. 2009. "Project de Transfert de Fonds Conditionné pour la Scolarisation et la Formation Professionnelle de 5,000 OEV au Sénégal."

Duflo, Esther. 2000. "Child Health and Household Resources in South Africa: Evidence from the Old Age Pension Program." *American Economic Review* 90 (2): 393–98.

Edmonds, Eric. 2006. "Child Labor and Schooling Responses to Anticipated Income in South Africa." *Journal of Development Economics* 81 (2): 386–414.

Edmonds, Eric, Kristen Mammen, and Douglas Miller. 2005. "Rearranging the Family? Income Support and Elderly Living Arrangements in a Low-Income Country." *Journal of Human Resources* 40 (1): 186–207.

ELCRN (Evangelical Lutheran Church in the Republic of Namibia). 2007. "Access to Government Grants." Desk for Social Development, ELCRN, Windhoek.

Ellis, Frank. 2007. "Food Subsidy Programme, Mozambique." REBA Case Study Brief 7, Regional Evidence Building Agenda, Regional Hunger Vulnerability Programme, Johannesburg.

EPRI (Economic Policy Research Institute). 2008. "Quantitative Analysis of the Impact of the Child Support Grant." EPRI, Cape Town, South Africa.

European Commission. 2009. *Advisor on Social Protection: Social Cash Transfers to Ministry of Gender, Children and Community Development, Interim Report*. Lilongwe: European Commission.

European University Institute. 2010. *Social Protection for Inclusive Development: A New Perspective in EU Cooperation with Africa*. San Domenico di Fiesole, Italy: Robert Schuman Centre for Advanced Studies, European University Institute.

Evans, David. 2008. "Tanzania Community-Based Conditional Cash Transfer (CB-CCT) Pilot." PowerPoint presentation, World Bank, Washington, DC, November 12.

Gaolathe, Baledzi. 2009. "Turning Challenges into Opportunities: Building on the Achievements of NDP 9." 2009 budget speech delivered to the National Assembly, Gaborone, February 2.

German Agency for Technical Cooperation. 2007. "Social Cash Transfers in Zambia: Setup, Lessons Learned, and Challenges." PowerPoint presentation at the Africa Regional Workshop on Cash Transfer (CT) Programmes for Vulnerable Groups, Mombasa, Kenya, February 26–28.

Gilligan, Daniel O., John Hoddinott, Neha Rati Kumar, and Alemayehu Seyoum Taffesse. 2009a. *An Impact Evaluation of Ethiopia's Productive Safety Nets Program*. Washington, DC: International Food Policy Research Institute.

Gilligan, Daniel O., John Hoddinott, Neha Rati Kumar, Alemayehu Seyoum Taffesse, Samson Dejene, Fikru Gezahegn, and Yisehac Yohannes. 2009b. *Ethiopia Food Security Program: Report on 2008 Survey*. Washington, DC: International Food Policy Research Institute.

Government of Cape Verde. 2011. "Ministério do Trabalho, Formação Profissional e Solidaridade Social."

Government of Kenya. 2006. "Cash Transfers for Orphan and Vulnerable Children (OVC)." Cash Transfer Pilot Project, Office of the Vice President and Ministry of Home Affairs, Nairobi.

———. 2007. "OVC in Kenya." 2007. PowerPoint presentation by the Ministry of Home Affairs at the Africa Regional Workshop on Cash Transfer Programmes for Vulnerable Groups, Mombasa, Kenya, February 26–28.

Government of Mauritius. 2008. "Mauritius: Ageing in Place." Paper presented by the Ministry of Social Security, National Solidarity, and Senior Citizens Welfare and Reform Institutions at the International Federation on Ageing's Ninth Global Conference, Montreal, Canada, September 4–7.

———. 2009. "Mauritius Pension System Ahead of World Bank Model, Says Minister Bappoo." Government Information Service, Prime Minister's Office, Port Louis. http://www.gov.mu/.

Hamonga, Jean. 2006. "Community-Based Targeting Case Study: Zambia." Presented at the Third International Conference on Conditional Cash Transfers, Istanbul, June 29.

Hartwig, Renate. 2010. "The Vision 2020 Umurenge Programme (VUP) in Rwanda: A Background Paper." International Institute of Social Studies, The Hague, Netherlands.

HelpAge International. n.d. "Cost of Pension as Percentage of GDP." Graph, HelpAge International, London.

Hoddinott, John. n.d. "Ethiopia's Productive Safety Net Programme." PowerPoint presentation, International Food Policy Research Institute, Washington, DC.

Horvath, Christophe, Mayke Huijbregts, and Douglas Webb. 2008. "Malawi's Experiences with Social Cash Transfer Systems." Presented at the Conference on Children and HIV/AIDS: Action Now, Action How, Mexico City, August 2.

HSNP (Hunger Safety Net Programme). n.d. "Welcome to Hunger Safety Net Programme." HSNP, Nairobi. http://www.hsnp.or.ke/.

———. 2008. "Know Hunger Safety Net Programme: Delivering Payments." HSNP, Nairobi.

Hurrell, Alex, Patrick Ward, and Fred Merttens. 2008. *Kenya OVC-CT Programme Operational and Impact Evaluation: Baseline Survey Report*. Oxford Policy Management, Oxford, U.K.

Hussein, Ahmed. 2006. "Conditional Cash Transfers in Low-Income Countries: Applicability and Challenges—Kenya." Presented at Third International Conference on Conditional Cash Transfers, Istanbul, June 26–30.

ILO (International Labour Organization). 2008. *Zambia Social Protection Expenditure and Performance Review and Social Budget*. Geneva: ILO Social Security Department.

IMF (International Monetary Fund). 2006. "Cape Verde: Poverty Reduction Strategy Paper—First Annual Progress Report." Country Report 06/332, IMF, Washington, DC.

International Poverty Centre. n.d. "Cash Transfers and Social Protection: Interview with Foday Conteh, Senior Monitoring and Evaluation Officer of the Social Safety Net Programme from the Ministry of Employment and Social Security, Sierra Leone." International Poverty Centre, Brasília. http://www.ipc-undp.org/publications/cct/Interview_Foday_Conteh_SierraLeone.pdf.

IPC-IG (International Policy Centre for Inclusive Growth). 2008. "Social Protection in Ghana: The Livelihood Empowerment against Poverty (LEAP)." *Brasil and Africa Newsletter* 1: 1–2.

IRIN (Integrated Regional Information Networks). 2009. "Burundi: Repatriation of Refugees from Tanzania Resumes." IRIN, Nairobi. http://www.irinnews.org/Report.aspx?ReportID=84089.

Jensen, Robert. 2004. "Do Private Transfers 'Displace' the Benefits of Public Transfers? Evidence from South Africa." *Journal of Public Economics* 88 (1–2): 89–112.

Jones, Nicola, with William Ahadzie and Daniel Doh. 2009. *Social Protection for Children: Opportunities and Challenges in Ghana*. London: Overseas Development Institute.

Lallmahomed, Ahmed. 2008. "African Pensions Roundtable: Mauritius." Presentation for Organisation for Economic Co-operation and Development/International Organisation of Pension Supervisors Global Forum, Mombasa, Kenya, October 30–31.

Levine, Sebastian, Servaas van der Berg, and Derek Yu. 2009. "Measuring the Impact of Social Cash Transfers on Poverty and Inequality in Namibia." Stellenbosch Economic Working Paper 25/09, Department of Economics and Bureau for Economic Research, University of Stellenbosch, Stellenbosch, South Africa.

Lund, Francie. 2007. "The South African Child Support Grant." PowerPoint presentation on Social Work 1V Research Methods, School of Development Studies, University of KwaZulu-Natal, Durban, South Africa, March.

Massingarela, Cláudio, and Virgulino Nhate. 2006. "The Politics of What Works: A Case Study of Food Subsidies and the Bolsa Escola in Mozambique." Background paper for the *Chronic Poverty Report 2008–2009*. Manchester, U.K.: Chronic Poverty Research Centre.

Mboozi, Bestone. n.d. "Zambia Social Protection Case Study." Ministry of Community Development and Social Services, Lusaka.

McGrath, Marie. 2006. "Exit Strategies in OVC Programming in Namibia." *Field Exchange* 29 (December): 16–18. http://fex.ennonline.net/29/exitstrategies.aspx.

MDRP (Multi-country Demobilization and Reintegration Program). 2006. "Reinsertion: Bridging the Gap between Demobilization and Reintegration." *In Focus* 3 (September): 1–4. http://www.mdrp.org/PDFs/In_Focus_3.pdf.

Miller, Candace. 2006. "Social Welfare in Africa: Meeting the Needs of Households Caring for Orphans and Affected by AIDS." Presentation for the United Nations Children's Fund and the Graduate Program in International Affairs at the New School University conference on Social Protection Initiatives for Children, Women, and Families: An Analysis of Recent Experiences, New York, October 30–31.

Miller, Candace, and Maxton Tsoka. n.d. "Evaluating the Mchinji Social Cash Transfer Pilot." Center for International Health and Development, Boston University, Boston, and Centre for Social Research, University of Malawi, Zomba.

Miller, Candace, Maxton Tsoka, and Mchinji Evaluation Team. 2007a. "Evaluation of the Mchinji Cash Transfer: Baseline Report—Preliminary Findings." Center for International Health and Development, Boston University, Boston, and Centre for Social Research, University of Malawi, Zomba.

———. 2007b. "Evaluation of the Mchinji Cash Transfer: Report II—Targeting and Impact." Center for International Health and Development, Boston University, Boston, and Centre for Social Research, University of Malawi, Zomba.

Miller, Candace, Maxton Tsoka, and Kathryn Reichert. 2008a. "Operations Report: External Evaluation of the Mchinji Social Cash Transfer Pilot." Center for International Health and Development, Boston University, Boston, and Centre for Social Research, University of Malawi, Zomba.

———. 2008b. "Targeting Report: External Evaluation of the Mchinji Social Cash Transfer Pilot." Center for International Health and Development, Boston University, Boston, and Centre for Social Research, University of Malawi, Zomba.

———. 2010. "Targeting Cash to Malawi's Ultra-Poor: A Mixed Methods Evaluation." *Development Policy Review* 28 (4): 481–502.

Ministry of Community Development and Social Services. 2007. "Implementation Framework for Scaling Up to a National System of Social Transfers in Zambia." Ministry of Community Development and Social Services, Lusaka.

———. 2008. *Manual of Operations for the Social Cash Transfer Scheme*. Lusaka: Ministry of Community Development and Social Services.

Ministry of Community Development and Social Services and German Agency for Technical Cooperation. 2005. "An Assessment Study in the Framework of the Development of a Social Protection Strategy." Ministry of Community Development and Social Services and German Agency for Technical Cooperation, Lusaka.

———. 2007a. "Final Evaluation Report: Kalomo Social Cash Transfer Scheme." Ministry of Community Development and Social Services, Lusaka.

———. 2007b. "The Pilot Social Cash Transfer Scheme in Zambia: Summary Report." Ministry of Community Development and Social Services and German Agency for Technical Cooperation, Lusaka.

Mukuka, Lawrence. 2008. "Linkages between Social Cash Transfers and Other Programmes." University of Zambia, Lusaka.

Munro, Lauchlan T. 2005. "A Social Safety Net for the Chronically Poor? Zimbabwe's Public Assistance Programme in the 1990s." *European Journal of Development Research* 17 (1): 111–31.

Musoni, Protais. n.d. "Decentralisation Process in Rwanda: Achievements, Challenges, and Way Forward, 2007–2011—Consolidating Successful Implementation of Rwanda Decentralisation Policy and Promoting Vision 2020 Based Local Economic Development." Ministry of Local Government, Good Governance, Community Development and Social Affairs, Kigali.

Nekundi, Loide Mbabyona. 2007. "A Comparative Study of Orphans and Vulnerable Children (OVC) Support in Oshakati District, Oshana Region, Namibia." Master's thesis, University of the Free State, Bloemfontein, South Africa.

Oxford Policy Management. 2009. "Kenya OVC Cash Transfer: OPM Independent Evaluation Quantitative and Qualitative Work, 2009." Oxford Policy Management, Oxford, U.K.

Pauw, Kalie, and Liberty Mncube. 2007. "Expanding the Social Security Net in South Africa: Opportunities, Challenges, and Constraints." Country Study 8, International Poverty Centre, Brasília.

Plaatjies, Daniel. 2006. "Conditional Cash Transfer Programs in South Africa." Presented at the Third International Conference on Conditional Cash Transfers, Istanbul, June 26–30.

PlusNews. 2009. "Lesotho: Cash for Kids." Integrated Regional Information Network, May 3. http://www.irinnews.org/report.aspx?ReportId=83855.

Posel, Dori, James Fairburn, and Frances Lund. 2006. "Labour Migration and Households: A Reconsideration of the Effects of the Social Pension on Labour Supply in South Africa." *Economic Modelling* 23 (5): 836–53.

"Productive Safety Nets Programme in Ethiopia: The Public Works Component." n.d. PowerPoint presentation, World Bank, Washington, DC.

PRP (Protracted Relief Programme). 2011. "About PRP." PRP, Harare. http://www.prpzim.info/default/default.cfm?linkid=1&CFID=10064608&CFTOKEN=72819016#.

"Q&A: Child Cash Grants Programme." 2008. UNICEF, Lesotho.

Republic of Namibia. 2007. *Namibia National Plan of Action for Orphans and Vulnerable Children.* Vol. 1. Windhoek: Ministry of Gender Equality and Child Welfare.

Republic of Rwanda. 2009. "Vision 2020 Umurenge Programme (VUP): Direct Support Operational Framework and Procedure Manual." Ministry of Local Government, Good Governance, Community Development, and Social Affairs, Kigali.

RHVP (Regional Hunger and Vulnerability Programme). 2007a. "Old Age and Public Assistance Grants, Swaziland." REBA Case Study Brief 6, Regional Evidence Building Agenda, RHVP, Johannesburg.

———. 2007b. "Zimbabwe: Summary Data on Social Protection Schemes." RHVP, Johannesburg.

———. 2009. "Impact of Social Cash Transfers on Household Welfare, Investment, and Education in Zambia." Wahenga Brief 17, RHVP, Johannesburg. http://www.wahenga.net/node/223.

RNA (RuralNet Associates). 2007. "Case Study on the Chipata and Kazungula Social Cash Transfer Schemes by CARE International." Regional Hunger and Vulnerability Programme, Johannesburg.

Sabates-Wheeler, Rachel, and Stephen Devereux. 2010. "Cash Transfers and High Food Prices: Explaining Outcomes on Ethiopia's Productive Safety Net Programme." *Food Policy* 35 (4): 274–85.

Samson, Michael. 2007. "African Perspectives on Cash Transfers: The Developmental Impact of Social Transfers." PowerPoint presentation at the Africa Regional Workshop on Cash Transfer Programmes for Vulnerable Groups, Mombasa, Kenya, February 26–28.

Samson, Michael, and Shesangai Kaniki. 2008. "Social Pensions as Developmental Social Security for Africa." *Poverty in Focus* 15 (August): 22–23.

Samson, Michael, Una Lee, Asanda Ndlebe, Kenneth Mac Quene, Ingrid van Niekerk, Viral Gandhi, Tomoko Harigaya, and Celeste Abrahams. 2004. *The Social and Economic Impact of South Africa's Social Security System.* Cape Town, South Africa: Economic Policy Research Institute.

SASSA (South African Social Security Agency). 2009. "Statistical Report on Social Grants." Report 17, Strategy and Business Development Branch, Monitoring and Evaluation Department, SASSA, Pretoria.

Save the Children UK. 2009. *How Cash Transfers Can Improve the Nutrition of the Poorest Children: Evaluation of a Pilot Safety Net Project in Southern Niger.* London: Save the Children.

Schubert, Bernd. 2003. "Social Welfare Interventions for AIDS Affected Households in Zambia." German Agency for Technical Cooperation, Lusaka.

———. 2007a. "Manual of Operations for the Malawi Pilot Social Cash Transfer Scheme." United Nations Children's Fund, Lilongwe.

———. 2007b. "Piloting the Scale Up of the Malawi Social Cash Transfer Scheme (Fifth Report: January–June 2007)." United Nations Children's Fund, Lilongwe.

———. 2009. "Targeting Social Cash Transfers: The Process of Defining Target Groups and the Targeting Mechanism for the Malawi Social Cash Transfer Scheme." Regional Hunger and Vulnerability Programme, Johannesburg.

Schubert, Bernd, and Mayke Huijbregts. 2006. "The Malawi Social Cash Transfer Pilot Scheme, Preliminary Lessons Learned." Presented at the conference on Social Protection Initiatives for Children, Women, and Families: An Analysis of Recent Experiences, New York, October 30–31.

Schüring, Esther. 2010. "Strings Attached or Loose Ends? The Role of Conditionality in Zambia's Social Cash Transfer Scheme." Maastricht Graduate School of Governance, Maastricht, Netherlands.

Sharp, Kay, Taylor Brown, and Amdissa Teshome. 2006. *Targeting Ethiopia's Productive Safety Net Programme (PSNP).* Addis Ababa: Overseas Development Institute, IDL Group, and A-Z Capacity Building Consult.

Slater, Rachel, Steve Ashley, Mulugeta Tefera, Mengistu Buta, and Delelegne Esubalew. 2006. "PSNP Policy, Programme, and Institutional Linkages." Overseas Development Institute, IDL Group UK, and Indak International, London.

Soares, Fábio Veras, Guilherme Issamu Hirata, and Rafael Rivas. n.d. "The Programa Subsidio de Alimentos in Mozambique: Baseline Evaluation." International Policy Centre for Inclusive Growth, Brasília.

Soares, Fábio Veras, and Clarissa Teixeira. 2010. "Impact Evaluation of the Expansion of the Food Subsidy Programme in Mozambique." Research Brief 17, International Policy Centre for Inclusive Growth, Brasília.

South African Government Services. 2009. "Social Services." South African Government Services, Pretoria. http://www.services.gov.za/.

Streak, Judith. 2007. "Brief Overview of Cash Transfer System in South Africa and Introduction to HSRC Going to Scale Research Project." PowerPoint presentation at the Africa Regional Workshop on Cash Transfer Programmes for Vulnerable Groups, Mombasa, Kenya, February 26–28.

Sultan, Sonya M., and Tamar T. Schrofer. 2008. "Building Support to Have Targeted Social Protection Interventions for the Poorest: The Case of Ghana." Presented at the Conference on Social Protection for the Poorest in Africa: Learning from Experience, Kampala, September 8–10.

Tandeo, Andrew. 2005. "Internal Monitoring System: Summary Report on the Use of Transfers."

Tanzania Team. 2007. "Cash Transfer Programmes: Experiences, Challenges, and the Way Forward for Tanzania." PowerPoint presentation at the Africa Regional Workshop on Cash Transfer Programmes for Vulnerable Groups, Mombasa, Kenya, February 26–28.

TASAF (Tanzania Social Action Fund). 2008. "Tanzania Community-Based Conditional Cash Transfer Pilot." TASAF, Dar es Salaam.

Troger, Franziska, and Vicky Tennant. 2008. "The Use of Cash Grants in UNHCR Voluntary Repatriation Operations: Report of a 'Lessons Learned' Workshop." Policy Development and Evaluation Service, United Nations High Commissioner for Refugees, Geneva.

UNHCR (Office of the United Nations High Commissioner for Refugees). 2007. "Burundi." In *Global Report 2007*, 169–73. Geneva: UNHCR.

UNICEF (United Nations Children's Fund). n.d.a. "The Lesotho Child Grants Programme." UNICEF, Maseru.

———. n.d.b. "Services for Children in Need." UNICEF, Windhoek.

———. 2008. "Review of the Child Support Grant: Uses, Implementation, and Obstacles." Community Agency for Social Enquiry, Johannesburg.

———. 2009. "La Protection Sociale et les Enfants en Afrique de l'Ouest et du Centre: Le Cas du Mali." Ministry of Social Development, Solidarity, and Elderly People and UNICEF, Bamako.

UNICEF (United Nations Children's Fund) and Government of Malawi. 2009. "The Malawi Experience: Social Cash Transfer and Their Multiple Impacts on Child Health, Nutrition, Food Security and Education." PowerPoint presentation, Lilongwe, March 10.

U.S. Social Security Administration. 2009. *Social Security Programs throughout the World: Africa, 2009*. Washington, DC: Office of Retirement and Disability Policy Office of Research, Evaluation, and Statistics.

Waterhouse, Rachel. 2007. "Briefing Paper: Coordination and Coverage of Social Protection Initiatives in Mozambique." International Policy Centre for Inclusive Growth, Brasília. http://www.ipc-undp.org/.

Watkins, Ben. 2008a. "Addendum to the Report 'Alternative Methods for Targeting Social Assistance to Highly Vulnerable Groups.'" Kimetrica, Washington, DC.

———. 2008b. "Alternative Methods for Targeting Social Assistance to Highly Vulnerable Groups: Independent Monitoring and Evaluation Study." Final report, Kimetrica, Washington, DC.

Williams, Martin J. 2007. "The Social and Economic Impacts of South Africa's Child Support Grant." Working Paper 39, Economic Policy Research Institute, Cape Town, South Africa.

Willmore, Larry. 2003. "Universal Pensions in Mauritius: Lessons for the Rest of Us." DESA Discussion Paper 32, Department of Economic and Social Affairs, United Nations, New York.

Wiseman, Will, and Ulrich Hess. 2008. "Incorporating Weather Indices into Early Warning Systems for Emergency Response and Social Protection: Ethiopia." Presentation at the World Bank, Washington, DC, October 1.

Woolard, Ingrid, and Murray Leibbrandt. 2010. "The Evolution and Impact of Unconditional Cash Transfers in South Africa." Southern Africa Labour and Development Research Unit, University of Cape Town, Cape Town, South Africa.

World Bank. n.d. "CCT in Nigeria: Preliminary Concept Note." World Bank, Washington, DC.

———. 2005. "Conditional Cash Transfers for Vulnerable Children in Kenya: Frequently Asked Questions." World Bank, Washington, DC.

———. 2008. "Joint World Bank–DFID–ESSPIN–UNICEF Partners Mission on Girls' Education Conditional Cash Transfers Pilot Programme for Northern Nigeria (Kano and Bauchi States)." World Bank, Washington, DC.

———. 2009a. "A Brief on the Current State of Social Protection in Mozambique." Social Protection Unit, Human Development Network, Eastern and Southern Africa, Africa Region, World Bank, Washington, DC.

———. 2009b. "Emergency Project Paper under the Global Food Crisis Response Program on a Proposed Grant from the Multi-Donor Trust Fund in the Amount of US$8 Million and a Proposed Credit in the Amount of SDR 6.8 Million (US$10 Million Equivalent) to the Republic of Senegal for a Rapid Response Child-Focused Social Cash Transfer and Nutrition Security Project." Human Development II, Country Department AFCF1, Africa Region, World Bank, Washington, DC.

———. 2009c. Nigeria: Conditional Grant and Cash Transfer Project." Project Concept Note, Social Protection, Africa Region, World Bank, Washington, DC.

———. 2009d. "Program Document on a Proposed Grant in the Amount of SDR 4 Million (US$6 Million Equivalent) Funding to the Republic of Rwanda for a First Community Living Standards Grant (CLSG-1)." Human Development III, Eastern Africa Country Cluster II, Africa Region, World Bank, Washington, DC.

———. 2009e. "Project Appraisal Document for a Cash Transfer for Orphans and Vulnerable Children Project." World Bank, Washington, DC.

———. 2010a. *Designing and Implementing a Rural Safety Net in a Low Income Setting: Lessons Learned from Ethiopia's Productive Safety Net Program 2005–2009*. Washington, DC: World Bank.

———. 2010b. "Malawi and Tanzania Research Shows Promise in Preventing HIV and Sexually Transmitted Infections." World Bank, Washington, DC. http://web.worldbank.org/WBSITE/EXTERNAL/COUNTRIES/AFRICAEXT/EXTAFRHEANUTPOP/EXTAFRREGTOPHIVAIDS/0,,contentMDK:22649337~menuPK:717155~pagePK:34004173~piPK:34003707~theSitePK:717148,00.html.

———. 2010c. Project Appraisal Document on a Proposed Credit in the Amount of SDR 58.4 Million (US$88.6 Million Equivalent) in the Amount of SDR 31.3 Million (US$47.6 Million Equivalent) in Pilot CRW Resources to the Republic of Ghana for a Social Opportunities Project." Western Africa I, Social Protection, Africa Region, World Bank, Washington, DC.

———. 2010d. "Review of the Tanzania Community-Based Conditional Cash Transfer Pilot Program." Annex to *Aide-Memoire*. Tanzania Social Action Fund Project. Washington, DC: World Bank.

———. 2011. "Managing Risk, Promoting Growth: Developing Systems for Social Protection in Africa—Africa Social Protection Strategy 2011–2021." Concept Note, World Bank, Washington, DC.

WFP (World Food Programme). 2009. "Protracted Relief and Recovery Operations Approved by Correspondence Between the First Regular Session and the Annual Session 2009: Uganda 10121.3." Executive Board Annual Session, WFP, Rome, June 8–12.

APPENDIX B

Overview Tables

Note: In charts listing individual programs, extremely small, short-term programs are typically not displayed.

Table B.1 Number of Cash Transfers Identified by Country, 2000–09

Country	Number of cash transfers
Botswana	3
Burkina Faso	2
Burundi	2
Cape Verde	1
Central African Republic	1
Congo, Dem. Rep.	2
Congo, Rep.	2
Côte d'Ivoire	1
Eritrea	1
Ethiopia	7
Ghana	1
Kenya	4
Lesotho	3
Liberia	3
Malawi	8
Mali	1
Mauritius	8
Mozambique	4
Namibia	6
Niger	3
Nigeria	2
Rwanda	4
São Tomé and Príncipe	1
Senegal	5
Seychelles	2
Sierra Leone	3
Somalia	8
South Africa	6
Sudan	1
Swaziland	3
Tanzania	6
Togo	1
Uganda	1
Zambia	9
Zimbabwe	8
Total	**123**

Source: Authors' compilation.

Table B.2 Focus of Selected Cash Transfer Programs

Long-term focus		Crisis focus	
Poverty or food security	Human capital	Natural disaster or food security	Human-made disasters
Botswana Old Age Pension	Burkina Faso Conditional Cash Transfer–Cash Transfer	Kenya Isiolo Emergency Drought Transfers	Burundi UNHCR Cash Grants
Botswana Program for Destitute Persons	Eritrea Results-Based Financing	Lesotho Cash and Food Transfers Pilot Project	Central African Republic UNHCR Repatriation Grants
Cape Verde Minimum Social Pension	Kenya Cash Transfer for Orphans and Vulnerable Children	Malawi Dowa Emergency Cash Transfer Project	Republic of Congo Repatriation Grants
Ethiopia Productive Safety Net Programme–Direct Support			
Ghana Livelihood Empowerment against Poverty	Malawi Zomba Cash Transfer	Malawi Food and Cash Transfer Programme	Côte d'Ivoire Repatriation Grants
Kenya Hunger Safety Net Programme	Mali Bourse Maman	Malawi Oxfam Emergency Transfers	Democratic Republic of Congo Emergency Cash Grants
Lesotho Child Grants Programme	Nigeria COPE (In Care of the Poor) Conditional Cash Transfer	Mozambique Cash Grants for Disaster Response	Liberia Cash Grants for Ex-combatants
Lesotho Old Age Pension	Nigeria Kano Conditional Cash Transfer for Girls' Education	Mozambique Emergency Flood Transfers	Liberia Repatriation Cash Grants
Malawi Social Cash Transfer	São Tomé and Príncipe Bolsa Escola	Niger CARE Disaster Risk Reduction Transfers	Rwanda Child Soldiers Reintegration Grant
Mauritius Food Aid	Senegal Conditional Cash Transfer for Orphans and Vulnerable Children	Niger Tanout Cash Transfer Project	Sierra Leone Reinsertion Benefits
Mozambique Food Subsidy Program	Tanzania Community-Based Conditional Cash Transfer	Swaziland Emergency Drought Response	Somalia UNHCR Transfers
Namibia Grants System		Tanzania Save the Children UK Transfers	Sudan Cash Transfer for Ex-combatants

(continued next page)

Table B.2 *(continued)*

Long-term focus		Crisis focus	
Poverty or food security	Human capital	Natural disaster or food security	Human-made disasters
Nigeria COPE (In Care of the Poor) Conditional Cash Transfer		Zambia Cash Grants I (Mongu and Kaoma Transfers)	Togo UNHCR Grants
Rwanda Vision 2020 Umurenge Programme		Zambia Flood Cash Grants I	
South African Grants System			
Zambia Social Cash Transfers (Chipata, Kalomo, Katete, Kazungula, and Monze)			
Zimbabwe Care for the Elderly			
Zimbabwe Drought Relief			
Zimbabwe Protracted Relief Program			
Zimbabwe Support to Families in Distress			

Source: Authors' compilation.
Note: UNHCR = Office of the United Nations High Commissioner for Refugees.

Table B.3 Presence of Conditional and Unconditional Transfers by Country

Country	Conditional transfer	Unconditional transfer
Botswana		✓
Burkina Faso	✓	✓
Burundi		✓
Cape Verde		✓
Central African Republic		✓
Congo, Dem. Rep.		✓
Congo, Rep.		✓
Côte d'Ivoire		✓
Eritrea	✓	
Ethiopia	✓	✓
Ghana	✓	
Kenya	✓	✓
Lesotho		✓
Liberia		✓
Malawi	✓	✓
Mali	✓	✓
Mauritius		✓
Mozambique		✓
Namibia		✓
Niger	✓	✓
Nigeria	✓	
Rwanda		✓
São Tomé and Príncipe	✓	
Senegal	✓	✓
Seychelles		✓
Sierra Leone		✓
Somalia		✓
South Africa		✓
Sudan		✓
Swaziland		✓
Tanzania	✓	✓
Zambia	✓	✓
Zimbabwe		✓

Source: Authors' compilation.

Table B.4 Conditional and Unconditional Transfers by Program

Program	Type of transfer
Botswana Old Age Pension	Unconditional
Botswana Orphan Care Program	Unconditional
Botswana Program for Destitute Persons	Unconditional
Burkina Faso Pilot Conditional Cash Transfer–Cash Transfer	Conditional or unconditional
Burundi UNHCR Cash Grants	Unconditional
Cape Verde Minimum Social Pension	Unconditional
Democratic Republic of Congo Emergency Cash Grants	Unconditional
Eritrea Results-Based Financing	Conditional
Ethiopia Productive Safety Net Programme–Direct Support	Unconditional
Ghana Livelihood Empowerment Against Poverty[a]	Conditional
Kenya Cash Transfer for Orphans and Vulnerable Children[a]	Conditional
Kenya Hunger Safety Net Programme	Unconditional
Lesotho Child Grants Programme	Unconditional
Lesotho Old Age Pension	Unconditional
Malawi Social Cash Transfer	Unconditional
Malawi Zomba Cash Transfer	Conditional or unconditional
Mali Bourse Maman	Conditional
Mauritius Basic Invalid's Pension	Unconditional
Mauritius Basic Orphan's Pension	Unconditional
Mauritius Basic Widow's Pension	Unconditional
Mauritius Carer's Allowance	Unconditional
Mauritius Child Allowance	Unconditional
Mauritius Food Aid	Unconditional
Mauritius Old Age Pension	Unconditional
Mauritius Social Aid	Unconditional
Mozambique Food Subsidy Program	Unconditional
Namibia Child Maintenance Grant	Unconditional
Namibia Disability Grant	Unconditional
Namibia Foster Care Grant	Unconditional
Namibia Old Age Pension	Unconditional
Namibia Special Maintenance Grant	Unconditional
Nigeria COPE (In Care of the Poor) Conditional Cash Transfer	Conditional
Nigeria Kano Conditional Cash Transfer for Girls' Education	Conditional
Rwanda Vision 2020 Umurenge Program	Unconditional
Senegal Conditional Cash Transfer for Orphans and Vulnerable Children	Conditional
Senegal Child-Focused Social Cash Transfer	Unconditional
Senegal Old Age Pension	Unconditional
Seychelles Old Age Pension	Unconditional
Seychelles Orphan Transfer	Unconditional
Sierra Leone Unconditional Cash Transfer for the Old and Needy	Unconditional
South Africa Care Dependency Grant	Unconditional

(continued next page)

Table B.4 *(continued)*

Program	Type of transfer
South Africa Child Support Grant	Unconditional
South Africa Disability Grant	Unconditional
South Africa Foster Care Grant	Unconditional
South Africa Grant for Carers of the Aged	Unconditional
South Africa Old Age Pension	Unconditional
Swaziland Old Age Grant	Unconditional
Swaziland Public Assistance Grant	Unconditional
Tanzania Community-Based Conditional Cash Transfer	Conditional
Tanzania Rewarding STI Prevention and Control in Tanzania (RESPECT)	Conditional
Zambia Chipata Social Cash Transfer	Conditional
Zambia Kalomo Social Cash Transfer	Unconditional
Zambia Katete Social Cash Transfer	Unconditional
Zambia Kazungula Social Cash Transfer	Unconditional
Zambia Monze Social Cash Transfer	Unconditional
Zimbabwe Care for the Elderly	Unconditional
Zimbabwe Drought Relief	Unconditional
Zimbabwe Maintenance of Disabled Persons	Unconditional
Zimbabwe Maintenance of Hero's Dependents	Unconditional
Zimbabwe Protracted Relief Program	Unconditional
Zimbabwe Support to Children in Difficult Circumstances	Unconditional
Zimbabwe Support to Families in Distress	Unconditional

Source: Authors' compilation.
Note: UNHCR = Office of the United Nations High Commissioner for Refugees.
a. Ghana's LEAP program and Kenya's Cash Transfer for Orphans and Vulnerable Children have only begun to enforce conditions over time.

Table B.5 Program Approach, Selected Cash Transfers

Program approach	Transfers to specific vulnerable groups
Conditional cash transfers	Eritrea Results-Based Financing Ghana Livelihood Empowerment against Poverty Kenya Cash Transfer for Orphans and Vulnerable Children Malawi Zomba Cash Transfer Mali Bourse Maman Nigeria Kano Conditional Cash Transfer for Girls' Education Senegal Conditional Cash Transfer for Orphans and Vulnerable Children Tanzania Rewarding STI Prevention and Control in Tanzania (RESPECT)

(continued next page)

Table B.5 *(continued)*

Program approach	Transfers to specific vulnerable groups
Unconditional cash transfers	Botswana Orphan Care Program Botswana Old Age Pension Burundi UNHCR Cash Grants Democratic Republic of Congo Emergency Cash Grants Lesotho Child Grants Programme Lesotho Old Age Pension Malawi Zomba Cash Transfer Mauritius Basic Orphan's Pension Mauritius Basic Widow's Pension Mauritius Carer's Allowance Mauritius Child Allowance Mozambique Food Subsidy Program Namibia Disability Grant Namibia Foster Care Grant Namibia Old Age Pension Namibia Special Maintenance Grant Rwanda Vision 2020 Umurenge Program Senegal Child-Focused Social Cash Transfer Seychelles Old Age Pension Seychelles Orphan Transfer Sierra Leone Unconditional Cash Transfer for the Old and Needy South Africa Foster Care Grant Swaziland Old Age Grant Zambia Chipata Social Cash Transfer Zambia Kalomo Social Cash Transfer Zambia Katete Social Cash Transfer Zambia Kazungula Social Cash Transfer Zambia Monze Social Cash Transfer Zimbabwe Care for the Elderly Zimbabwe Drought Relief Zimbabwe Maintenance of Disabled Persons Zimbabwe Maintenance of Hero's Dependents Zimbabwe Support to Children in Difficult Circumstances Zimbabwe Support to Families in Distress
Program approach	**Poverty-targeted social assistance**
Unconditional cash transfers	Cape Verde Minimum Social Pension Mauritius Social Aid
Program approach	**Mixture of vulnerability and poverty targeting**
Conditional cash transfers	Burkina Faso Pilot Conditional Cash Transfer–Cash Transfer Nigeria COPE (In Care of the Poor) Conditional Cash Transfer Tanzania Community-Based Conditional Cash Transfer

(continued next page)

Table B.5 *(continued)*

Program approach	Transfers to specific vulnerable groups
Unconditional cash transfers	Botswana Program for Destitute Persons
	Burkina Faso Pilot Conditional Cash Transfer–Cash Transfer
	Ethiopia Productive Safety Net Programme–Direct Support
	Malawi Social Cash Transfer
	Namibia Child Maintenance Grant
	Niger Pilot Cash Transfer
	Senegal Old Age Pension
	South Africa Care Dependency Grant
	South Africa Child Support Grant
	South Africa Disability Grant
	South Africa Grant for Carers of the Aged
	South Africa Old Age Pension
	Swaziland Public Assistance Grant
	Zimbabwe Protracted Relief Program

Source: Authors' compilation.
Note: UNHCR = Office of the United Nations High Commissioner for Refugees.

Table B.6 Programs by Scale, Selected Cash Transfers

Program scale	Program
Pilot	Burkina Faso Pilot Conditional Cash Transfer–Cash Transfer
	Eritrea Results-Based Financing
	Ghana Livelihood Empowerment against Poverty
	Kenya Hunger Safety Net Programme
	Lesotho Child Grants Programme
	Malawi Zomba Cash Transfer
	Mali Bourse Maman
	Malawi Social Cash Transfer
	Niger Pilot Cash Transfer
	Nigeria Kano Conditional Cash Transfer for Girls' Education
	Nigeria COPE (In Care of the Poor) Conditional Cash Transfer
	Rwanda Vision 2020 Umurenge Program
	Senegal Conditional Cash Transfer for Orphans and Vulnerable Children
	Senegal Child-Focused Social Cash Transfer
	Sierra Leone Unconditional Cash Transfer for the Old and Needy
	Tanzania Community-Based Conditional Cash Transfer
	Tanzania Rewarding STI Prevention and Control in Tanzania (RESPECT)
	Zambia Chipata Social Cash Transfer
	Zambia Kalomo Social Cash Transfer
	Zambia Katete Social Cash Transfer
	Zambia Kazungula Social Cash Transfer
	Zambia Monze Social Cash Transfer
	Zimbabwe Protracted Relief Program

(continued next page)

Table B.6 *(continued)*

Program scale	Program
Niche	Burundi UNHCR Cash Grants
	Democratic Republic of Congo Emergency Cash Grants
	Swaziland Public Assistance Grant
	Zimbabwe Drought Relief
Nationwide or large scale	Botswana Old Age Pension
	Botswana Orphan Care Program
	Botswana Program for Destitute Persons
	Cape Verde Minimum Social Pension
	Ethiopia Productive Safety Net Programme–Direct Support
	Kenya Cash Transfer for Orphans and Vulnerable Children
	Lesotho Old Age Pension
	Mauritius Basic Orphan's Pension
	Mauritius Basic Invalid's Pension
	Mauritius Basic Widow's Pension
	Mauritius Carer's Allowance
	Mauritius Child Allowance
	Mauritius Food Aid
	Mauritius Social Aid
	Mozambique Food Subsidy Program
	Namibia Child Maintenance Grant
	Namibia Disability Grant
	Namibia Foster Care Grant
	Namibia Old Age Pension
	Namibia Special Maintenance Grant
	Senegal Old Age Pension
	Seychelles Old Age Pension
	Seychelles Orphan Transfer
	South Africa Care Dependency Grant
	South Africa Child Support Grant
	South Africa Disability Grant
	South Africa Foster Care Grant
	South Africa Grant for Carers of the Aged
	South Africa Old Age Pension
	Swaziland Old Age Grant
	Zimbabwe Care for the Elderly
	Zimbabwe Maintenance of Disabled Persons
	Zimbabwe Maintenance of Hero's Dependents
	Zimbabwe Support to Children in Difficult Circumstances
	Zimbabwe Support to Families in Distress

Source: Authors' compilation.
Note: UNHCR = Office of the United Nations High Commissioner for Refugees.

Table B.7 Programs by Life Stage Focus, Selected Cash Transfers

Maternal or early childhood	Children or young adults	Adult	Elderly	Mixture
Eritrea Results-Based Financing	Botswana Orphan Care Program	Mauritius Basic Invalid's Pension	Botswana Old Age Pension	Ghana Livelihood Empowerment against Poverty
Senegal Child-Focused Social Cash Transfer	Burkina Faso Pilot Conditional Cash Transfer–Cash Transfer	Mauritius Social Aid	Cape Verde Minimum Social Pension	Mozambique Food Subsidy Program
	Kenya Cash Transfer for Orphans and Vulnerable Children	Namibia Disability Grant	Lesotho Old Age Pension	Nigeria COPE (In Care of the Poor) Conditional Cash Transfer
	Lesotho Child Grants Programme	South Africa Disability Grant	Mauritius Basic Widow's Pension	Tanzania Community-Based Conditional Cash Transfer
	Malawi Zomba Cash Transfer		Mauritius Old Age Pension	
	Mali Bourse Maman	Tanzania Rewarding STI Prevention and Control in Tanzania (RESPECT)		
		Zimbabwe Maintenance of Disabled Persons	Namibia Old Age Pension	
	Mauritius Carer's Allowance		Senegal Old Age Pension	
			Seychelles Old Age Pension	
	Mauritius Child Allowance		Sierra Leone Unconditional Cash Transfer for the Old and Needy	
	Namibia Child Maintenance Grant			
	Namibia Special Maintenance Grant			
			South Africa Grant for Carers of the Aged	
	Nigeria Kano Conditional Cash Transfer for Girls' Education		South Africa Old Age Pension	
	Senegal Conditional Cash Transfer for Orphans and Vulnerable Children		Swaziland Old Age Grant	
	Seychelles Orphan Transfer		Zimbabwe Care for the Elderly	
	South Africa Care Dependency Grant		Zimbabwe Maintenance of Hero's Dependents	
	South Africa Child Support Grant			
	Zimbabwe Support to Children in Difficult Circumstances			

Source: Authors' compilation.

Table B.8 Approximate Number of Beneficiaries Covered by Programs

Program	Individual beneficiaries	Number of households	Notes or date when available
Botswana Old Age Pension	89,471	—	February 2009
Botswana Orphan Care Program	49,852	—	February 2009
Botswana Program for Destitute Persons	40,525	—	February 2009
Burkina Faso Pilot Conditional Cash Transfer—Cash Transfer	—	2,000	2008
Cape Verde Minimum Social Pension	8,040	—	2006
Democratic Republic of Congo Emergency Cash Transfers	120,000	—	2004
Ethiopia Productive Safety Net Programme—Direct Support	1,200,000	242,383	2009
Ghana Livelihood Empowerment against Poverty	—	8,200	May 2009
Kenya Cash Transfer for Orphans and Vulnerable Children	—	74,000	June 2009
Kenya Hunger Safety Net Programme	—	60,000	2009
Lesotho Child Grants Programme	5,000	1,250	2009
Lesotho Old Age Pension	78,064	—	March 2009
Malawi Social Cash Transfer	94,386	24,051	July 2009
Malawi Zomba Cash Transfer	1,230	—	2008
Mali Bourse Maman	—	430–500 annually	2002–07
Mauritius Old Age Pension	148,800	—	2007
Mozambique Food Subsidy Program	287,454	—	2008
Namibia Child Maintenance Grant	86,100	—	2008
Namibia Disability Grant	20,400	—	2008
Namibia Foster Care Grant	13,400	—	2008
Namibia Old Age Pension	130,500	—	2008
Niger Pilot Cash Transfer	—	1,500	2008

Nigeria COPE (In Care of the Poor) Conditional Cash Transfer	—	12,000	2007
Nigeria Kano Conditional Cash Transfer for Girls' Education	12,000	10,000	2009
Senegal Conditional Cash Transfer for Orphans and Vulnerable Children	5,000	—	2008
Sierra Leone Unconditional Cash Transfer for the Old and Needy	35,000	—	2009 (anticipated)
South Africa Child Support Grant	8,826,000	—	April 2009
South Africa Disability Grant	1,282,000	—	April 2009
South Africa Foster Care Grant	483,000	—	April 2009
South Africa Old Age Pension	2,414,000	—	April 2009
Swaziland Old Age Grant	60,000	—	2007
Swaziland Public Assistance Grant	2,255	—	2007
Tanzania Rewarding STI Prevention and Control in Tanzania (RESPECT)	1,500	—	2009 (reflects conditional cash transfer recipients only)
Zambia Chipata Social Cash Transfer	—	1,163	Mid-2009
Zambia Kalomo Social Cash Transfer	—	3,575	Mid-2009
Zambia Katete Social Cash Transfer	4,500	—	Mid-2009
Zambia Kazungula Social Cash Transfer	—	735	Mid-2009
Zambia Monze Social Cash Transfer	—	2,069	Mid-2010 (anticipated)
Zimbabwe Care for the Elderly	39,468	—	2005
Zimbabwe Maintenance of Disabled Persons	21,535	—	2005

Source: Authors' compilation.
Note: — = not available.

Table B.9 Groups Targeted, Selected Cash Transfers

Group targeted	Program
Mothers or young children	Eritrea Results-Based Financing
	Senegal Child-Focused Social Cash Transfer
Orphans and vulnerable children	Botswana Orphan Care Program
	Kenya Cash Transfer for Orphans and Vulnerable Children
	Lesotho Child Grants Programme
	Mauritius Basic Orphan's Pension
	Mauritius Child Allowance
	Senegal Conditional Cash Transfer for Orphans and Vulnerable Children
	Seychelles Orphan Transfer
	Zimbabwe Support to Children in Difficult Circumstances
Children and adolescents, general	Malawi Zomba Cash Transfer
	Mali Bourse Maman
	Nigeria Kano Conditional Cash Transfer for Girls' Education
	South Africa Child Support Grant
Caregivers of children	Mauritius Carer's Allowance
	Namibia Foster Care Grant
	South Africa Foster Care Grant
Refugees	Burundi UNHCR Cash Grants
Ex-combatants	Democratic Republic of Congo Emergency Cash Grants
People with disabilities	Mauritius Basic Invalid's Pension
	Namibia Disability Grant
	Namibia Special Maintenance Grant
	South Africa Care Dependency Grant
	South Africa Disability Grant
	Zimbabwe Maintenance of Disabled Persons
Food-insecure people	Kenya Hunger Safety Net Programme
	Zimbabwe Drought Relief
Labor-constrained people	Botswana Program for Destitute Persons
	Cape Verde Minimum Social Pension
	Ethiopia Productive Safety Net Programme–Direct Support
	Mozambique Food Subsidy Program
	Zambia Chipata Social Cash Transfer
	Zambia Kalomo Social Cash Transfer
	Zambia Kazungula Social Cash Transfer
	Zambia Monze Social Cash Transfer
	Zimbabwe Support to Families in Distress
Poor people	Mauritius Social Aid

(continued next page)

Table B.9 *(continued)*

Group targeted	Program
Elderly people	Botswana Old Age Pension
	Lesotho Old Age Pension
	Mauritius Old Age Pension
	Namibia Old Age Pension
	Senegal Old Age Pension
	Seychelles Old Age Pension
	Sierra Leone Unconditional Cash Transfer for the Old and Needy
	South Africa Old Age Pension
	Swaziland Old Age Grant
	Zambia Katete Social Cash Transfer
	Zimbabwe Care for the Elderly
Mixture	Burkina Faso Pilot Conditional Cash Transfer–Cash Transfer
	Cape Verde Minimum Social Pension
	Ghana Livelihood Empowerment against Poverty
	Malawi Social Cash Transfer
	Namibia Child Maintenance Grant
	Niger Pilot Cash Transfer
	Nigeria COPE (In Care of the Poor) Conditional Cash Transfer
	Rwanda Vision 2020 Umurenge Programme
	South Africa Care Dependency Grant
	Swaziland Public Assistance Grant
	Tanzania Community-Based Conditional Cash Transfer
	Zimbabwe Maintenance Allowance in the Public Assistance Program
	Zimbabwe Protracted Relief Program
Other	Mauritius Basic Widow's Pension
	South Africa Grant for Carers of the Aged
	Tanzania Rewarding STI Prevention and Control in Tanzania (RESPECT)
	Zimbabwe Maintenance of Hero's Dependents

Source: Authors' compilation.
Note: UNHCR = Office of the United Nations High Commissioner for Refugees.

Table B.10 Targeting Methods, Selected Cash Transfers

Program	Categorical (excludes geographic category)	Means tested	Proxy means	Geographic	Community	Self-targeted
Botswana Orphan Care Program	✓					
Botswana Program for Destitute Persons	✓	✓			✓	✓
Botswana Old Age Pension	✓				✓	
Burkina Faso Pilot Conditional Cash Transfer–Cash Transfer	✓		✓			
Burundi UNHCR Cash Grants	✓					
Cape Verde Minimum Social Pension	✓	✓				
Democratic Republic of Congo Emergency Cash Transfers	✓			✓		
Eritrea Results-Based Financing	✓					
Ethiopia Productive Safety Net Programme–Direct Support	✓			✓	✓	
Ghana Livelihood Empowerment against Poverty	✓		✓	✓	✓	
Kenya Cash Transfer for Orphans and Vulnerable Children	✓		✓	✓	✓	
Kenya Hunger Safety Net Programme[a]	✓			✓	✓	
Lesotho Child Grants Programme[b]	✓			✓	✓	
Lesotho Old Age Pension	✓				✓	✓
Malawi Social Cash Transfer	✓				✓	

Program								
Mali Bourse Maman	✓			✓				
Mauritius Old Age Pension	✓	✓		✓				
Mozambique Food Subsidy Program[c]	✓	✓		✓				
Namibia Child Maintenance Grant[d]	✓	✓	✓					
Namibia Disability Grant	✓		✓	✓				
Namibia Foster Care Grant	✓	✓		✓				
Namibia Old Age Pension[d]	✓	✓		✓				
Namibia Special Maintenance Grant	✓			✓				
Niger Pilot Cash Transfer	✓			✓				
Nigeria COPE (In Care of the Poor) Conditional Cash Transfer[e]				Varies by state				
Nigeria Kano Conditional Cash Transfer for Girls' Education[f]	✓				✓			
Rwanda Vision 2020 Umurenge Programme	✓	✓			✓			
Senegal Conditional Cash Transfer for Orphans and Vulnerable Children	✓	✓				✓		
Senegal Child-Focused Social Cash Transfer[g]	✓					✓		
Senegal Old Age Pension	✓	✓						
Sierra Leone Unconditional Cash Transfer for the Old and Needy	✓	✓	✓				✓	
South Africa Care Dependency Grant	✓	✓	✓					✓
South Africa Child Support Grant	✓							✓
South Africa Disability Grant	✓							✓
South Africa Foster Care Grant	✓							✓

(continued next page)

Table B.10 (continued)

Program	Categorical (excludes geographic category)	Means tested	Proxy means	Geographic	Community	Self-targeted
South Africa Old Age Grant	✓	✓				
Swaziland Old Age Grant[h]	✓		✓			
Swaziland Public Assistance Grant[i]		✓				
Tanzania Community-Based Conditional Cash Transfer	✓					
Tanzania Rewarding STI Prevention and Control in Tanzania (RESPECT)	✓					✓
Zambia Chipata Social Cash Transfer[j]			✓	✓		
Zambia Kalomo Social Cash Transfer[j]	✓		✓		✓	
Zambia Katete Social Cash Transfer[j]	✓				✓	
Zambia Kazungula Social Cash Transfer[j]			✓		✓	
Zambia Monze Social Cash Transfer[j]			✓		✓	
Zimbabwe Care for the Elderly	✓					
Zimbabwe Drought Relief and Public Works Program	✓				✓	✓
Zimbabwe Maintenance of Disabled Persons	✓					✓

| Zimbabwe Support to Children in Difficult Circumstances | | ✓ |
| Zimbabwe Support to Families in Distress[k] | | ✓ |

Source: Authors' compilation.

Note: UNHCR = Office of the United Nations High Commissioner for Refugees.

a. Various methods of targeting will be tested.
b. Children are supposed to apply for the program. Village leaders and social or child welfare officers must locate children in eligible households that have not applied.
c. The program is supposedly means tested, but it is likely unenforced. The community relies on individual health workers and other professionals.
d. A means test is legislated but not implemented.
e. Targeting varies by state and probably utilizes multiple methods.
f. Various methods of targeting have been tested.
g. Program engages in community targeting, and nongovernmental organizations and other groups identify potential beneficiaries.
h. Poverty- and vulnerability-related targeting criteria are not enforced.
i. There is community-based targeting as a result of social workers' involvement.
j. Zambian programs (excluding Katete) are classified as proxy means and community-based targeting because communities rely on multiple specified criteria to select eligible beneficiaries within their localities. These programs meet the geographic targeting criteria because they are piloted in one district; however, they do not use geographic targeting within the selected district.
k. The additional methods used to select beneficiaries for the listed Zimbabwean programs are unclear, particularly in the case of Zimbabwe Support to Families in Distress.

Table B.11 Frequency of Cash Transfer Distribution

Program	Number of transfers per year
Botswana Orphan Care Program	1
Botswana Program for Destitute Persons	1
Botswana Old Age Pension	12
Burkina Faso Pilot Conditional Cash Transfer–Cash Transfer	4
Burundi UNHCR Cash Grants	1
Cape Verde Minimum Social Pension	12
Democratic Republic of Congo Emergency Cash Grants	12
Ethiopia Productive Safety Net Programme–Direct Support	6
Ghana Livelihood Empowerment against Poverty	6
Kenya Cash Transfer for Orphans and Vulnerable Children	6
Kenya Hunger Safety Net Programme	12
Lesotho Child Grants Programme	4
Lesotho Old Age Pension	12
Malawi Social Cash Transfer	12
Malawi Zomba Cash Transfer	10
Mali Bourse Maman	8
Mauritius Old Age Pension	12
Mozambique Food Subsidy Program	12
Namibia Child Maintenance Grant	12
Namibia Disability Grant	12
Namibia Foster Care Grant	12
Namibia Old Age Pension	12
Namibia Special Maintenance Grant	12
Nigeria COPE (In Care of the Poor) Conditional Cash Transfer	12
Nigeria Kano Conditional Cash Transfer for Girls' Education	10
Rwanda Vision 2020 Umurenge Programme	12
Senegal Child-Focused Social Cash Transfer	6
Senegal Conditional Cash Transfer for Orphans and Vulnerable Children	4
Seychelles Orphan Transfer	12
Sierra Leone Unconditional Cash Transfer for the Old and Needy	2
South Africa Care Dependency Grant	12
South Africa Child Support Grant	12
South Africa Disability Grant	12
South Africa Foster Care Grant	12
South Africa Grant for Carers of the Aged	12
South Africa Old Age Pension	12
Swaziland Old Age Grant	4
Tanzania Community-Based Conditional Cash Transfer	6
Tanzania Rewarding STI Prevention and Control in Tanzania (RESPECT)	4
Zambia Chipata Social Cash Transfer	6
Zambia Kalomo Social Cash Transfer	6
Zambia Katete Social Cash Transfer	6
Zambia Kazungula Social Cash Transfer	6

(continued next page)

Table B.11 *(continued)*

Program	Number of transfers per year
Zambia Monze Social Cash Transfer	6
Zimbabwe Care for the Elderly	12
Zimbabwe Drought Relief	12
Zimbabwe Maintenance of Disabled Persons	12
Zimbabwe Maintenance of Hero's Dependents	12
Zimbabwe Protracted Relief Program	12
Zimbabwe Support to Families in Distress	12

Source: Authors' compilation.
Note: UNHCR = Office of the United Nations High Commissioner for Refugees.

Table B.12 Transfer Size, Selected Cash Transfers

Program	Monthly transfer (US$)	Transfer size information	Source
Botswana Old Age Pension	27.00	Real value ranges from US$27 to US$30.	BFTU (2007)
Botswana Orphan Care Program	5.00	Program provides much larger in-kind transfer.	Bar-On (2002)
Burkina Faso Conditional Cash Transfer–Cash Transfer	0.66 (minimum) 2.66 (maximum)	Transfer size depends on children's ages; transfers are given quarterly. Transfer amounts do not surpass 7.5% of GDP per capita in 1 household with 1 child in the oldest targeted group.	de Walque (2009)
Cape Verde Minimum Social Pension	43.00		Government of Cape Verde (2011)
Democratic Republic of Congo Emergency Cash Grants	25.00	US$110 was provided initially; then US$25 was provided monthly for 1 year.	MDRP (2006)
Ethiopia Productive Safety Net Programme–Direct Support (PSNP-DS)	23.00	Size is based on the annual total transfer value, which equals approximately 10% of the 2007/08 national poverty line. Transfers are given for six months each year. For most PSNP-DS participants, transfers cover more than 10% of household needs. Recent evidence in PSNP-DS communities suggests that transfers cover about 40% of annual food needs.	World Bank (2010a)
Ghana Livelihood Empowerment against Poverty	8.00 (minimum) 15.00 (maximum)	Size equals 20% of the bottom quintile's average household consumption.	World Bank (2010b)
Kenya Cash Transfer for Orphans and Vulnerable Children	14.00 (minimum) 42.00 (maximum)	Size equals approximately 20% of household expenditures of poor households in Kenya.	World Bank (2009c)
Kenya Hunger Safety Net Programme	27.00	Size equals between 30% and 40% of beneficiary households' food expenditures.	HSNP (n.d.)

Program	Value	Description	Source
Lesotho Child Grants Programme	13.00	US$38 is given quarterly.	UNICEF (n.d.)
Lesotho Old Age Pension	35.00	Transfer was originally intended to cover 75% of the cost of meeting the minimum required caloric intake of a 5-person household.	European University Institute (2010)
Malawi Social Cash Transfer	4.00 (minimum) 13.00 (maximum)		Schubert and Huijbregts (2006)
Malawi Zomba Cash Transfer	5.00 (minimum) 15.00 (maximum)	Size equals approximately 15% of cost of eligible households' total monthly consumption. The transfer is given for 10-month periods.	Baird and others (2009)
Mali Bourse Maman	12.00	Transfer is given through the 8-month school year.	UNICEF (2009)
Mauritius Old Age Pension	100.00	Transfer equaled approximately 20% of the country's average wage in 2008.	Central Statistics Office (2007)
Mozambique Food Subsidy Program	4.00 (minimum) 11.00 (maximum)	Transfer equaled 4% to 6% of the country's minimum wage in 2007.	Ellis (2007)
Namibia Old Age Pension	57.00		Levine, van der Berg, and Yu (2009)
Nigeria COPE (In Care of the Poor) Conditional Cash Transfer	13.00 (minimum) 43.00 (maximum)	Size varies by number of children. Additional annual transfer of US$717 is given through the Poverty Reduction Accelerator Investment.	World Bank (2009b)
Nigeria Kano Conditional Cash Transfer for Girls' Education	6.00 (minimum) 12.00 (maximum)	Transfer equaled approximately 20% of gross domestic product per capita in 2007.	Ayala (2009)
Rwanda Vision 2020 Umurenge Programme	13.00 (minimum) 37.00 (maximum)	For households already receiving similar transfers from other programs, transfer size is supposed to be reduced by the amount of the other transfers.	Republic of Rwanda (2009)

(continued next page)

Table B.12 *(continued)*

Program	Monthly transfer (US$)	Transfer size information	Source
Senegal Child-Focused Social Cash Transfer	14.00	Size equals about 14% of average food consumption cost for a household with 4 adults.	World Bank (2009a)
Seychelles Orphan Transfer	116.00		Miller (2006)
Sierra Leone Unconditional Cash Transfer for the Old and Needy	11.33	US$68 is given to each beneficiary every 6 months.	International Poverty Centre (n.d.)
South Africa Child Support Grant	27.00	Size equaled 40% of the median per capita income in 2010.	South African Government Services (2009); Woolard and Leibbrandt (2010)
South Africa Foster Care Grant	76.00	Size equaled 1.15 times the median per capita income in 2010.	South African Government Services (2009), Woolard and Leibbrandt (2010)
South Africa Old Age Pension	112.00	Size equaled 1.75 times the median per capita income in 2010.	South African Government Services (2009), Woolard and Leibbrandt (2010)
Swaziland Old Age Grant	15.00		RHVP (2007)
Tanzania Community-Based Conditional Cash Transfer	6.00 (minimum) 18.00 (maximum)	Transfer equals half of the 2000/01 food poverty line value for each child and equals the 2000/01 food poverty line value for the elderly.	Evans (2008)
Tanzania Rewarding STI Prevention and Control in Tanzania (RESPECT)	3.33 (minimum) 6.66 (maximum)	Transfer equaled up to 24% of annual individual earnings of the study group. US$10 (minimum) or US$20 (maximum) is given quarterly.	de Walque and others (2010)

Zambia Chipata Social Cash Transfer	6.25 (minimum) 11.25 (maximum)	Bimonthly household benefits are K 50,000 (US$12.50). A flat bonus of K 10,000 (US$2.50) is given to households with 2 or more individuals. If households have a child enrolled in primary school, they earn K 10,000 (US$2.50) extra, and children enrolled in secondary school entitle the household to an additional K 20,000 (US$5).	RNA (2007)
Zambia Kalomo Social Cash Transfer	5.00 (minimum) 6.25 (maximum)	Transfer is US$10.00 per household plus US$2.50 for households with a child, given bimonthly.	Ministry of Community Development and Social Services (2007)
Zambia Katete Social Cash Transfer	15.00		Ministry of Community Development and Social Services and German Agency for Technical Cooperation (2007)
Zambia Kazungula Social Cash Transfer	Varies	Bimonthly transfer is US$12.50 per household plus US$5.00 for each child.	Ministry of Community Development and Social Services and German Agency for Technical Cooperation (2007)

Source: Authors' compilation.

Table B.13 Other Benefits Given, Selected Cash Transfers

Country	Program	Benefits given to some or all beneficiaries in addition to regular cash transfers
Botswana	Orphan Care Program	Monthly food rations of P 216 plus additional in-kind support, fee waivers, and other benefits
Botswana	Program for Destitute Persons	P 181 in food rations per month for temporarily destitute, P 256 in food rations for permanently destitute, contact with social worker, and rehabilitation strategies (since 2006)
Burundi	UNHCR Cash Grants	Other in-kind benefits
Cape Verde	Minimum Social Pension	Health care support
Eritrea	Results-Based Financing	Competition to receive monetary prizes through the "Spin the Wheel for Healthy Mothers" contest—22 prizes (US$667 each) awarded; around-the-clock access to emergency transportation to a health center for women in communities with registered drivers; and health care
Kenya	Kenya Cash Transfer for Orphans and Vulnerable Children	Annual awareness sessions covering various health topics
Nigeria	Nigeria COPE (In Care of the Poor) Conditional Cash Transfer	Poverty Reduction Accelerator Investment, a compulsory savings component, which provides approximately US$717 annually after households receive training to create a microenterprise
Senegal	Conditional Cash Transfer for Orphans and Vulnerable Children	Psychosocial support
Sierra Leone	Unconditional Cash Transfer for the Old and Needy	Originally provided a bag of rice with the cash transfer, but rice no longer provided
Tanzania	Community-Based Conditional Cash Transfer	Community banking component
Tanzania	Rewarding STI Prevention and Control in Tanzania (RESPECT)	Psychosocial support, STI testing and treatment
Zimbabwe	Protracted Relief Program	In-kind transfers of farming inputs, training in agricultural activities, home care for the chronically ill, and other benefits
Zimbabwe	Drought Relief and Public Works Program	Bag of grain given until 2006, when all benefits were converted to cash

Source: Authors' compilation.
Note: UNHCR = Office of the United Nations High Commissioner for Refugees.

Table B.14 Gender of Cash Recipient

Program	Female or both[a]
Botswana Old Age Pension	Both
Botswana Orphan Care Program	Both
Botswana Program for Destitute Persons	Both
Burkina Faso Pilot Conditional Cash Transfer–Cash Transfer	Both
Cape Verde Minimum Social Pension	Both
Eritrea Results-Based Financing	Female
Ethiopia Productive Safety Net Programme–Direct Support	Both
Ghana Livelihood Empowerment against Poverty	Both
Kenya Cash Transfer for Orphans and Vulnerable Children	Both
Kenya Hunger Safety Net Programme	Both
Lesotho Child Grants Programme	Both
Lesotho Old Age Pension	Both
Malawi Social Cash Transfer	Both
Malawi Zomba Cash Transfer	Both
Mali Bourse Maman	Female
Mauritius Basic Invalid's Pension	Both
Mauritius Basic Widow's Pension	Female
Mauritius Old Age Pension	Both
Mozambique Food Subsidy Program	Both
Namibia Child Maintenance Grant	Both
Namibia Disability Grant	Both
Namibia Foster Care Grant	Both
Namibia Old Age Pension	Both
Namibia Special Maintenance Grant	Both
Niger Pilot Cash Transfer	Female
Nigeria COPE (In Care of the Poor) Conditional Cash Transfer	Female
Nigeria Kano Conditional Cash Transfer for Girls' Education	Female
Rwanda Vision 2020 Umurenge Programme	Both
Senegal Conditional Cash Transfer for Orphans and Vulnerable Children	Both
Senegal Child-Focused Social Cash Transfer	Female
Senegal Old Age Pension	Both
Seychelles Old Age Pension	Both
Sierra Leone Unconditional Cash Transfer for the Old and Needy	Both
South Africa Care Dependency Grant	Both
South Africa Child Support Grant	Both
South Africa Disability Grant	Both
South Africa Foster Care Grant	Both
South Africa Grant for Carers of the Aged	Both
South Africa Old Age Pension	Both
Swaziland Old Age Grant	Both
Swaziland Public Assistance Grant	Both
Tanzania Rewarding STI Prevention and Control in Tanzania (RESPECT)	Both

(continued next page)

Table B.14 *(continued)*

Program	Female or both[a]
Zambia Chipata Social Cash Transfer	Both
Zambia Kalomo Social Cash Transfer	Both
Zambia Katete Social Cash Transfer	Both
Zambia Kazungula Social Cash Transfer	Both
Zambia Monze Social Cash Transfer	Both

Source: Authors' compilation.
a. "Both" indicates that the program makes payments to either male or female heads of households, caretakers, or other beneficiaries.

Table B.15 Payment Mechanism by Program

Program	Paypoint facility	Local office or bank	Bank account or direct deposit	Mobile phone	Mobile automatic teller machine	Community committee distribution	Other
Botswana Old Age Pension		✓					
Burkina Faso Pilot Conditional Cash Transfer–Cash Transfer						✓	
Burundi UNHCR Cash Grants		✓					
Cape Verde Minimum Social Pension		✓					
Democratic Republic of Congo Emergency Cash Grants				✓			
Eritrea Results-Based Financing		✓					
Ethiopia Productive Safety Net Programme–Direct Support	✓						
Ghana Livelihood Empowerment against Poverty		✓					
Kenya Cash Transfer for Orphans and Vulnerable Children		✓					
Kenya Hunger Safety Net Programme				✓	✓		✓
Lesotho Child Grants Programme	✓						
Lesotho Old Age Pension	✓	✓					
Malawi Zomba Cash Transfer	✓						
Malawi Social Cash Transfer							✓
Mali Bourse Maman	✓						
Mozambique Food Subsidy Program							

(continued next page)

Table B.15 *(continued)*

Program	Paypoint facility	Local office or bank	Bank account or direct deposit	Mobile phone	Mobile automatic teller machine	Community committee distribution	Other
Namibia Child Maintenance Grant		✓					
Namibia Disability Grant		✓	✓				
Namibia Foster Care Grant		✓	✓				
Namibia Old Age Pension		✓	✓				
Namibia Special Maintenance Grant		✓	✓				
Nigeria COPE (In Care of the Poor) Conditional Cash Transfer		✓					
Nigeria Kano Conditional Cash Transfer for Girls' Education		✓		✓			
Rwanda Vision 2020 Umurenge Programme	✓			✓		✓	
Senegal Conditional Cash Transfer for Orphans and Vulnerable Children		✓					
Senegal Child-Focused Social Cash Transfer	✓	✓					
Sierra Leone Unconditional Cash Transfer for the Old and Needy							
South Africa Care Dependency Grant	✓	✓	✓			✓	
South Africa Child Support Grant	✓	✓	✓		✓		
South Africa Disability Grant	✓	✓	✓		✓		
South Africa Foster Care Grant	✓	✓	✓		✓		

Program				
South Africa Grant for Carers of the Aged			✓	
South Africa Old Age Pension	✓		✓	
Swaziland Old Age Grant				
Swaziland Public Assistance Grant				
Tanzania Community-Based Conditional Cash Transfer				✓
Zambia Chipata Social Cash Transfer	✓	✓		
Zambia Kalomo Social Cash Transfer	✓	✓	✓	
Zambia Katete Social Cash Transfer	✓	✓	✓	
Zambia Kazungula Social Cash Transfer	✓	✓	✓	
Zambia Monze Social Cash Transfer	✓	✓	✓	
Zimbabwe Care for the Elderly			✓	
Zimbabwe Drought Relief			✓	
Zimbabwe Maintenance of Disabled Persons			✓	
Zimbabwe Maintenance of Hero's Dependents			✓	
Zimbabwe Support to Children in Difficult Circumstances			✓	
Zimbabwe Support to Families in Distress			✓	

Source: Authors' compilation.
Note: UNHCR = Office of the United Nations High Commissioner for Refugees.

Table B.16 Program Conditions

Program	School enrollment	School attendance	Health requirements for young children	Maternal medical requirements	Household training	National registration	Other
Burkina Faso Pilot Conditional Cash Transfer–Cash Transfer	✓	✓					
Eritrea Results-Based Financing			✓	✓			
Ghana Livelihood Empowerment against Poverty	✓	✓	✓				
Kenya Cash Transfer for Orphans and Vulnerable Children	✓	✓	✓			✓	✓
Malawi Zomba Cash Transfer	✓	✓			✓		
Mali Bourse Maman	✓	✓					
Niger Pilot Cash Transfer					✓		✓
Nigeria Kano Conditional Cash Transfer for Girls' Education	✓	✓	✓				
Nigeria COPE (In Care of the Poor) Conditional Cash Transfer	✓	✓	✓				
Senegal Conditional Cash Transfer for Orphans and Vulnerable Children	✓	✓		✓	✓		
Tanzania Community-Based Conditional Cash Transfer	✓	✓					✓
Tanzania Rewarding STI Prevention and Control in Tanzania (RESPECT)							✓
Zambia Chipata Cash Transfer (soft conditions)[a]		✓					✓

Source: Authors' compilation.

a. Soft conditions require that beneficiary households agree verbally or in writing that they will abide by program conditions. However, there is no penalty for noncompliance.

Table B.17 **Monitoring of Conditions, Selected Cash Transfers**

Program	Monitoring procedure
Burkina Faso Pilot Conditional Cash Transfer–Cash Transfer	Health care centers and schools fill out booklets to track fulfillment of conditions. Village committees conduct additional monitoring.
Eritrea Results-Based Financing	Health and growth monitoring cards are marked by local health care officials. Cards are taken to administrative offices.
Ghana Livelihood Empowerment against Poverty	Most conditions were not yet monitored at time of writing.
Kenya Cash Transfer for Orphans and Vulnerable Children	Children under 1 year have conditions monitored every 2 months, and children between ages 1 and 3 are monitored twice annually. School enrollment of children between ages 6 and 17 is monitored once annually, but school attendance is verified every 3 months (at the end of the school term). Parents' attendance at education sessions is monitored once annually. Teachers and health care workers fill out monitoring forms, which are collected and transported to volunteers and then to the district children officer. The district children officer reports this information to main offices.
Malawi Zomba Cash Transfer	Local NGO collects attendance data and progress report information on students.
Mali Bourse Maman	NGOs and local school officials conduct monitoring.
Nigeria COPE (In Care of the Poor) Conditional Cash Transfer	Monitoring varies by state. Typically, households turn in forms, with the signatures of representatives from relevant institutions, to local program offices.
Nigeria Kano Conditional Cash Transfer for Girls' Education	School-based management committees monitor conditions in some cases. Centralized monitoring is used in other cases. Mobile phones may potentially be used to monitor conditions.
Senegal Conditional Cash Transfer for Orphans and Vulnerable Children	NGOs are contracted to monitor school attendance and to provide support. Schools must provide proof of a child's enrollment and fee payment. CNLS also may work with regional units or representatives to monitor arrangement with NGOs.
Tanzania Community-Based Conditional Cash Transfer	Health centers and schools must complete monitoring forms, which are entered in the MIS. Conditions are monitored once annually for school enrollment and elderly checkups and 3 times annually for other conditions.

Source: Authors' compilation.
Note: CNLS = Conseil National de Lutte contre le SIDA (National Council in the Fight against AIDS); MIS = management information system; NGO = nongovernmental organization.

Table B.18 Other Internal Monitoring, Selected Cash Transfers

Program	Other internal monitoring procedures
Burkina Faso Pilot Conditional Cash Transfer–Cash Transfer	Spot-checks are conducted at health care centers and schools.
Burundi UNHCR Cash Grants	Monitoring system keeps track of integration of refugees. Regular meetings are held between beneficiaries and offices, and internal databases are used to ensure beneficiaries receive transfers only once.
Eritrea Results-Based Financing	A data entry officer will be in charge of internal monitoring.
Ethiopia Productive Safety Net Programme–Direct Support	Program uses MIS from Ethiopia's Food Security Program. Payroll and Attendance Sheet Systems are used to track transfer payments. The Information Center, which captures data on food prices and transfer status every 2 weeks in 81 selected *woredas* (administrative districts), was created to supplement government monitoring.
Kenya Cash Transfer for Orphans and Vulnerable Children	Program has a centralized MIS, which will be decentralized to the district level. Postal Cooperation of Kenya and MIS data are reconciled. Spot-checks of conditions are used, and an appeals and complaint process has been set up. Financial MIS component will be added.
Kenya Hunger Safety Net Programme	There is an extensive MIS with decentralized inputs. Biometric smart cards act as internal controls.
Lesotho Child Grants Programme	Community committees help monitor the way funds are spent. A consultant contracted by UNICEF oversees MIS.
Malawi Social Cash Transfer	Monthly reports on costs, activities, outputs, and so on are provided. Complaints and appeals process is being planned.
Malawi Zomba Cash Transfer	School visits, calls to principals, school records, and random spot-checks are used to provide additional verification of conditions.

Mozambique Food Subsidy Program	Community workers support paydays and verify the list of payment recipients. The program's computer information system, LINDEX, does not work within a network; therefore, various regions run their own version of the program.
Niger Pilot Cash Transfer	Accuracy of targeting was verified in some areas.
Nigeria COPE (In Care of the Poor) Conditional Cash Transfer	Program is implemented separately by states and has significant variation at the state level.
Nigeria Kano Conditional Cash Transfer for Girls' Education	Community validation meetings are held to review targeting potential. Mobile phone–based monitoring and evaluation will be used along with other controls.
Rwanda Vision 2020 Umurenge Program	Villages monitor payment distribution. Appeals process is in place.
Senegal Child-Focused Social Cash Transfers	Program will use monitoring and evaluation already developed by the Nutrition Enhancement Program and will examine the need for a single registry during the pilot program.
Tanzania Community-Based Conditional Cash Transfer	Communities (especially community management committees) help with monitoring, and an MIS is used. Further eligibility checks include field visits and data consistency checks. Appeals are addressed during a community validation process for targeting.
Zambia Chipata Social Cash Transfer	Little internal monitoring occurs because of lack of capacity at the district and community levels.
Zambia Kalomo Social Cash Transfer	Little internal monitoring occurs because of lack of capacity at the district and community levels.
Zambia Katete Social Cash Transfer	Little internal monitoring occurs because of lack of capacity at the district and community levels.
Zambia Kazungula Social Cash Transfers	Little internal monitoring occurs because of lack of capacity at the district and community levels.
Zambia Monze Social Cash Transfer	Little internal monitoring occurs because of lack of capacity at the district and community levels.

Source: Authors' compilation.
Note: CNLS = Conseil National de Lutte contre le SIDA (National Council in the Fight against AIDS); MIS = management information system; NGO = nongovernmental organization; UNHCR = Office of the United Nations High Commissioner for Refugees.

Table B.19 Communications Campaign and Strategy, Selected Cash Transfers

Program	Information and communications components
Burundi UNHCR Cash Grants	Media and mass information campaigns are used.
Eritrea Results-Based Financing	There are information, education, and communications program components, which include the "Spin the Wheel for Healthy Mothers" competition.
Kenya Cash Transfer for Orphans and Vulnerable Children	Attention to developing a communications strategy was given in phase 2 of the pilot program. The strategy aimed to give participating communities information about the program, tell communities which households qualify, and hold meetings for relevant stakeholders in cash transfer locations.
Lesotho Child Grants Programme	Initial awareness campaign was conducted to encourage households to apply.
Malawi Social Cash Transfer	Community meetings inform local inhabitants and leaders about, and sensitize them regarding, the program and program eligibility.
Malawi Zomba Cash Transfer	Efforts were made to ensure participants understood the rules of their particular program.
Mali Bourse Maman	Campaign was launched to help households better understand targeting following protests by nonbeneficiaries who felt they were eligible.
Mozambique Food Subsidy Program	Community meetings inform potential beneficiaries about the program.
Namibia Child Maintenance Grant	Communications campaign increases potential beneficiaries' awareness of the grant and of eligibility criteria.
Namibia Disability Grant	Communications campaign increases potential beneficiaries' awareness of the grant and of eligibility criteria.
Namibia Foster Care Grant	Communications campaign increases potential beneficiaries' awareness of the grant and of eligibility criteria.

Namibia Old Age Grant	Communications campaign increases potential beneficiaries' awareness of the grant and of eligibility criteria.
Namibia Special Maintenance Grant	Communications campaign increases potential beneficiaries' awareness of the grant and of eligibility criteria.
Niger Pilot Cash Transfer	Households are required to participate in awareness sessions.
Nigeria COPE (In Care of the Poor) Conditional Cash Transfer	Strategy varies by state.
Nigeria Kano Conditional Cash Transfer for Girls' Education	Strong communications strategy will be used to combat cultural norms opposed to girls' education. Mobile phones will possibly be used for this strategy.
Rwanda Vision 2020 Umurenge Programme	Sensitization programs are used.
Senegal Child-Focused Social Cash Transfer	Information and communications, which will highlight maternal and child nutrition, are major components of the program.
South Africa Child Support Grant	Campaigns are used to raise awareness of the program and to increase coverage of the eligible population.
Tanzania Community-Based Conditional Cash Transfer	Community management committees are supposed to communicate with beneficiaries about the program.

Source: Authors' compilation.
Note: UNHCR = Office of the United Nations High Commissioner for Refugees.

Table B.20 Institutional Home

Program	Department	Ministry
Botswana Old Age Pension		Ministry of Local Government
Botswana Orphan Care Program	Department of Social Services	Ministry of Local Government
Botswana Program for Destitute Persons	Department of Social Services	Ministry of Local Government
Burkina Faso Pilot Conditional Cash Transfer–Cash Transfer		National Council against AIDS/STI
Cape Verde Minimum Social Pension		National Social Pension Center
Eritrea Results-Based Financing		Ministry of Health
Ethiopia Productive Safety Net Programme–Direct Support		Ministry of Agriculture and Rural Development
Ghana Livelihood Empowerment against Poverty	Social Welfare Department	Ministry of Employment and Social Welfare
Kenya Cash Transfer for Orphans and Vulnerable Children		Ministry of Gender, Children, and Social Development
Kenya Hunger Safety Net Programme		Ministry for the Development of Northern Kenya and Other Arid Lands
Lesotho Child Grants Programme	Child Welfare Division, Department of Social Welfare	Ministry of Health and Social Welfare
Lesotho Old Age Pension	Department of Social Welfare	Ministry of Health and Social Welfare
Malawi Social Cash Transfer	Department of Child Development Affairs	Ministry of Gender, Children, and Community Development
Mauritius Basic Invalid's Pension		Ministry of Social Security, National Solidarity, and Senior Citizens' Welfare and Reform Institutions

Program	Agency
Mauritius Basic Orphan's Pension	Ministry of Social Security, National Solidarity, and Senior Citizens' Welfare and Reform Institutions
Mauritius Basic Widow's Pension	Ministry of Social Security, National Solidarity, and Senior Citizens' Welfare and Reform Institutions
Mauritius Carer's Allowance	Ministry of Social Security, National Solidarity, and Senior Citizens' Welfare and Reform Institutions
Mauritius Child Allowance	Ministry of Social Security, National Solidarity, and Senior Citizens' Welfare and Reform Institutions
Mauritius Food Aid	Ministry of Social Security, National Solidarity, and Senior Citizens' Welfare and Reform Institutions
Mauritius Old Age Pension	Ministry of Social Security, National Solidarity, and Senior Citizens' Welfare and Reform Institutions
Mauritius Social Aid	Ministry of Social Security, National Solidarity, and Senior Citizens' Welfare and Reform Institutions
Mozambique Food Subsidy Program	National Institute for Social Action
Namibia Child Maintenance Grant	Ministry of Women and Social Action
Namibia Disability Grant	Ministry of Gender Equality and Child Welfare
Namibia Foster Care Grant	Ministry of Gender Equality and Child Welfare
Namibia Old Age Pension	Ministry of Gender Equality and Child Welfare
Namibia Special Maintenance Grant	Ministry of Gender Equality and Child Welfare
Nigeria COPE (In Care of the Poor) Conditional Cash Transfer	National Poverty Eradication Program and the Ministry of Poverty Eradication and Value Reorientation
Nigeria Kano Conditional Cash Transfer for Girls' Education	Ministry of Education

(continued next page)

Table B.20 *(continued)*

Program	Department	Ministry
Rwanda Vision 2020 Umurenge Programme		Ministry of Local Government, Good Governance, Community Development, and Social Affairs
Senegal Conditional Cash Transfer for Orphans and Vulnerable Children		Conseil National de Lutte contre le SIDA (National Council in the Fight against AIDS)
Senegal Child-Focused Social Cash Transfer		Cellule de Lutte contre la Malnutrition (Unit in the Fight against Malnutrition)
Sierra Leone Unconditional Cash Transfer for the Old and Needy	National Social Safety Net	Ministry of Employment and Social Security
South Africa Care Dependency Grant	Department of Social Development	South African Social Security Agency
South Africa Child Support Grant	Department of Social Development	South African Social Security Agency
South Africa Disability Grant	Department of Social Development	South African Social Security Agency
South Africa Foster Care Grant	Department of Social Development	South African Social Security Agency
South Africa Grant for Carers of the Aged	Department of Social Development	South African Social Security Agency
South Africa Old Age Pension	Department of Social Development	South African Social Security Agency
Swaziland Old Age Grant	Department of Social Welfare	Ministry of Health and Social Welfare
Swaziland Public Assistance Grant	Department of Social Welfare	Ministry of Health and Social Welfare
Tanzania Community-Based Conditional Cash Transfer		Tanzania Social Action Fund
Zambia Chipata Social Cash Transfer	Department of Social Welfare	Ministry of Community Development and Social Services
Zambia Kalomo Social Cash Transfer	Department of Social Welfare	Ministry of Community Development and Social Services

Zambia Katete Social Cash Transfer	Department of Social Welfare	Ministry of Community Development and Social Services
Zambia Kazungula Social Cash Transfer	Department of Social Welfare	Ministry of Community Development and Social Services
Zambia Monze Social Cash Transfer	Department of Social Welfare	Ministry of Community Development and Social Services
Zimbabwe Care for the Elderly	Department of Social Services	Ministry of Public Service, Labour, and Social Welfare
Zimbabwe Drought Relief	Department of Social Services	Ministry of Public Service, Labour, and Social Welfare
Zimbabwe Maintenance of Disabled Persons	Department of Social Services	Ministry of Public Service, Labour, and Social Welfare
Zimbabwe Maintenance of Hero's Dependents	Department of Social Services	Ministry of Public Service, Labour, and Social Welfare
Zimbabwe Support to Children in Difficult Circumstances	Department of Social Services	Ministry of Public Service, Labour, and Social Welfare
Zimbabwe Support to Families in Distress	Department of Social Services	Ministry of Public Service, Labour, and Social Welfare

Source: Authors' compilation.
Note: STI = sexually transmitted infection.

Table B.21 Funders by Program, Selected Cash Transfers

Program	Government	World Bank	DFID	UNICEF	EU/ECHO	USAID	CARE	Other
Botswana Old Age Pension	✓							
Botswana Orphan Care Program	✓							
Botswana Program for Destitute Persons	✓							
Burkina Faso Pilot Conditional Cash Transfer–Cash Transfer	✓	✓						
Burundi UNHCR Cash Grants			✓					✓
Cape Verde Minimum Social Pension	✓							
Democratic Republic of Congo Emergency Cash Grants		✓	✓		✓			✓
Eritrea Results-Based Financing	✓	✓						
Ethiopia Productive Safety Net Programme–Direct Support	✓	✓	✓		✓	✓		✓
Ghana Livelihood Empowerment against Poverty	✓	✓	✓	✓				✓
Kenya Cash Transfer for Orphans and Vulnerable Children	✓	✓	✓	✓				✓
Kenya Hunger Safety Net Programme	✓		✓		✓	✓	✓	✓
Lesotho Child Grants Programme	✓			✓	✓			
Lesotho Old Age Pension	✓							
Malawi Social Cash Transfer	✓			✓	✓			✓
Mali Bourse Maman				✓				
Mauritius Basic Invalid's Pension	✓							
Mauritius Basic Orphan's Pension	✓							
Mauritius Basic Widow's Pension	✓							
Mauritius Carer's Allowance	✓							
Mauritius Child Allowance	✓							
Mauritius Food Aid	✓							
Mauritius Social Aid	✓							

Program					
Mauritius Old Age Pension				✓	
Mozambique Food Subsidy Program	✓				
Namibia Child Maintenance Grant	✓				
Namibia Disability Grant	✓				
Namibia Foster Care Grant	✓				
Namibia Old Age Grant				✓	
Niger Pilot Cash Transfer	✓				
Nigeria COPE (In Care of the Poor) Conditional Cash Transfer			✓		
Nigeria Kano Conditional Cash Transfer for Girls' Education				✓	
Rwanda Vision 2020 Umurenge Programme				✓	
Senegal Conditional Cash Transfer for Orphans and Vulnerable Children		✓			
Senegal Child-Focused Social Cash Transfer		✓			
Senegal Old Age Pension	✓				
Seychelles Old Age Pension	✓				
Seychelles Orphan Transfer	✓				
Sierra Leone Unconditional Cash Transfer for the Old and Needy					✓
South Africa Care Dependency Grant	✓				
South Africa Child Support Grant	✓				
South Africa Disability Grant	✓				
South Africa Foster Care Grant	✓				
South Africa Grant for Carers of the Aged	✓				
South Africa Old Age Pension	✓				

(continued next page)

Table B.21 *(continued)*

Program	Government	World Bank	DFID	UNICEF	EU/ECHO	USAID	CARE	Other
Swaziland Old Age Grant	✓							
Swaziland Public Assistance Grant	✓							
Tanzania Community-Based Conditional Cash Transfer	✓	✓						✓
Zambia Chipata Social Cash Transfer	✓		✓	✓				✓
Zambia Kalomo Social Cash Transfer	✓		✓	✓				✓
Zambia Katete Social Cash Transfer	✓		✓	✓				✓
Zambia Kazungula Social Cash Transfer	✓		✓	✓				✓
Zambia Monze Social Cash Transfer	✓		✓	✓				✓
Zimbabwe Care for the Elderly	✓							
Zimbabwe Drought Relief	✓							
Zimbabwe Maintenance of Disabled Persons	✓							
Zimbabwe Maintenance of Hero's Dependents	✓							
Zimbabwe Protracted Relief Program			✓					
Zimbabwe Support to Children in Difficult Circumstances	✓							
Zimbabwe Support to Families in Distress	✓							

Source: Authors' compilation.

Note: "Other" includes the following institutions: African Development Bank, Canadian International Development Agency, Danish International Development Agency, Development Corporation of Ireland, Dutch Aid, Food and Agriculture Organization (United Nations), German Agency for Technical Cooperation, Government of Norway, Japan Social Development Fund, Office of the United Nations High Commissioner for Refugees, Oxfam International, Save the Children, Swedish International Development Agency, and World Food Program (United Nations). CARE = Cooperative for Assistance and Relief Everywhere; DFID = Department for International Development; EU/ECHO = European Commission's Humanitarian Aid and Civil Protection; UNHCR = Office of the United Nations High Commissioner for Refugees; UNICEF = United Nations Children's Fund; USAID = United States Agency for International Development.

Table B.22 Annual Estimated Program Costs

Program	Country financing (US$)	Donor financing (US$)	Total cost (US$)	Notes
Botswana Old Age Pension	55,200,000	0	55,200,000	
Burkina Faso Pilot Conditional Cash Transfer–Cash Transfer	366,000	256,250	622,250	
Cape Verde Minimum Social Pension	3,600,000	0	3,600,000	
Eritrea Results-Based Financing	Data unavailable	2,366,666	2,366,666	
Ethiopia Productive Safety Net Programme–Direct Support	82,800,000	331,200,000	414,000,000	The program cost US$360 million in 2009, 8% of which was financed by the government of Ethiopia. There was an additional cost of US$54 million for government of Ethiopia staff time.
Kenya Cash Transfer for Orphans and Vulnerable Children	6,190,476	19,809,524	26,000,000	Data are for fiscal year 2010.
Kenya Hunger Safety Net Programme	Data unavailable	Data unavailable	12,366,240	Data are calculated by dividing total cost by 10 years for program life.
Lesotho Child Grants Programme	Data unavailable	2,467,500	2,467,500	
Lesotho Old Age Pension	22,680,000	0	22,680,000	Lesotho's 2008 nominal GDP was US$1,620 million. Old Age Pension is 1.4% of GDP.
Malawi Social Cash Transfer	Data unavailable	Data unavailable	4,146,736	Data are calculated by multiplying the total reported annual cost per household (US$176) by the number of households in the program (23,561) at time of calculation.
Mali Bourse Maman	Data unavailable	36,800	36,800	Data show annual reported cost.

(continued next page)

Table B.22 (continued)

Program	Country financing (US$)	Donor financing (US$)	Total cost (US$)	Notes
Mauritius Old Age Pension	174,760,000	0	174,760,000	Data equal 2% of GDP using GDP estimate for 2008 (US$8.738 billion).
Mozambique Food Subsidy Program	7,300,000	2,810,509	10,110,509	Data are calculated by adding the National Institute for Social Welfare's 2008 budget for the Food Subsidy Program (US$7.3 million) and the Department for International Development's yearly financing amount (assuming equal use each year).
Namibia Old Age Pension	544,670,000	0	544,670,000	
Nigeria COPE (In Care of the Poor) Conditional Cash Transfer	36,000,000	20,000,000	56,000,000	Amounts are based on data for the 5-year program.
Rwanda Vision 2020 Umurenge Programme	1,537,135	1,221,498	2,760,633	Data are calculated by dividing the cost of the direct support component by 5 (number of program years).
Senegal Child-Focused Social Cash Transfer	Data unavailable	2,100,000	2,100,000	Data equal one-third of total cost because program is from 2009 to 2011.
Sierra Leone Unconditional Cash Transfer for the Old and Needy	4,735,150	0	4,735,150	
South Africa Child Support Grant	1,000,000,000	0	1,000,000,000	Data shown are from the budget for 2005/06.
South Africa Old Age Pension	3,880,632,000	0	3,880,632,000	Number reached by multiplying the estimated 2008 GDP of US$277,188 million by 0.014 for estimated cost of Old Age Pension.

Swaziland Old Age Grant	9,230,000	0	9,230,000	Data show 2007 budget (most recent data available).
Swaziland Public Assistance Grant	333,138	0	333,138	Data show 2007 budget (most recent data available).
Tanzania Community-Based Conditional Cash Transfer	Data unavailable	1,800,000	1,800,000	Data equal US$4.5 million for project divided by 2.5 years for program length.
Zambia Chipata Social Cash Transfer	70,000	247,590	317,590	Government of Zambia data value is 2007 amount divided by the number of programs. It assumes equal allocation across districts. Total for Chipata is the program's 2-year cost divided by 2; 2-year cost is calculated using the average exchange rate for July 1, 2006 to July 1, 2007.
Zambia Kalomo Social Cash Transfer	70,000	239,875	309,875	Donor data are calculated by multiplying US$165 per household (the reported cost, which is probably an underestimate) by the number of covered households. Government amount was 2007 commitment for the cash transfer (see note for Zambia Chipata Social Cash Transfer).
Zambia Katete Social Cash Transfer	70,000	655,541	725,541	Donor data are calculated by annualizing donor financing based on available data and applying corresponding exchange rate. Government amount was 2007 commitment for the cash transfer (see note for Zambia Chipata Social Cash Transfer).
Zambia Kazungula Cash Transfer	70,000	75,462	145,462	Government amount was 2007 commitment for the cash transfer (see note for Zambia Chipata Social Cash Transfer).

(continued next page)

Table B.22 *(continued)*

Program	Country financing (US$)	Donor financing (US$)	Total cost (US$)	Notes
Zambia Monze Cash Transfer	70,000	232,689	302,689	Donor data are calculated by annualizing donor financing based on available data and applying corresponding exchange rate. Government amount was 2007 commitment for the cash transfer (note for Zambia Chipata Social Cash Transfer).
Zimbabwe Care for the Elderly	1,156,267	0	1,156,267	Data convert the Z$25 billion cost to U.S. dollars using the average 2005 exchange rate. Data are outdated.
Zimbabwe Drought Relief	1,588,162	0	1,588,162	
Zimbabwe Maintenance of Disabled Persons	1,850,053	0	1,850,053	Data convert the Z$40 billion cost to U.S. dollars using the average 2005 exchange rate. Data are outdated.
Zimbabwe Support to Children in Difficult Circumstances	222,000	0	222,000	Data convert the Z$4.8 billion cost to U.S. dollars using the average 2005 exchange rate. Data are outdated.
Zimbabwe Support to Families in Distress	1,387,539	0	1,387,539	Data convert the Z$30 billion cost to U.S. dollars using the average 2005 exchange rate. Data are outdated.

Source: Authors' compilation.
Note: GDP = gross domestic product.

Table B.23 Total Estimated Program Costs, Various Years

Program	Total country financing (US$)	Total donor financing (US$)	Total program cost (US$)	Notes
Burkina Faso Pilot Conditional Cash Transfer–Cash Transfer	732,000	512,500	1,244,500	The amount of counterpart funds is unclear.
Eritrea Results-Based Financing			7,100,000	Donor funding is from 2005 to 2009 (Adaptable Program Loan I and II).
Ethiopia Productive Safety Net Programme–Direct Support		1,449,201,103	1,449,201,103	Data are for phase 3 of the program.
Kenya Cash Transfer for Orphans and Vulnerable Children	30,000,000	96,000,000	126,000,000	K Sh 80 million was converted to U.S. dollars using the average 2009 exchange rate.
Kenya Hunger Safety Net Programme			125,274,400	
Lesotho Child Grants Programme			6,973,150	€5 million was converted to U.S. dollars using the average 2009 exchange rate.
Mozambique Food Subsidy Program		30,915,600		The Department for International Development (United Kingdom) and the Royal Netherlands Embassy will give support over 11 years.
Nigeria COPE (In Care of the Poor) Conditional Cash Transfer	180,000,000	100,000,000	280,000,000	Data are the totals anticipated for the 5-year program.
Nigeria Kano Conditional Cash Transfer for Girls' Education			9,078,500	Data are the totals for a 3-year program.
Rwanda Vision 2020 Umurenge Programme	7,695,676	6,107,488	13,803,164	Data are the total projected scale-up cost for 2008–13, multiplied by 0.20 for the direct support component.
Senegal Child-Focused Social Cash Transfer		6,300,000	6,300,000	
Tanzania Community-Based Conditional Cash Transfer		4,500,000	4,500,000	Data are the total anticipated for a 2.5-year program.

Source: Authors' compilation.
Note: Blank spaces indicate that it is unclear what amount of the funding was donor financed and what amount was country financed.

Table B.24 Process Evaluation Information, Selected Cash Transfers

Program	External process or program evaluation
Eritrea Results-Based Financing	Spot-checks and financial audits are planned.
Ethiopia Productive Safety Net Programme–Direct Support	Multiple studies were conducted in 2006 to guide the second part of the first phase, and another major evaluation was conducted in 2008 in 8 *woredas* (districts). Qualitative and quantitative process evaluations are used.
Kenya Cash Transfer for Orphans and Vulnerable Children	At the time of writing, an outside organization was expected to conduct community censuses, complete "citizen report cards," do spot-checks, and control the appeals and complaints process. A cost study also will be completed. Another evaluation of processes and program impact was set to begin in fiscal year 2009 to evaluate the donor- and country-financed programs.
Lesotho Child Grants Programme	UNICEF will contract with an outside firm to complete a process evaluation.
Lesotho Old Age Pension	The Pension Impact Group in Lesotho has provided an external evaluation.
Mali Bourse Maman	An evaluation process was conducted through UNICEF.
Mozambique Food Subsidy Program	The International Food Policy Research Institute examined program issues; other evaluations have also been completed.
Niger Pilot Cash Transfer	An evaluation was completed by Save the Children.
Rwanda Vision 2020 Umurenge Programme	An evaluation has been planned.
Senegal Child-Focused Social Cash Transfer	The evaluation process will examine targeting errors, the percentage of planned transfers made to providers, and the placement of the cash transfer in the National Social Protection Strategy.
Sierra Leone Unconditional Cash Transfer for the Old and Needy	An evaluation was completed.
South Africa Child Support Grant	An evaluation was completed by the Community Agency for Social Enquiry in 2008.
Tanzania Community-Based Conditional Cash Transfer	An evaluation has been planned.
Zambia Chipata Social Cash Transfer	An evaluation was completed.
Zambia Kalomo Cash Transfer	An evaluation was completed.
Zambia Katete Cash Transfer	An evaluation was completed.
Zambia Kazungula Cash Transfer	An evaluation was completed.

Source: Authors' compilation.
Note: UNICEF = United Nations Children's Fund.

Table B.25 Completed Impact Evaluations by Program

Program	Completed impact evaluation
Burundi UNHCR Cash Grants	A qualitative evaluation was conducted (interviews of returned refugees).
Ethiopia Productive Safety Net Programme[a]	The Food Security Programme collected household panel data in 2006 and 2008. The process evaluation will be merged with this survey in the future.
Malawi Social Cash Transfer	UNICEF and the United States Agency for International Development (through their Child and Family Applied Research Project) funded an experimental evaluation. Baseline data were collected in March 2007 by a team from the Boston University Center for Social Research; follow-ups were completed in 2007 and 2008.
Malawi Zomba Cash Transfer	An experimental impact evaluation examines the impact of using conditions versus not using conditions, as well as the impact of transfer amounts, provision of transfer to adolescent girls (and households), spillover effects, and so on. Baseline data were collected beginning in October 2007. Follow-ups were completed in 2008 and 2009.
Mozambique Food Subsidy Program	The International Food Policy Research Institute conducted an evaluation in 1997. UNICEF and the International Policy Centre for Inclusive Growth are working with the National Institute of Social Welfare to evaluate the impact of increased transfer levels. Surveys were conducted in late 2008 and 2009.
Namibia Child Maintenance Grant	UNDP and a group from the University of Stellenbosch conducted an evaluation. MGECW conducted a qualitative evaluation.
Namibia Disability Grant	UNDP and a group from the University of Stellenbosch conducted an evaluation.
Namibia Foster Care Grant	UNDP and a group from the University of Stellenbosch conducted an evaluation. MGECW conducted a qualitative evaluation.
Namibia Old Age Pension	UNDP and a group from the University of Stellenbosch conducted an evaluation.
Namibia Special Maintenance Grant	UNDP and a group from the University of Stellenbosch conducted an evaluation.
South Africa Child Support Grant	Some evaluations relied on the gradual program phase-in. No formal experimental evaluation was conducted. Other nonexperimental evaluations were commissioned by the Department of Social Development in 2004 and 2008. Qualitative evaluations were conducted in 2000 and 2003.

(continued next page)

Table B.25 *(continued)*

Program	Completed impact evaluation
South Africa Old Age Pension	Evaluations have made use of variation in benefit levels (especially the increase in benefits to the African population) to identify program impacts.
Zambia Chipata Social Cash Transfer	Several studies use comparison, but not control, groups. A retrospective study was completed for the Chipata, Kalomo, and Kazungula districts using propensity-score-matching and odds-ratio weighted regressions.
Zambia Kalomo Cash Transfer	Several studies use comparison, but not control, groups. A retrospective study was completed for the Chipata, Kalomo, and Kazungula districts using propensity-score-matching and odds-ratio weighted regressions.
Zambia Kazungula Cash Transfer	Several studies use comparison, but not control, groups. A retrospective study was completed for Chipata, Kalomo, and Kazungula districts using propensity score matching and odds-ratio weighted regressions.

Source: Authors' compilation.
Note: MGECW = Ministry of Gender Equality and Child Welfare; UNDP = United Nations Development Programme; UNHCR = Office of the United Nations High Commissioner for Refugees; UNICEF = United Nations Children's Fund.
a. Describes the entire PSNP, not just the PSNP-DS.

Table B.26 Ongoing Experimental Evaluations by Program

Program	Year results are expected	Key information evaluated
Burkina Faso Conditional Cash Transfer–Cash Transfer	2010	Impact of conditional versus unconditional transfers and payments to mothers versus fathers on education, health, and consumption outcomes
Eritrea Results-Based Financing	Midterm results: 2010; final results: 2012	Impact of conditional transfers that are awarded as health conditions are fulfilled; impact of supply-side health transfers (pay for performance)
Kenya Cash Transfer for Orphans and Vulnerable Children	2010	Impact of conditional versus unconditional transfers
Kenya Hunger Safety Net Programme	First results in 2010; additional results later	Impact of unconditional transfers targeting various groups in extremely remote areas
Nigeria Kano Conditional Cash Transfer for Girls' Education	Late 2012	Impact of soft versus hard conditions;[a] different transfer sizes and centralized versus decentralized monitoring; impact of various communications strategies, including mobile phone technology
Rwanda Vision 2020 Umurenge Programme	2010	Impact of unconditional transfers in a larger social protection program, which includes support for insertion into the financial system and labor market when possible
Senegal Child-Focused Social Cash Transfer	2011	Impact of unconditional transfers on consumption, nutrition, and health outcomes in the presence of a successful community nutrition program
Tanzania Community-Based Conditional Cash Transfer	2010/11	Impact of conditional cash transfers in a program supported by communities trained in community-driven development and based within a social fund
Tanzania Rewarding STI Prevention and Control in Tanzania (RESPECT)	2010/11	Impact of cash transfer that is conditioned on payee remaining free of curable sexually transmitted infections (STIs) on human immunodeficiency virus status, STI status, and other measures; initial results already available and additional results expected
Zambia Monze Social Cash Transfer	2010/11	Impact of unconditional cash transfers on household outcomes

Source: Authors' compilation.

Note: Other programs for which experimental impact evaluations are expected to occur include Ghana Livelihood Empowerment against Poverty, Lesotho Child Grants Programme, and Senegal Conditional Cash Transfer for Orphans and Vulnerable Children. Whether these evaluations have been conducted is unclear.

a. Soft conditions require that beneficiary households agree verbally or in writing that they will abide by program conditions. However, there is no penalty for noncompliance. Hard conditions penalize beneficiaries for noncompliance.

Table B.27 Results from Evaluations of Cash Transfers in Sub-Saharan Africa

Program	Results of evaluation	Source
Burundi UNHCR Cash Grants	• Cash transfers encouraged refugees' return to Burundi. • More than 50% of returnees used cash to invest in agriculture or construction. • Some refugees used cash for investment in assets, transportation costs, and the purchase of food or medicine. • Some refugees invested cash in businesses.	UNHCR (n.d.)
Ethiopia Productive Safety Net Programme[a]	• Most of the transfers went to purchase necessary food. Households also used cash to invest in education, agriculture, debt repayment, health care, and small businesses. • Program increased households' months of food security and livestock ownership. • Program improved households' self-reported welfare. • Many of the positive effects found in the impact evaluation were severely dampened in households that received low or irregular transfers. Results also were muted if households did not have access to other food security programs.	Devereux and others (2008); Gilligan and others (2009)
Malawi Social Cash Transfer	• The listed results occurred after almost 6 months of transfers. • Beneficiary households went less than 1 day per month without enough food, as compared to 5 days for nonbeneficiary households. • Asset ownership in beneficiary households increased to more than that of nonbeneficiary households. • Beneficiary households' food consumption and diversity improved more than that of nonbeneficiary households. • Beneficiary households reported improvements in 62.7% of their children's health in the past 6 months. (The corresponding amount for nonbeneficiary households was 5.5%.) The corresponding percentage for beneficiary household heads was 71%; the amount for nonbeneficiary household heads was 5.5%. • School enrollment in nonbeneficiary households declined, whereas it did not decline in beneficiary households.	Miller, Tsoka, and Mchinji Evaluation Team (2007)

Malawi Zomba Cash Transfer	• The listed results occurred after 2 years in the program. • Improvement in school enrollment in the group receiving unconditional cash transfers was less than half (43%) of the improvement for the conditional cash transfer group. School attendance was also higher for conditional cash transfer than for unconditional cash transfer beneficiaries. • The conditional cash transfer improved English test scores and cognitive ability and marginally increased Trends in International Mathematics and Science Study math scores. The improvement in conditional cash transfer English scores was statistically above that of the improvement in English scores for unconditional cash transfer beneficiaries. • The unconditional cash transfer significantly decreased the probability that girls would become pregnant or marry. The effect was primarily due to the unconditional cash transfer's impact on adolescent girls who dropped out of school. No effects of the unconditional cash transfer or conditional cash transfer were found for this outcome for girls who remained students.	Baird, McIntosh, and Özler (2011)
Mozambique Food Subsidy Program	• Program increased the proportion of expenditures on food by 22%. Positive effects on food share, as well as the probability of consuming flour, were even larger in female-headed households. • Program increased the likelihood that women ate additional meals daily, and it marginally increased daily additional meals for boys ages 5 to 9. • Adults in beneficiary households increased their probability of working (17% for male adults and the elderly and 24% for adult women, although this was only marginally significant), whereas boys ages 5 to 9 were 29% less likely to work. • The number of hours that adults in beneficiary households spent in their own fields decreased, indicating additional labor time was being spent outside the household. • One indicator showed that children's acute malnutrition (wasting) decreased by 30%, but the study concluded this result may have been an anomaly, given no other results supported such strong nutritional impacts.	Soares and Teixeira (2010)

(continued next page)

Table B.27 (continued)

Program	Results of evaluation	Source
South Africa Child Support Grant	• Using instrumental variables regressions, an evaluation found that the grant decreased poverty and child hunger and increased food consumption and school attendance. • Using exogenous variations in grant eligibility or duration, studies have determined that the grant improved school attendance, labor force participation, self-reported measures of children's hunger, and children's height-for-age reports. • Using propensity score matching and difference-in-differences, an evaluation found that the grant decreased children's hunger by 4% to 7% and increased school attendance by 6% to 8%. The grant also helped beneficiary households continue agricultural activities and increased mobile phone use among beneficiary households. The grant was not found to impact children's labor activities, household employment, or likelihood of using a social worker.	Agüero, Carter, and Woolard (2007); EPRI (2008); Samson and others (2004); Williams (2007)
South Africa Old Age Pension	• Most evaluations rely on extension of pension benefits to all South Africans. • One study suggested that the pension affected household composition (notably, by adding children under age 5 and young women of childbearing age, whereas older working-age women departed). Other research suggests no effect of the pension on household composition. • Female pension receipt was associated with increases in girls' nutritional outcomes, but not boys' nutritional outcomes. • Pension eligibility of a male in South African households was associated with increased school attendance and decreased market labor among children over age 5. • Impacts of the pension on households with orphans were mixed. • There were mixed results in studies of the impact of the pension on labor supply. Some studies found pension receipt was associated with lower labor supply in certain household adults; other studies found that pensions were associated with increased adult labor supply, often through migration; some studies suggest the pension has not impacted labor supply and migration.	Ardington, Case, and Hosegood (2009); Bertrand, Mullainathan, and Miller (2003); Case and Ardington (2006); Duflo (2000); Edmonds (2006); Edmonds, Mammen, and Miller (2005); Posel, Fairburn, and Lund (2006)

Program	Findings	Source
Tanzania Rewarding STI Prevention and Control in Tanzania (RESPECT)	• The listed results occurred after 1 year of treatment. • Treatment group receiving the larger cash transfer size showed a 25% reduction in sexually transmitted infection prevalence. • No impact was found among those receiving the smaller transfers.	de Walque and others (2010)
Zambia Chipata Social Cash Transfer, Zambia Kalomo Social Cash Transfer, Zambia Kazungula Social Cash Transfer	• Results are from evaluation of Chipata, Kalomo, and Kazungula cash transfers using retrospective data as well as propensity score matching and odds-weighted regressions. • Positive effects of transfers were found on consumption, especially nonfood consumption. • Greatest impacts were seen in areas with the highest vulnerability (for example, consumption effects were 150% higher in the poorest district, Kazungula, than in the other districts). • Wealthier households appeared to be able to use the transfers to increase household assets, whereas households with fewer beginning assets were not able to do so. • The programs' impacts on education were mixed. School attendance increased across the board only for Chipata district, which imposed a soft conditionality of school attendance and an extra payment for school enrollment.	Tembo and Freeland (2009)

Source: Authors' compilation.
Note: UNHCR = Office of the United Nations High Commissioner for Refugees.
a. Describes the entire PSNP, not just the PSNP-DS.

Table B.28   Key Contacts for Desk Review

Country	Source for country information
Angola	Margaret Brown, UNICEF
	Nilsa de Fátima Pereira Batalha, Ministry of Social Assistance and Reinsertion
Burkina Faso	Harold Alderman, World Bank
	Tshiya Subayi-Cuppen, World Bank
Cape Verde	Rene Ferreira, National Centre for Pensions
	José Carlos Moniz, Ministry of Labor and Social Solidarity, Portugal
Ethiopia	Cristiana Sparacino, International Fund for Agricultural Development
	Sarah Coll-Black, World Bank
	Wout Soer, World Bank
	Will Wiseman, World Bank
Ghana	Julianna Lindsey, UNICEF
	Lawrence Ofori-Addo, Ministry of Employment and Social Welfare
Kenya	Mark Agoya, DFID
	Sammy Keter, Ministry of Arid and Semi-arid Lands, HSNP
	Michael Mills, World Bank
	Ada Mwangola, DFID-HSNP
	Roger Pearson, UNICEF
	Emma Sorensson, World Bank
	Leigh Stubblefield, DFID
	Patrick Ward, Oxford Policy Management
Lesotho	Mohammed Farooq, UNICEF
	Xiao-yan Liang, World Bank
	Aidan Mulkeen, World Bank
Madagascar	Mukesh Chawla, World Bank
	Dorothee Klaus, UNICEF
	Nadine Poupart, World Bank
	Ando Raobelison, World Bank
Malawi	Blessings Chinsinga, Future Agricultures Consortium
	Mayke Huijbregts, UNICEF
	Reagan Kaluluma, Ministry of Gender, Children, and Community Development, Social Cash Transfer Scheme National Secretariat
	Johanne Lebede, European Commission
	Harry Mwamlima, Ministry of Economic Planning and Development
	Khwima Nthara, World Bank
	Berk Özler, World Bank
	Eliana Toro, European Commission
Mozambique	Theresa Kilbane, UNICEF
	Riham Shendy, World Bank
Namibia	Benjamin Roberts, Human Sciences Research Council

(continued next page)

Table B.28 *(continued)*

Country	Source for country information
Nigeria	Ian Attfield, DFID
	Foluso Okunmadewa, World Bank
Rwanda	Isabelle Cardinal, DFID
	Alex Kamurase, World Bank
São Tomé and Príncipe	Jacy Braga Rodrigues, Bolsa Escola
Senegal	Gilberte Hounsounou, Senegal Conditional Cash Transfer for Orphans and Vulnerable Children
	Rémy Pigois, UNICEF
	Vincent Turbat, World Bank
Sierra Leone	Helen Appleton, DFID
	Foday Cohteh, National Safety Net Program, Unconditional Cash Transfer for the Poor and Needy
Swaziland	Kumiko Imai, UNICEF
Tanzania	Gertrude Mapunda Kihunrwa, DFID
	Ida Manjolo, World Bank
Uganda	Joanne Bosworth, DFID
	Suleiman Namara, World Bank
Zambia	Charlotte Harland, UNICEF
	Sebastian Martinez, World Bank
	Bestone Mboozi, Ministry of Community Development and Social Services, Zambia Social Cash Transfer
	Morris Moono, Zambia Social Cash Transfer
	Gelson Tembo, University of Zambia
Zimbabwe	Jane Maponga, Action Aid International
	Philippa Thomas, DFID
	Rachel Yates, DFID
	Kerina Zvobgo, GRM International, Protracted Relief Program
Multiple countries	Melissa Andrade, International Policy Centre for Inclusive Growth
	Catherine Arnold, DFID
	Francisco Ayala, Ayala Consulting
	Armando Barrientos, Brooks World Poverty Institute and Chronic Poverty Research Centre
	Jeanine Braithwaite, World Bank
	Dominic Crowley, Concern Worldwide
	Fagoon Dave, DFID
	Carlo del Ninno, World Bank
	Darren Evans, Concern Worldwide
	Marito Garcia, World Bank
	Margaret Grosh, World Bank
	Paul Harvey, Humanitarian Outcomes
	Stephen Kidd, HelpAge International
	Camilla Knox-Peebles, Oxfam Great Britain
	Nupur Kukrety, Oxfam Great Britain
	Paulina LaVerde, Ayala Consulting

(continued next page)

Table B.28 *(continued)*

Country	Source for country information
	Mads Lofvall, WFP
	Waheed Lor-Mehdiabadi, WFP
	Mirey Ovadiya, World Bank
	Dennis Pain, DFID
	Alex Rees, Save the Children United Kingdom
	Norbert Schady, World Bank
	Sanna Stockstrom de Pella, German Agency for Technical Cooperation
	Jason Thompson, Ayala Consulting
	Héloise Troc, European Commission
	Marika Uotila, European Commission
	Fábio Veras Soares, International Policy Centre for Inclusive Growth
	Ruth Wutete, World Bank
Multiple countries, especially pastoral areas	Tim Waites, DFID
Multiple countries: Eastern and Southern African countries	Benjamin Davis, UNICEF
Multiple countries: Ghana and Nigeria	Graham Gass, DFID
Multiple countries: Ghana and other West African countries	Setareh Razmara, World Bank
Multiple countries: Republic of Congo, Ghana, Guinea, Mali, and Senegal	Rebecca Holmes, ODI Nicola Jones, ODI
Multiple countries: Ghana and Zambia	Esther Schüring, German Agency for Technical Cooperation Sonya Sultan, DFID
Multiple countries: Malawi, Uganda, and Zimbabwe	Mungai Lenneiye, World Bank
Multiple countries: Liberia, Malawi, Mozambique, and Zambia	Bernd Schubert, Team Consult
Multiple countries: Namibia and Uganda	Sebastian Levine, United Nations Development Programme
Multiple countries: Senegal and other West African countries	Menno Mulder-Sibanda, World Bank Maurizia Tovo, World Bank

(continued next page)

Table B.28 *(continued)*

Country	Source for country information
Multiple countries: Sierra Leone and other West African countries	Giuseppe Zampaglione, World Bank
Multiple countries: West African countries	Cécile Cherrier, World Bank Jan Eijkenaar, European Commission's Humanitarian Aid and Civil Protection
Multiple countries: West and Central African countries	Anthony (Tony) Hodges, UNICEF
Multiple countries: Zambia and Ghana	Sonya Sultan, DFID

Source: Authors' compilation.
Note: DFID = U.K. Department for International Development; HSNP = Hunger Safety Net Programme; ODI = Overseas Development Institute; UNICEF = United Nations Children's Fund; WFP = United Nations World Food Programme.

References

Agüero, Jorge, Michael Carter, and Ingrid Woolard. 2007. "The Impact of Unconditional Cash Transfers on Nutrition: The South African Child Support Grant." Working Paper 39, International Poverty Centre, Brasília.

Ardington, Cally, Anne Case, and Victoria Hosegood. 2009. "Labor Supply Responses to Large Social Transfers: Longitudinal Evidence from South Africa." *American Economic Journal: Applied Economics* 1 (1): 22–48.

Ayala, Francisco. 2009. "Design Proposal for a Kano State Pilot CCT for Girls' Education." Federal Republic of Nigeria, Nairobi.

Baird, Sarah, Ephraim Chirwa, Craig McIntosh, and Berk Özler. 2009. "Unpacking the Impacts of a Randomized CCT Program in Sub-Saharan Africa." Research proposal, University of California–San Diego and World Bank, Washington, DC.

Baird, Sarah, Craig McIntosh, and Berk Özler. 2011. "Cash or Condition? Evidence from a Cash Transfer Experiment." World Bank, Washington, DC. http://ipl.econ.duke.edu/bread/papers/0511conf/Baird.pdf.

Bar-On, Arnon. 2002. "Going against World Trends: Social Protection in Botswana." *Social Policy Journal* 1 (4): 23–41.

Bertrand, Marianne, Sendhil Mullainathan, and Douglas Miller. 2003. "Public Policy and Extended Families: Evidence from Pensions in South Africa." *World Bank Economic Review* 17 (1): 27–50.

BFTU (Botswana Federation of Trade Unions). 2007. "Policy Position Paper on Social Security and Social Protection in Botswana." BFTU, Gaborone.

Case, Anne, and Cally Ardington. 2006. "The Impact of Parental Death on School Outcomes: Longitudinal Evidence from South Africa." *Demography* 43 (3): 401–20.

Central Statistics Office. 2007. *Social Security Statistics, 2000/2000–2005/2006.* Port Louis: Ministry of Finance and Economic Development.

Devereux, Stephen, Rachel Sabates-Wheeler, Rachel Slater, Mulugeta Tefera, Taylor Brown, and Amdissa Teshome. 2008. *Ethiopia's Productive Safety Net Programme (PSNP): 2008 Assessment Report.* Sussex, U.K.: Institute of Development Studies, Overseas Development Institute, Dadimos Development Consultants, IDL Group, and A–Z Consult.

de Walque, Damien. 2009. "Evaluating the Impact of Conditional and Unconditional Cash Transfers in Rural Burkina Faso." PowerPoint presentation, Development Economics Research Group, World Bank, Washington, DC, January 12.

de Walque, Damien, William H. Dow, Rose Nathan, Carol Medlin, and RESPECT Study Team. 2010. "The RESPECT Study: Evaluating Conditional Cash Transfers for HIV/STI Prevention in Tanzania." World Bank, Washington, DC.

Duflo, Esther. 2000. "Child Health and Household Resources in South Africa: Evidence from the Old Age Pension Program." *American Economic Review* 90 (2): 393–98.

Edmonds, Eric. 2006. "Child Labor and Schooling Responses to Anticipated Income in South Africa." *Journal of Development Economics* 81 (2): 386–414.

Edmonds, Eric, Kristen Mammen, and Douglas Miller. 2005. "Rearranging the Family? Income Support and Elderly Living Arrangements in a Low-Income Country." *Journal of Human Resources* 40 (1): 186–207.

Ellis, Frank. 2007. "Food Subsidy Programme, Mozambique." REBA Case Study Brief 7, Regional Evidence Building Agenda, Regional Hunger Vulnerability Programme, Johannesburg.

EPRI (Economic Policy Research Institute). 2008. "Quantitative Analysis of the Impact of the Child Support Grant." EPRI, Cape Town, South Africa.

European University Institute. 2010. *Social Protection for Inclusive Development: A New Perspective in EU Cooperation with Africa.* San Domenico di Fiesole, Italy: Robert Schuman Centre for Advanced Studies, European University Institute.

Evans, David. 2008. "Tanzania Community-Based Conditional Cash Transfer (CB-CCT) Pilot." PowerPoint presentation, World Bank, Washington, DC, November 12.

Gilligan, Daniel O., John Hoddinott, Neha Rati Kumar, and Alemayehu Seyoum Taffesse. 2009. *An Impact Evaluation of Ethiopia's Productive Safety Nets Program*. Washington, DC: International Food Policy Research Institute.

Government of Cape Verde. 2011. "Ministério do Trabalho, Formação Profissional e Solidaridade Social." http://www.mtfs.gov.cv/.

HSNP (Hunger Safety Net Programme). n.d. "Welcome to Hunger Safety Net Programme." HSNP, Nairobi.

International Poverty Centre. n.d. "Cash Transfers and Social Protection: Interview with Foday Conteh, Senior Monitoring and Evaluation Officer of the Social Safety Net Programme from the Ministry of Employment and Social Security, Sierra Leone." International Poverty Centre, Brasília. http://www.ipc-undp.org/publications/cct/Interview_Foday_Conteh_SierraLeone.pdf.

Levine, Sebastian, Servaas van der Berg, and Derek Yu. 2009. "Measuring the Impact of Social Cash Transfers on Poverty and Inequality in Namibia." Stellenbosch Economic Working Paper 25/09, Department of Economics and Bureau for Economic Research, University of Stellenbosch, Stellenbosch, South Africa.

MDRP (Multi-country Demobilization and Reintegration Program). 2006. "Reinsertion: Bridging the Gap between Demobilization and Reintegration." *In Focus* 3 (September): 1–4. http://www.mdrp.org/PDFs/In_Focus_3.pdf.

Miller, Candace. 2006. "Social Welfare in Africa: Meeting the Needs of Households Caring for Orphans and Affected by AIDS." Presentation for the United Nations Children's Fund and the Graduate Program in International Affairs at the New School University conference on Social Protection Initiatives for Children, Women, and Families: An Analysis of Recent Experiences, New York, October 30–31.

Miller, Candace, Maxton Tsoka, and the Mchinji Evaluation Team. 2007. "Evaluation of the Mchinji Cash Transfer: Report II—Targeting and Impact." Center for International Health and Development, Boston University, Boston, and Centre for Social Research, University of Malawi, Zomba.

Ministry of Community Development and Social Services. 2007. "Implementation Framework for Scaling Up to a National System of Social Transfers in Zambia." Ministry of Community Development and Social Services, Lusaka.

Ministry of Community Development and Social Services and German Agency for Technical Cooperation. 2007. "The Pilot Social Cash Transfer Scheme in Zambia: Summary Report." Ministry of Community Development and Social Services and German Agency for Technical Cooperation, Lusaka.

Posel, Dori, James Fairburn, and Frances Lund. 2006. "Labour Migration and Households: A Reconsideration of the Effects of the Social Pension on Labour Supply in South Africa." *Economic Modelling* 23 (5): 836–53.

Republic of Rwanda. 2009. "Vision 2020 Umurenge Programme (VUP): Direct Support Operational Framework and Procedure Manual." Ministry of Local Government, Good Governance, Community Development, and Social Affairs, Kigali.

RHVP (Regional Hunger and Vulnerability Programme). 2007. "Old Age and Public Assistance Grants, Swaziland." REBA Case Study Brief 6, Regional Evidence Building Agenda, RHVP, Johannesburg.

RNA (RuralNet Associates). 2007. "Case Study on the Chipata and Kazungula Social Cash Transfer Schemes by CARE International." Regional Hunger and Vulnerability Programme, Johannesburg.

Samson, Michael, Una Lee, Asanda Ndlebe, Kenneth Mac Quene, Ingrid van Niekerk, Viral Gandhi, Tomoko Harigaya, and Celeste Abrahams. 2004. *The Social and Economic Impact of South Africa's Social Security System*. Cape Town, South Africa: Economic Policy Research Institute.

Schubert, Bernd, and Mayke Huijbregts. 2006. "The Malawi Social Cash Transfer Pilot Scheme, Preliminary Lessons Learned." Presented at the conference on Social Protection Initiatives for Children, Women, and Families: An Analysis of Recent Experiences, New York, October 30–31.

Soares, Fábio Veras, and Clarissa Teixeira. 2010. "Impact Evaluation of the Expansion of the Food Subsidy Programme in Mozambique." Research Brief 17, International Policy Centre for Inclusive Growth, Brasília.

South African Government Services. 2009. "Social Services." South African Government Services, Pretoria. http://www.services.gov.za/.

Tembo, Gelson, and Nicholas Freeland. 2009. "Impact of Social Cash Transfers on Investment, Welfare and Education Outcomes: A Retrospective Study of the Social Cash Transfer Schemes in Chipata, Kalomo and Kazungula Districts of Zambia." Lusaka, Zambia: Ministry of Community Development and Social Services.

UNHCR (Office of the United Nations High Commissioner for Refugees). n.d. "Impact of Cash Grants: A First Assessment." UNHCR, Geneva.

UNICEF (United Nations Children's Fund). n.d. "The Lesotho Child Grants Programme." UNICEF, Maseru.

———. 2009. "La Protection Sociale et les Enfants en Afrique de l'Ouest et du Centre: Le Cas du Mali." Ministry of Social Development, Solidarity, and Elderly People and UNICEF, Bamako.

Williams, Martin J. 2007. "The Social and Economic Impacts of South Africa's Child Support Grant." Working Paper 39, Economic Policy Research Institute, Cape Town, South Africa.

Woolard, Ingrid, and Murray Leibbrandt. 2010. "The Evolution and Impact of Unconditional Cash Transfers in South Africa." Southern Africa Labour and

Development Research Unit, University of Cape Town, Cape Town, South Africa.

World Bank. 2009a. "Emergency Project Paper under the Global Food Crisis Response Program on a Proposed Grant from the Multi-Donor Trust Fund in the Amount of US$8 Million and a Proposed Credit in the Amount of SDR 6.8 Million (US$10 Million Equivalent) to the Republic of Senegal for a Rapid Response Child-Focused Social Cash Transfer and Nutrition Security Project." Human Development II, Country Department AFCF1, Africa Region, World Bank, Washington, DC.

———. 2009b. "Nigeria: Conditional Grant and Cash Transfer Project." Project Concept Note, Social Protection, Africa Region, World Bank, Washington, DC.

———. 2009c. "Project Appraisal Document for a Cash Transfer for Orphans and Vulnerable Children Project." World Bank, Washington, DC.

———. 2010a. *Designing and Implementing a Rural Safety Net in a Low Income Setting: Lessons Learned from Ethiopia's Productive Safety Net Program 2005–2009*. Washington, DC: World Bank.

———. 2010b. "Project Appraisal Document on a Proposed Credit in the Amount of SDR 58.4 Million (US$88.6 Million Equivalent) in the Amount of SDR 31.3 Million (US$47.6 Million Equivalent) in Pilot CRW Resources to the Republic of Ghana for a Social Opportunities Project." Western Africa I, Social Protection, Africa Region, World Bank, Washington, DC.

ECO-AUDIT
Environmental Benefits Statement

The World Bank is committed to preserving endangered forests and natural resources. The Office of the Publisher has chosen to print *The Cash Dividend: The Rise of Cash Transfer Programs in Sub-Saharan Africa* on recycled paper with 50 percent postconsumer fiber in accordance with the recommended standards for paper usage set by the Green Press Initiative, a nonprofit program supporting publishers in using fiber that is not sourced from endangered forests. For more information, visit www.greenpressinitiative.org.

Saved:
- 7 trees
- 4 million BTUs of total energy
- 876 pounds of net greenhouse gases
- 3,951 gallons of waste water
- 251 pounds of solid waste